W9-CBK-399

macOS Big Sur™

by Bob LeVitus

Houston Chronicle "Dr. Mac" columnist

for **dummies**®

A Wiley Brand

macOS Big Sur™ For Dummies®

Published by: **John Wiley & Sons, Inc.**, 111 River Street, Hoboken, NJ 07030-5774, www.wiley.com

Copyright © 2021 by John Wiley & Sons, Inc., Hoboken, New Jersey

Published simultaneously in Canada

No part of this publication may be reproduced, stored in a retrieval system or transmitted in any form or by any means, electronic, mechanical, photocopying, recording, scanning or otherwise, except as permitted under Sections 107 or 108 of the 1976 United States Copyright Act, without the prior written permission of the Publisher. Requests to the Publisher for permission should be addressed to the Permissions Department, John Wiley & Sons, Inc., 111 River Street, Hoboken, NJ 07030, (201) 748-6011, fax (201) 748-6008, or online at http://www.wiley.com/go/permissions.

Trademarks: Wiley, For Dummies, the Dummies Man logo, Dummies.com, Making Everything Easier, and related trade dress are trademarks or registered trademarks of John Wiley & Sons, Inc. and may not be used without written permission. macOS Big Sur is a trademark of Apple, Inc. All other trademarks are the property of their respective owners. John Wiley & Sons, Inc. is not associated with any product or vendor mentioned in this book. *macOS Big Sur™ For Dummies* is an independent publication and has not been authorized, sponsored, or otherwise approved by Apple, Inc.

LIMIT OF LIABILITY/DISCLAIMER OF WARRANTY: THE PUBLISHER AND THE AUTHOR MAKE NO REPRESENTATIONS OR WARRANTIES WITH RESPECT TO THE ACCURACY OR COMPLETENESS OF THE CONTENTS OF THIS WORK AND SPECIFICALLY DISCLAIM ALL WARRANTIES, INCLUDING WITHOUT LIMITATION WARRANTIES OF FITNESS FOR A PARTICULAR PURPOSE. NO WARRANTY MAY BE CREATED OR EXTENDED BY SALES OR PROMOTIONAL MATERIALS. THE ADVICE AND STRATEGIES CONTAINED HEREIN MAY NOT BE SUITABLE FOR EVERY SITUATION. THIS WORK IS SOLD WITH THE UNDERSTANDING THAT THE PUBLISHER IS NOT ENGAGED IN RENDERING LEGAL, ACCOUNTING, OR OTHER PROFESSIONAL SERVICES. IF PROFESSIONAL ASSISTANCE IS REQUIRED, THE SERVICES OF A COMPETENT PROFESSIONAL PERSON SHOULD BE SOUGHT. NEITHER THE PUBLISHER NOR THE AUTHOR SHALL BE LIABLE FOR DAMAGES ARISING HEREFROM. THE FACT THAT AN ORGANIZATION OR WEBSITE IS REFERRED TO IN THIS WORK AS A CITATION AND/OR A POTENTIAL SOURCE OF FURTHER INFORMATION DOES NOT MEAN THAT THE AUTHOR OR THE PUBLISHER ENDORSES THE INFORMATION THE ORGANIZATION OR WEBSITE MAY PROVIDE OR RECOMMENDATIONS IT MAY MAKE. FURTHER, READERS SHOULD BE AWARE THAT INTERNET WEBSITES LISTED IN THIS WORK MAY HAVE CHANGED OR DISAPPEARED BETWEEN WHEN THIS WORK WAS WRITTEN AND WHEN IT IS READ.

For general information on our other products and services, please contact our Customer Care Department within the U.S. at 877-762-2974, outside the U.S. at 317-572-3993, or fax 317-572-4002. For technical support, please visit https://hub.wiley.com/community/support/dummies.

Wiley publishes in a variety of print and electronic formats and by print-on-demand. Some material included with standard print versions of this book may not be included in e-books or in print-on-demand. If this book refers to media such as a CD or DVD that is not included in the version you purchased, you may download this material at http://booksupport.wiley.com. For more information about Wiley products, visit www.wiley.com.

Library of Congress Control Number: 2020945957

ISBN 978-1-119-73010-1 (pbk); ISBN 978-1-119-73011-8 (ebk); ISBN 978-1-119-73013-2 (ebk)

Manufactured in the United States of America

SKY10021639_100820

macOS Big Sur™ For Dummies®

Published by: **John Wiley & Sons, Inc.**, 111 River Street, Hoboken, NJ 07030-5774, www.wiley.com

Copyright © 2021 by John Wiley & Sons, Inc., Hoboken, New Jersey

Published simultaneously in Canada

No part of this publication may be reproduced, stored in a retrieval system or transmitted in any form or by any means, electronic, mechanical, photocopying, recording, scanning or otherwise, except as permitted under Sections 107 or 108 of the 1976 United States Copyright Act, without the prior written permission of the Publisher. Requests to the Publisher for permission should be addressed to the Permissions Department, John Wiley & Sons, Inc., 111 River Street, Hoboken, NJ 07030, (201) 748-6011, fax (201) 748-6008, or online at http://www.wiley.com/go/permissions.

Trademarks: Wiley, For Dummies, the Dummies Man logo, Dummies.com, Making Everything Easier, and related trade dress are trademarks or registered trademarks of John Wiley & Sons, Inc. and may not be used without written permission. macOS Big Sur is a trademark of Apple, Inc. All other trademarks are the property of their respective owners. John Wiley & Sons, Inc. is not associated with any product or vendor mentioned in this book. *macOS Big Sur™ For Dummies* is an independent publication and has not been authorized, sponsored, or otherwise approved by Apple, Inc.

LIMIT OF LIABILITY/DISCLAIMER OF WARRANTY: THE PUBLISHER AND THE AUTHOR MAKE NO REPRESENTATIONS OR WARRANTIES WITH RESPECT TO THE ACCURACY OR COMPLETENESS OF THE CONTENTS OF THIS WORK AND SPECIFICALLY DISCLAIM ALL WARRANTIES, INCLUDING WITHOUT LIMITATION WARRANTIES OF FITNESS FOR A PARTICULAR PURPOSE. NO WARRANTY MAY BE CREATED OR EXTENDED BY SALES OR PROMOTIONAL MATERIALS. THE ADVICE AND STRATEGIES CONTAINED HEREIN MAY NOT BE SUITABLE FOR EVERY SITUATION. THIS WORK IS SOLD WITH THE UNDERSTANDING THAT THE PUBLISHER IS NOT ENGAGED IN RENDERING LEGAL, ACCOUNTING, OR OTHER PROFESSIONAL SERVICES. IF PROFESSIONAL ASSISTANCE IS REQUIRED, THE SERVICES OF A COMPETENT PROFESSIONAL PERSON SHOULD BE SOUGHT. NEITHER THE PUBLISHER NOR THE AUTHOR SHALL BE LIABLE FOR DAMAGES ARISING HEREFROM. THE FACT THAT AN ORGANIZATION OR WEBSITE IS REFERRED TO IN THIS WORK AS A CITATION AND/OR A POTENTIAL SOURCE OF FURTHER INFORMATION DOES NOT MEAN THAT THE AUTHOR OR THE PUBLISHER ENDORSES THE INFORMATION THE ORGANIZATION OR WEBSITE MAY PROVIDE OR RECOMMENDATIONS IT MAY MAKE. FURTHER, READERS SHOULD BE AWARE THAT INTERNET WEBSITES LISTED IN THIS WORK MAY HAVE CHANGED OR DISAPPEARED BETWEEN WHEN THIS WORK WAS WRITTEN AND WHEN IT IS READ.

For general information on our other products and services, please contact our Customer Care Department within the U.S. at 877-762-2974, outside the U.S. at 317-572-3993, or fax 317-572-4002. For technical support, please visit https://hub.wiley.com/community/support/dummies.

Wiley publishes in a variety of print and electronic formats and by print-on-demand. Some material included with standard print versions of this book may not be included in e-books or in print-on-demand. If this book refers to media such as a CD or DVD that is not included in the version you purchased, you may download this material at http://booksupport.wiley.com. For more information about Wiley products, visit www.wiley.com.

Library of Congress Control Number: 2020945957

ISBN 978-1-119-73010-1 (pbk); ISBN 978-1-119-73011-8 (ebk); ISBN 978-1-119-73013-2 (ebk)

Manufactured in the United States of America

SKY10021639_100820

Contents at a Glance

Table of Contents

Introduction

You made the right choice twice: macOS Big Sur (version 11.0) and this book. Take a deep breath and get ready to have a rollicking good time. That's right. This is a computer book, but it's fun. What a concept! Whether you're brand spanking new to the Mac or a grizzled Mac vet, I guarantee that reading this book to discover the ins and outs of macOS Big Sur will make learning easy. If it weren't true, I couldn't say it right on the cover!

About This Book

This book's roots lie with my international best seller *Macintosh System 7.5 For Dummies,* an award-winning book so good that long-deceased Mac clone-maker Power Computing gave away a copy with every Mac clone it sold (back in the '90s before Steve came back and killed off all Mac clones).

macOS Big Sur For Dummies is the latest revision and has been, once again, completely and thoroughly updated to include all the tasty goodness in macOS Big Sur. In other words, this edition combines all the old, familiar features of literally dozens of previous editions — but, as always, I've lovingly updated every page to reflect the latest and greatest offering from Apple as well as feedback from readers. If you have comments — good or bad — email me. (My email address appears in the last section.)

Why write a *For Dummies* book about Big Sur? Well, Big Sur is a big, somewhat complicated personal-computer operating system. So, I made *macOS Big Sur For Dummies* a not-so-big, not-too-complicated book that shows you what Big Sur is all about without boring you to tears, confusing you, or poking you with sharp objects.

In fact, I think you'll be so darned comfortable that I wanted the title to be *macOS Big Sur Made Easy,* but the publishers wouldn't let me. Apparently, my publisher has rules, and using *Dummies* in this book's title is one of them.

And speaking of dummies — remember, that's just a word. I don't think you're a dummy at all — quite the opposite! My second choice for this book's title was *macOS Big Sur For People Smart Enough to Know They Need This Book*, but you can just imagine what Wiley thought of that.

The book is chock-full of information and advice, explaining everything you need to know about macOS Big Sur in language you can understand — along with time-saving tips, tricks, techniques, and step-by-step instructions, all served up in generous quantities.

Another rule we *Dummies* authors must follow is that our books cannot exceed a certain number of pages. (Brevity is the soul of wit, and all that.) So, while I wish I could have included some things that didn't fit, I feel confident you'll find what you need to know about using macOS Big Sur in this book.

Still, a few things bear further looking into, such as these:

>> **Information about many of the applications (programs) that come with macOS Big Sur:** An installation of macOS Big Sur includes more than 50 applications, mostly located in the Applications and Utilities folders. I'd love to walk you through each one of them, but that would have required a book a whole lot bigger, heavier, and more expensive than this one.

I brief you on the handful of bundled applications essential to using macOS Big Sur — namely, Calendar, Contacts, Messages, Mail, Safari, Siri, TextEdit, and the like — as well as several important utilities you may need to know how to use someday.

>> **Information about Microsoft Office, Apple lifestyle and productivity apps (iMovie, Numbers, Pages, GarageBand, and so on), Adobe Photoshop, Quicken, and other third-party applications:** Okay, if all the gory details of all the bundled (read: *free)* macOS Big Sur applications don't fit here, I think you'll understand why digging into third-party applications that cost extra was out of the question.

>> **Information about programming for the Mac:** This book is about *using* macOS Big Sur, not writing code for it. Dozens of books — most of which are two or three times the size of this book — cover programming on the Mac; this one does not.

Within this book, you may note that some web addresses break across two lines of text. If you're reading this book in print and want to visit one of these web pages, simply key in the web address exactly as it's noted in the text, pretending as though the line break doesn't exist. If you're reading this as an e-book, you've got it easy — just click the web address to be taken directly to the web page.

Foolish Assumptions

Although I know what happens when you make assumptions, I've made a few anyway.

First, I assume that you, gentle reader, know nothing about using macOS — beyond knowing what a Mac is, that you want to use macOS, that you want to understand macOS without having to digest an incomprehensible technical manual, and that you made the right choice by selecting this particular book. And so I do my best to explain each new concept in full and loving detail. Maybe that's foolish, but . . . that's how I roll.

Oh, and I also assume that you can read. If you can't, ignore this paragraph.

Icons Used in This Book

Little pictures (icons) appear off to the left side of the text throughout this book. Consider these icons miniature road signs, telling you a little something extra about the topic at hand. Here's what the different icons look like and what they all mean.

Look for Tip icons to find the juiciest morsels: shortcuts, tips, and undocumented secrets about Big Sur. Try them all; impress your friends!

When you see this icon, it means that this particular morsel is something that I think you should memorize (or at least write on your shirt cuff).

Put on your propeller-beanie hat and pocket protector; these parts include the truly geeky stuff. It's certainly not required reading, but it must be interesting or informative, or I wouldn't have wasted your time with it.

Read these notes very, very, very carefully. (Did I say *very*?) Warning icons flag important cautionary information. The author and publisher won't be responsible if your Mac explodes or spews flaming parts because you ignored a Warning icon. Just kidding. Macs don't explode or spew these days. But I got your attention, didn't I?

Well, now, what could this icon possibly be about? Named by famous editorial consultant Mr. Obvious, this icon highlights things new and different in macOS Big Sur.

Beyond the Book

In addition to what you're reading right now, this product also comes with a free access-anywhere Cheat Sheet that provides handy shortcuts for use with macOS Big Sur, offers my backup recommendations, and more. To get this Cheat Sheet, simply go to www.dummies.com and type **macOS Big Sur For Dummies Cheat Sheet** in the Search box.

Where to Go from Here

The first few chapters of this book are where I describe the basic things that you need to understand to operate your Mac effectively. If you're new to Macs and macOS Big Sur, start there.

Although macOS Big Sur looks different from previous Mac operating systems, it works the same as always (for the most part). So, the first part of the book presents concepts so basic that if you've been using a Mac for long, you might think you know it all — and okay, you might know some (or most) of it. But remember that not-so-old-timers need a solid foundation, too. So here's my advice: Skim through stuff you already know and you'll get to the better stuff sooner.

I would love to hear how this book worked for you. As mentioned, sending me your thoughts, platitudes, likes, dislikes, and comments will make me a happy author. Did this book work for you? What did you like? What didn't you like? What questions were unanswered? Did you want to know more (or less) about something?

I have received more than 100 suggestions about previous editions, many of which are incorporated here. So please (please!) keep the tradition alive and email me at BigSur4Dummies@boblevitus.com.

I appreciate your feedback, and I *try* to respond to all reasonably polite email within a few days.

So what are you waiting for? Go on and enjoy the book!

1

macOS Basics

IN THIS PART . . .

Find the most basic of basics, including how to turn on your Mac.

Make the dock work harder for you.

Get a gentle introduction to Finder and its desktop.

Find everything you need to know about Big Sur's windows, icons, and menus (oh my)!

Get all the bad puns and wisecracks you've come to expect.

Discover a plethora of Finder tips and tricks to make life with Big Sur even easier (and more fulfilling).

Chapter **1**

macOS Big Sur 101 (Prerequisites: None)

ongratulate yourself on choosing macOS Big Sur version 11.0, the 17th release of the venerable operating system (OS) formerly known as OS X (pronounced "oh-ess-ten"). Congratulate yourself for scoring more than just an OS upgrade. See, macOS Big Sur includes a few new features that make using your Mac even easier, hundreds of tweaks to help you do more work in less time, plus a user interface overhaul that affects almost every pixel on the screen.

In this chapter, I start at the very beginning and talk about macOS in mostly abstract terms; then I move on to explain what you need to know to use macOS Big Sur successfully. A number of features I describe haven't changed in years (other than adopting updated Big Sur graphics), so if you've been using macOS (the operating system formerly known as Mac OS X) for a while, most of the information in this chapter may seem hauntingly familiar.

But if you decide to skip this chapter because you think you have all the new stuff figured out, I assure you that you'll miss at least a couple of things that Apple didn't bother to tell you (as if you read every word in macOS Help — the only user manual Apple provides in the box — anyway!).

Tantalized? Let's rock.

Gnawing to the Core of macOS

The operating system (that is, the *OS* part of *macOS*) is what makes your Mac a Mac. Without it, your Mac is nothing but a pile of silicon and circuits — no smarter than a toaster.

"So what does an operating system do?" you ask. Good question. The short answer is that an OS controls the basic and most important functions of your computer. In the case of macOS and your Mac, the operating system

>> Manages memory

>> Controls how windows, icons, and menus work

>> Keeps track of files

>> Manages networking and security

>> Does housekeeping (No kidding!)

Other forms of software, such as word processors and web browsers, rely on the OS to create and maintain the environment in which they work their magic. When you create a memo, for example, the word processor provides the tools for you to type and format the information and save it in a file. In the background, the OS is the muscle for the word processor, performing the following crucial functions:

>> Providing the mechanism for drawing and moving the onscreen window in which you write the memo

>> Keeping track of the file when you save it

>> Helping the word processor create drop-down menus and dialogs for you to interact with

>> Communicating with other programs

>> And much, much more (stuff that only geeks could care about)

So, armed with a little background in operating systems, take a gander at the next section before you do anything else with your Mac.

One last thing: As I mention in this book's Introduction (I'm repeating it here in case you normally don't read introductions), macOS Big Sur comes with more than 50 applications in its Applications and Utilities folders. Although I'd love to tell you all about each and every one, I have only so many pages at my disposal.

THE MAC ADVANTAGE

Most of the world's personal computers use Microsoft Windows (although more and more people are switching to the Mac). But you're among the lucky ones who have a computer with an OS that's intuitive, easy to use, and (dare I say?) fun. If you don't believe me, try using Windows for a day or two. Go ahead. You probably won't suffer any permanent damage. In fact, you'll really begin to appreciate how good you have it. Feel free to hug your Mac. Or give it a peck on the mouse or trackpad.

As someone once told me, "Claiming that macOS is inferior to Windows because more people use Windows is like saying that all other restaurants serve food that's inferior to McDonald's."

We might be a minority, but Mac users have the best, most stable, most modern all-purpose operating system in the world, and here's why: Unix, on which macOS is based, is widely regarded as the best industrial-strength operating system on the planet. For now, just know that being based on Unix means that a Mac running macOS benefits from more than three decades of UNIX development, which means less downtime. Being Unix-based also means getting far fewer viruses and encounters with malicious software. But perhaps the biggest advantage macOS has is that when an application crashes, it doesn't crash your entire computer, and you don't usually have to restart the computer to continue working.

By the way, since the advent of Intel-powered Macs more than a decade ago, you can run Windows natively also on any Mac powered by an Intel processor, as I describe in Chapter 23. Note that the opposite isn't true: You can run Windows on your Mac if you care to, but you *cannot* run macOS on a Dell or HP or any other computer not made by Apple (at least not without serious hacking, which is probably illegal anyway).

And don't let that Unix or Windows stuff scare you. It's there if you want it, but if you don't want it or don't care (like most users), you'll rarely even know it's there. In fact, you'll rarely (if ever) see the word *Unix* or *Windows* again in this book. As far as you're concerned, Unix under the hood means your Mac will just run and run and run without crashing and crashing and crashing. As for Windows, your Mac can run it if you need it; otherwise, it's just another checklist item on the list of reasons Macs are better than PCs.

WARNING

In June 2020, Apple announced that the Mac will transition from Intel processors to Apple's custom silicon "to deliver industry-leading performance and powerful new technologies." Since the first Apple-processor-equipped Macs won't be available until long after this book is printed, all I can do is guess. And my guess is that Macs with Apple processors won't support Boot Camp but should allow you to run Windows (and other operating systems) through virtualization.

A Safety Net for the Absolute Beginner (or Any User)

In the following sections, I deal with the stuff that macOS Help doesn't cover — or doesn't cover in nearly enough detail. If you're a first-time Mac user, please, *please* read this section of the book carefully; it could save your life. Okay, okay, perhaps I'm being overly dramatic. What I mean to say is that reading this section could save your Mac or your sanity. Even if you're an experienced Mac user, you may want to read this section. Chances are you'll see at least a few things you've forgotten that will come in handy now that you've been reminded of them.

Turning the dang thing on

Okay. This is the big moment — turning on your Mac! Gaze at it longingly first, and say something cheesy, such as, "You're the most awesome computer I've ever known." If that doesn't turn on your Mac (and it probably won't), keep reading.

Apple, in its infinite wisdom, has manufactured Macs with power buttons on every conceivable surface: on the front, side, and back of the computer itself, and even on the keyboard and monitor.

So if you don't know how to turn on your Mac, don't feel bad; just look in the manual or booklet that came with your Mac. It's at least one thing that the documentation *always* covers.

You don't have that little booklet? Most Macs have the power button in the upper-right corner of the keyboard (notebooks), the back of the screen (iMacs), or the back of the enclosure (Mac Mini); it usually looks like the little circle thingy you see in the margin.

Don't bother choosing Help ➪ macOS Help, which opens the Help Viewer program. It can't tell you where the switch is. Although the Help program is good for finding out a lot of things, the location of the power button isn't among them. If you haven't found the switch and turned on the Mac, of course, you can't access Help anyway. (D'oh!)

TIP

Launch the Books (formerly iBooks) app and click the Book Store icon (top left) to search its built-in store for the name of your Mac plus the word *Essentials* (for example, "MacBook Essentials," "iMac Essentials," or "MacBook Pro Essentials"). Click the Only Show Free Titles check box near the upper-right corner of the Books window, and grab the free Essentials e-book with your Mac's name, by Apple. At around 150 pages each, these booklets aren't in any way comprehensive, but they do include information you won't find elsewhere, including where to find the power button on your particular Mac.

What you should see on startup

When you finally do turn on your Mac, you set in motion a sophisticated and complex series of events that culminates in the loading of macOS and the appearance of the macOS desktop. After a small bit of whirring, buzzing, and flashing (meaning that the OS is loading), macOS first tests all your hardware — slots, ports, disks, random access memory (RAM), and so on. If everything passes, you'll see a tasteful whitish Apple logo in the middle of your screen, as shown in Figure 1-1.

FIGURE 1-1:
This is what you'll see if everything is fine and dandy when you turn on your Mac.

Here are the things that you might see when you power-up your Mac:

>> **Login screen:** You might or might not see the macOS login screen. Here, you choose your user account, enter your name and password, and press Return or Enter (or click the little right-arrow-in-a-circle in the password field), and away you go.

TIP

If you don't want to type your name and password every time you start or restart your Mac (or even if you do), check out Chapter 23 for the scoop on how to turn the login screen on or off.

WARNING

You should turn off the login screen only if you're confident you'll be the only one touching the machine. With the login screen disabled, your Mac and everything in it is completely available to anyone who turns it on, which is usually *not* a good thing. So I don't recommend turning off the login screen if your Mac is a laptop. And even desktop Mac users should think twice before turning it off.

Either way, the desktop soon materializes before your eyes. If you haven't customized, configured, or tinkered with your desktop, it should look pretty much like Figure 1-2. Now is a good time to take a moment for positive thoughts about the person who convinced you that you wanted a Mac. That person was right!

FIGURE 1-2:
The desktop after a brand-spanking-new installation of macOS Big Sur.

» **Blue/black/gray screen of death:** If any of your hardware fails when it's tested, you may see a blue, black, or gray screen.

Some older Macs played the sound of a horrible car wreck instead of the chimes, complete with crying tires and busting glass. It was exceptionally unnerving, which might be why Apple doesn't use it anymore.

REMEMBER

The fact that something went wrong is no reflection on your prowess as a Mac user. Something is broken, and your Mac may need repairs. If this is happening to you right now, check out Chapter 26 to try to get your Mac well again.

TIP

If your computer is under warranty, set up a Genius Bar appointment at your nearest Apple Store or dial 1-800-SOS-APPL, and a customer service person can tell you what to do. Before you do anything, though, skip ahead to Chapter 26. It's entirely possible that one of the suggestions there will get you back on track without your having to spend even a moment on hold.

» **Prohibitory sign or flashing question mark in a folder:** Most users eventually encounter the prohibitory sign or flashing question mark in a folder (as shown in the margin). These icons mean that your Mac can't find a startup disk, hard drive, network server, or DVD-ROM containing a valid Mac operating system. See Chapter 26 for ways to ease your Mac's ills.

» **Kernel panic:** You may occasionally see a block of text in several languages, including English, as shown in Figure 1-3. This means that your Mac has experienced a *kernel panic,* the most severe type of system crash. If you restart your Mac and see either message again, look in Chapter 26 for a myriad of possible cures for all kinds of ailments, including this one.

You need to restart your computer. Hold down the Power button for several seconds or press the Restart button.

Veuillez redémarrer votre ordinateur. Maintenez la touche de démarrage enfoncée pendant plusieurs secondes ou bien appuyez sur le bouton de réinitialisation.

Sie müssen Ihren Computer neu starten. Halten Sie dazu die Einschalttaste einige Sekunden gedrückt oder drücken Sie die Neustart-Taste.

コンピュータを再起動する必要があります。パワーボタンを数秒間押し続けるか、リセットボタンを押してください。

Your computer restarted because of a problem. Press a key or wait a few seconds to continue starting up.

Votre ordinateur a redémarré en raison d'un problème. Pour poursuivre le redémarrage, appuyez sur une touche ou patientez quelques secondes.

El ordenador se ha reiniciado debido a un problema. Para continuar con el arranque, pulse cualquier tecla o espere unos segundos.

Ihr Computer wurde aufgrund eines Problems neu gestartet. Drücken Sie zum Fortfahren eine Taste oder warten Sie einige Sekunden.

問題が起きたためコンピュータを再起動しました。このまま起動する場合は、いずれかのキーを押すか、数秒間そのままお待ちください。

FIGURE 1-3:
If you're seeing this, things are definitely not fine and dandy.

How do you know which version of the macOS your computer has? Simple:

1. **Choose About This Mac from the menu (the menu with the symbol in the top-left corner of the menu bar).**

   A window pops up on your screen, as shown in Figure 1-4. The version you're running appears just below *macOS* near the top of the window. Version 11.0 is the release we know as *Big Sur.*

TECHNICAL STUFF

   If you're curious or just want to impress your friends, you'll might want to know that OS X version 10.15 was called Catalina; 10.14 was called Mojave; 10.13 was known as High Sierra; 10.12 was Sierra; 10.11 was El Capitan; 10.10 was Yosemite; 10.9 was Mavericks; 10.8 was Mountain Lion; 10.7 was Lion; 10.6 was Snow Leopard; 10.5 was Leopard; 10.4 was Tiger; 10.3 was Panther; 10.2 was Jaguar; 10.1 was Puma; and 10.0 was Cheetah.

Overview Displays Storage Support Service

macOS Big Sur
Version 11.0 (20A4299v)

MacBook Air (11-inch, Early 2014)
Processor 1.4 GHz Dual-Core Intel Core i5
Memory 8 GB 1600 MHz DDR3
Graphics Intel HD Graphics 5000 1536 MB
Serial Number

System Report...   Software Update...

™ and © 1983-2020 Apple Inc. All Rights Reserved. License Agreement

FIGURE 1-4:
See which version
of macOS you're
running.

2. **(Optional) Click the Displays, Storage, Support, or Service tabs to see additional details about your Mac.**

3. **Click the System Report button to launch the System Information application and see even more details.**

The System Information app shows you even more about your Mac, including bus speed, number of processors, caches, installed memory, networking, storage devices, and much more. You can find more about this useful program in Chapter 25.

ETERNALLY YOURS . . . *NOW*

macOS is designed so that you never have to shut it down. You can configure it to sleep after a specified period of inactivity. (See Chapter 23 for more info on Energy Saver.) If you do so, your Mac will consume very little electricity when it's sleeping and will usually be ready to use (when you press any key or click the mouse) in a few seconds. On the other hand, if you're not going to be using your Mac for a few days, you might want to shut it down anyway.

Note: If you leave your Mac on constantly, and you're gone when a lightning storm or rolling blackout hits, your Mac might get hit by a power surge or worse. So be sure you have adequate protection — say, a decent surge protector designed for computers — if you decide to leave your Mac on and unattended for long periods. See the section "A few things you should definitely not do with your Mac," elsewhere in this chapter, for more info on lightning and your Mac.

One last thing: If your Mac is a laptop and will be enclosed in a bag or briefcase for more than a few hours, turn it off. Otherwise, it could overheat — even in Sleep mode.

Shutting down properly

Turning off the power without shutting down your Mac properly is one of the worst things you can do to your poor Mac. Shutting down your Mac improperly can really screw up your hard or solid-state drive, scramble the contents of your most important files, or both.

WARNING

If a thunderstorm is rumbling nearby, or you're unfortunate enough to have rolling blackouts where you live, you may really want to shut down your Mac and unplug it from the wall. (See the next section, where I briefly discuss lightning and your Mac.) If it's a laptop, you can just disconnect it from its charging cable and continue using it if you like.

To turn off your Mac, always use the Shut Down command from the (Apple) menu or shut down in one of these kind and gentle ways:

>> Press the power button for approximately two seconds and then click the Shut Down button in the Are You Sure You Want to Shut Down Your Computer Now? dialog.

>> On keyboards that don't have a power key, press Control+Eject instead, and then click the Shut Down button that appears in the Are You Sure You Want to Shut Down Your Computer Now? dialog.

TIP

You can use a handy keyboard shortcut when the Shut Down button (or any button, for that matter) is highlighted in blue and pulsating slightly. Pressing the Return (or Enter) key is (usually) the same as clicking whichever button is highlighted.

The Are You Sure You Want to Shut Down Your Computer Now? dialog sports a check box option: Reopen Windows When Logging Back In. If you select this check box, your Mac will start back up with the same windows (and applications) that were open when you shut down or restarted. I think that's pretty darn sweet, but you can clear the check box and disable this option if that's not what you want!

Most Mac users have been forced to shut down improperly more than once without anything horrible happening, of course — but don't be lulled into a false sense of security. Break the rules one time too many (or under the wrong circumstances), and your most important files could be toast. The *only* time you should turn off your Mac without shutting down properly is when your screen is completely frozen or when your system crashed due to a kernel panic and you've already tried everything else. (See Chapter 26 for a list of those "everything elses.") A stubborn crash doesn't happen often — and less often under macOS than ever before — but when it does, forcing your Mac to turn off and then back on might be the only solution.

A few things you should definitely not do with your Mac

In this section, I cover the bad stuff that can happen to your computer if you do the wrong things with it. If something bad has already happened to you . . . . I know, I'm beginning to sound like a broken record, but see Chapter 26.

>> **Don't unplug your Mac when it's turned on.** Very bad things can happen, such as having your OS break. See the preceding section, where I discuss shutting down your system properly.

   Note that this warning doesn't apply to laptops as long as their battery is at least partially charged. As long as there's enough juice in the battery to power your Mac, you can connect and disconnect its power adapter to your heart's content.

>> **Don't use your Mac when lightning is near.** Here's a simple life equation for you: Mac + lightning = dead Mac. 'Nuff said. Oh, and don't place much faith in inexpensive surge protectors. A good jolt of lightning will fry the surge protector and everything plugged into it, including computers, modems, printers, and hubs. Some surge protectors can withstand most lightning strikes, but those warriors aren't the cheapies that you buy at your local computer emporium. Unplugging your Mac from the wall during electrical storms is safer and less expensive. (Don't forget to unplug your external modem, network hubs, printers, and other hardware that plugs into the wall as well; lightning can fry them, too.)

   For laptops, disconnect the power adapter and all other cables because whatever those cables are connected to could fry — and fry your laptop right along with it. After you do that, you can use your laptop during a storm if you care to. Just make sure that it's 100 percent wireless and cableless when you do.

>> **Don't jostle, bump, shake, kick, throw, dribble, or punt your Mac, especially while it's running.** Many older Macs contain a hard drive that spins at 5,200 revolutions per minute (rpm) or more. A jolt to a hard drive while it's reading or writing a file can cause the head to crash into the disk, which can render many — or all — files on it unrecoverable. Ouch!

TIP

   Don't think you're exempt if your Mac uses a solid-state drive with no moving parts. A good bump to your Mac could damage other components. Treat your Mac like it's a carton of eggs, and you'll never be sorry.

>> **Don't forget to back up your data!** If the files on your hard drive mean anything to you, you must back up. Not maybe. *Must.* Even if your most important file is your last saved game of Bejeweled, you still need to back up your files. Fortunately, macOS includes an awesome backup utility called Time

Machine. (Unfortunately, you need an external hard drive to take advantage of it.) So I beg you: Please read Chapter 24 now, and find out how to back up before something horrible happens to your valuable data!

TIP

I *strongly* recommend that you read Chapter 24 sooner rather than later — preferably before you do any significant work on your Mac. Dr. Mac says, "There are only two kinds of Mac users: Those who have lost data and those who will." Which kind do you want to be?

>> **Don't kiss your monitor while wearing stuff on your lips.** For obvious reasons!

WARNING

Definitely do not use household window cleaners or paper towels. Either one can harm your display. Use a soft clean cloth (preferably microfiber), and if you're going to use a cleaner, make sure it's specifically designed not to harm computer displays. Finally, spray the cleaner on the *cloth,* not on the screen.

Point-and-click 101

Are you new to the Mac? Just figuring out how to move the mouse around? Now is a good time to go over some fundamental stuff that you need to know for just about everything you'll be doing on the Mac. Spend a few minutes reading this section, and soon you'll be clicking, double-clicking, pressing, and pointing all over the place. If you think you have the whole mousing thing pretty much figured out, feel free to skip this section. I'll catch you on the other side.

Still with me? Good. Now for some basic terminology:

>> **Point:** Before you can click or press anything, you have to *point* to it. Place your hand on your mouse, and move it so that the cursor arrow is over the object you want — such as on top of an icon or a button.

If you're using a trackpad, slide your finger lightly across the pad until the cursor arrow is over the object you want.

>> **Click:** Also called *single click.* Use your index finger to push the mouse button (or the left mouse button if your mouse has more than one) all the way down and then let go so that the button (usually) produces a satisfying clicking sound. (If you have one of the optical Apple mice, you push the whole thing down to click.) Use a single click to highlight an icon, press a button, or activate a check box or window.

In other words, first you point and then you click — *point and click,* in computer lingo.

If you're using a trackpad, press down on it to click.

» **Double-click:** *Click twice* in rapid succession. With a little practice, you can perfect this technique in no time. Use a double-click to open a folder or to launch a file or application.

Trackpad users: Press down on the pad two times in rapid succession.

» **Control-click:** Hold down the Control key while single-clicking. (Also called *secondary-click* or *right-click*.)

Trackpad users can either hold down the Control key while pressing down on the pad with one finger, or tap the trackpad with two fingers without holding down the Control key.

If tapping your trackpad with two fingers didn't bring up the little menu, check your Trackpad System Preferences pane (see Chapter 6).

Control-clicking displays a *contextual* menu (also known as a *shortcut menu*). In fact, if you're blessed with a two-or-more-button mouse (such as the Apple Magic Mouse), you can right-click and avoid having to hold down the Control key. If it doesn't work, you can enable this feature in the Mouse System Preferences pane.)

» **Drag:** *Dragging* something usually means you have to click it first and hold down the mouse or trackpad button. Then you move the mouse on your desk or mouse pad (or your finger on the trackpad) so that the cursor and what-ever you select moves across the screen. The combination of holding down the button and dragging the mouse is usually referred to as *clicking and dragging*.

» **Wiggle (or jiggle):** This welcome improvement, introduced in El Capitan (and terrific if I do say so myself), is awesome when you lose track of the pointer on your screen. Just wiggle your mouse back and forth (or jiggle your finger back and forth on the trackpad) for a few seconds and the pointer will magically get much bigger, making it easier to see on the screen. And, of course, when you stop wiggling or jiggling, the pointer returns to its normal size.

» **Choosing an item from a menu:** To get to macOS menu commands, you must first open a menu and then choose the option you want. Point at the name of the menu you want with your cursor, press the mouse button, and then drag downward until you select the command you want. When the command is highlighted, finish selecting by letting go of the mouse button.

TIP

If you're a longtime Mac user, you probably hold down the mouse button the whole time between clicking the name of the menu and selecting the command you want. You can still do it that way, but you can also click the menu name to open it, release the mouse button, point at the item you want to select, *and then click again.* In other words, macOS menus stay open after you click their names, even if you're not holding down the mouse button. After you click a menu's name to open it, you can even type the first letter (or letters) of the item to select it and then execute that item by pressing the spacebar or the Return key. Furthermore, menus remain open until you click something else.

Go ahead and give it a try . . . I'll wait.

REMEMBER

The terms given in the preceding list apply to all Mac laptop, desktop, and pro systems. If you use a MacBook, MacBook Pro, MacBook Air, or Apple Magic Track-pad, however, you'll want to add to your lexicon a few more terms — such as *tap*, *swipe*, *rotate*, *pinch*, and *spread*. You can read all about them in Chapters 2 and 13.

Not Just a Beatles Movie: Help and the Help Menu

One of the best features of all Macs is the excellent built-in help, and macOS Big Sur doesn't cheat you on that legacy: This system has online help in abundance. When you have a question about how to do something, Help Center is the first place you should visit (after this book, of course).

Clicking the Help menu reveals the Search field at the top of the menu and the macOS Help item. Choosing MacOS Help opens the window shown in Figure 1-5.

Table of contents icon

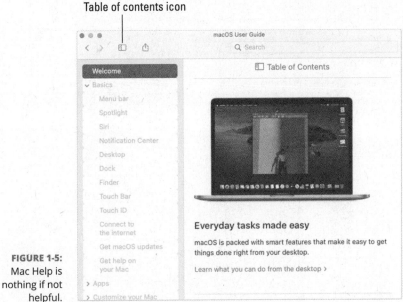

FIGURE 1-5:
Mac Help is nothing if not helpful.

Although the keyboard shortcut for Help no long appears on the Help menu, the same shortcut as always, Shift+⌘+?, still opens Help.

You can browse Help by clicking a topic in the table of contents and then clicking a subtopic. If you don't see the table of contents, click the Table of contents icon, labeled in Figure 1-5.

To search Mac Help, simply type a word or phrase in either Search field — the one in the Help menu itself or the one near the top of the Help window on the right side — and then press Return. In a few seconds, your Mac provides one or more articles to read, which (theoretically) are related to your question. Usually. If you type **menus** and press Return, for example, you get the results shown in Figure 1-6.

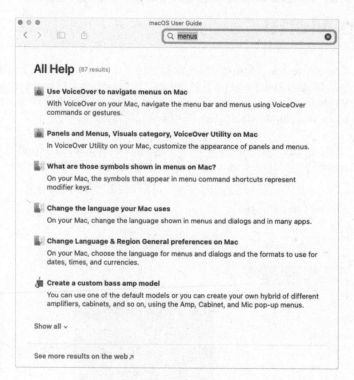

FIGURE 1-6:
You have
questions? Mac
Help has
answers.

As long as your Mac is connected to the Internet, search results include articles from the Apple online support database.

REMEMBER

Although you don't have to be connected to the Internet to use Mac Help, you do need an Internet connection to get the most out of it. (Chapter 15 can help you set up an Internet connection, if you don't have one.) That's because macOS installs only certain help articles on your hard drive. If you ask a question that those articles don't answer, Mac Help connects to the Apple website and downloads the answer (assuming that you have an active Internet connection). These answers appear when you click Show All near the bottom of Figure 1-6. Click one of these entries, and Help Viewer retrieves the text over the Internet. This is sometimes inconvenient but also quite smart, because Apple can update the Help system at any time without requiring any action from you.

Furthermore, after you ask a question and Mac Help has grabbed the answer from the Apple website, the answer remains on your hard drive forever. If you ask for it again — even at a later date — your computer won't have to download it from the Apple website again.

Click See More Results on the Web (refer to the bottom of Figure 1-6) to launch Safari and perform a web search for the phrase you typed.

TIP

macOS also has a cool feature I like to call *automatic visual help cues*. Here's how they work:

1. **In the Help menu's Search field, type a word or phrase.**

2. **Select any item that has a menu icon to its left (such as the items with *Trash* in their names in Figure 1-7).**

   The automatic visual cue — an arrow — appears, pointing at that command in the appropriate menu.

Finally, don't forget that most apps have their own Help systems, so if you want general help with your Mac, you need to first click the Finder icon in the dock, click the desktop, or use the app-switching shortcut ⌘+Tab to activate Finder. Only then can you choose Mac Help from Finder's Help menu.

FIGURE 1-7:
If you choose an item with a menu icon, an arrow points to that item in context.

Chapter **2**

Desktop and Windows and Menus (Oh My!)

This chapter introduces important features of macOS, starting with the first things you see when you log in: Finder and its desktop. After a quick look around the desktop, you get a look into two of its most useful features: windows and menus.

Windows are (and have always been) an integral part of Mac computing. Windows in Finder (or, as a PC user might say, "on the desktop") show you the contents of the hard drive, optical drive, flash (thumb) drive, network drive, disk image, and folder icons. Windows in applications do many things. The point is that windows are part of what makes your Mac a Mac; knowing how they work — and how to use them — is essential.

Menus are another quintessential part of the Mac experience. The latter part of this chapter starts you out with a few menu basics. As needed, I direct you to other parts of the book for greater detail. So relax and don't worry. By the end of this chapter, you'll be ready to work with windows and menus in any application that uses them (and most applications, games excluded, do).

Touring Finder and Its Desktop

Finder is the program that creates the desktop, keeps track of your files and folders, and is always running. Just about everything you do on your Mac begins and ends with Finder. It's where you manage files, store documents, launch programs, and much more. If you ever expect to master your Mac, the first step is to master Finder and desktop.

Finder is the center of your macOS experience, so before I go any further, here's a quick description of its most prominent features:

» **Desktop:** The *desktop* is the area behind the windows and the dock. In macOS 11.0 the default desktop picture again honors its namesake, showing the California coast's Big Sur region.

It's also where your startup disk icon (ordinarily) lives.

If you don't see a disk icon on the desktop, never fear — you learn how to enable this behavior in Chapter 4.

The desktop isn't a window, yet it acts like one. Like a folder or disk window, the desktop can contain icons. But unlike most windows, which require a bit of navigation to get to, the desktop is always there behind any open windows, making it a great place for icons you use a lot, such as oft-used folders, applications, or documents.

Some folks use the terms *desktop* and *Finder* interchangeably to refer to the total Mac environment you see after you log in — the icons, windows, menus, and all that other cool stuff. Just to make things confusing, the background you see on your screen — the picture behind your hard drive icon and your open windows — is *also* called the desktop. In this book, I refer to the application you use when the desktop is showing as *Finder*. When I say *desktop,* I'm talking about the picture background behind your windows and the dock, which you can use as a storage place for icons if you like.

Don't panic. The desktop metaphor used by Big Sur will become crystal clear in upcoming pages and chapters.

» **Dock:** The dock is Finder's main navigation shortcut tool. It makes getting to frequently used icons easy, even when you have a screen full of windows. Plus, it's extremely customizable, as you find out in Chapter 3.

» **Icons:** Icons are the little pictures you see in folder and disk windows and on your desktop. Icons represent the things you work with on your Mac, such as applications (programs), documents, folders, utilities, and more.

» **Windows:** Opening most icons (by double-clicking them) makes a window appear. Windows in Finder show you the contents of disk drive and folder icons; windows in applications usually show the contents of documents. In the sections that follow, you can find the full scoop on Big Sur windows.

>> **Menus:** Menus let you choose to do things, such as create new folders; duplicate files; and cut, copy, or paste text. I introduce menu basics later in this chapter in the "Menu Basics" section; you find details about working with menus for specific tasks throughout this book.

Whereas this chapter offers a basic introduction to Finder and desktop, Chapter 8 explains in detail how to navigate and manage your files in Finder. But before you start using Finder, it helps to know the basics of working with windows and menus; if these Mac features are new to you, I suggest that you read this entire chapter now and pay special attention to Chapter 8 later.

Anatomy of a Window

Windows are a ubiquitous part of using a Mac. When you open a folder, you see a window. When you write a letter, the document that you're working on appears in a window. When you browse the Internet, web pages appear in a window . . . and so on.

For the most part, windows are windows from program to program. You'll probably notice that some programs (Adobe Photoshop or Microsoft Word, for example) take liberties with windows by adding features such as custom toolbars or textual information (such as zoom percentage or file size) around the edges of the document window and in toolbars.

Don't let it bug you; that extra fluff is just window dressing (pun intended). Maintaining the window metaphor, many information windows display different kinds of information in different *panes*, or discrete sections within the window.

When you finish this chapter, which focuses exclusively on macOS Finder windows, you'll know how to use most windows in most applications. And so, without further ado, the following list gives you a look at the main features of a typical Finder window (as shown in Figure 2-1). I discuss these features in greater detail in later sections of this chapter.

TIP

If your windows don't look exactly like Figure 2-1, don't be concerned. You can make your windows look and feel any way you like. As I explain later in the "Working with Windows" section, moving and resizing windows are easy tasks.

FIGURE 2-1:
A typical Finder window in macOS Big Sur.

Meanwhile, here's what you see on the toolbar (clockwise from top left):

>> **Close, Minimize, and Zoom buttons:** Shut 'em, shrink 'em, and grow 'em.

>> **View icons:** Choose among four exciting views of your window: Icon, List, Column, and Gallery. Find out more about views in Chapter 4.

>> **Group By menu:** Click this little doohickey to group this window's icons by Name, Kind, Application, Date Modified, Date Created, Date Last Opened, Date Added, Size, or Tags. Or, of course, by None, which is the default.

>> **Action menu:** This icon is really a pop-up menu of commands you can apply to currently selected items in the Finder window or on the desktop. It's nearly the same list of commands you'll find in the contextual (shortcut) menu when you right-click or Control-click that item or items.

Note that some menu icons and items in these menus aren't available (appear dimmed) until you select one or more icons in the Finder window. If nothing happens when you click a toolbar icon, click a file or folder icon to select it and try again.

>> **Window title:** Shows the name of the window (*bigsurbob* in Figure 2-1).

TIP

⌘-click (or Control-click) the window title to see a pop-up menu with the complete path to this folder. (Try it now.) This tip applies to most windows you'll encounter, not just Finder windows. So ⌘- or Control-click a window's title (a right-click or two-fingered tap on a trackpad will work, too), and you'll (usually) see the path to its enclosing folder on your disk, though some third-party apps don't follow this convention.

TIP

To see the path from your hard or solid-state drive to the active window, choose View ⇨ Show Path Bar. The path will appear at the bottom of all Finder windows until you choose View ⇨ Hide Path Bar.

» **Share menu:** Another icon that's a menu. Click it to share selected files or folders via Mail, Messages, AirDrop, or Notes. Additional commands, such as Add (the selected item) to Photos or Contacts.

» **Tags menu:** Yet another menu; click it to assign a tag to the selected files or folders.

» **Search:** Click the magnifying glass icon and then type a string of characters in the field that appears. Big Sur's Spotlight search feature digs into your system to find items that match by filename or document contents (yes, it will find words within most documents).

» **Scroll bars:** Use the scroll bars for moving around a window.

» **Sidebar:** Frequently used items live here.

» **Forward and Back icons:** These icons take you to the next or previous folder, respectively, displayed in this particular window. The first time you open a window, neither icon is active; in Figure 2-1, only the Back icon is active.

As you navigate from folder to folder, these icons remember your bread-crumb trail so you can quickly traverse backward or forward, window by window. You can even navigate this way from the keyboard by using the shortcuts ⌘ +[for Back and ⌘+] for Forward.

REMEMBER

The Forward and Back icons remember only the other folders you've visited that appear in *that* open window. If you've set a Finder preference so that folders always open in a new window — or if you forced a folder to open in a new window, which I describe in a bit — the Forward and Back icons won't work. In other words, you have to use the modern macOS-style window option, which uses a single window and tabs; otherwise, the Forward and Back icons are useless.

Top o' the window to ya!

Take a gander at the top of a window — any window. You see three buttons in the top-left corner and the name of the window to the right of the Back and Forward icons. The three buttons (called *gumdrop buttons* by some folks because they look like, well, gumdrops) are officially known as Close, Minimize, and Zoom, and their colors (red, yellow, and green, respectively) are designed to pop off the screen.

Here's what they do:

>> **Close (red):** Click this button to close the window.

>> **Minimize (yellow):** Click this button to minimize the window. Clicking Minimize appears to close the window, but instead of making it disappear, Minimize adds an icon for the window to the right side of the dock.

TIP

See the section about minimizing windows into application icons in Chapter 3 if a document icon doesn't appear in your dock when you minimize the document's window.

To view the window again, click the dock icon for the window that you minimized. If the window happens to be a QuickTime movie, the movie audio continues to play and a tiny still image from the video appears as its icon in the dock. (I discuss the dock in detail in Chapter 3.)

>> **Zoom (green):** Click a window's green Zoom button, and the window expands to cover the whole screen, including the menu bar.

TIP

If you prefer the old behavior, where a window zoomed to the largest size it could but didn't cover the full screen, hold down the Option key when you click the green button.

To shrink the window back to its previous dimensions, slide the cursor up to the very top of the screen, wait for the menu bar to appear, and then click the green Zoom button.

Another way to escape from a full-screen window, at least in Finder, is to press the Esc key on your keyboard. Sadly, this trick doesn't work with all apps, though it's quite useful in apps that support it (most Apple apps and many others) as well as in Finder.

Split View is semi-hidden beneath the green Zoom button. To see Split View in action, click the green button for a moment — that is, perform the first half of a click but don't release the button yet. A pop-up menu with three options appears; select Enter Full Screen, Tile Window to Left of Screen, or Tile Window to Right of Screen.

Another way to invoke Split View is to *hover* the cursor over the Zoom button for a moment (don't click). The same pop-up menu appears with the same three options.

After assigning a window to the left or right half of the screen, the other half displays miniature versions of all open windows. Hover the cursor over a miniature window to see its name; click a miniature window and it fills that half of the screen.

To work in Split View, click either window to activate it and do what you have to do. To activate the other window, click it. To exit Split View, do one of the following:

- Press Esc.

- Move the pointer to the top of the screen; when the buttons (for both windows) reappear, click any button.

- Quit either application.

A scroll new world

Yet another way to see more of what's in a window or pane is to scroll through it. Scroll bars appear at the bottom and right sides of any window or pane that contains more stuff — icons, text, pixels, or whatever — than you can see in the window. Figure 2-2, for example, shows two instances of the same window: Dragging the scroll bar on the right side of the smaller window would reveal the icons above and below the six (whole) icons that are currently visible. Dragging the scroll bar on the bottom of the smaller window would reveal items to the left and right of the six that are currently visible.

Scroll bars (gray)

FIGURE 2-2:
The same window twice. Use the scroll bars in the front window to see the icons above, below, to the left, or to the right.

Scroll areas (white)

Simply click and drag a scroll bar to move it up or down or side to side.

If your scroll bars don't look exactly like the ones in Figure 2-2 or work as described in the following list, don't worry. These are System Preferences you can configure to your heart's desire, as you discover in Chapter 6.

Here are some ways you can scroll in a window:

>> **Click a scroll bar and drag.** The content of the window scrolls proportionally to how far you drag the scroll bar.

>> **Click in the scroll bar area but don't click the scroll bar itself.** The window scrolls either one page up (if you click above the scroll bar) or down (if you click below the scroll bar). You can change a setting in your General System Preferences pane to cause the window to scroll proportionally to where you click.

TIP

For what it's worth, the Page Up and Page Down keys on your keyboard function the same way as clicking the white scroll area (the vertical scroll bar only) in Finder and many applications. These keys don't work in every program, though, so don't become too dependent on them. Also, if you purchased a mouse, a trackball, or another pointing device that has a scroll wheel, you can scroll vertically in the active (front) window with the scroll wheel or press and hold down the Shift key to scroll horizontally. Alas, this horizontal scrolling-with-the-Shift-key works in Finder windows but not in all applications. For example, it works in the Apple TextEdit application, but not in Microsoft Word.

>> **Use the keyboard.** In Finder, first click an icon in the window and then use the arrow keys to move up, down, left, or right. Using an arrow key selects the next icon in the direction it indicates — and automatically scrolls the window, if necessary. In other programs, you might or might not be able to use the keyboard to scroll. The best advice I can give you is to try it — either it will work or it won't.

>> **Use a two-finger swipe (on a trackpad).** If you have a notebook with a trackpad or use a Magic Trackpad or Magic Mouse, just move the arrow cursor over the window and then swipe the trackpad with two fingers to scroll.

(Hyper)active windows

To work within a window, the window must be active. The *active* window is always the frontmost window, and *inactive* windows always appear behind the active window. Only one window can be active at a time. To make a window active, click it anywhere — in the middle, on the title bar, or on a scroll bar. It doesn't matter where; just click anywhere to activate it.

TIP

The exceptions are the Close, Minimize, and Zoom buttons on inactive windows, which always do what they do, regardless of whether a window is active or inactive.

Look at Figure 2-3 for an example of an active window in front of an inactive window (the Applications window and the Utilities window, respectively).

Inactive window

Active window

FIGURE 2-3:
An active window in front of an inactive window.

The following is a list of the major visual cues that distinguish active from inactive windows:

» **The active window's title bar:** By default, the Close, Minimize, and Zoom buttons are bright red, yellow, and green, respectively, and the inactive windows' buttons are light gray.

TIP

This is a nice visual cue. Colored items are active, and gray ones are inactive. Better still, if you move your mouse cursor over an inactive window's gumdrop buttons, they light up in their usual colors so you can close, minimize, or zoom an inactive window without first clicking it to making it active. Neat!

» **The active window's toolbar:** Toolbar icons are darker and more distinctive; the inactive window's toolbar icons are light gray and more subdued.

» **The active window's drop shadow:** Notice how the active window has a more prominent shadow? This tricks your eye into thinking the active window is in front of the inactive one.

One last thing: If you're wondering how to resize a window, just hover the cursor over a window's edge or corner or over the dividing line between two panes in the same window (such as the sidebar and the main area of Finder windows). A helpful little arrow appears as a visual cue that you can now drag the edge, corner, or dividing line to resize the window or pane.

Dialog Dealie-Boppers

Dialogs are special windows that pop up over the active window. You generally see them when you select a menu item that ends in an ellipsis (. . .).

Dialogs can contain a number of standard Mac features (I call them *dealie-boppers*), such as radio buttons, pop-up menus, tabs, text-entry fields, and check boxes. You see these features again and again in dialogs. Take a moment to look at each of these dealie-boppers in Figure 2-4.

>> **Radio buttons:** *Radio buttons* are so named because, like the buttons on your car radio (if you have a very old car), only one at a time can be active. (When they're active, they appear to be pushed in, just like the old radio buttons.) Radio buttons always appear in a group of two or more; when you select one, all the others are automatically deselected.

TIP

Here's a nifty and undocumented shortcut: You can usually select check boxes and radio buttons by clicking their names (instead of the buttons or boxes).

>> **Tabs:** When a dialog contains more information than can fit in a single window, the info may be divided among panes denoted by tabs. In Figure 2-4, the New Document tab is selected on the left, and the Open and Save tab is selected on the right.

>> **Pop-up menus:** These menus are appropriately named because they pop up when you click them. In Figure 2-4, right, the Styling menu has been clicked and is popped up; the other pop-up menus — Opening Files, Saving Files, Document Type, and Encoding (mostly obscured by the popped-up Styling menu) — are unclicked and unpopped.

You can always recognize a pop-up menu because it appears in a slightly rounded rectangle and has a double-ended arrow symbol (or a pair of triangles, if you like) on the right.

Have you figured out yet what radio buttons, tabs, and pop-up menus have in common? *Hint:* All three enable you to make a single selection from a group of options. (Well, okay, that was more of an answer than a hint.)

» **Text-entry fields:** In text-entry fields, you type text (including numbers) from the keyboard. In Figure 2-4, left, the Width, Height, Author, Organization, and Copyright options are text-entry fields.

» **Check boxes:** The last dealie-bopper that you see frequently is the check box. In a group of check boxes, you can select as many options as you like. Check boxes are selected when they contain a check mark, and they're deselected when they're empty, as shown in Figure 2-4.

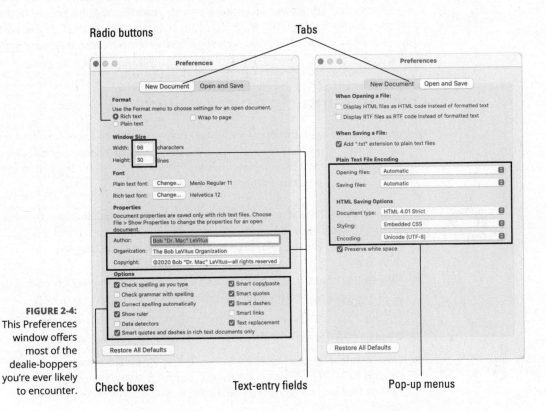

Radio buttons

Tabs

Check boxes

Text-entry fields

Pop-up menus

FIGURE 2-4:
This Preferences window offers most of the dealie-boppers you're ever likely to encounter.

I couldn't find a dialog or window that included all the aforementioned dealie-boppers as well as the one other dealie-bopper you should become familiar with, the disclosure triangle. If you see a triangle in a dialog or sheet, try clicking it. If it's a disclosure triangle, it will reveal additional options (or its contents if it's a folder in Finder's List view, as you see in Chapter 8).

TECHNICAL STUFF

Some applications have *tri-state* check boxes (and no, I'm not talking geography here). These special check boxes are empty when nothing in the group is selected, sport an X when everything in the group is selected, and sport a minus sign (–) when some items in the group are selected and some are not.

Working with Windows

In the following sections, I give you a closer look at windows themselves: how you move them, size them, and use them. And although Big Sur windows are similar to windows you've used in other versions of macOS (and even, dare I say it, Windows), you may just discover a new wrinkle or two.

TIP

If you're relatively new to the Mac, you may want to read this section while sitting at your computer, trying the techniques as you read them. Most people find it easier to remember something they've read if they actually do it. If you've been using your Mac for a while, you've probably figured out how windows work by now.

Opening and closing windows

To start peering into windows on your Mac, first you need to know how to open and close them. When you're working in Finder, you can choose the following commands from the File menu. Note that you'll probably find similar commands on the File menu of programs other than Finder.

TIP

You'll use many of these commands frequently, so it would behoove you to memorize their keyboard shortcuts. If you're not sure how keyboard shortcuts work, check out "Using keyboard shortcut commands," later in this chapter.

>> **New Finder Window (⌘+N):** Opens a new Finder window. In other programs, ⌘+N might open a new document, project, or whatever that program helps you create.

>> **Open (⌘+O):** Opens the selected item, be it an icon, a window, or a folder.

>> **Close Window (⌘+W):** Closes the active window. If no windows are open or if no window is selected, the Close Window command appears dimmed and can't be chosen. Or if you prefer, you can close a window by clicking the red Close button in the top-left corner.

REMEMBER

If you hold down the Option key with the File menu open, the Close Window command changes to Close All. This useful command enables you to close all open Finder windows. But it shows up only when you press the Option key or use its keyboard shortcut (⌘+Option+W); otherwise, it remains hidden.

TIP

Note that several other commands in the File menu transmogrify when you press the Option key. It would be off topic to get into them here, but here's a tip: Press the Option key, and browse all Finder menus. At least a dozen useful commands appear only when the Option key is pressed. Press it early and often for hidden (often time-saving) commands.

Resizing windows and window panes

If you want to see more (or less) of what's in a window, just hover the pointer over any edge or corner and drag. When the cursor turns into a little double-headed arrow, as shown in Figure 2-5, click and drag to resize the window.

FIGURE 2-5:
Hover the pointer over any corner or edge; when the double-headed arrow (resizer) cursor appears, click and drag to resize the window.

Note that I've put arrow cursors on all sides and corners of the window in Figure 2-5. That's for illustration purposes; in real life you'll only see one at a time (below your mouse cursor).

 Display windows, like those in Finder, frequently consist of multiple panes. If you look at Figure 2-5, a line divides the sidebar pane to the left of it and the contents pane to the right. When your mouse pointer hovers over the line, the cursor changes to a vertical bar (or it could be horizontal if the panes are one above the other) with little arrows pointing out of both sides, as shown in the margin.

When you see this cursor, you can click and drag anywhere in the dividing line that separates the sidebar from the rest of the window. Doing so resizes the two panes relative to each other; one gets larger and one gets smaller.

Moving windows

To move a window, click anywhere in a window's gray title bar or toolbar (except on a button, an icon, a menu, or a Search field) and drag the window to wherever you want it. The window moves wherever you move the mouse, stopping dead in its tracks when you release the mouse button.

If you can't find the cursor on the screen, wiggle your finger on the trackpad or jiggle the mouse. In Big Sur, these movements magnify the pointer to make it easier to find onscreen.

TIP

Shuffling windows

I've already spent plenty of pages giving you the scoop on how to work with windows. But wait. There's more! The commands on the Window menu provide tools you can use to manage your windows.

Here is a brief look at each of the items on the Window menu. (And if you're unfamiliar with menus and keyboard shortcuts, you find out how they work later in this chapter.)

» **Minimize (⌘+M):** Use this command to minimize the active Finder window to the dock and unclutter your desktop. It's the same as clicking the yellow gumdrop button.

» **Zoom:** This command does the same thing as the green gumdrop button. If you've forgotten what the green gumdrop does already, just turn back a few pages to the "Top o' the window to ya!" section and read it again.

» **Cycle through Windows (⌘+`):** Each time you choose this command or use the keyboard shortcut for it, a different window becomes active. So if you have three windows — call 'em Window 1, Window 2, and Window 3 — and you're using Window 1, this command deactivates Window 1 and activates Window 2. If you choose it again, the command deactivates Window 2 and activates Window 3. Choose it one more time, and it deactivates Window 3 and reactivates Window 1.

The next four commands in the Window menu help you manage Big Sur Finder window tabs. If you're a fan of tabbed browsing (*à la* Safari), you'll love tabs in a Finder window.

Tabs let you view multiple folders or disks or both in a single window, with each folder or disk in its own tab, as shown in Figure 2-6.

Tabbed windows are an ingenious way to cram a lot of information into a little space. I've tried a number of third-party utilities that purported to provide tabbed Finder windows, but I've never found one that's reliable and robust enough to continue using. This one, on the other hand, just works.

Big Sur, like its last few predecessors, includes system-wide tabbed windows, which should work in almost every application that uses windows. The cool part is the app doesn't have to be updated in any way — Big Sur grafts tabbed windows onto almost every app that displays multiple windows.

FIGURE 2-6:
I can view the contents of my Documents (shown), Applications, or Downloads folder by merely clicking the appropriate tab.

The remaining commands in the Window menu are as follows:

>> **Show Previous Tab (Control+Shift+Tab):** Each time you choose this command or use its keyboard shortcut, the previous tab — the one to its left, unless it's the leftmost tab — becomes active. For example, in Figure 2-6, Documents is the active tab. Use this command, and Applications becomes the active tab. Use it a third time, and Downloads becomes active. Because Downloads is the leftmost tab, if you use this command yet again, it wraps around and Documents becomes the active tab again.

>> **Show Next Tab (Control+Tab):** Same as Show Previous Tab except in reverse. Instead of showing the previous tab (the one to the left), this command shows the next tab (the one to the right). Use this command three times in a row (refer to the order shown in Figure 2-6), and you see the Downloads tab, then the Applications tab, and finally the Documents tab again.

>> **Move Tab to New Window (no keyboard shortcut):** Does just what it says; it moves the active tab into a new window of its own.

>> **Merge All Windows (no keyboard shortcut):** Combines all open windows and tabs in one window.

TIP

You can click a tab and drag it left or right to change the order. You can also drag and drop a tab from one Finder window to another. The trick is to click directly on a tab and drag it *onto the tabs in the target window*. If you release it anywhere else, the tab will be displayed in a new window.

One more thing: In Big Sur, all these commands and keyboard shortcuts appear in most apps that display windows.

»» Bring All to Front (no keyboard shortcut): Windows from different applications can interleave. For example, you can have (from front to back) a Finder window, a Microsoft Word window, an Adobe Photoshop window, another Microsoft Word window, and another Finder window. In this example, choosing Bring All to Front while Finder is the active application enables you to have both Finder windows move in front of those belonging to Word and Photoshop.

If you want to bring all the windows belonging to Finder (or any other program, for that matter) to the front at the same time, you can also click the appropriate dock icon (Finder, in this case).

If you hold down the Option key when you click the Window menu, Minimize Window changes to Minimize All, and the Zoom command changes to Zoom All.

»» Other items: The remaining items on the Window menu — if any — are the names of all currently open Finder windows. Click a window's name to bring it to the front.

TIP

Menu Basics

Mac menus are often referred to as *pull-down menus*. To check out the macOS menus, click the Finder button on the dock to activate Finder and then look at the top of your screen. From left to right, you see the Apple menu, the Finder menu, and six other menus. To use an macOS menu, click its name to make the menu appear and then pull (drag) down to select a menu item. Piece of cake!

Note that menus stay down after you click their names, and stay open until you either select an item or click outside the menu's boundaries.

The ever-changing menu bar

Before you start working with macOS menus, you really, really should know this: *Menu items can change unexpectedly.* Why? Well, the menus you see on the menu bar at the top of the screen always reflect the program that's *active* at the time. When you switch from Finder to a particular program — or from one program to another — the menus change immediately to match whatever program you switched to.

REMEMBER

Figure 2-7 shows the menu bars for Finder, Preview, and TextEdit applications.

FIGURE 2-7:
Menu bars
change to reflect
the active
application.

🍎	**Finder**	File	Edit	View	Go	Window	Help	

🍎	**Preview**	File	Edit	View	Go	Tools	Window	Help

🍎	**TextEdit**	File	Edit	Format	View	Window	Help	

An easy way to tell which program is active is to look at the application menu — it's the leftmost menu with a name, just to the right of the Apple menu. When you're in Finder, of course, the application menu reads *Finder.* But if you switch to another program (by clicking its icon on the dock or by clicking any window associated with the program) or launch a new program, that menu changes to the name of the active program.

When you have an application open, the commands on the menu change, too — but just a little bit. What makes this cool is that you have access to some standard application menu items whether you're running Mail, Safari, or almost any other app. For example, most (but not all) applications have Cut, Copy, and Paste commands in their Edit menus, and Open, Save, and Print commands in their File menus. You can find much more about commands for applications in Part 3, which explains how applications that come with macOS Big Sur can help you get things done.

Contextual (shortcut) menus: They're sooo contextual!

Contextual menus (also called *shortcut menus*) list commands that apply only to the item that is currently selected. Contextual menus might be available in windows, on icons, and in most places on the desktop.

To see whether a contextual menu is available, either hold down the Control key and click — which you can call a *Control-click* to sound cool to your Mac friends — or, for those with two or more buttons on their mice, *right-click.* Finally, most Mac laptops (as well as the Magic Trackpad and the Magic Mouse) let you click the trackpad using two fingers to simulate a right-click or a Control-click.

TIP

If this doesn't work for you, launch System Preferences and click the Trackpad icon. Click the Point & Click tab and make sure that Click with Two Fingers is selected as your Secondary Click and (of course), the Secondary Click check box is enabled.

Another reason the contextual menu might not appear is that it is available only if any of its commands make sense for the item that you Control-click or right-click. That's why people call 'em *contextual!* They're specific to the current context, which is whatever is selected or Control-clicked.

Figure 2-8, left, shows the contextual menu that appears when you Control-click (or right-click) a document icon. Figure 2-8, right, shows the contextual menu you see when you Control-click the desktop.

FIGURE 2-8:
Only relevant
items appear in a
contextual menu.

Contextual menus are also available in most applications. Open your favorite app and try Control-clicking to find out whether those menus are there. In most cases, using a contextual menu is a quick way to avoid going to the menu bar to choose a command. In some programs — such as iMovie and Music — contextual menus are the *only* way to access some commands.

To make the Finder-related contextual menus available to users who didn't have the foresight to purchase this book, Apple added the Action icon (shown in the margin) to the toolbar. As a result, people who don't know about Control-clicking or right-clicking (or have only one free hand) can access most contextual menu commands by clicking the Action button and displaying its context-sensitive menu of shortcuts. You, on the other hand, gentle reader, know how to get at these commands without having to run your mouse all the way up to the Action icon in the toolbar. Plus, a handful of commands appear in the Control-click/right-click contextual menu but don't appear in the Action icon/menu.

Get in the habit of Control-clicking (or right-clicking or two-finger clicking) items on your screen. Before you know it, using contextual menus will become second nature to you.

REMEMBER

Recognizing disabled options

Menu items that appear in black on a menu are currently available. Menu items that aren't currently available are grayed out, to indicate that they're disabled for the time being. You can't select a disabled menu item.

In Figure 2-9, the File menu on the left is pulled down while nothing is selected in Finder; this is why many of the menu items are disabled (in gray). These items are disabled because an item (such as a window or an icon) must be selected for you to use one of these menu items. For example, the Show Original command is grayed out because it works only if the selected item is an alias. On the right side of Figure 2-9, I selected a document before I pulled down the menu; note that many of the formerly disabled commands are enabled when an icon is selected. (The Show Original command is still grayed out because the selected icon is not an alias.)

FIGURE 2-9:
File menu with nothing selected (left) and with a document icon selected (right); the disabled items appear grayed out.

Finally, note that items that end in an ellipsis (. . .), such as the Tags command in Figure 2-9, will open a dialog with additional options.

Navigating submenus

Some menu items have more menus attached to them, and these are called *submenus*, which are menus that are subordinate to a menu item. If a menu has a black triangle to the right of its name, it has a submenu.

To use a submenu, click a menu name once (to drop the menu down) and then slide your cursor down to any item with a black triangle. When the item is highlighted, move your mouse to the right just slightly. The submenu should pop out of the original menu's item, as shown in Figure 2-10.

FIGURE 2-10:
The Apple menu's
Recent Items
selection, with its
submenu
popped out.

Under the Apple menu tree

On the far-left side of the menu bar sits a little , which displays a menu when clicked. No matter what application is active, the menu is always available in the top-left corner of your menu bar.

TIP

The menu bar is always available, even with apps that hide it in full-screen mode. To make it reappear, move the pointer to the top of the screen, wait a second or two, and watch the menu bar magically reappear.

From top to bottom, the menu gives you a number of options, including the following:

>> **About This Mac:** Choose this item to see what version of macOS you're running, what kind of Mac and processor you're using, how much memory your Mac has, the name of your startup disk, and much more. The window sports multiple tabs across the top of the window — Overview, Displays, Storage, and so on.

Click the System Report button on the Overview tab to launch the Apple System Information utility; there, you can find out more than you'll probably ever want or need to know about your Mac's hardware and software.

Click the Software Update button on the Overview tab to have your Mac check with the mothership (Apple) to see whether any updates are available for macOS, its included applications, third-party applications purchased at the Mac App Store, other Apple-branded applications (such as GarageBand, Final Cut Pro, Pages), or even Apple-branded peripheral devices, such as the iPod or iPhone.

>> **System Preferences:** Choose this item to open the System Preferences app (which I discuss further in Chapter 6 and elsewhere).

>> **App Store:** Choose this item to launch the Mac App Store.

>> **Recent Items:** This option lets you quickly access applications, documents, and servers you've used recently, as shown previously in Figure 2-10.

>> **Force Quit:** Use this option only in emergencies. What's an emergency? Use it when an application becomes recalcitrant or otherwise misbehaves or refuses to quit when you say Quit.

TIP

Memorize the keyboard shortcut for Force Quit (⌘+Option+Esc). Sometimes a program gets so badly hosed that you can't click anywhere and other keyboard shortcuts won't do anything at all. It doesn't happen often, nor does it happen to everyone. If it should happen to you, calmly press the magic key combo you memorized (⌘+Option+Esc), and the Force Quit Applications dialog (usually) appears. Click the name of the program that's acting up and then click the Force Quit button or press the Return key to make the balky application stop balking.

WARNING

The reason Force Quit should be used only in an emergency is that if you use it on an application that's working fine and have any unsaved documents, your work since the last time you saved the file will be blown away.

Or not. The Auto Save and Versions features are *still* the default for Apple's own applications. You read more about these features in Chapter 7; if the app you're using supports Auto Save features, you shouldn't lose much (if any) work regardless of when you last saved.

>> **Shut Down options:** These five commands do exactly what their names imply:

- *Sleep:* Puts your Mac into an energy-efficient state of suspended animation. See the section about Energy Saver in Chapter 23 for details on the Energy Saver System Preferences pane and sleeping.

- *Restart:* Quits all open programs and restarts your Mac. It's quite polite about this task, asking if you want to save any unsaved changes in open documents before complying.

- *Shut Down:* Turns off your Mac. Refer to Chapter 1 for details.

- *Lock Screen (⌘+Control+Q):* Locks your screen instantly, and then requires your account password to unlock it.

- *Log Out <your account name> (⌘+Shift+Q):* Quits all open programs and logs you out. Again, your Mac will be ever so polite, asking if you want to save unsaved changes in open documents before complying. When it's done, the login screen appears.

Using keyboard shortcut commands

Most menu items, or at least the most common ones, have *keyboard shortcuts* to help you quickly navigate your Mac without having to haggle so much with the mouse. Using these key combinations activates menu items without using the mouse; to use them, you press the Command (⌘) key and then press another key (or keys) without releasing the ⌘ key. Memorize the shortcuts that you use often.

Learn how to change keyboard shortcuts and even how to create ones of your own in Chapter 6.

REMEMBER

Some people refer to the Command key as the *Apple key.* That's because on many keyboards that key has both the pretzel-like Command key symbol (⌘) and an Apple logo () on it. To avoid confusion, I always refer to ⌘ as the Command key.

Chapter **3**

What's Up, Dock?

The dock appears at the bottom of your screen by default, providing quick access to your most often-used applications, documents, and folders.

TIP

Many users prefer to have the dock located on the left or right side of the screen instead of at the bottom. You see how to relocate your dock (and more) in the coming pages.

Folder icons on the dock are called *stacks,* and they can display your choice of a fan, a grid, or a list of contents when clicked.

Other icons on the dock open an application or document with one click.

The dock is your friend. It's a great place to put files, folders, and apps you use a lot so that they're always just one click away.

TIP

A dock icon is merely a pointer (also known as an *alias* or a *shortcut*) to applications, documents, and folders stored on your hard drive. So, you can add and remove icons from your dock (as you discover shortly) without affecting the actual applications, documents, and folders. Don't be shy about adding items you use often as well as removing items you don't use.

A Quick Introduction to Your Dock

Take a minute to look at the row of icons at the bottom of your display. That row, gentle reader, is the *dock* (shown in Figure 3-1), and those individual pictures are known as *icons* (which I discuss in greater detail momentarily). Note that I chopped the dock in Figure 3-1 into two pieces (with the left half on top) to make the icons bigger and easier to see.

FIGURE 3-1:
The dock and all its default icons.

Icons in the dock and Launchpad (see Chapter 10) are odd ducks; you activate them with a single click. Most other Finder icons are selected (highlighted) when you single-click and opened only when you double-click them.

So dock icons (and their Launchpad brethren) are kind of like links on a web page; you need only a single click to open them.

Here's the rundown on what happens when you click dock icons:

>> If it's an **application icon,** the application opens and becomes active. If the application is already open, it becomes active, which brings its menu and all its windows to the front.

>> If it's a **document icon,** that document opens in its appropriate application, which becomes the active application. If that application is already open, it becomes the active application with this document in the front.

If the item is an application or document and is already open when you click its dock icon, the app or document becomes active.

REMEMBER

>> If it's a **folder icon or disk icon,** a stack, fan, or grid with its contents appears so you can choose an item. If you choose Show in Finder from this menu, the folder's window opens in Finder.

The default icons of the dock

By default, the dock contains a number of commonly used macOS applications, and you can also store your own applications, files, or folders there. (I show you how to do that in the "Adding dock icons" section, later in this chapter.)

But first, look at the items you find in a standard macOS Big Sur dock. If they aren't familiar to you, they certainly will be as you get to know Big Sur.

I admit that I can't do justice to all the programs that come with macOS Big Sur that aren't, strictly speaking, part of the operating system (OS). Alas, some of the programs in the default dock are ones you won't be seeing much more of. But I'd hate to leave you wondering what all those icons in the dock are, so the following list gives you a brief description of each default dock icon (moving from left to right onscreen). If additional coverage of an item appears elsewhere in the book, the list tells you where:

>> **Finder:** The always running application that manages the desktop, files, folders, disks, and more (this chapter and Chapters 4-8)

>> **Launchpad:** A display of all your applications on a grid that looks suspiciously like an iPad or iPhone (Chapter 10)

>> **Safari**: A web browser (Chapter 15)

>> **Mail:** An email program (Chapter 17)

>> **FaceTime**: A video chat program (Chapter 15)

>> **Messages:** A program for sending and receiving text and multimedia messages as well as transferring files to and from and remotely controlling other Macs (Chapter 17)

>> **Maps:** A program with maps and driving directions (Chapter 13)

>> **Photos:** A program for managing and editing photographs (Chapter 20)

>> **Contacts** A contact manager application (Chapter 16)

>> **Calendar:** A calendar program for managing appointments and events (Chapter 11)

>> **Reminders**: A to-do list and reminder application (Chapter 11)

- **»** **Notes:** A program for making notes (Chapter 11)

- **»** **Music:** An audio player and store (Chapter 19)

- **»** **Podcasts:** A podcast player (Chapter 20)

- **»** **TV:** A video player and store (Chapter 20)

- **»** **News:** A news reader (Chapter 14)

- **»** **Mac App Store:** Where you buy Mac apps from Apple (Chapter 23)

- **»** **System Preferences:** An application to configure the way many aspects of your Mac work (Chapters 6, 18, and 23)

- **»** **Divider:** The line that separates apps on the left and documents or folders on the right (this chapter)

- **»** **Downloads folder:** A folder that contains files downloaded by Safari or Mail (Chapter 4)

- **»** **Trash:** Where you drag files and folders to delete them, or drag removable media to eject it (this chapter)

TIP

To get a quick look at the name of a dock icon, just move (hover) your pointer over any item in the dock. Like magic, that item's name appears above it (like *Safari* on the left side of Figure 3-4, later in this chapter).

It's likely that your dock won't look *exactly* like the one shown in Figure 3-1. If you added icons to your dock before you upgraded to Big Sur, for example, you'll see those icons. If you have Apple apps such as iMovie, GarageBand, Pages, Numbers, or Keynote installed, or you get a new Mac with Big Sur preinstalled, you may see their icons in your dock. And if you've deleted one of the default icons shown in Figure 3-1 from your dock under a previous version of macOS, it won't come back when you upgrade to Big Sur.

TIP

If you don't understand what I just said or want to make your dock look exactly like the one shown in Figure 3-1, I have good news: You find out how to do that and much more before the end of this chapter.

Also, if you see a question mark instead of an icon in the dock, the file (application, document, or folder) it represents has been deleted.

Trash talkin'

The *Trash* is a special container where you put the icons you no longer want to hang around on your hard drive(s). Got four copies of a document named *Letter to the Editor re: Bird Waste Issue* on your hard drive? Drag three of them to the Trash. Tired of tripping over old PDF and DMG files you've downloaded but no longer need? Drag them to the Trash, too.

To put something in the Trash, just drag its icon onto the Trash icon in the dock and it will move into the Trash. As with other icons, when the Trash icon is highlighted you know that you've connected with the Trash while dragging. And as with other dock icons, the Trash icon's name appears when you move the cursor over the icon.

Two other ways to put items into the Trash are to select the items you want to dispose of and then choose File⇨Move to Trash or press ⌘+Delete (⌘+Backspace on some keyboards).

TIP

If you accidentally move something to the Trash and want it back right now, you can magically put it back where it came from in two ways.

Way #1

Choose Edit⇨Undo or press ⌘+Z.

Finder usually remembers more than one action for Undo and can often undo the last *few* things you did in Finder. That's the good news. The bad news is that it redoes things in reverse order, so don't wait too long. If you perform several other file-related activities in Finder, you'll have to Undo all those actions before you can Undo your accidental Move to Trash.

In other words, as soon as you create or rename a folder, move a file from one place to another, drag a different file to the Trash, create an alias, or almost anything that affects a file or folder, choosing Edit⇨Undo or pressing ⌘+Z will undo *that* action first.

You'll find that some Finder actions — most of the items in the View menu, for example — don't affect Undo. So if you drag a file to the Trash and then switch views (see Chapter 4), Undo will still un-trash the file.

Even if you do something and can't use Undo, files you drag to the Trash aren't deleted immediately. You know how the garbage in the can on the street curb sits there until the sanitation engineers come by and pick it up each Thursday? Big Sur's Trash works the same way, but without the smell. Items sit in the Trash, waiting for a sanitation engineer (you) to come along and empty it.

Way #2

So, if you miss the window of opportunity to use the Undo command, don't worry; you can still retrieve the file from the Trash:

>> **To open the Trash and see what's in there,** just click its icon on the dock. A Finder window called Trash opens, showing you the files it contains (namely, files and folders put in the Trash since the last time it was emptied).

>> **To retrieve an item that's already in the Trash,** drag it back out, either onto the desktop or back into the folder where it belongs.

TIP

Or use the secret keyboard shortcut: Select the item(s) in the Trash that you want to retrieve and press ⌘+Delete. This technique has the added benefit of magically transporting the files or folders you select from the Trash back into the folder from which they came. And, unlike Undo, the secret keyboard shortcut will work on a file or folder at any time, or at least until the next time you empty the Trash. Try it — it's sweet.

And if that doesn't work, you can right-click or Control-click a file and choose Put Back from the contextual menu.

>> **To empty the Trash,** choose Finder⇨Empty Trash or press Shift+⌘+Delete. If the Trash window is open and files are in the Trash, you see an Empty button just below its toolbar on the right. Clicking the button, of course, also empties the Trash.

You can also empty the Trash from the dock by positioning the pointer on the Trash icon and right-clicking (or Control-clicking) the Trash icon. The Empty Trash menu item pops up like magic. Move the pointer over Empty Trash to select it and then release the mouse button.

WARNING

Think twice before you invoke the Empty Trash command. After you empty the Trash, the files that it contained are pretty much gone forever, or at least gone from your hard drive. There is no Undo for Empty Trash. So my advice is: Before you get too bold, read Chapter 24, and back up your hard drive at least once (several times is better). After you get proficient at backups, chances improve greatly that even though the files are technically gone forever from your hard drive, you can get them back if you really want to (from your backups).

The Trash icon shows you when it has files waiting for you there; as in real life, Trash that contains files or folders looks like it's full of crumpled paper (see Figure 3-2). Conversely, when your Trash is empty, the Trash icon looks, well, empty.

FIGURE 3-2:
The Options
menu for an
application icon
(Mac App Store)
on the dock.

Finally, although you can't open a file that's in the Trash, you can select it and use Quick Look (shortcut: ⌘+Y) to see its contents before you decide to use Empty Trash and permanently delete it.

And that's pretty much all there is to know about the Trash.

Opening application menus on the dock

Single-clicking an application icon on the dock launches that application — or, if the application is already open, switches you to that application and brings forward all open windows in that application.

But application icons on the dock — such as Calendar, Safari, and Music — also hide menus containing some handy commands. (Folder icons in the dock have a different but no less handy menu, which I discuss in a moment.)

You can make menus for applications on the dock appear in two ways:

>> Press and continue to hold down the mouse button.

>> Right-click or Control-click.

TIP

If you use a trackpad or a Magic Mouse, a two-finger tap should do the trick. (If it doesn't do the trick, check out the Mouse and Trackpad System Preferences sections in Chapter 6).

Do any of the preceding and you'll see a menu for that dock icon, as shown in Figure 3-2 for the App Store icon.

The Options submenu offers three choices:

>> **Remove from Dock:** Removes that application's icon from the dock (waiting until after you quit the application if it's running). If an application is running and its icon *isn't* already in the dock, you'll see Add to Dock rather than Remove from Dock.

>> **Open at Login:** Launches this application automatically every time you log in to this user account. This is handy for apps you want to keep running all the time, such as Mail or Safari.

>> **Show in Finder:** Opens the enclosing folder (in this instance, that would be the Applications folder) and selects the application's icon.

The other options in the menu follow:

>> **Show Recents (if available):** Displays recently used windows for this app if there are any.

>> **Open:** Launches the application or opens the folder.

So there you have it: The default Options menu for applications, which is what you'll see for most applications when they aren't open.

One last thing: When you right-click/Control-click the dock icon for an application that's currently running (look for the little dot below its icon), you may see different menus, like the ones shown in Figure 3-3 (clockwise from top left: Safari, Preview, System Preferences, TextEdit, and Music).

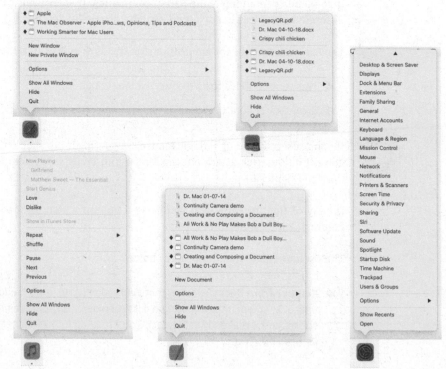

FIGURE 3-3: Press and hold down or right-click/Control-click an open application's dock icon, and menus such as these appear.

As you can see, some open applications provide useful program-specific commands or options.

TIP

Music has one of my favorite dock menus, letting me control my music from the dock with options such as Play/Pause, Next or Previous Track, Repeat, and Shuffle.

Other programs, including Preview and Safari in Figure 3-3, offer you a list of open windows with a check mark to indicate the active window or diamonds (as shown) to indicate windows minimized to the dock.

Finally, the items above the list of open windows for TextEdit are recently used documents.

Reading dock icon body language

As you use the dock or when you're just doing regular stuff on your Mac, the dock icons like to communicate with you. They can't talk, so they have a few moves and symbols that indicate things you might want to know. Figure 3-4 and Table 3-1 should make those moves and symbols crystal clear.

FIGURE 3-4:
The Safari dock icon at rest (left) and caught doing the bouncy dance (right).

TABLE 3-1   **What Dock Icons Are Telling You**

Icon Movement or Symbol	What It Means
The icon moves up and out of its place in the dock for a moment.	You single-clicked a dock icon, and it's letting you know that you activated it.
The icon does a little bouncy dance when that program is open but isn't *active* (that is, the menu bar isn't showing, and it isn't the frontmost program).	The program desires your attention; give its icon a click to find out what it wants.
A dot appears below its dock icon.	This application is open.
An icon that isn't ordinarily in the dock magically appears.	You see a temporary dock icon for every program that's currently open until you quit that application. The icon appears because you've opened something. When you quit, its icon magically disappears.

Opening files from the dock

REMEMBER

One useful function of the dock is that you can use it to open an application quickly and easily. The following tips explain several handy ways to open what you need from the dock:

>> **You can drag a document icon onto an application's dock icon.** If the application knows how to handle that type of document, its dock icon is highlighted, and the document opens in that application. If the application can't handle that particular type of document, the dock icon isn't highlighted, and you can't drop the document onto it.

TIP

I'm getting ahead of myself here, but if the application can't handle a document, try opening the document this way: Select the document icon and choose File⇨Open With, or right-click/Control-click the document icon and use the Open With menu to choose the application you want to open the document with. And if you hold down the Option key, the Open With command changes to Always Open With, which enables you to change the default application that opens this document permanently.

>> **You can find the original icon of any item you see in the dock by choosing Show in Finder from its dock menu.** This trick opens the window containing the item's actual icon and thoughtfully selects that icon for you.

Customizing Your Dock

The dock is a convenient way to get at oft-used icons. By default, the dock comes stocked with icons that Apple thinks you'll need most frequently (refer to Table 3-1), but you can customize it to contain any icons that you choose, as you discover in the following sections. You also find out how to resize the dock to fit your new set of icons and how to tell dock icons what your preferences are.

Adding dock icons

REMEMBER

You can customize your dock with favorite applications, a document you update daily, or maybe a folder containing your favorite recipes. Use the dock for anything you need quick access to.

Adding an application, file, or folder to the dock is as easy as 1-2-3:

1. **Open a Finder window that contains an application, a document file, or a folder you use frequently.**

   TIP

   You can also drag an icon — including a hard drive icon — from the desktop or any Finder window.

2. **Click the item you want to add to the dock.**

   As shown in Figure 3-5, I chose the TextEdit application. (It's highlighted.)

FIGURE 3-5:
Adding an icon to the dock is as easy as 1-2-3. Just drag the icon onto the dock.

3. **Drag the icon out of the Finder window and onto the dock.**

   The icons to the left and right of the new icon magically part to make room for it. Note that the dock item isn't the actual item. That item remains wherever it was — in a window or on the desktop. The icon you see in the dock is a shortcut that opens the item. I briefly mentioned aliases (known as *shortcuts* in the Windows world) earlier, but the icon on the dock is actually an alias of the icon you dragged onto the dock.

   Furthermore, when you remove an icon from the dock, as you find out how to do in a moment, you aren't removing the actual application, document, or folder. You're removing *only its shortcut* from the dock.

Folder, disk, document, and URL icons must sit on the right side of the divider line in the dock; application icons must sit on the left side of it. Why does the dock force these rules upon you? I suppose that someone at Apple thinks this is what's best for you. Who knows? But that's the rule: apps on the left; folders, disks, documents, and URLs on the right.

TIP

As long as you follow the rule, you can add several items to either side of the divider line at the same time by selecting them all and dragging the group to that side of the dock. You can delete only one icon at a time from the dock, however.

Adding a URL to the dock works slightly differently. Here's a quick way to add a URL to the dock:

1. **Open Safari, and go to the page with a URL that you want to save in the dock.**

2. **Click the small icon that you find to the left of the URL in the address bar and drag it to the right side of the dividing line in the dock.**

3. **Release the mouse button when the icon is right where you want it in the dock.**

   The icons in the dock slide over and make room, as shown in Figure 3-6, and the URL appears as a dock icon. From now on, when you click the URL icon that you moved to your dock, Safari opens to that page.

Drag from here...   ...to here

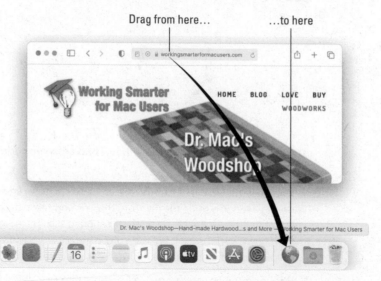

FIGURE 3-6:
Drag the icon
from Safari's
address bar to
the right side of
the dock.

TIP

If you open an icon that normally doesn't appear in the dock, and you want to keep its temporary icon in the dock permanently, you have two ways to tell it to stick around after you quit the program:

» Control-click (or click and hold down) and choose Keep in Dock from the menu that pops up.

» Drag the icon (for an application that's currently open) off and then back to the dock (or to a different position in the dock) without letting go of the mouse button.

Removing an icon from the dock

Removing an item from the dock is as easy as 1-2-3 but without the 3:

1. **Drag its icon off the dock and onto the desktop.**

2. **When you see the Remove bubble (see Figure 3-7), release the icon (mouse button).**

3. **There is no Step 3.**

FIGURE 3-7:
To remove an icon, drag it off the dock until it says Remove.

You can also choose Remove from Dock in the item's dock menu to get it out of your dock, but this way is way more fun.

REMEMBER

You can't remove the icon of a program that's currently running from the dock by dragging it. Either wait until you quit the program or choose Remove from Dock in its dock menu.

Also, note that by moving an icon off the dock, you aren't moving, deleting, or copying the item itself; you're just removing its icon from the dock. The item is unchanged. The icon is sort of like a library catalog card: Just because you remove the card from the card catalog doesn't mean that the book is gone from the library.

TIP

The dock used to come with your Documents and Applications folders installed by default. Ever since Mountain Lion, the dock does not include those folders, at least not by default. I mention this only because having those folders on the dock is convenient, and you should consider adding them to your dock if they aren't already there.

On the other hand, for those with Macs that once ran OS X 10.7 (Lion) or earlier versions and have since been upgraded to Big Sur, your Documents and Applications folders should still be on your Big Sur dock unless you removed them at some point.

Resizing the dock

If the default size of the dock bugs you, you can make the dock smaller and save yourself a lot of screen real estate. This space comes in especially handy when you add your own stuff to the dock.

To shrink or enlarge the dock (and its icons) without opening the Dock Preferences window, follow these steps:

1. **Make the Sizer appear by moving your cursor over the divider line that you find between apps and documents near the right side of the dock.**

2. **Drag the Sizer down to make the dock smaller, holding down the mouse button until you find the size you like.**

   The more you drag this control down, the smaller the dock gets.

3. **To enlarge the dock again, just drag the Sizer back up.**

   Bam! Big dock! You can enlarge the dock until it fills your screen from side to side.

What should you put on your dock?

Put things on the dock that you need quick access to and that you use often, or add items that aren't quickly available from menus or a Finder window's sidebar. If you like using the dock better than the Finder window's sidebar (for example), add your Documents, Movies, Pictures, Music, or even your Home folder or hard drive to the dock.

I suggest adding these items to your dock:

>> **A word-processing application:** Most people use word-processing software more than any other applications. Just drag the icon for yours to the left side of the dock, and you're good to go.

If you don't have a word processor such as Microsoft Word or Apple Pages already, give TextEdit a try. It's in every macOS Applications folder, and it's more powerful than you expect from a freebie.

TIP

>> **A project folder:** You know — the folder that contains all the documents for your thesis, or all the notes for the biggest project you have at work, or your massive recipe collection . . . whatever. If you add that folder to the dock, you can access it more quickly than if you have to open several folders to find it.

>> **A special utility or application:** The Preview application is an essential part of my work because I receive a lot of different image files every day. You may also want to add Internet-enabled programs you use (such as Skype, Spotify, and Twitter), your favorite graphics applications (such as Adobe Photoshop or Photoshop Elements), or the game you play every afternoon when you think the boss isn't watching.

>> **Your favorite URLs:** Save links to sites that you visit every day — the ones you use in your job, your favorite Mac news sites, or your personalized page from an Internet service provider (ISP). Sure, you can make one of these pages your browser's start page or bookmark it, but the dock lets you add one or more additional URLs. (Refer to the "Adding dock icons" section, earlier in this chapter, for details.)

TIP

You can add several URL icons to the dock, but bear in mind that the dock and its icons shrink to accommodate added icons, which makes them harder to see. Perhaps the best idea — if you want easy access to several URLs — is to create a folder full of URLs and put that folder on the dock. Then you can just press and hold your cursor on the folder (or Control-click the folder) to pop up a menu with all your URLs.

REMEMBER

Even though you can make the dock smaller, you're still limited to one row of icons. The smaller you make the dock, the larger the crowd of icons you can amass. You have to determine for yourself what's best for you: having lots of icons available in the dock (even though they might be difficult to see because they're so tiny) or having less clutter but fewer icons on your dock.

Figure 3-8 shows my dock, customized to my liking. Note that it's been split in half for this figure, to make it easier for you to discern the individual icons.

TIP

After you figure out which programs you use and don't use, it's a good idea to relieve overcrowding by removing the ones you never (or rarely) use from the dock.

FIGURE 3-8:
I keep icons for the apps I use most in my dock, which is split into two parts for this illustration.

Left side of my dock:

Right side of my dock:

Setting your dock preferences

You can change a few things about the dock to make it look and behave just the way you want it to. First, I cover global preferences that apply to the dock itself. After that, I discuss some preferences that apply only to folder and disk icons in the dock.

Global dock preferences

To change global dock preferences, choose 🍎⇨ System Preferences and then click the Dock & Menu Bar icon. The System Preferences application opens to the Dock & Menu Bar pane (see Figure 3-9).

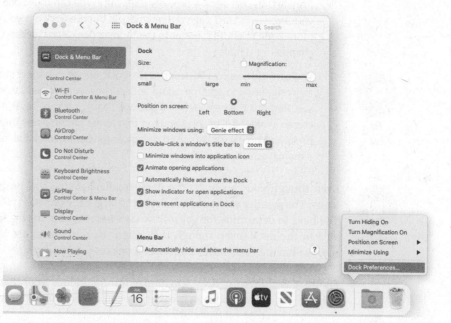

FIGURE 3-9:
The Dock & Menu Bar System Preferences pane (left) and the dock resizer shortcut menu (right).

TIP

You can open the Dock & Menu Bar System Preferences pane also by right-clicking or Control-clicking the dock resizer and choosing Dock Preferences from the shortcut menu.

Now you can adjust your dock with the following preferences:

>> **Size:** Note the slider bar here. Move this slider to the right (larger) or left (smaller) to adjust the size of the dock in your Finder. As you move the slider, watch the dock change size. (Now, *there's* a fun way to spend a Saturday afternoon!)

REMEMBER

As you add items to the dock, the icons — and the dock itself — shrink to accommodate the new ones.

>> **Magnification:** This slider controls how big icons grow when you pass the arrow cursor over them. Or you can deselect this check box to turn off magnification entirely.

>> **Position on Screen:** Choose one of these three radio buttons to attach the dock to the left side, the right side, or the bottom of your screen (the default). I prefer it on the bottom, but you should probably try all three before you decide.

>> **Double-Click a Window's Title Bar to Minimize (or Zoom):** If you select this option, double-clicking anywhere in a window's title bar minimizes (or zooms) the window. If this option isn't selected, each window you minimize gets its own personal icon on the right side of your dock.

REMEMBER

This option achieves the same result as clicking the (usually) yellow Minimize button in a window's upper-left corner. The difference is that the Minimize button is a tiny target and way over on the upper-left side of the window, whereas the title bar — the area to the right of the three gumdrops, which include the window's title (*Dock* & Menu Bar in Figure 3-9) — is a much easier target.

>> **Minimize Windows Using:** From this handy pop-up menu (PC users would call it a *drop-down list,* but what the heck; there's no gravity in a computer screen anyway), choose the animation that you see when you click a window's Minimize (yellow by default) button. The Genie Effect is the default, but the Scale Effect seems a bit faster to me.

>> **Minimize Windows into Application Icon:** If you select this option, when you minimize a window by clicking its yellow Minimize button, you won't see a separate dock icon for that window.

>> **Animate Opening Applications:** macOS animates *(bounces)* dock icons when you click them to open an item. If you don't like the animation, deselect (that is, uncheck) this check box, and the bouncing ceases evermore.

>> **Automatically Hide and Show the Dock:** Don't like the dock? Maybe you want to free the screen real estate on your monitor? Then choose the Automatically Hide and Show the Dock check box; after that, the dock displays itself only when you move the cursor to the bottom of the screen where the dock would ordinarily appear. It's like magic! (Okay, it's like Windows that way, but I hate to admit it.)

If the dock isn't visible, deselect the Automatically Hide and Show the Dock check box to bring back the dock. The option remains turned off unless you change it by selecting the Automatically Hide and Show the Dock check box. Choose ⌘⇨ Dock ⇨ Turn Hiding On (or use its keyboard shortcut ⌘+Option+D).

TIP

The keyboard shortcut ⌘+Option+D is a toggle, so it reverses the state of this option each time you use it.

>> **Show Indicators for Open Applications:** Select this option if you want all open applications to display a little black indicator dot below their icon on the dock, like the Finder icon in Figure 3-1. This program is open, whereas the others — the ones without black dots — are not. If you disable this option (although I can't imagine why you'd ever want to), none of your dock icons will ever display an indicator dot.

>> **Show Recent Applications in Dock:** This setting automatically adds icons for apps you've used recently to a special new Recent Applications section on the dock. It sits between your application icons on the left and the folder and Trash icons on the right, as shown in Figure 3-10.

Notice the dividing lines, which represent the left and right edges of the Recent Applications section.

FIGURE 3-10:
The three apps
I used most
recently are in
the Recent
Applications
section of
the dock.

The last three apps I launched

Divider line   Divider line

Folder and disk dock icon menu preferences

If you click a folder or disk icon in the dock, its contents are displayed in a fan, grid, or list menu, as shown in Figure 3-11.

If you right-click or Control-click a folder or disk icon in the dock, its Options menu appears, as shown in Figure 3-12.

Here are the choices on the Options menu:

>> **Sort By** determines the order in which items in the folder or drive appear when you click its dock icon.

>> **Display As** determines what the dock icon for a folder or drive looks like. If you choose Stack, the icon takes on the appearance of the last item moved into the folder or drive. If you choose Folder, the dock icon looks like a folder, as does the Documents folder icon in Figure 3-11.

FIGURE 3-11:
My Documents folder's dock menu as a fan, list, and grid.

FIGURE 3-12:
The Options menu for my Documents folder.

TIP

>> **View Contents As** lets you choose Fan, Grid, or List as the menu type for the folder or drive.

The default is Automatic, which is to say that the dock tries to choose the menu for you. I much prefer choosing the menu I consider most appropriate for a particular folder or drive. I like list menus best, especially for folders or drives with a lot of subfolders. As you can see in Figure 3-11, the list menu is the only one that lets you see and access folders inside folders (and subfold-ers inside other subfolders). For folders with images, I like the grid menu because it displays easily discernible icons for the folder or drive's contents. The fan menu is fantastic (ha!) when the folder or drive contains only a few items.

» **The Options submenu** contains the following items:

- *Remove from Dock* removes the icon from the dock.

- *Show in Finder* opens the window containing the item and selects the item. So, for example, in Figures 3-11 and 3-12, my Home (or iCloud) folder would open, and the Documents folder inside it would be selected.

The dock is your friend. Now that you know how it works, make it work the way you want it to. Put those programs and folders you use most in the dock, and you'll save yourself a significant amount of time and effort.

Chapter **4**

Getting to Know Finder and Its Desktop

On your Mac, Finder is your starting point — the centerpiece of your Mac experience, if you will — and it's always available. In Finder windows or the desktop, you can double-click your way to your favorite application, your documents, or your folders. So, in this chapter, I show you how to get the most from Finder and its desktop.

By the way, Big Sur's Finder has so many features that I divided them into two chapters — this one and Chapter 5, in which you discover additional Big Sur desktop and Finder features to save you time and effort.

I suggest reading (or at least skimming) this chapter first. That's not just because this is Chapter 4 and 4 comes before 5. Rather, this chapter covers basic Finder and desktop features you need to grok before the features in Chapter 5 will make sense.

Introducing Finder and Its Minions: The Desktop and Icons

The Finder is a special application unlike any other. Its most significant difference from other applications is that it launches automatically when you log in, is always running in the background, and doesn't include a Quit command. Put another way, the Finder is omnipresent.

The desktop is a special part of Finder unlike any other.

Finally, icons and windows are the units of currency used by Finder and the desktop.

Before I tackle any deep thoughts — such as what Finder does or what the desktop is — I start with a quick overview of some of the icons you're likely to encounter as you get to know Finder and the desktop.

Introducing the desktop

The *desktop* is the backdrop for Finder — everything you see behind the dock and any open windows. The desktop is always available and is where you can usually find your hard drive icon(s).

TIP

If your desktop doesn't display hard drive icons and you wish it did, stay tuned.

Explaining the Finder and desktop will be a whole lot easier with a picture for reference, so take a gander at Figure 4-1, which is a glorious depiction of a typical macOS Big Sur Finder.

If you're not familiar with Finder and its desktop, here are a few tips that will come in handy as you become familiar with the icons that hang out there:

>> **Icons on the desktop behave the same as icons in a window.** You move them and copy them just as you would icons in a window. The only difference is that icons on the desktop aren't in a window. Because they're on the desktop, they're more convenient to use.

>> **The first icon you need to get to know is the icon for your startup disk (a hard drive or SSD; see Figure 4-2).** You used to be able to find it on the top-right side of the desktop, as mine is in Figure 4-1. Yours probably has the name Macintosh HD unless you've renamed it. (I renamed mine *Big Sur* in Figure 4-2; see the section on renaming icons in Chapter 8 if you'd like to rename your own hard drive.)

Sample file (inside Desktop folder)

Sample folder (on desktop)

Sample folder (inside Desktop folder)

Sample file (on desktop)

SSD icon (on desktop)

Big Sur SSD
(in sidebar)

Desktop folder (inside bob folder)

Path bar

Desktop

bob (Home) folder (inside Users folder)

Status bar

Preview column

Users folder (inside Big Sur SSD)

FIGURE 4-1:
A typical Finder
and desktop.

You can see how selected and deselected hard or solid-state drive icons look in Figure 4-2, too.

Big Sur doesn't display the startup disk's icon on the desktop by default. So, if you don't see your startup (boot) disk's icon on the desktop but you'd like to, select the check box for hard drives in Finder Preferences as described in the "Setting Finder preferences" section, later in this chapter.

» **Other disc or hard drive icons appear on the desktop by default.** When you insert a CD or DVD or connect an external hard drive or a thumb drive, the disc or drive icon does appear on the desktop near the top-right corner. This feature *is* enabled by default; if yours isn't enabled, just open Finder Preferences and select its check box as described later in the chapter.

» **You can move an item to the desktop to make it easier to find.** Simply click any icon in any window and then, without releasing the mouse button, drag it out of the window and onto the desktop. Then release the mouse button. This will move the icon from wherever it was to the desktop. You can now drag the icon elsewhere on the desktop if necessary.

FIGURE 4-2:
Selected (top) and
unselected
(bottom) SSD
(solid-state
drive) icons.

WARNING

If you drag an item from an external volume to any location on your startup disk (including the desktop), the item is copied, not moved. Put another way, the item is moved if it's on the same disk or volume, and copied if it's on another disk or volume.

TECHNICAL STUFF

Volume is the generic term for any storage container — a hard drive, solid-state drive, CD, DVD, disk image, or remote disk — that appears in the sidebar's Locations section.

TIP

At the bottom of the Finder window in Figure 4-1 are two optional bars. The lower of the two is called the *status bar*; it tells you how many items are in each window and, if any are selected, how many you've selected out of the total, as well as how much space is available on the hard drive containing this window. And just above the status bar is the *path bar*, which shows the path from the top level of your hard drive to the selected file (which is Sample File on Desktop.jpg in Figure 4-1). You can show or hide the status bar by choosing View⇨Hide/Show Status Bar and show or hide the path bar by choosing View⇨Hide/Show Path Bar. Finally, when the toolbar is hidden (see the next section, "Bellying up to the toolbar"), the status bar moves to the top of the window (the path bar remains at the bottom of the window no matter what).

Bellying up to the toolbar

In addition to the sidebar (introduced in Chapter 2) and some good old-fashioned double-clicking, the macOS Finder window offers additional navigation aids on the toolbar — namely, the Back and Forward icons, as well as the extra-helpful View icons. You can find other handy features on the Go menu, discussed a little later in this chapter.

In case you didn't know, the toolbar is the area (see Figure 4-3) at the top of all Finder windows, which (among other things) displays the window's name. On the toolbar you'll find icons to navigate quickly and act on selected icons.

68   PART 1 **macOS Basics**

FIGURE 4-3:
A Finder window's
default toolbar.

To activate a toolbar icon, click it once.

You say you don't want to see the toolbar at the top of the window? Okay! Just choose View➪Hide Toolbar or use its keyboard shortcut (⌘+Option+T), and it's gone. (If only life were always so easy!) Want it back? Choose View➪Show Toolbar or use the same keyboard shortcut: ⌘+Option+T.

Alas, hiding the toolbar also hides the useful sidebar. If only you could choose to hide them independently. . .. I find this fact annoying because I use the sidebar a lot but don't use the toolbar much. To make matters worse, View➪Hide Sidebar (shortcut: ⌘+Option+S) lets you hide the sidebar without hiding the toolbar. It's been like this for a long time, and for whatever reason, you *still* can't hide the toolbar while keeping the sidebar visible! Boo. Hiss.

REMEMBER

When you hide the toolbar, opening a folder spawns a *new* Finder window. The default, which is probably what you're used to, is for folders to open in place, displaying their contents in a tab in the current window.

The toolbar's default icons are shown in Figure 4-3. So if you customized your toolbar by choosing View➪Customize Toolbar, yours won't look exactly like Figure 4-3.

Here is the lowdown on the toolbar's default icons, from left to right:

>> **Forward and Back icons:** Clicking the Forward and Back icons displays the folders that you've viewed in this window in sequential order. It's a lot like using a web browser.

Here's an example of how the Back icon works. Say you're in your Home folder; you click the Favorites icon, and a split-second later, you realize that you actually need something in the Home folder. Just a quick click of the Back icon and — *poof!* — you're back Home. As for the Forward icon, well, it moves you in the opposite direction, through folders that you've visited in this window. Play around with them both; you'll find them invaluable. The keyboard shortcuts ⌘+[for Back and ⌘+] for Forward are even more useful (in my opinion) than the icons.

>> **View icons:** The four View icons change the way that the window displays its contents.

You have four ways to view a window: Icon, List, Column, and Gallery. Some people like columns, some like icons, and others love lists or galleries. To each her own. Play with the four Finder views to see which one works best for you. For what it's worth, I usually prefer Column view with a dash of List view thrown in when I need a folder's contents sorted by creation date or size. And the Gallery view is great for folders with documents because you can see the contents of many document types right in the window, as I explain shortly.

TIP

Don't forget that each view also has a handy keyboard shortcut: ⌘+1 for Icon view, ⌘ +2 for List view, ⌘+3 for Column view, and ⌘+4 for Gallery view. (Views are so useful you'll find an entire section devoted to them later in this chapter.)

» **Group By/Sort By:** Click this icon to see a pop-up menu with options for grouping this window's contents. Hold down the Option key to change the sort order (within the selected group). Note that the Group By/Sort By menu works in all four views. Read more about Group By/Sort By in "What's next on the (View) menu?" later in this chapter.

» **Share:** Click here to share the selected items with others. A pop-up menu lets you choose to share via Mail, Messages, AirDrop, or Notes.

Big Sur's extensible architecture lets you add other services (such as Vimeo or LinkedIn) and apps (such as Photos and Aperture) to your Share menu. To manage these extensions, choose More from the Share pop-up menu. Alternatively, you can launch the System Preferences application, click the Extensions icon, and then click the Share Menu item on the left side of the window.

» **Add Tags:** Click here to assign one or more colored tags to selected items. You find out more about tags and tagging in the "Customizing Finder Windows" section, later in this chapter.

» **Action:** Click this icon to see a pop-up menu of all the context-sensitive actions you can perform on selected icons, as shown in Figure 4-4.

TIP

If you see angle brackets (>>) at the right edge of the toolbar, as shown in Figure 4-4, at least one toolbar item is not visible. Click the angle brackets and a menu displays all hidden items (Group By, Share, Add Tags, and Action in Figure 4-4). Or expand the window so it's wide enough to display all the items in the toolbar.

» **Search:** Click the little magnifying glass and the Search box appears. This is a nifty way to quickly search for files or folders. Just type a word (or even just a few letters), and in a few seconds, the window fills with a list of files that match. You can also start a search by choosing File⇨Find (shortcut: ⌘+F). You find out all about searching in Chapter 10.

Angle brackets

FIGURE 4-4:
Use the Action
pop-up menu to
perform common
actions on
selected items.

Figuring out what an icon is

What's an icon? Glad you asked. Each Finder icon represents an item or a container on your hard drive. *Containers* — hard drives, USB thumb drives, folders, CDs, DVDs, shared network volumes, and so on — can contain a virtually unlimited number of application files, document files, and folders (which can contain an unlimited number of application files, document files, and folders).

Icons on the dock and the sidebar of Finder windows are not the same as the Finder icons I describe in this chapter. They're simply convenient pointers to actual Finder icons. Technically, dock and sidebar icons are aliases. (If you don't yet know what an alias is, you're going to find out long before the thrilling conclusion of this chapter.)

Anyway, working with icons is easy:

>> Single-click to select.

>> Double-click to open.

>> Click and drag to move.

>> Release mouse button to drop.

But enough talk. It's time to see what these puppies look like.

Identifying your Finder icons in the wild

Although icons all work the same, they come in different kinds, shapes, and sizes. When you've been around the Mac for a while, you develop a sixth sense about icons and can guess what an unfamiliar icon contains just by looking at it.

Here are the major icon types:

» **Application icons** are *programs* — the software you use to accomplish tasks on your Mac. Mail, Safari, and Calendar are applications. So are Microsoft Word and Adobe Photoshop.

Application icons come in a variety of shapes. For example, application icons are often square-ish, diamond-shaped, rectangular, or just oddly shaped. The first row of icons in Figure 4-5 displays application icons of various shapes.

» **Document icons** are files created by applications. Letters created with TextEdit are documents. This chapter began life as a document created in Microsoft Word. And spreadsheet, PDF, video, image, and song files are all documents.

Document icons are often reminiscent of a piece of paper, as shown in the second row of icons in Figure 4-5.

TIP

If your document icons are generic, like the first three icons in the second row of Figure 4-5, but you'd prefer icons that reflect their contents, like the last three icons in the second row of Figure 4-5, open View Options or use the ⌘+J shortcut, and then select the Show Icon Preview check box (see Chapter 23 for additional details about View Options).

» **Folder and disk icons** are the Mac's organizational containers. You can put icons — and the applications or documents they stand for — in folders or disks. You can put folders in disks or in other folders, but you can't put a disk inside another disk.

WARNING

Folders look like, well, manila folders (what a concept) and can contain just about any other icon. You use folders to organize your files and applications on your hard drive. You can have as many folders as you want, so don't be afraid to create new ones. The thought behind the whole folders thing is pretty obvious: If your hard drive is a filing cabinet, folders are its drawers and folders (duh!). The third row in Figure 4-5 shows some typical folder icons.

And while disks behave pretty much like folders, their icons often look like disks, as shown in the last row in Figure 4-5.

» **Alias icons** are wonderful — no, make that *fabulous* — organizational tools. I like aliases so much that they get an entire section to themselves.

FIGURE 4-5:
Icons come in many shapes and designs.

TIP

If you're looking for details about how to organize your icons in folders, move them around, delete them, and so on, hang in there. Chapter 8 is about organizing and managing files and folders.

Aliases Are Awesome!

An *alias* is a tiny file that automatically opens the file, folder, disk, or network volume that it represents. Although an alias is technically an icon, it's different from other icons; it actually does nothing but open a different icon when you double-click. Put another way, aliases are organizational tools that let you store an icon in more than one place without creating multiple copies of the file.

An alias is very different than a duplicated file. For example, the Preview application uses around 40 megabytes (MB) of disk space. If I were to *duplicate* Preview, I'd have two files on my hard drive, each requiring around 40MB of disk space apiece.

An *alias* of Preview, on the other hand, looks just like the original Preview icon and opens Preview when you double-click it — but it uses a mere 736 bytes (4K) of disk space — a tiny fraction of its parent icon's size. So try placing aliases of programs and files you use most often in convenient places such as the desktop or a folder in your Home folder.

Why else do I think that aliases are so great? Well, they open any file or folder (or application) on any hard drive from anywhere else on any hard drive — which is a very good trick. But there are other reasons why I think aliases are awesome:

» **Convenience:** Aliases enable you to make items appear to be in more than one place, which on many occasions is exactly what you want to do. For example, keep an alias of your word-processing program on your desktop and another in your Documents folder for quick access. Aliases enable you to open your word processor right away without having to navigate into the depths of your Applications folder every time you need it.

TIP

While you're at it, you might want to put an icon for your word processor in both the dock and the sidebar to make it even easier to open your word processor without a lot of clicking.

>> **Flexibility and organization:** You can create aliases and store them anywhere on your hard drive to represent the same document in several different folders.

>> **Integrity:** Some programs must remain in the same folder as their supporting files and folders. These programs won't function properly unless they're in the same folder as their dictionaries, thesauruses, data files (for games), templates, and so on. Thus, you can't put the actual icons for such programs on the desktop without impairing their functionality. An alias lets you access a program like that from anywhere on your hard drive. (And it's probably best to leave all your apps in the Applications folder, where they belong.)

I admit I'm somewhat old-school when it comes to organizing my files in the proper folders (see Chapter 8), but Big Sur's speedy Spotlight search mechanism along with tools such as Launchpad and Mission Control (all, not coincidentally, discussed in Chapter 10), as well as the sidebar's Recents item, let you find pretty much any file on your disk in seconds.

Creating aliases

When you create an alias, its icon looks the same as the original icon it represents, but the suffix *alias* is tacked onto its name, and a tiny arrow called a *badge* (as shown in the margin) appears in the bottom-left corner of its icon. Figure 4-6 shows an alias and its *parent* icon — the icon that opens if you double-click the alias.

FIGURE 4-6:
An alias (right) and its parent.

To create an alias for an icon, do one of the following:

>> Click the parent icon and choose File⇨Make Alias.

>> Click the parent icon and press ⌘+Control+A.

>> Click the parent icon and use the Action menu's Make Alias command (in the toolbar of all Finder windows).

>> Click an icon while holding down the Control key (or right-click it or tap it with two fingers on a trackpad) and then choose the Make Alias command from the contextual menu that appears. (You can explore contextual shortcut menus — which are very cool — in Chapter 2.)

>> Click any file or folder, press and hold down ⌘+Option, and then drag the file or folder while continuing to hold down ⌘+Option. Presto! An alias appears where you release the mouse button.

TIP

When I first create a file, I save it in its proper folder inside the Documents folder in my Home folder. If it's a document that I plan to work on for more than a day or two (such as a magazine article or book chapter), I make an alias of the document (or folder) and plop it on my desktop. After I finish the article or chapter and submit it to an editor, I trash the alias, leaving the original file safe and sound, filed away in its proper folder, and leaving my desktop clean and uncluttered.

Deleting aliases

This is a short section because deleting an alias is such an easy chore. To delete an alias, simply drag it onto the Trash icon on the dock. That's it! You can also Control-click it and choose Move to Trash from the contextual menu that appears (right-click or Control-click or two-finger tap), or select the icon and press ⌘+Delete.

Deleting an alias does *not* delete the parent item. (If you want to delete the parent item, you have to go hunt it down and kill it yourself.)

Hunting down an alias's parent

Suppose that you create an alias of a file, and later you want to delete both the alias and its parent file, but you can't find the parent file. What do you do? Well, you can use Finder's Find function to find it (try saying that three times real fast), but here are four faster ways to find the parent icon of an alias:

>> Select the alias icon and choose File⇨Show Original.

>> Select the alias icon and press ⌘+Option+Control+A.

>> Select the alias icon and use the Action menu's Show Original command.

>> Control-click (or right-click or two-fingered tap on a trackpad) the alias icon and choose Show Original from the contextual menu.

Any of these methods opens the window containing the parent document with its icon preselected for your convenience.

The View(s) from a Window

Views are part of what makes your Mac feel like *your* Mac. Big Sur offers four views so you can select the best one for any occasion. Some people like one view so much that they rarely (or never) use others. Other people, like me, memorize the keyboard shortcuts to switch views instantly without reaching for the mouse. Try 'em all, and use the one(s) you prefer.

Moving through folders fast in Column view

Column view is a darn handy way to quickly look through a lot of folders at once, and it's especially useful when those folders are filled with graphics files. The Column view is my favorite way to display windows in Finder.

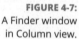

To display a window in Column view, shown in Figure 4-7, click the Column view icon on the toolbar (as shown in the margin), choose View➪As Columns from Finder's menu bar, or press ⌘+3.

FIGURE 4-7:
A Finder window in Column view.

Here's how I clicked around in Column view to see the list of folders and files you see in Figure 4-7:

1. When I clicked the Documents icon in the sidebar, its contents appeared in the column to the right.

2. When I clicked the folder titled Desktop Pix in this column, its contents appeared in the second column.

3. When I clicked Writers write pen.png in the second column, the contents of that file appeared in the third column along with information about the file, such as its size (10 KB) and the date and time it was created, modified, and last opened.

TIP

The third column is displaying a Preview, a feature available in all views by choosing View⇨Show/Hide Preview. You can modify the information you see in the Preview by choosing View⇨Show Preview Options and enabling the items you want displayed in the Preview column.

Here are some helpful tips when you're poking around Column view:

TIP

>> **You can have as many columns in a Column view window as your screen can handle.** Just drag any edge or corner of the window to enlarge it so new columns have room to open. You can also click the green Zoom (Maximize) button to make the window fill the screen. (*Hint:* To get out of full-screen mode, press Esc or move your cursor to the top of the screen and click the green Zoom button that appears near the top-left corner.)

If you Option-click the green Zoom button, the window will expand just enough to display all columns with content in them.

>> **You can use the little column divider lines at the bottom of every column to resize the column width.**

WARNING

You'll see the resizer cursor when your mouse pointer is directly over a column divider line, as shown in Figure 4-7.

To be specific:

• If you drag the resizer left or right, the column to its left resizes.

• If you hold down the Option key when you drag a divider line, *all* columns resize at the same time.

• If you double-click a divider line, the column to its left expands to the Right Size, which is the width of the widest item in the column.

• If you right- or Control-click a divider line, you see a pop-up menu with four or five options: Right Size This Column, Right Size All Columns Individually, Right Size All Columns Equally, and Set Desktop Picture. You'll see the fifth option, Import from iPhone or iPad, only if an iPhone or iPad is connected to your Mac.

» **The preview column displays information about the highlighted item to its left, but only if that item isn't a folder or disk.** Why? Well, if it were a folder or disk, its contents would be in this column.

For many items, the picture you see in the preview column is an enlarged view of the file's icon. You only see a preview (as shown in Figure 4-7) when the selected item is saved in a format that Quick Look (which you discover in Chapter 10) can interpret (which is to say, most image file formats, including TIFF, JPEG, PNG, GIF, and PDF to name a few, as well as many other file formats, including Microsoft Word and Pages).

TIP

If you don't like having the preview displayed in Column view (but want it to remain in all other views), choose View ➪ Show View Options and deselect the check box for Show Preview Column. You can do the same for any other view, or turn the preview off in all views by choosing View ➪ Hide Preview.

Perusing in Icon view

Icon view is a free-form view that allows you to move your icons around within a window to your heart's content. Refer to Figure 4-4 to see icons in my Documents folder displayed in Icon view.

To display a window in Icon view, click the Icon view icon in the toolbar (shown in the margin), choose View ➪ As Icons from Finder's menu bar, or press ⌘+1.

TIP

The best part of Icon view, at least in my humble opinion, is the Icon Size slider in the lower-right corner of Icon view windows (or in the top-right corner if the sidebar and toolbar are hidden).

Listless? Try touring folders in List view

Now I come to my second-favorite view, List view (shown in Figure 4-8). I like it so much because of the little angle bracket to the left of each folder. These angle brackets, which were called *disclosure triangles* in earlier macOS releases, let you see the contents of a folder without actually opening it. This view also allows you to select items from multiple folders at once and move or copy items between folders in a single window. Finally, it's the view used to present Spotlight search results.

To display a window in List view, click the List view icon on the toolbar (shown in the margin), choose View ➪ As List from the Finder menu bar, or press ⌘+2.

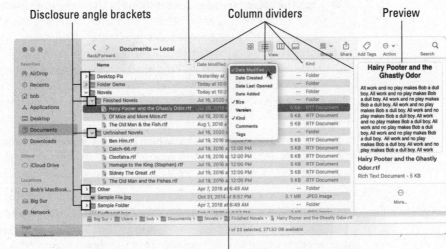

Sorting Indicator (for Name column)

Disclosure angle brackets   Column dividers   Preview

FIGURE 4-8:
A window in
List view.

Right- or Control Click in header to select columns for display

When you're in List view, the following tips can help you breeze through your folders to find what you're looking for:

>> **To disclose a folder's contents, click the angle bracket to its left or, if it's selected, press the right-arrow key.** Figure 4-8 shows the result of either clicking the angle bracket to the left of the Novels folder or selecting (highlighting) the Novels folder and pressing the right-arrow key.

TIP

I pressed Option+→ in Figure 4-8, so all the Novels folder's subfolders (the Finished Novels and Unfinished Novels folders in this case) also expanded. And if either of these subfolders (or any other subfolder in the Novels folder) had subfolders, they too would have been expanded when I pressed Option+→.

To close an open folder, click the angle bracket again or select the folder and press left-arrow. To close all open folders in a List view window, choose Edit➪ Select All (or press ⌘+A) and then press Option+←.

WARNING

The angle brackets don't appear if you're using groups. To see the angle brackets, choose View ➪ Use Groups or the keyboard shortcut ⌘+Control+0 (zero). These are toggles, and will turn groups off if they're enabled or on if they're disabled. You could also choose None from the Group icon/menu in the toolbar.

Disclosure angle brackets and groups are an either/or situation — you either have disclosure angle brackets or groups but not both at the same time (in the same window).

» **Click the column header to sort items in List view.** Note the little upside-down *v* at the right edge of the selected column (the Name column in Figure 4-8). That's the column's sorting indicator. If the *v* points upward, as it does in Figure 4-8, the items in the corresponding column are sorted in alphabetical order; if you click the header (Name) again, the triangle will flip upside down and point downward and the items will be listed in the opposite (reverse alphabetical) order. This behavior is true for all columns in List view windows.

» **You can change the order in which columns appear in a window.** To do so, press and hold down on a column's name, and then drag it to the left or right until it's where you want it. Release the mouse button, and the column moves.

The exception (isn't there always an exception?) is that the Name column always appears first in List view windows; you can move all other columns about at will. In fact, you can even hide and show columns other than Name if you like using the View Options window.

TIP

It's even easier to hide or show columns by right- or Control-clicking anywhere on any column header (as shown below the Date Modified column in Figure 4-8). Column names with check marks are displayed; column names that are unchecked are hidden.

TIP

You can fine-tune all four views and the desktop by using the View Options window. Just choose View⇨Show View Options or press ⌘+J. The options you see apply to the active window or the desktop. Click the Use as Defaults button to apply these options to all windows in that view (that is, Icon, List, Column, or Gallery).

» **To widen or shrink a column, hover the cursor over the dividing line between that column and drag left or right.** When your cursor is over the dividing line in the header, it changes to a double-headed resizer, as shown in the margin.

Hangin' in the Gallery (view)

Gallery view is the latest iteration of Cover Flow view in High Sierra and earlier. To display a window in Gallery view, click the Gallery view icon on the toolbar (shown in the margin), choose View⇨As Gallery from Finder's menu bar, or press ⌘+4. Figure 4-9 shows Gallery view.

FIGURE 4-9:
A window in
Gallery view.

Although Gallery view is useful only for folders with documents or images, it does offer at least three cool features:

>> The selected item (Writers Write Pen.png in Figure 4-9) appears in a preview in the top part of the window.

>> The Preview column displays additional information about the selected item.

>> You can quickly flip through the previews by clicking the images to the left or right of the current preview image or by pressing the left- or right-arrow key.

What's next on the (View) menu?

The Finder View menu offers several commands in addition to the four views. These commands might help you peruse your icons more easily:

>> **Use Groups:** Active window only. When enabled, it subdivides the items in the active window into groups, as shown in Figure 4-10, which is grouped by Date Last Opened.

>> **Group By:** This submenu offers nine options for grouping items in the active window:

- Name (shortcut: ⌘+Control+1)

- Kind (shortcut: ⌘+Control+2)

- Application (strangely, there's no shortcut for this command)

- Date Last Opened (shortcut: ⌘+Control+3)

- Date Added (shortcut: ⌘+Control+4)

- Date Modified (shortcut: ⌘+Control+5)

- Date Created (strangely, there's no shortcut for this command either)

- Size (shortcut: ⌘+Control+6)

- Tags (shortcut: ⌘+Control+7)

» **Clean Up:** Clean Up is available only in Icon view or on the desktop when no windows are active. Choose this command to align icons to an invisible grid; you use it to keep your windows and desktop neat and tidy. (If you like this invisible grid, don't forget that you can turn it on or off for the desktop and individual windows by using View Options.) If no windows are active, the command instead cleans up your desktop. (To deactivate all open windows, just click anywhere on the desktop or close all open windows.)

TIP

If any icons are selected (highlighted) when you pull down the View menu, you see Clean Up Selection rather than Clean Up. If you choose this command, it moves only the icons that are currently selected.

» **Clean Up By:** This command combines the tidiness of the Clean Up command with the organizational yumminess of the Sort By command, which I mention earlier in this chapter and discuss in more detail shortly.

This command sorts the icons by your choice of criteria, namely:

- Name (shortcut: ⌘+Option+1)

- Kind (shortcut: ⌘+Option+2)

- Date Modified (shortcut: ⌘+Option+5)

- Date Created (no shortcut)

- Size (shortcut: ⌘+Option+6)

- Tags (shortcut: ⌘+Option+7)

Clean Up By is similar to the Sort By command, but unlike Sort By, Clean Up By is a one-time affair. After you've used it, you can once again move icons around and reorganize them any way you like.

» **Sort By:** This command rearranges the icons in the active window in your choice from among nine ways, which happen to be the same nine options (ten, if you count None) in the Sort By pop-up menu (shown earlier in Figure 4-4).

Unlike Clean Up By, which is a one-shot command, Sort By is persistent and will continue to reorganize your icons automatically. In other words, you can't move icons around manually in an arranged window.

One last thing: The Clean Up and Clean Up By commands are available only for windows viewed as icons. The Sort By command is available in all four views and remains in effect if you switch to a different view or close the window. To stop Finder from arranging icons in a window, choose None from the View➪Sort By submenu or Option + click the toolbar's Group pop-up menu and choose None.

WARNING

If you're like me, you've taken great pains to place icons carefully in specific places on your desktop. If so, the Clean Up By and Sort By commands will mess up your perfectly arranged desktop icons. And alas, cleaning up your desktop is still not something macOS lets you undo.

Finder on the Menu

Finder's menu bar is packed with useful goodies; in the following sections, I look at those that pertain specifically to using Finder.

The actual Finder menu

Here are a few of the main items you can find on the Finder menu:

>> **About Finder:** Choose this command to find out which version of Finder is running on your Mac. This menu item isn't particularly useful — or at least not

for very long. But when a different application is running, the About Finder item becomes About application name and usually gives information about the program's version number, the developers, and any other tidbits that those developers decide to throw in. Sometimes these tidbits are useful, sometimes they're interesting, and sometimes they're both.

>> **Preferences:** Use the choices here to control how Finder looks and acts. Find out the details in the "Setting Finder preferences" section, later in this chapter.

>> **Services:** One of the cool features of macOS applications is the accessibility of Services. If nothing is selected in Finder, the Services menu is empty, as shown in the top panel of Figure 4-11. When an icon or icons are selected, you can choose from four Services, as shown in the middle panel of Figure 4-11. Finally, if a word or words are selected, you have five different options, as shown in bottom pane of Figure 4-11.

In other words, the items you see in the Services menu are context-sensitive, so what you see in yours will depend on what you have selected. If you look in the Services menu and don't find anything interesting, try selecting something else and looking again; you might be pleasantly surprised.

Choose the last item in the menu, Services Preferences, and you can enable dozens of useful Services that aren't available by default.

>> **Hide Finder (⌘+H):** Use this command when Finder windows are open and are distracting you. Choosing it makes Finder inactive (another program becomes active) and hides any open Finder windows. To make Finder visible again, either choose Show All from the application's self-named menu (the one that bears the name of the active application, such as Finder, TextEdit, or System Preferences) or click the Finder icon, shown in the margin here, on the dock.

TIP

The advantage to hiding Finder — rather than closing or minimizing all your windows to get a clean screen — is that you don't have to open them all again when you're ready to get the windows back. Instead, just choose Show All (to see all windows in all apps) or click the Finder icon on the dock to see all Finder windows.

>> **Hide Others (Option+⌘+H):** This command hides all windows associated with all running programs except the active program. It appears in most applications' self-named menus and is good for hiding distractions so you can focus on one thing: the unhidden application.

TIP

Another easy way to hide all open applications and windows while activating Finder is to hold down the ⌘ and Option keys and click the Finder icon on the dock. This technique works with whatever application is active, not just Finder. So if you're surfing the web and decide you want to see only Safari's windows on your screen, ⌘+Option-click the Safari icon on the dock, and it will happen instantly.

» **Show All:** Use this command as the antidote to both of the Hide commands. Choose this, and nothing is hidden anymore.

Note that all three of these commands require that at least one application be running in addition to Finder. Put another way, when Finder is the only app running, these three commands are grayed out and unavailable.

TIP

You can achieve much the same effect as all this hide-and-show jazz with Mission Control, which I discuss in Chapter 10.

Finally, if you noticed that Finder menu's Empty Trash command isn't mentioned here, that's because it gets detailed coverage in Chapter 8.

Like a road map: The current folder's pop-up menu

On every window's title bar is the name of the folder (or disk) that you're viewing in this window: the highlighted folder. You know that already. What you might not know is that it offers a hidden road map to this folder from the top level. The following steps explain how it works:

1. **⌘-click or Control-click the folder's name in the title bar.**

    A pop-up menu appears, with the current folder (Desktop in Figure 4-12) at the top.

2. **Select any folder in the menu, and release the mouse button to display that folder's contents.**

    As shown in Figure 4-12, the contents of the Desktop folder — three screen shot files — are displayed in the window. If I highlight the bob folder (as I have in Figure 4-12) and release the mouse button, the contents of the bob folder would replace the contents of the Desktop folder in this window.

3. **After jumping to a new folder, you can click the Back button.**

    Hey, you're right back where you were before you touched that pop-up menu!

TIP

Don't forget that you can display the path bar near the bottom of the window (it's displayed in Figure 4-12) by choosing View➪Show Path Bar. Then you can double-click any folder displayed in the path bar to open it. This last trick works not only on Finder windows but also with the title bar of most document windows (Word, Photoshop, and so on), showing you the path to the folder containing the document you're working on.

Going places with the Go menu

The Go menu is chock-full of shortcuts. The items on this menu take you to places on your Mac — many of the same places you can go with the Finder window's toolbar — and a few other places.

The following list gives you a brief look at the items on the Go menu:

» **Back (⌘+[):** Use this menu option to return to the last open Finder window. It's equivalent to the Back button on the Finder toolbar, in case you have the toolbar hidden.

FIGURE 4-12:
Traverse folders
from this
convenient
pop-up menu.

>> **Forward (⌘+]):** This command is the opposite of using the Back command, moving you forward through every folder you open. Remember that if you haven't gone back, you can't go forward.

>> **Enclosing Folder (⌘+↑):** This command tells the Finder window to display the folder where the currently selected item is located.

>> **Recents (Shift+⌘+F):** This command shows you all your document files at once.

This is a good time to use the Arrange pop-up menu to sort these files into some semblance of order.

>> **Documents (Shift+⌘+O):** You'll probably use this command often because the Documents folder is a great place to save documents you create.

>> **Desktop (Shift+⌘+D):** Use this command to display the Desktop folder, which contains the same icons as the desktop you see behind open windows.

>> **Downloads (Option+⌘+L):** This opens your Downloads folder, which is where files you download in Safari, save as attachments in Mail, or receive via AirDrop (explained shortly) are saved by default.

>> **Home (Shift+⌘+H):** Use this command to have the Finder window display your Home folder (which is named with your short name).

>> **Computer (Shift+⌘+C):** This command tells the Finder window to display the Computer level, showing your network and all your disks.

>> **AirDrop (Shift+⌘+R):** AirDrop lets you share files wirelessly with anyone around you. No setup or special settings are required. Just click the AirDrop icon in the Finder sidebar, use this menu item, or use the keyboard shortcut, and your Mac automatically discovers other people nearby who are using AirDrop. Bear in mind that not all Macs capable of running Big Sur support AirDrop. *Note:* If your Mac is 2009 vintage (or older), AirDrop might not work.

AirDrop now works between Macs and late-model iDevices running iOS 8. Which late model devices, you ask? AirDrop in Big Sur supports file sharing with the iPhone 5 and later, fourth-gen and later iPads, all iPad Minis, and fifth-gen and later iPod touches.

>> **Network (Shift+⌘+K):** This command displays whatever is accessible on your network in the Finder window.

>> **iCloud Drive (Shift+⌘+I):** This command opens a window that displays the contents of your iCloud drive (which you read more about in Chapter 8).

>> **Applications (Shift+⌘+A):** This command displays your Applications folder, the usual storehouse for all the programs that came with your Mac (and the most likely place to find the programs you install).

>> **Utilities (Shift+⌘+U):** This command gets you to the Utilities folder inside the Applications folder in one fell swoop. The Utilities folder is the repository of such useful items as Disk Utility (which lets you erase, format, verify, and repair disks) and Disk Copy (which you use to create and mount disk-image files).

>> **Recent Folders:** Use this submenu to quickly go back to a folder that you recently visited. Every time you open a folder, OS X creates an alias to it and stores it in the Recent Folders folder. You can open any of these aliases from the Recent Folders command on the Go menu.

>> **Go to Folder (Shift+⌘+G):** This command summons the Go to the Folder dialog, shown in Figure 4-13. Look at your desktop. Maybe it's cluttered with lots of windows, or maybe it's empty. Either way, suppose you're several clicks away from a folder that you want to open. If you know the path from your hard drive to that folder, you can type the path to the folder in the Go to the Folder text box — separating folder names with forward slashes (/) — and then click Go to move (relatively) quickly to the folder you need.

TIP

The first character you type must also be a forward slash, as shown in Figure 4-13.

This particular dialog is a tad clairvoyant in that it tries to guess which folder you mean by the first letter or two that you type. For example, in Figure 4-13, I typed the letter **A** and paused, and the window guessed that I wanted *Applications.* Then I pressed the right-arrow key to accept the guess and typed **/U,** and the window guessed the rest *(tilities)* and filled it in for me.

>> **Connect to Server (⌘+K):** If your Mac is connected to a network or to the Internet, use this command to reach those remote resources.

FIGURE 4-13:
Go to a folder by
typing its path.

One last thing: If you're looking for the Library folder inside your Home folder, which used to appear in the Go menu (before OS X 10.7 Lion), it's now hidden for your protection (as I explain in Chapter 7). To reveal it, hold down the Option key before you open the Go menu.

Customizing Finder Windows

Finder is outrageously handy. It not only gives you convenient access to multiple windows but also offers ways to tweak what you see until you get what works best for you. So whereas earlier sections in this chapter explain what Finder is and how it works, the following sections ask, "How would you like it to be?"

Adding folders to the sidebar

Adding any file or folder you like to the sidebar is easy. All you need to do is select the file or folder you want to add and choose File⇨Add to Sidebar from the menu bar (or use its shortcut ⌘+Control+T). You can now use the item anytime you like by clicking it in the sidebar of any Finder window. Better still, you can move files or folders into folders in the sidebar by dragging them onto the folder's sidebar icon.

You can add folders (but not files) to the sidebar by dragging them onto the sidebar.

TIP

WARNING

Be careful not to drag a folder *onto* another folder or it will be moved into that folder instead of being added to the sidebar. You'll see a little line above or below existing folders in the sidebar; that shows you where this folder will appear if you release the mouse button. If a folder in the sidebar is highlighted and you don't see the little line, releasing the mouse button will not add the folder to the sidebar, but will move it into the highlighted folder.

To remove an item from the sidebar, right- or Control-click the item and choose Remove from Sidebar. Or drag the item off the sidebar and release the mouse button when the little x-in-a-circle appears.

Setting Finder preferences

You can find Finder and Desktop preferences by choosing Finder ⇨ Preferences. In the Finder Preferences window that appears, click the icons in the toolbar to select one of the four Finder Preferences panes: General, Tags, Sidebar, and Advanced, all of which are shown in Figure 4-14.

General pane

In the General pane, you find the following options:

» **Show These Items on the Desktop check boxes:** Select or deselect these check boxes to choose whether icons for hard drives; external disks; CDs, DVDs, and iPods; and connected servers appear on the desktop. macOS Big Sur deselects all four options by default. If you don't want disk icons cluttering your beautiful desktop, deselect (clear) these check boxes as shown in Figure 4-14. When they're deselected, you can still work with hard drives, CDs, DVDs, and other types of disks. You just have to open a Finder window and select the disk or disc you want in the sidebar.

» **New Finder Windows Show:** Here, you can choose whether opening a new Finder window displays Recents, your Home folder (which is my preference), the Documents or Desktop folders, or any other disk or folder. (Recents is the default.)

» **Open Folders in Tabs Instead of New Windows check box:** Selecting this check box spawns a new tab in the current window when you press ⌘ and double-click a folder or disk.

TIP

If you don't enable it, ⌘+double-clicking a folder or disk icon opens it in a new window.

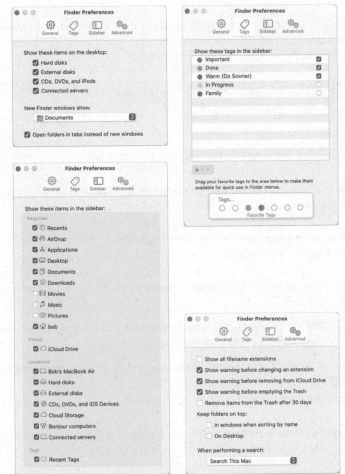

FIGURE 4-14:
Set Finder preferences here.

The default behavior is for folders to open in place when you double-click (open) them, which prevents window clutter. If you want a new window or tab instead, press ⌘ before you double-click. This forces the folder to open in a new window or tab (depending on whether the box is checked or not). Between this feature and Column view, I rarely need more than two windows onscreen, and I get by most of the time with a single window with multiple tabs.

Tags pane

The Tags pane is where you manage your tags, which appear in Finder's File menu, the right- or Control-click shortcut menu, the sidebar, and the toolbar. You can see a file or folder's tags in Finder windows, Get Info windows and inspectors, and applications' Open and Save dialogs and sheets, and you can use them as criteria for searches and smart folders.

TECHNICAL STUFF

A sheet is nothing more than a dialog that is attached to a document window's title bar and can't be moved. Some apps use sheets, other apps use dialogs, but either way you'll see the same options.

>> To rename a tag, click its name and type a new one.

>> To change a tag's color, click the colored circle to the left of its name and choose a different color.

>> Select the boxes for tags that you want to appear in the sidebar and toolbar.

TIP

To see your deselected tags in the sidebar or toolbar, click All Tags in (Sidebar) or Show All (toolbar).

Now, here's how to use 'em. To assign tags to icons, first select the icon(s) and then follow these steps:

1. **Choose File⇨Tags and click one or more of the colored dots in the Tags section.**

2. **Right- or Control-click and click one or more of the colored dots in the Tags section of the shortcut menu.**

3. **Click the Tags icon on the toolbar and click one or more tags.**

Here are a few more handy tricks with tags:

>> **To create a custom tag on the fly:** Right- or Control-click an item, choose Tags, type a label for the new tag, and then press Return.

>> **To untag an item:** Right- or Control-click the item, choose Tags, select the tag you want to remove, and then press Delete.

>> **To remove every instance of a tag from every file and folder on your disk:** Right- or Control-click the tag in the Tags pane of Finder Preferences, and then choose Delete Tag. Don't worry. Deleting a tag won't delete the items; it just removes that tag from every item.

TIP

Click the tags in your sidebar to see every file on all connected hard drives with that tag.

Sidebar pane

The Sidebar pane lets you choose which items are displayed in the sidebar. Select the check box to display the item; deselect the check box to not display it.

Advanced pane

The Advanced pane is just big enough to offer the following check boxes and a pop-up menu:

>> **Show All Filename Extensions check box (off by default):** Tells Finder to display the little two-, three-, four-, or more character filename suffixes (such as .doc in summary.doc) that make your Mac's file lists look more like those of a Linux (or Windows) user. The Finder hides those from you by default, but if you want to be able to see them in Finder when you open or save files, you need to turn on this option.

>> **Show Warning Before Changing an Extension check box (on by default):** Allows you to turn off the nagging dialog that appears if you attempt to change the two-, three-, four-, or more character file extension.

>> **Show Warning Before Removing from iCloud Drive (on by default):** Does what it says — warns you before you remove a file or folder from your iCloud drive.

>> **Show Warning Before Emptying the Trash check box (on by default):** Allows you to turn off the nagging dialog telling you how many items are in the Trash and asking whether you really want to delete them.

>> **Remove Items from the Trash After 30 Days check box (off by default):** This option does exactly what it says: It automatically deletes any item in the Trash for more than 30 days. Think of it as automatic emptying of the Trash for items that have been there 30 days or longer.

>> **Keep Folders on Top when Sorting by Name (off by default):** This one sorts folders and then files in windows sorted by Name. I love it and encourage you to enable it and give it a try.

>> **When Performing a Search drop-down menu:** Lets you choose the default search location when you initiate a search as described earlier in this chapter. Your choices are Search This Mac (the default), Search the Current Folder, and Use the Previous Search Scope.

Digging for Icon Data in the Info Window

Every icon has an Info window that gives you — big surprise! — information about that icon and enables you to choose which other users (if any) you want to have the privilege of using this icon. (I discuss sharing files and privileges in detail in Chapter 18.) The Info window is also where you can lock an icon so that it can't be renamed or dragged to the Trash.

To see an icon's Info window, click the icon and choose File⇨Get Info (or press ⌘+I). The Info window for that icon appears. Figure 4-15 shows the Info window for an image (a .jpg file named Kiss).

FIGURE 4-15:
A typical Info window for an image (Kiss.jpg).

Documents, folders, and disks each have slightly different Info windows. In this section, I give you highlights on the type of information and options that you can find.

The gray triangles reveal what information for an icon is available in this particular Info window. The sections that you see for most icons include the following:

» **Add Tags:** Click in this field to add tags to this item.

» **General:** For information of the general kind, such as

- *Kind:* What kind of file this is — an application, document, disk, folder, and so on

- *Size:* How much hard drive space this file uses

- *Where:* The path to the folder that contains this file

- *Created:* The date and time this file was created

- *Modified:* The date and time this file was last modified (that is, saved)

Six other check boxes may or may not appear in the General section of a particular Info window. Here's the scoop on this sextet of optional options:

- *Version:* Copyright information and the file's version number.

- *Shared Folder* (check box): Designates the folder as Shared, so other users are allowed to see and use its contents. You find out all about sharing in Chapter 18.

- *Stationery Pad* (check box): This one appears only in the Info window of document icons. If you select it, the file becomes a template. When you open a Stationery Pad document, a copy of its contents appears in a new Untitled document that you would typically save with a descriptive name.

- *Locked* (check box): If this box is selected, you receive the following warning if you try to put the item in the Trash: *This Item Is Locked. Do You Want to Move It to the Trash Anyway?* Your options are Stop and Continue. If you continue, the item goes into the Trash as usual. Then, when you try to empty the Trash, you receive another warning: *There Are Some Locked Items in the Trash. Do You Want to Remove All the Items, Including the Locked Ones, or Just the Unlocked Ones?* Your choices this time are Cancel, Remove Unlocked Items, and Remove All Items. If you choose to Remove All Items, the locked item(s) is/are deleted. If you choose Remove Unlocked Items, the locked item(s) remain(s) in the Trash, and you receive the *There Are Some Locked Items* warning again the next time you try to empty it.

  To remove the locked item from the Trash, click the Trash icon in the dock and drag the locked item out of the Trash and into a folder or onto the desktop.

- *Prevent App Nap* (check box): macOS can tell when an app is completely hidden behind other windows. If an app isn't currently doing something — playing music, downloading files, or checking your email, for example — App Nap conserves valuable battery life on laptops by slowing the app down. As soon as you activate the app again, it shifts back to full speed instantly.

- While App Nap can reduce CPU energy use by up to 23 percent, it may interfere with some programs' operation. If it does, try enabling this check box.

>> **More Info:** When the file was created, modified, and last opened (documents only).

>> **Name & Extension:** Tells the full name, including the (possibly hidden) extension.

>> **Comments:** Provides a field in which you can type your own comments about this icon for Spotlight to use in its searches.

I talk about searching a little earlier in this chapter and discuss Spotlight searches in greater detail in Chapter 10.

» **Preview:** When you select a document icon, the menu offers a Preview option that you use to see a glimpse of what's in that document. You can also see this preview when you select a document icon in Column view; it magically appears in the rightmost column. If you select a QuickTime movie or sound, you can play your selection right there in the preview pane without launching a separate application. And when you select most pictures, you see a preview of the actual picture (me in Kiss makeup on Halloween in Figure 4-15).

» **Sharing & Permissions:** Governs which users have access to this icon and how much access they are allowed. (See Chapter 18 for more about access privileges.)

TIP

If you press the Option key before you pull down Finder's File menu, the Get Info command changes to Show Inspector (alternatively, press ⌘+Option+I). The Get Info Inspector window looks and acts almost exactly like Get Info windows with two whopping exceptions:

» **Inspector displays info for only the currently selected icon.** If you click a different icon, Inspector instantly displays the info for the icon you clicked. That means you can Get Info on lots of icons in a row using the arrow keys or by pressing Tab or Shift+Tab. Try it — it's cool.

» **Cumulative info is displayed if multiple icons are selected.** In other words, if more than one icon is selected, Inspector displays the total size for all the selected files or folders or both.

And that's about it for icons, which are among the most fundamental parts of what makes your Mac a Mac (and not a toaster or an Xbox).

» Editing image, video, and audio files without an application

» Automating tasks with Quick Actions

» Making movies of your screen

» Tips, hints, and techniques to help you do more work with less effort

Chapter **5**

Delving Even Deeper into Big Sur's Desktop and Finder

I n this chapter, you discover cool features you may not be familiar with — such as Stacks and Quick Actions — as well as features you (should) already know and love, such as Quick Look and the Preview pane. Along the way I also point out a handful of useful interface features that make Finder better.

And now, without further ado, let's dive into the power and magic of Stacks on your desktop.

Cleaning Up Your Desktop Automatically with Stacks

I've seen a lot of users' Mac desktops over the years, and many of them look something like Figure 5-1.

FIGURE 5-1:
A messy,
disorganized
desktop.

In the past, my advice to people with messy desktops was to select all the icons on the desktop, put them in one folder, and then rename the folder something like Former Desktop icons. It worked okay but using Big Sur's Stacks is better and easier.

You can organize your desktop using Stacks in three ways:

>> Choose View ⇨ Use Stacks.

>> Use the keyboard shortcut ⌘+Control+0 (that's a zero).

>> Right- or Control-click anywhere on the desktop, and then choose Use Stacks from the shortcut menu.

REMEMBER

The Use Stacks command is available only when the desktop is active, so if an active window is on your screen, you'll see Use Groups rather than Use Stacks.

When you choose Use Stacks, your desktop transforms instantly from the mess shown in Figure 5-1 to the four nicely organized stacks shown in Figure 5-2. Folders on the desktop are not affected by using Stacks; all other icons on the desktop are organized automatically into stacks (Images, PDF Documents, Music, and Screen Shots in Figure 5-2).

Single-click a stack to see its contents, as shown in Figure 5-3 for the Images stack.

FIGURE 5-2:
Stacks create
order out
of chaos.

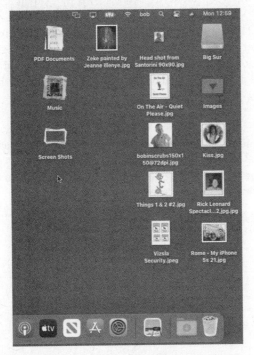

FIGURE 5-3:
Single-click a
stack (Images) to
see its contents.

Note that the expanded stack (Images, directly below the Big Sur disk icon) now displays a down-facing arrow (or a triangle, depending on how you look at it) in Figure 5-3. That indicates that the stack is expanded. Click the stack again to close it. Finally, note that stacks ignore your disk icons (if any).

Managing your Stacks

Choosing Use Stacks is just the start of things. When you're using Stacks, you can group items by choosing View⇨Group Stacks By, which offers the following choices:

» None (no keyboard shortcut)

» Kind (Control+⌘+2)

» Date Last Opened (Control+⌘+3)

» Date Added (Control+⌘+4)

» Date Modified (Control+⌘+5)

» Date Created (no keyboard shortcut)

» Tags (Control+⌘+7)

All figures in this chapter so far have their stacks grouped by Kind, but it may be easier to find what you're looking for if you use one of the other options. For example, if you know when you added, modified, or last opened the file, you can choose one of the date-based options, such as Date Created, which is shown in Figure 5-4.

TIP

You can also right- or Control-click and choose Group Stacks By, which offers all the same commands except None, which also, strangely, lacks a keyboard shortcut.

Finally, if you're not already using Tags (discussed in Chapter 4) to organize your files, Stacks may be just the incentive you need to start.

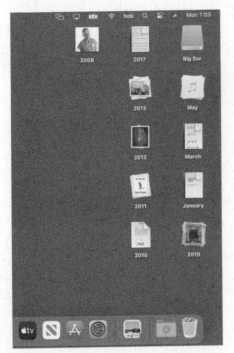

FIGURE 5-4:
Grouping stacks by Date Created gives you a different perspective than grouping them by Kind.

Quick Actions: Now Playing All Over Big Sur

Quick Actions are mini-apps that let you perform certain tasks without launching a real application. You'll find them in the Preview pane of Finder windows, in Quick Look windows, and in shortcut menus. They're super useful and can save you the time and effort of opening a program to perform a simple task, such as adding circles and arrows to an image (and much more), trimming video, and rotating pictures.

Getting the most out of Markup

In Big Sur, the Markup icon (shown in the margin) and the Rotate icon (see Figure 5-5) are available in Quick Look windows and the Preview pane of Finder windows, and the commands are in Finder's shortcut menu (right- or Control-click).

TIP

When you click the Rotate icon, the default is to rotate your document counter-clockwise by 90°. If you'd rather rotate clockwise, press Option before you click.

Show Markup toolbar   Rotate

FIGURE 5-5:
Click the Markup
icon to see the
Markup toolbar;
click the Rotate
icon to rotate
your image in 90°
increments.

When you have an image selected and you click the Markup icon in a Quick Look overlay, in a Preview pane in a Finder window, or in a Finder shortcut menu, an overlay appears displaying the image below the Markup toolbar, as shown in Figure 5-6.

Markup toolbar   Shape style   Text style

Shapes   Draw   Border color   Rotate counterclockwise

Sketch   Text   Sign   Fill color   Crop

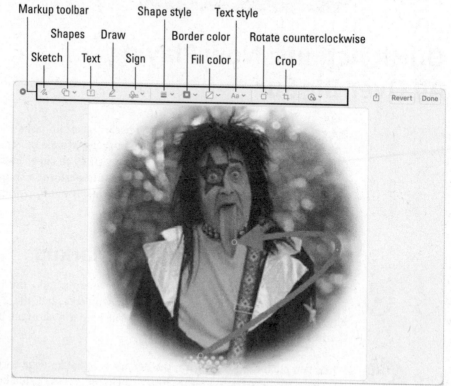

FIGURE 5-6:
The Markup
toolbar above an
image to which I
added text and
an arrow by using
Markup.

And here's how the tools work:

- » **Sketch:** Sketch a shape with a single stroke. Here's the cool part: If your drawing is recognized as a standard shape — a circle, a rectangle, an arrow, or such — it's replace d by a perfectly drawn rendition of the shape. If you don't like it perfect, you can use what you drew instead by choosing it from the palette that appears after you use the tool.

- » **Shapes:** Click a shape to place it on the image, and then drag the shape where you want. To resize a shape, use its blue handles. If the shape has green handles, you can use them to alter the shape.

  You can also zoom in or out and highlight specific shapes using the pair of tools at the bottom of the Shapes drop-down (and shown in Figure 5-7):

  - *Highlight:* Drag the highlight where you want. To resize it, use the blue handles.

  - *Loupe:* Drag the loupe over the area you want to magnify. To increase or decrease the magnification level, drag the green handle; to increase or decrease the size of the loupe, drag the blue handle. To further magnify an area, you can create additional loupes and stack them, using the yellow guides that appear to align them.

- » **Text:** Type your text, and then drag the text box where you want.

- » **Draw:** Use your finger to draw a shape with a single stroke. Press more firmly on the trackpad to draw thicker, heavier lines. Note that this tool is available only on computers with a Force Touch trackpad.

- » **Sign:** If signatures are listed, click one and drag it where you want. To resize it, use the blue handles.

  To create a signature:

  - *Using your trackpad:* Click the Sign tool, click Create Signature if shown, and then click Trackpad. Click the text as prompted, sign your name on the trackpad using your finger, and then click Done. If you don't like the results, click Clear and try again. If your trackpad supports it, press your finger more firmly on the trackpad to sign with a heavier, darker line.

  - *Using a camera:* Click the Sign tool, click Create Signature if shown, and then click Camera (Mac camera) or iPhone or iPad (camera). Hold your signature (on white paper) facing the camera so that your signature is level with the blue line in the window. When your signature appears in the window, click Done. If you don't like the results, click Clear and try again.

- » **Shape style:** Change the thickness and type of lines used in a shape or add a shadow to a shape.

- » **Border color:** Change the color of the a shape's border.

- » **Fill color:** Change the color of a shape's fill.

- » **Text style:** Change the font type, style, and color.

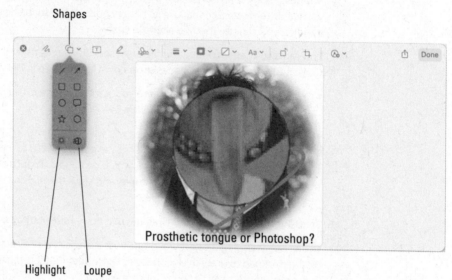

Shapes

FIGURE 5-7:
The shapes drop-down (left) and the loupe in action (right).

Highlight Loupe

Prosthetic tongue or Photoshop?

Trimming video without launching an app

Although QuickTime Player has allowed you to trim videos for years, you have to launch it and usually wait a few seconds for the video to appear. Big Sur includes a faster, easier way to trim your videos without launching QuickTime Player (or another app).

When a video file is selected, you'll find the new Trim icon (shown in the margin) available in Quick Look windows, in Finder preview panes, and in the shortcut menu (right- or Control-click a video and choose Quick Actions ⇨ Trim).

Click the Trim icon and a filmstrip appears below the video with handles for setting the beginning and end of the video, as shown in Figure 5-8.

Video to be deleted

The Macworld All-Star Band Redux - Feelin' Alright.mp4   Revert Done

Start of Video   End of Video

FIGURE 5-8:
Drag the handles
to set the start
and end points.

Drag the left handle to where you want the video to begin, and then drag the right handle to where you want the video to end. Click Done and you're done. Your video has been trimmed of excess footage without launching an app.

One more thing: All tools discussed in this section are part of a Big Sur feature called Quick Actions.

Do It Quicker with Finder Quick Actions

You've already seen several of Big Sur's Finder Quick Actions — Rotate, Markup, and Trim, to be precise — but there are a couple of actions that can help you get more out of your Quick Actions.

The first is the Create PDF Quick Action, which does what its name implies and more; the second is creating your own Quick Actions with Automator (discussed in Chapter 23), which may be the coolest thing about Quick Actions.

Creating PDFs without launching an app

In most applications, you can create a PDF from the Print sheet (see Chapter 22). But wouldn't it be nice if you could create PDFs without launching an application and choosing Print?

In Big Sur it's no problem. Just use the Create PDF Quick Action, which you'll find in Quick Look windows, in the Preview pane of Finder windows, and in the shortcut menu (right- or Control-click).

Actually, it is a problem if you want to use the Create PDF Quick Action on files other than images. It won't work with a Word, Pages, Excel, or TextEdit document, or other document types. But, if your files are images — JPEG, TIFF, PNG, and such — you can turn them into PDFs with a click.

You can tell if the file can be converted because the Create PDF command or icon appears only when suitable files are selected, as shown in Figure 5-9.

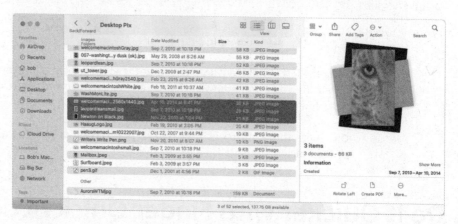

FIGURE 5-9: I've selected three image files, so the Create PDF Quick Action icon appears.

TIP

If the Create PDF Quick Action icon doesn't appear in the Preview pane when you select an image or images, try clicking the More icon (where the Create PDF Quick Action occasionally hides).

Here's a cool feature: If you select multiple image files, as I did in Figure 5-9 before using Create PDF, the result is a multipage PDF file with one image on each page — a kind of virtual contact sheet. Neat!

Creating custom Finder Quick Actions

The Markup, Rotate, Trim, and Create PDF Quick Actions are useful and a welcome addition to Finder, but wouldn't you love to be able to create your own Quick Actions to appear in Quick Look windows, in the Preview pane of Finder windows, and in the shortcut menu (right- or Control-click)?

You'll be happy to know that you can, and doing so is relatively easy using Automator, which comes with Big Sur. That's all I have to say here. See near the end of Chapter 23 for a nice tutorial on building Quick Actions with Automator.

Four More Cool Big Sur Tricks

In addition to Stacks and Quick Actions, Big Sur includes several other enhancements, such as a nifty mechanism for capturing still and video images from your Mac screen, desktop pictures that change to reflect the time of day, the recently used apps section of the dock, and using Gallery view as a photo browser.

Shooting screens

If you've used a Mac for long, you probably know that you can grab a picture of what's on your screen by using the shortcuts ⌘+Shift+3 for the whole screen or ⌘+Shift+4 to select a window or part of the screen. Those shortcuts and features have been around since time immemorial.

When you take a screenshot using your old-school shortcuts — ⌘+Shift+3 or ⌘+Shift+4 — a thumbnail of the screenshot appears in the lower-right corner of the screen.

If you do nothing, the thumbnail disappears after about 5 seconds, and then the screenshot is saved on your desktop. To see additional options, right- or Control-click the thumbnail and choose from the shortcut menu, as shown in Figure 5-10.

Or just single-click the thumbnail before it disappears and the image opens in a window with Markup tools so you can annotate the image before you save it.

When you have finished annotating, click Done to save the screenshot and annotations to the desktop, or click Revert to close the overlay without saving your annotations.

TIP

If you don't want to save a file at all, add the Control key to the keyboard shortcut (⌘+Shift+Control+3 or ⌘+Shift+Control+3). Instead of saving the screenshot to a file, it will be sent to the clipboard, so you can paste it into any document that will accept an image from the clipboard.

FIGURE 5-10:
After you take a screenshot, a thumbnail appears in the lower-right corner of the screen; right- or Control-click for additional options.

But it gets even better with one more fabulous screen-shooting shortcut that provides even more control over screenshots and adds the capability to record screen movies. This magical shortcut is ⌘+Shift+5, and it's the only shortcut you really have to memorize because its floating toolbar, shown in Figure 5-11, includes all the functionality of the ⌘+Shift+3 and ⌘+Shift+4 shortcuts and more.

Capture selected window

Capture entire screen   Capture selected portion

Record entire screen   Selected portion

Record selected portion

FIGURE 5-11:
The screenshot toolbar appears when you press ⌘+Shift+5.

Notice the Options pop-up menu, which lets you do the following:

» Change the destination for screenshots from Desktop (the default) to Documents, Clipboard, Mail, Messages, Preview, or Other Location.

» Set a timer for shots.

» Turn on and off the floating thumbnail.

» Remember the last selection you made (or not).

» Show or hide the mouse pointer.

After configuring the options, you capture screenshots by clicking the Capture icon. If you've chosen one of the movie options — Record Entire Screen or Record Selected Portion — the Capture icon becomes the Record icon; click it to begin recording. When you do, the Stop Recording icon appears in the menu bar (and shown in the margin). Click it to end your recording.

Bottom line: Memorize Big Sur's one keyboard shortcut to rule them all — ⌘+Shift+5 — and use it for all your screen-capturing needs.

Dynamic desktop images

Although I cover using desktop pictures in Chapter 6, I'd like to highlight a feature here: dynamic desktops.

When you choose your desktop picture, you'll find a pair of dynamic desktop options above all the normal desktop pictures in the Desktop & Screen Saver System Preferences pane.

Because a picture is worth a thousand words, take a gander at Figure 5-12, which explains it all.

That's all.

Recently used apps in the dock

Although I discuss the dock in Chapter 3, I'd be remiss if I didn't point out a relatively new feature to the dock: the Recently Used Apps section, which displays icons for the last three apps you've launched, regardless of whether their icons are in the dock permanently.

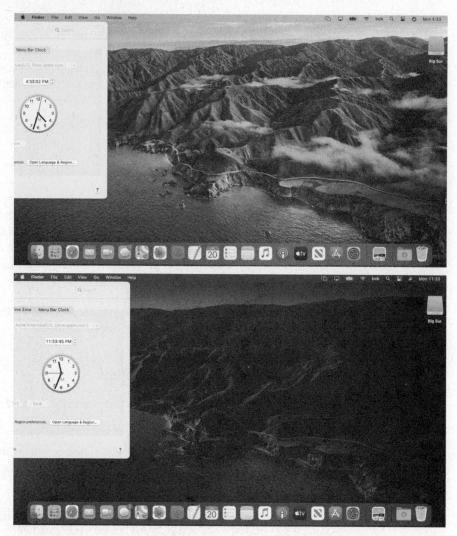

FIGURE 5-12:
A dynamic desktop at 4:33 PM (top) and 11:33 PM (bottom).

Mentions of Gallery view

One last thing: Although I discuss Gallery view in Chapter 4, here's a tip I recently discovered for its use: Gallery view is great for browsing folders full of images.

Click an image and then use the arrow keys to see the next or previous image; click the Markup, Rotate, or More icon to edit the current image.

And that retires the side, at least as far as features in Big Sur's Finder are concerned. Onward!

2

How Stuff Works

IN THIS PART . . .

Customize and organize macOS Big Sur to suit your style.

Understand what goes where, and why.

Save and open files.

Get the secret to finding anything, anywhere, on any disk.

Mastering Mission Control — try saying that three times real fast.

Find time-saving secrets of Quick Look and Launchpad.

Master the Big Sur Clipboard.

Chapter **6**

Having It Your Way

Everyone works a bit differently, and everyone likes to use the Mac in a particular way. In this chapter, you find out how to tweak various options so everything is just the way you like it. The first things many people like to do are set their background and screen saver to something more interesting. You can begin with that stuff, but keep in mind that you can do much more.

You can change the colors in windows, the standard font, and more if you like. Your Mac lets you choose how onscreen elements behave and how your hardware — such as the keyboard, mouse, and wireless Bluetooth gadgets — interact with your Mac.

Introducing System Preferences

You should start by becoming familiar with System Preferences, which lives in the Applications folder and appears on the menu and in the dock.

The following steps explain how to move around the System Preferences window, no matter what you're trying to tweak:

1. **Open the System Preferences window, shown in Figure 6-1.**

   You can open System Preferences in at least four ways:

   - Double-click the System Preferences icon in your Applications folder.
   - Choose ⌫ System Preferences.
   - Click the System Preferences icon in Launchpad.
   - Click the System Preferences icon on your dock.

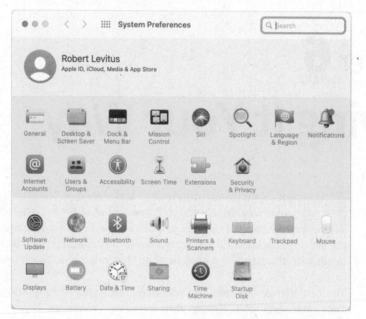

FIGURE 6-1: System Preferences is where you change many Big Sur options (organized by category here).

2. **Click any of the icons in the System Preferences window.**

   The contents of the window change to reflect the options for whichever icon you click. When this happens, I call the window a *pane.* So, for example, when you click the General icon in the System Preferences window, the icons disappear and are replaced by the General preference pane.

   When you finish working with System Preferences panes, you should (of course) quit by choosing System Preferences ⌫ Quit System Preferences (shortcut: ⌘+Q) or clicking the red gumdrop (close) button.

REMEMBER

Although System Preferences quits when you close its window, *many other apps DON'T quit when you close their last open window*. Worse, there's no easy way to know if an app will or won't quit when you close its last window (so pay attention).

3. **Click the Show All icon in the toolbar to exit the pane and return to the icons in the System Preferences window.**

   You can accomplish the same thing by choosing View⇨Show All Preferences, or by pressing ⌘+L; both return you to the window with icons for all your System Preferences panes.

   Alternatively, you can choose a different preference pane right from the View menu or the dock icon menu, both shown in Figure 6-2.

TIP

If you right- or Control-click the System Preferences icon on the dock (or just press and hold down for a couple of seconds), a menu pops up listing all available preference panes. The cool part is that this works even if the System Preferences window isn't open. When you know which pane you need, this shortcut is often the fastest way to get to it.

Last but not least, note that you can navigate to the next or previous pane you've viewed with the Back and Forward icons beside the red and yellow gumdrops (shortcuts ⌘+[and ⌘+], respectively). Back and Forward commands also appear on the View menu.

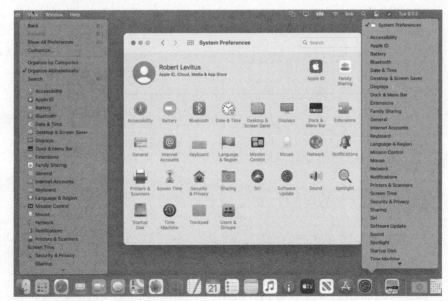

FIGURE 6-2:
The View menu (left), the System Preferences window organized alphabetically (center), and the dock icon menu (right).

TIP

You can get rid of the categories (shown in Figure 6-1) and display the icons in alphabetical order (shown in Figure 6-2). To switch to alphabetical view, choose View⇨Organize Alphabetically. The categories disappear, the window shrinks, and the icons are alphabetized. To switch from alphabetical view back to category view, choose View⇨Organize by Categories.

TIP

Big Sur lets you hide little-used System Preferences pane icons. To manage icons, choose View⇨Customize, and a little check box appears next to each icon. Deselect the box if you want to hide the icon; select the box to make the icon reappear.

Choose View⇨Customize again when you're finished selecting and deselecting.

The Desktop & Screen Saver System Preferences Pane

Figure 6-3 shows my desktop with a portrait of my dog Zeke painted by talented artist Jeanne Illenye. (Refer to the default Big Sur desktop background in Figure 1-2.)

FIGURE 6-3: My beautified desktop.

The Desktop tab

Here's how you can change your desktop picture:

1. From the desktop, choose **System Preferences.**

Or right- or Control-click the desktop, choose Change Desktop Background from the contextual menu, and skip to Step 3.

The System Preferences window appears.

2. Click the Desktop & Screen Saver icon.

When the Desktop & Screen Saver pane appears, click the Desktop tab (if it's not selected already, as it is in Figure 6-3).

3. Click a folder in the column on the left, and then click a picture in the area on the right.

In Figure 6-3, I clicked a picture *called Zeke painted by Jeanne Illenye notail*, one of the items in the Pictures folder inside my Home folder.

You have at least three other ways to change your desktop picture:

>> Drag a picture file from the Finder onto the *image well* (the little rectangular picture to the left of the picture's name, as shown in Figure 6-3).

>> Click the Desktop tab in the Desktop & Screen Saver System Preferences pane and then click the + icon at the bottom of the list on the left. Choose a folder in the standard Open File sheet and that folder appears in the list; you can use any picture files it contains for your desktop picture.

>> Click the disclosure triangle next to Photos in the column on the left side of the Desktop & Screen Saver Preferences pane and choose from pictures stored in your Photos library.

Although I love having a beautiful desktop picture, I use a white or gray desktop (click Solid Colors in the list, and then click the white or gray color swatch) for most figures in this book to make it easier to discern fine details.

If you need a color other than the 16 hues displayed in the Desktop & Screen Saver System Preferences pane, click the Custom Color button. When the Color Picker window appears, either click a color to choose it or click the eyedropper icon and then click any color displayed on your screen to select and use that color.

The Screen Saver tab

macOS Big Sur comes with several screen-saver modules, and many more are available for free (search the Internet for *macOS Screen Saver*). To set up your screen saver, follow these steps:

1. **Open System Preferences, click the Desktop & Screen Saver icon, and then click the Screen Saver tab to see the options shown in Figure 6-4.**

2. **In the Screen Savers column on the left side of the pane, choose a screen saver that interests you.**

   Scroll down to see all the available Slideshows and Screen Savers.

   If you can't decide, scroll to the bottom of the screen savers list and choose Random to have your Mac choose a different screen saver at random each time the screen saver kicks in.

3. **(Optional) To see what the chosen module looks like in action, click the Preview image on the right.**

   A little Preview button appears on the image when you hover your cursor over it to remind you how to see a preview. Nice touch!

   Press any key or click anywhere to end the test.

4. **After you choose a screen saver, select the number of minutes you want the Mac to wait before activating the screen saver from the Start After pop-up menu.**

5. **Select the Show with Clock check box to display a digital clock along with the screen saver.**

6. **(Optional) Click the Hot Corners button to choose which corner of your screen activates the screen saver and which disables it.**

   If you enable this option, when you move your cursor to the chosen corner of the screen, you activate or disable the screen saver until you move the cursor elsewhere. Note that hot corners are optional and are turned off by default.

7. **When you're done, close the Desktop & Screen Saver pane.**

You can require a password to wake your Mac from a screen saver (or sleep). To do so, follow these steps:

1. **From the main System Preferences screen, click the Security & Privacy icon.**

   The Security & Privacy System Preferences pane appears.

2. **Click the General tab.**

FIGURE 6-4:
The Screen Saver
tab (foreground)
and Drift screen
saver
(background).

3. **Select the Require Password after Sleep or Screen Saver Begins check box.**

4. **Choose a length of time from the pop-up menu between the words Password and After.**

   Your options range from Immediately to 8 hours, with six other options between. If you wouldn't want someone to sit down at your computer and have access to all your stuff, you'd be wise to require a password and choose one of these options.

   Now you'll have to supply the user account password to wake up your computer after the length of time you selected.

The General System Preferences Pane

Computers don't care about appearances, but if you want your Mac to look a bit more festive (or, for that matter, businesslike), you have options in the General pane (see Figure 6-5) at your disposal. To open this pane, choose System Preferences, and then click the General icon.

First up are the general appearance options:

» **Appearance:** This option governs the appearance of buttons and other interface elements, including the menu bar and the three gumdrops (Close, Minimize, and Zoom) in the top-left corner of most windows.

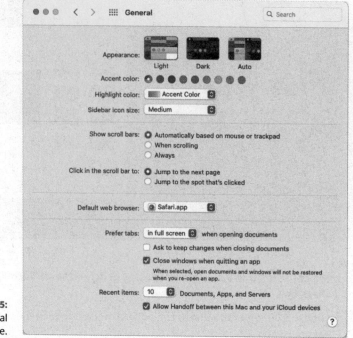

FIGURE 6-5:
The General
pane.

Apple, however, in its infinite wisdom, provides only three choices: Light, Dark, or Auto.

» **Accent Color buttons:** Change the color of buttons and other interface elements to one of eight choices.

TIP

To preview an accent color, click it. The check boxes, drop-down menus, and radio buttons in the General System Preferences pane instantly change to that accent color. Sweet!

» **Highlight Color pop-up menu:** From here, you can choose the color that text is surrounded by when you choose it in a document or select an icon. This time, Apple isn't so restrictive: You have eight highlight colors you can choose, plus Other, which brings up a color picker from which you can choose almost any color.

I'm partial to yellow, which makes selections look like they've been run over by a yellow highlighter.

» **Sidebar Icon Size pop-up menu:** Choose Small, Medium, or Large for icons in your Finder sidebar.

The next area in the General pane enables you to set the behavior of scroll bars:

>> **Show Scroll Bars radio buttons:** These buttons let you choose when you want to see scroll bars on windows. Your choices are Automatically Based on Mouse or Trackpad, When Scrolling, or Always. I prefer Always; your mileage may vary.

>> **Click in the Scroll Bar To radio buttons:** These buttons give you the option of moving your view of a window up or down by a page (the default) or to the position in the document roughly proportionate to where you clicked in the scroll bar. I prefer jumping to the spot that's clicked.

TIP

An easy way to try these options is to open a Finder window and place it side by side with the General pane, reducing the size of the window if necessary to make scroll bars appear. Select an option in the General pane, observe the behavior of the scroll bars, and then select a different option and observe again.

TIP

The Jump to the Spot That's Clicked option is handy for navigating long documents. And don't forget — the Page Down key does the same thing as choosing the Jump to the Next Page choice, so you lose nothing by choosing Jump to the Spot That's Clicked.

It would be even nicer if all third-party apps supported this feature, but some — including Microsoft Office 2011 (but not Office 2016 and later, which finally behave properly with respect to your scroll bar setting) — don't behave properly no matter what you choose for this setting.

Use the Default Web Browser drop-down menu to choose (what else?) your default browser. Unless you've installed another web browser, such as Chrome or Firefox, Safari is the only option.

>> **Prefer Tabs pop-up menu:** This option determines when to use tabbed windows; your choices are Never, In Full Screen, or Always. I like tabbed windows all the time, so my option is set to Always. Try all three and choose the one you like best.

>> **Ask to Keep Changes when Closing Documents check box:** Big Sur can save versions of your documents automatically and without any action on your part. So when you quit an application or close a document, your changes can be saved automatically. If you want to be able to close documents without having to manually save your changes, enable this option.

>> **Close Windows when Quitting an Application check box:** Your Mac's default behavior is to reopen documents and windows that were open when you quit that app. When you launch the app again, all the windows and documents magically reappear right where you left them. So enable this option to have your apps open to a clean slate, without reopening documents or windows from the previous session.

WARNING

These last two items may not work as expected with older third-party applications. As a rule, the longer it's been since a program's last update, the more likely it is that the app will ignore these two settings.

>> **Recent Items pop-up menu:** Use this to specify how many recent items will be remembered and displayed in your ⬢➪ Recent Items submenu. The default is 10, but I like having access to more than 10 applications and documents in my Recent Items submenu, so I set mine to 50.

>> **Allow Handoff between This Mac and Your iCloud Devices check box:** When enabled, you can start working on a document, an email, or a message on any Apple device and pick up where you left off on another device, as described in Chapter 23.

Adjusting the Keyboard, Mouse, Trackpad, and Other Hardware

No two Mac users use the keyboard, mouse, or trackpad in the same way. Some folks don't use a mouse at all. (You might not even use the keyboard if you use voice-recognition software or other devices, as I explain in Chapter 23.) If you're using macOS on a notebook, you have a *trackpad*, that little surface where you move your finger around to control the cursor. Or perhaps you have a Bluetooth-enabled keyboard and mouse so you can hook them up wirelessly. Regardless of what you have, you should give some thought to customizing the way they work so it feels just right for you.

The Keyboard, Mouse, and Trackpad System Preferences panes offer several tabs that enable you to modify the behavior of your keyboard, mouse, and trackpad so it feels just right for you. The first thing to do is open the Keyboard System Preferences pane by choosing ⬢➪ System Preferences and clicking the Keyboard icon.

The Keyboard System Preferences pane

The Keyboard System Preferences pane has five tabs: Keyboard, Text, Shortcuts, Input Sources, and Dictation.

Keyboard tab

On the Keyboard tab, you can adjust your settings in the following ways:

» Drag the Key Repeat slider to set how fast a key repeats when you hold it down. This feature comes into play when (for example) you hold down the hyphen (–) key to make a line or the asterisk (*) key to make a divider.

» Drag the Delay Until Repeat slider to set how long you have to hold down a key before it starts repeating.

If you have a notebook Mac (such as a MacBook, MacBook Pro, or MacBook Air), you also see one or more of these additional features:

» **Adjust Keyboard Brightness in Low Light:** This check box turns your laptop's ambient keyboard lighting on and off.

» **Turn Keyboard Backlight Off After (Choose 5, 10, or 30 seconds, or 1 or 5 minutes from the drop-down menu):** This option lets you determine how long the keyboard backlighting remains on when your computer isn't in use.

Of course, if your MacBook doesn't *have* ambient keyboard lighting, you don't see the last two items.

REMEMBER

Ambient keyboard lighting is a cool feature, but it reduces battery life. My recommendation is to use it only when you really need it.

» **Show Keyboard and Emoji Viewers in the Menu Bar:** This check box adds a new menu for opening either of these useful windows, as shown in Figure 6-6.

Click any character (smiley faces in Figure 6-6) to insert it in your document; click the little icons at the bottom of the window to view additional screens full of characters.

FIGURE 6-6:
(Clockwise) Keyboard tab, Character Viewer window, Keyboard and Character Viewer menu, and Keyboard Viewer window (U.S.) in all their glory.

NEW

For more Keyboard Viewer options, click the little gear in the upper-right corner of the window. A drop-down menu offers a slew of additional options (see Figure 6-6).

Some people prefer the look Character Viewer had prior to Mavericks (OS X 10.9). While both looks offer the same characters you know and love, the presentation has changed. Never fear. If you prefer the old column browser look and feel, click the little Character Viewer icon to the right of the Search field (and shown in the margin). This transforms Character Viewer back to its pre-Mavericks look, as shown in Figure 6-7.

FIGURE 6-7: The little Character Viewer icon near the Search field toggles the look of the Character Viewer window between the old look shown here and the newer look (smileys and people in Figure 6-6).

To return the window to its other state, just click the little icon again.

TIP

Click the Action menu (the little gear near the upper-left corner) and choose Customize List to enable additional character categories, including Braille Patterns, Dingbats, Musical Symbols, and Sign/Standard Symbols.

>> **Use All F1, F2 Keys as Standard Function Keys:** If this check box is selected, the F keys at the top of your keyboard control the active software application.

To use the special hardware features printed on each F key (display brightness, screen mirroring, sound volume, mute, and so on), you have to press the Fn (Function) key before pressing the F key. If the check box is left deselected, you have to press the Fn key if you want to use the F keys with a software application. Got it? Good.

Finally, these keys may not work if you use a third-party keyboard (one not manufactured by Apple).

>> **Set Up Bluetooth Keyboard button:** This button launches the Bluetooth assistant and walks you through pairing and setup as described in Chapter 23.

>> **Modifier Keys button:** With this button, you can change the action performed by the Caps Lock, Control, Option, and Command keys. This option is particularly useful if you use a non-Apple keyboard, although it works just fine on Apple keyboards, too.

TIP

I'm always engaging the Caps Lock key accidentally with my overactive left pinky, and I rarely engage it on purpose. So, I set *my* Caps Lock key to perform No Action. Now I never type half a sentence in ALL CAPS BECAUSE I ACCIDENTALLY PRESSED THE CAPS LOCK KEY.

Text tab

The Text tab is one of my favorite features in all of Macdom because it saves me countless keystrokes every day. Not because it's the tab with the Correct Spelling Automatically check box. Enable it (if it's not already enabled) and be done. Spelling correction is good, but the reason I love the Text tab so much is because it lets me create shortcuts to replace short phrases with longer ones.

When I type . . .	My Mac replaces it with . . .
wtf	what the heck
vty	Very truly yours,
	Bob "Dr. Mac" LeVitus
	Writer, Raconteur, and Troublemaker
blc	boblevitus@boblevitus.com

It's a handy trick, indeed. Plus, a preview pops up just below your typing so you can accept the replacement by pressing the spacebar or reject it by clicking the little X or pressing Esc.

To create your own shortcuts, click the little plus sign near the bottom-left corner of the window. Type the short phrase in the Replace field, click in the With field or press Tab, and then type the replacement phrase. You can see what happens when I type **wtf** in the TextEdit window in the foreground of Figure 6-8.

TIP

Although it's not obvious, you can create multiline substitutions. Just hold down Option and press Return to start a new line of text. You won't see the lines above (or below) the line you're typing, but with a bit of trial and error you can get it to work, as I did with my *vty* shortcut.

FIGURE 6-8:
The Text tab of
the Keyboard
System
Preferences pane
(left), and what I
see when I type
wtf in a TextEdit
document (right).

Shortcuts tab

If you really hate to use your mouse or if your mouse is broken, keyboard short-cuts can be handy. I tend to use them more on my laptop because I really don't like using the built-in-touch-mouse thing (technically, it's a *trackpad*, and I talk more about it in the next section).

I introduce some commonly used keyboard shortcuts in Chapter 2. You probably don't want to mess with those, but you can assign other commands you use often to just about any key combination you like. By creating your own keyboard short-cuts, you can have whatever commands you need literally at your fingertips.

Not only can you add, delete, or change keyboard shortcuts for many operating system functions (such as taking a picture of the screen or using the keyboard to choose menu and dock items), but you can also add, delete, and change keyboard shortcuts for your applications.

To begin, choose the Shortcuts tab in the Keyboard System Preferences pane. Now you can do any or all of the following:

» **To change a shortcut:** First, click the appropriate application, preference, or feature in the left column. Next, double-click the shortcut you want to change on the right side of the right column (for example, F3 or ⌘+G). The old shortcut becomes highlighted; when it does, press the new shortcut keys you want to use.

>> **To add a new shortcut:** Click App Shortcuts on the left and then click the + icon. Choose the appropriate application from the Application pop-up menu, type the exact name of the menu command you want to add in the Menu Title field, and then type the shortcut you want to assign to that command in the Keyboard Shortcut field. If the shortcut you press is in use by another application or preference, a yellow triangular caution symbol appears next to it. It really is that simple.

>> **To delete a shortcut you created:** Choose it and then click the – icon.

The Shortcuts tab also offers options for what happens when you press the Tab key in a window or dialog:

>> If you deselect (no checkmark) the Use Keyboard Navigation to Move Focus Between Controls check box, the Tab key moves the cursor from one text box to the next or from one list item to the next item (usually alphabetically). This action is the default.

>> If you select the Use Keyboard Navigation to Move Focus Between Controls check box, you can avoid using the mouse for the most part, if that's your preference.

When the check box is selected, the Tab key moves the focus from one item to the next in a window or dialog. So (for example) every time you press the Tab key in an Open File dialog or sheet, the focus moves — say, from the sidebar to the file list to the Cancel button to the Icon view icon. Each item is high-lighted to show it's selected, and you can activate the highlighted item from the keyboard by pressing the spacebar.

To move the focus backward (that is, to the previously selected item), press Shift+Tab.

TIP

You can toggle this setting by pressing Control+F7. And if you don't care for Control+F7 as its shortcut, you can change it by clicking Keyboard in the left column, double-clicking the Change the Way Tab Moves Focus item in the right column, and then pressing the new shortcut.

Input Sources tab

The Input Sources tab is where you can choose to display one or more foreign language keyboards in the Input menu.

The Input menu and the Keyboard and Character Viewer menu are one and the same. If you add one or more foreign keyboards, the icon in your menu bar changes from the rather tame icon shown in Figure 6-7 to the flag of the selected keyboard (that's the Dutch flag in the margin, by the way).

Last but not least, the Dictation tab is covered in Chapter 23; if you want to dictate to your Mac, you might want to read that section sooner rather than later.

The Mouse System Preferences pane

The Mouse System Preferences pane is where you set your mouse tracking speed, scrolling speed, and double-click delays.

If you use a notebook or an Apple Magic Trackpad, you'll use the System Preferences pane named Trackpad instead. I tell you more about it in the upcoming section, "The Trackpad System Preferences pane."

The first item in this pane is a check box titled Scroll Direction: Natural. If scrolling or navigating in windows feels backward to you, try deselecting this box.

Moving right along, here are the features you'll find in the Mouse System Preferences pane (if you have a mouse connected):

» Move the Tracking Speed slider to change the relationship between hand movement of the mouse and cursor movement onscreen. This slider works just like the slider for trackpads, as I explain in the upcoming section on trackpads.

» The Double-Click Speed setting determines how close together two clicks must be for the Mac to interpret them as a double-click and not as two separate clicks. Move the slider arrow to the leftmost setting, Very Slow, for the slowest. The rightmost position, Fast, is the fastest setting. I prefer the setting one tick shy of Fast.

» If your mouse has a scroll ball or scroll wheel, you also see a Scrolling Speed slider, which lets you adjust how fast the contents of a window scroll when you use the scroll wheel or ball.

» If your mouse has more than one button, you see a pair of Primary Mouse Button radio buttons. These let you choose which button — left or right — you use to make your primary (regular) click. Conversely, the other mouse button (the one you didn't choose) becomes your secondary (Control or right) click.

Many lefties like to change this setting. Set the primary button as the right button, and you can click with the index finger of your left hand.

Being right-handed, I've chosen the defaults in Figure 6-9, so the left button is the primary click and the right button is the secondary (right or Control) click.

TIP

FIGURE 6-9:
The Mouse
System
Preferences pane
set up for a
right-hander.

Note that the mouse I used for Figure 6-9 is a third-party mouse. If you use an Apple branded mouse, you'll see additional options specific to your mouse. Sadly, I don't have an Apple mouse to use for testing (and have no need to buy one), so you're on your own.

One last thing: Changes in the Mouse System Preferences pane take effect immediately, so you should definitely play around with various speed settings to determine what works best for you.

The Bluetooth System Preferences pane

Bluetooth is a technology that lets you make wireless connections between your Mac and devices such as Bluetooth mice and phones. Most Macs manufactured in the past few years have Bluetooth built in; some older models don't.

TIP

You configure Bluetooth devices you want to use with your Mac elsewhere in the Bluetooth System Preferences pane (as I describe in Chapters 18 and 23).

If your Mac has Bluetooth built in, the Bluetooth tab shows you the battery level of your Bluetooth mouse or keyboard. It also offers a check box to add a Bluetooth status menu to your menu bar and a check box to let Bluetooth devices wake your computer from sleep.

The Trackpad System Preferences pane

If you use a notebook Mac — a MacBook, MacBook Air, or MacBook Pro — or a desktop Mac with a Magic Trackpad (version 1 or 2), you'll have an additional System Preferences pane called Trackpad. This pane lets you configure tracking and clicking speed as well as the gesturing behavior of your Mac's built-in trackpad.

TIP

If you're looking for a replacement for your mouse, consider Apple's $129 Magic Trackpad 2. This nifty wireless device can be used with any Mac or PC that has Bluetooth. It's also the biggest glass Multi-Touch trackpad yet, nearly 80 percent larger than the MacBook Pro built-in trackpad. Yes, you can use the Magic Trackpad 2 with your MacBook Pro, and yes, that does mean you'll have dual trackpads.

I am trying to become more of a trackpad believer and make better use of the iPhone-like gestures available on my Mac. I have both a Magic Trackpad and a mouse on my desk and grab whichever is appropriate at the moment.

The Trackpad System Preferences pane has three tabs — Point & Click, Scroll & Zoom, and More Gestures — as shown in Figure 6-10.

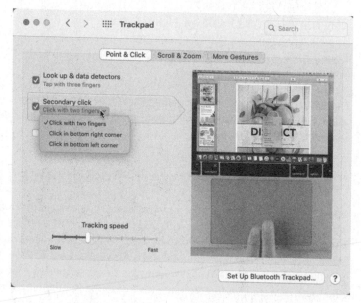

FIGURE 6-10: The Trackpad System Preferences pane offers controls for one-finger and multi-finger gestures.

WARNING

If you have an older notebook with the older-style trackpad, you may not see all the controls in Figure 6-10. (For what it's worth, a Magic Trackpad 2 would cure it.)

All three tabs work the same way as the Point & Click tab shown in Figure 6-10. To enable or disable a feature, select its check box. To see how a feature works, just move your cursor over it (you don't even have to click), and a movie demonstrates that gesture on the right side of the window. In Figure 6-10, I'm pointing to the Secondary Click feature on the left; how it works is demonstrated in the movie playing on the right. Pretty cool, don't you think?

You need to know a couple of other things about the Trackpad System Preferences pane before you move on:

>> If you see a little v to the right of a feature's description (Click with Two Fingers in Figure 6-10), a drop-down menu is available; click near the v to display the options for that feature.

>> The Tracking Speed slider lets you change the relationship between finger movement on the trackpad and cursor movement onscreen. A faster tracking-speed setting (moving the slider to the right) sends your cursor flying across the screen with a mere flick of the finger; slower tracking-speed settings (moving the slider to the left) make the cursor crawl across in seemingly slow motion, even when your finger is flying. Set this setting as fast as you can stand it — I like the fastest speed. Try it: You might like it.

The Sound System Preferences Pane

Out of the box, macOS Big Sur comes with a preset collection of beeps and controls. From the Sound System Preferences pane, however, you can change the way your Mac plays and records sound by changing settings on each of its three tabs: Sound Effects, Output, and Input.

Three items appear at the bottom of the Sound Effects pane, no matter which of the three tabs is active:

>> To make your Mac's volume louder or softer, use the Output Volume slider. You can also change or mute the volume with the designated volume and mute keys found on most Apple keyboards.

>> Select the Mute check box to turn off all sound.

>> Select the Show Volume in Menu Bar check box to add a volume control menu to your menu bar.

TIP

A shortcut to the Sound System Preferences pane is to press Option while pressing any of the volume keys (usually the F11 and F12 keys on newer laptops and keyboards and F4 and F5 keys on older ones).

Changing sound effects

On the Sound Effects tab, choose an alert (beep) sound by clicking its name; set its volume by using the Alert Volume slider control.

NEW

Finally, a long-overdue feature arrived in Big Sur. If your Mac can play a start up sound, you can enable or disable that sound with the Play Sound on Startup check box. YEA!

You can also specify the output device through which sound effects play (if you have more than one device) by choosing it from the Play Sound Effects Through pop-up menu.

The Play User Interface Sound Effects check box turns on sound effects for actions, such as dragging a file to the Trash. The Play Feedback when Volume Is Changed check box tells your Mac to beep once for each key press when you increase or decrease volume.

Choosing output and input options

If you have more than one sound-output device (in addition to the built-in speakers), you can choose it on the Outputs tab. The Balance slider makes one stereo speaker — left or right — louder than the other.

If you have more than one sound-input device (in addition to the built-in microphone on many Macs or an iSight camera, which contains its own mic), you can choose it on the Inputs tab. The Input Volume slider controls the Input Level (how loud input from that device will be), which is displayed as a row of blue dots. If the dots light up all the way to the right side, your input volume is too loud. Ideally, the input level should light up with about three-fourths of the little blue dots — and no more.

TECHNICAL STUFF

Some input sources (microphones) don't let you adjust their level in the Sound System Preferences pane.

Finally, you can choose to have Big Sur flash the screen when an alert sound occurs, or have stereo recordings play back in mono, or both by enabling these options in the Audio tab of the Accessibility System Preferences pane.

Chapter **7**

Opening and Saving Files

This might be the most important chapter in this book. If you don't under-stand how to open and save files by using the Open dialog and Save sheets or how to use the file and folder system, you'll have a heck of a time finding, opening, or saving files.

TECHNICAL STUFF

A *sheet* is nothing more than a dialog that is attached to a document window's title bar and can't be moved. Some apps use sheets, other apps use dialogs, but either way you'll see the same options.

This chapter is a tonic for finding the file or folder you want. Knowing where your files are is something every Mac user should *grok* (fully understand). Hang with me and pay attention; everything will soon become crystal clear.

Later in the chapter, I look at using Open dialogs and Save sheets within applica-tions to find files and folders. You see them only *after* you launch a program and use that program's File menu to open or save a file. (For more on launching appli-cations, read the parts of Chapter 4 about icons; for more on creating and opening documents, see the documentation or Help file for the program you're using.)

A Quick Primer on Finding Files

Before we even look at organizing your files, let's look at the problem organizing files and folders can solve. Ask any longtime Mac user; the old lament is common: "Well, I saved the file, but I don't know where I saved it." It happens all the time with new users (and occasionally with longtime users like my wife).

If they don't master these essential techniques, they often become confused about where files are located on their hard drives. Sure, the sidebar has an item called Recents that displays all files you've used recently, and Spotlight can find almost any file in milliseconds — but if you have thousands or tens of thousands of files, both can be more of a curse than a blessing.

Recents (in the sidebar of Finder windows) is a fast and easy way to find a file or folder (although the sheer number of files it displays may overwhelm you, no matter how you sort or arrange them).

TIP

Recents is especially handy when you know you either created or worked on the file recently. Just use List view sorted or grouped by Date Last Opened, and the most recently used files will be at or near the top of the Recents list.

Chapter 10 is chock-full of tools and tips for finding files and folders when you misplace them. Furthermore, although you can often find files or folders by using Spotlight, you have to remember enough details about the file or its contents for Spotlight to find it.

At the end of the day, all the aforementioned techniques are useful and good to know, but take it from me: It's often faster and easier if you know exactly where a file or folder is than to hunt for it.

Spotlight (covered in Chapter 10) is macOS's built-in search mechanism. It's available just about everywhere you look in Big Sur: the magnifying glass on the menu bar, the toolbar of Finder windows, and Open dialogs and Save sheets. The point is, if you can't find a file or folder manually as described in the rest of this chapter, try Spotlight.

Understanding the macOS Folder Structure

Start by looking at the folder structure of a typical macOS installation. Open a Finder window and click the icon for your hard drive (typically called Macintosh HD; mine's been renamed Big Sur) in the sidebar.

TIP

If you don't see your startup disk in the sidebar, choose Finder ➪ Preferences, click the Sidebar icon at the top of the window, and then enable the check box for hard disks.

You should now see at least four folders: Applications, Library, System, and Users. In the Users folder, each user with an account on this Mac (see Chapter 18 for the skinny on users and accounts) has his or her own set of folders containing documents, preferences, and other information that belongs to that user and account.

TECHNICAL
STUFF

If you're the sole person who accesses your Mac, you probably have only one user. Regardless, the folder structure that macOS uses is the same whether you have one user or dozens.

In the Users folder, you find your personal Home folder (which bears your account name), along with a Shared folder, where you can put files you want to share with other users. All these files are stored in a nested folder structure that's a bit tricky to understand at first. This structure makes more sense after you spend a little time with it and figure out some basic concepts.

TIP

The structure will start to make sense much sooner if you display the path bar at the bottom of the window, as shown in Figure 7-1. (Choose View ➪ Show Path Bar if yours isn't displayed.)

FIGURE 7-1:
A bird's-eye view
of key folders on
your Mac.

Take a look at Figure 7-1; you can see how these main folders are related to one another. In the sections that follow, you look at each of these folders in more depth and find out more about what's nested inside each one.

Understanding nested folders

Folders within other folders are often called *nested folders*. To get a feel for the way nested folders work in macOS, check out the example of nested folders on my desktop in Figure 7-2.

FIGURE 7-2:
Nested folders, going four levels deep.

You can see the following in Figure 7-2:

>> The Desktop is the top-level folder in this example; all other folders and files you see reside in the Desktop folder.

>> Folder 1 is inside the Desktop folder, which is one level deep.

>> Folder 2 is inside Folder 1, which is one level deeper than Folder 1, or two levels deep.

>> Folder 3 is inside Folder 2 and is three levels deep.

>> The two files inside Folder 3 are four levels deep.

REMEMBER

If the preceding list makes sense to you, you're golden. What's important here is that you can visualize the path to Folder 3. That is, to get to files inside Folder 3, you open Folder 1 and then open Folder 2 to be able to open Folder 3. Understanding this concept is important to understanding the relationships between files and folders. Keep reviewing this section and looking at the status bar, and eventually everything will click. You'll slap yourself in the head and say, "Now I get it!"

From the top: The Computer folder

I start with the Computer folder, which is the top level of the folder hierarchy. The Computer folder shows all the storage devices (hard drives, CD- or DVD-ROM, USB flash drive, and so forth) connected to your Mac. The following steps show how you can start at the Computer folder and drill down through the folder structure:

1. **Choose Go ⇨ Computer or press Shift+⌘+C.**

   Now you're at the Computer folder. In Figure 7-1, the Computer folder is called Bob's MacBook Air (look in the title bar), and it contains a solid-state Drive icon (Big Sur) and a Network icon, from which you can access servers or other computers on your local network.

   If that seems mysterious, read Chapter 18 for the scoop on sharing files (and more) with other users.

   You might have more or fewer icons in your Computer folder than you see in Figure 7-1, depending on how many disks you have mounted.

   You might also find an icon for your Mac in your sidebar (mine's called Bob's MacBook Air). If you don't have your Mac in the sidebar but would like to, choose Finder ⇨ Preferences, click the Sidebar tab at the top, and then select the check box for your computer.

   TIP

   You can change a Mac's name (Bob's MacBook Air in Figure 7-1) by opening the Sharing System Preferences pane (see Chapter 18) and changing the computer's name in the Computer Name field.

2. **Double-click the icon for the drive that holds your macOS stuff.**

   Technically, this drive is called your boot drive. In Figure 7-1, that drive is called Big Sur. I have no idea what yours is called, of course; if you haven't changed it, it's probably called Macintosh HD.

3. **Check out the folders you find there.**

   You should see four folders. In the next few sections, I walk you through what you can find in each one.

Peeking into the Applications folder

You can access the Applications folder, located at the root level of your boot drive (the one with macOS installed on it), by clicking the Applications icon in the sidebar, by choosing it in the Go menu, or by pressing Shift+⌘+A. In this folder, you find applications and utilities that Apple includes with macOS as well as most (if not all) third-party apps and utilities you've installed.

Most users of a Mac have access to all the items in the Applications folder, with the exception of managed accounts or accounts with Parental Controls, as discussed in Chapter 18.

Visiting the Library folders

The Library folder, at the root level of your macOS hard drive, is like a public library; it stores items available to everyone who logs into any account on this Mac.

There are actually three or more Library folders on your hard drive:

>> At the root level of your macOS disk

>> In the root-level System folder

>> One in each user's Home folder

TECHNICAL STUFF

In Big Sur, your Home/Library folder is hidden from view to protect you from yourself. Never fear: You'll discover the secret to making it visible if you need it in the "Your personal library card" section later in this chapter.

Now, here's the scoop on your various Library folders:

>> **Public Library:** You find a bunch of folders inside the Library folder at the root level (the public Library folder). Most of them contain files that you never need to open, move, or delete.

By and large, the public Library subfolder that gets the most use is the Fonts folder, which houses many of the fonts installed on the Mac.

>> **System Library:** This is the nerve center of your Mac. In other words, you should never have to touch this particular Library folder.

WARNING

Leave the /System/Library folder alone. Don't move, remove, or rename it, or do anything within it.

>> **Library in each user's Home folder:** This is where macOS stores configuration and preferences files for each user account.

The location of each of these libraries is illustrated in Figure 7-3.

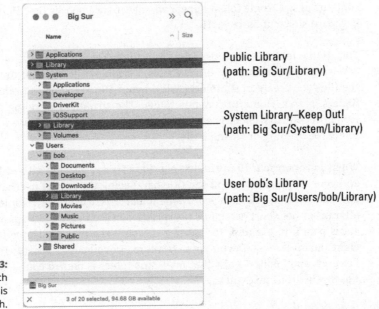

FIGURE 7-3:
A guide to which
Library folder is
which.

Public Library
(path: Big Sur/Library)

System Library–Keep Out!
(path: Big Sur/System/Library)

User bob's Library
(path: Big Sur/Users/bob/Library)

If your Mac is set up for multiple users, only users with administrator (admin) privileges can put stuff in the public (root-level) Library folder. (For more information on admin privileges, check out Chapter 18.)

Let it be: The System folder

The System folder contains the files that macOS needs to start up and keep working.

WARNING

Leave the System folder alone. Don't move, remove, or rename it or anything within it. It's part of the nerve center of your Mac.

So now you can forget everything outside your Home folder because with few exceptions, that's where all *your* stuff will reside.

There's no place like Home

Your Home folder is inside the Users folder. When the user logs on to this Mac, the contents of her Home folder appear whenever she chooses Go➪Home, or uses the keyboard shortcut Shift+⌘+H.

REMEMBER

Your Home folder is the most important folder for you as a user — or at least the one where you stash most of your files. I strongly recommend that you store all the files you create in subfolders within your Home folder — preferably, in sub-folders in your Home/Documents folder. The advantage of doing so is that your Home/Documents folder is easy to find, and many programs use it as the default folder for opening or saving a file.

When you open your Home folder, you see a Finder window with a little house icon and your short username in the title bar. Seeing your short username in the title bar tells you that you're in *your* Home folder. Every user has a Home folder named after his or her short username (as specified in the Users & Groups System Prefer-ences pane). If you refer to Figure 7-1, you'll see that my Home folder contains eight subfolders — Documents, Desktop, Downloads, Library, Movies, Music, Pictures, and Public — and that my Home folder is named *bob* — the short name I used when I first set up my Mac.

If your Mac has more than one user, you can see their Home folders in the Users folder (for example, *Woz* and *MacTheKnife* in Figure 7-1), but macOS prevents you from opening files from or saving files to other users' Home folders.

By default, your Home folder has several folders inside it created by macOS. The following four are the most important:

>> **Desktop:** If you put items (files, folders, applications, or aliases) on the desktop, they're actually stored in the Desktop folder.

>> **Documents:** This is the place to put all the documents (letters, spreadsheets, recipes, and novels) that you create.

>> **Library:** As I mention earlier in this chapter, this Library folder is invisible in macOS Big Sur; I show you how to deal with that shortly. Rest assured that even though it's hidden, it's still one of the most important folders in your Home folder, containing Preferences (files containing the settings you create in System Preferences and individual applications' preferences), fonts available only to you (as described earlier in this chapter), and other stuff that you — and only you — expect to use.

>> **Public:** If others on your local area network (LAN) use file sharing to connect with your Mac, they can't see or use the files or folders in your Home folder (unless you explicitly share them), but they can share files you store in your Home folder's Public folder. (Read more about file sharing and Public folders in Chapter 18.)

You can create more folders, if you like. In fact, every folder that you *ever* create (at least every one you create on this particular hard drive or volume) *should* be within your Home folder. I explain more about creating folders and subfolders and organizing your stuff inside them later in this chapter.

TIP

The following are a couple more tidbits to keep in mind as you dig around your Home folder:

>> If you decide that you don't want an item on the desktop anymore, delete it by dragging its icon from the Desktop folder to the Trash or by dragging its icon from the desktop itself to the Trash. Both techniques yield the same effect: The file is in the Trash, where it remains until you empty the Trash. Or if you don't want it on the desktop anymore but don't want to get rid of it either, you can drag it from the desktop into any other folder you like.

>> The other four folders that you should see in your Home folder are Downloads, Movies, Music, and Pictures. All these folders are empty until you (or programs such as Music, GarageBand, Photos, or iMovie, which create files inside these folders automatically the first time you launch them) put something in them.

Your personal library card

The invisible Library subfolder of your Home folder is the repository of everything that macOS needs to customize *your* Mac to *your* tastes. If you want to add something to a Library folder, it's usually best to add it to your Home/Library folder. You won't spend much time (if any) adding things to the Library folder or moving them around within it, and that's probably why it's now hidden from sight. Still, I think it's a good idea for you to know what's in your Home/Library.

Earlier in this chapter I mention the root-level (which I call *public*) Library folder (refer to Figure 7-3), which is used to specify preferences for all users on this Mac. *This* Library folder, however, is all about you and your stuff.

WARNING

Be cautious with all Library folders. macOS is persnickety about how the folders and files within it are organized. As I discuss earlier in the chapter, you can safely add items to and remove items from most public or Home/Library folders, but *leave the folders themselves alone.* If you remove or rename the wrong folder, you could render macOS inoperable. It's like the old joke about the guy who said to the doctor, "It hurts when I do that," and the doctor replies, "Then don't do that."

To find your hidden Home/Library folder, do this:

1. **Hold down the Option key on your keyboard and click the Go menu.**

The (formerly) invisible Library folder appears in the Go menu as long as the Option key is pressed.

2. **Select Library and release the mouse button.**

You should see several folders in the Home/Library folder; the exact number depends on the software that you install on your Mac. You probably have folders called Mail, Safari, Logs, and Preferences, for example.

TIP

If you don't want to do this dance every time you open your Home/Library folder, select your Home folder in Finder and choose View ⇨ Show View Options (or press ⌘+J). Enable the Show Library Folder check box and your Home Library will be visible evermore (or at least until you deselect the check box).

Some of the most important standard folders in the Library folder include the following:

>> **Application Support:** Some applications store their support files here; others store theirs in the main (root-level) public Library folder.

>> **Fonts:** This folder is empty until you install your own fonts here. The easiest way to install a font is to double-click its icon and let the Font Book utility handle it for you, as described in Chapter 21. But I'd be remiss if I didn't also mention how to install a font manually:

- *To install a font that only you can use:* Drag the font file's icon to the Fonts folder in your Home/Library. The font is available only to this user account (because other users can't use fonts stored in *your* Home/Library folder).

- *To install a font for all users of this Mac:* Drag the font file's icon into the Fonts folder in the public Library folder — the one at root level that you see when you open your hard drive's icon.

TIP

It might not be a great idea to add too many fonts for all users because the Fonts menu will become long and unwieldy. Plus, too many fonts may cause degraded performance on older Macs.

WARNING

» **Preferences:** The files here hold the information about whichever things you customize in macOS or in the applications you run. Whenever you change a system or application preference, that info is saved to a file in the Preferences folder.

Don't mess with the Preferences folder! You should never need to open or use this folder unless something bad happens — say, you suspect that a particular preferences file has become *corrupted* (that is, damaged). My advice is to just forget that you know about this folder and let it do its job. If you don't know why you're doing something to a folder (other than the Fonts folder) in your Home/Library, *don't do it.* There must be some good reasons why Apple decided to hide the Home/Library folder in macOS Big Sur, and I'm sure that one of them is to keep you (or me) from accidentally screwing something up.

Saving Your Document Before It's Too Late

Now that you have a feel for the macOS folder structure, it's time to get down to the important stuff — namely, how to save documents and where to save them. You can create as many documents as you want, using one program or dozens of 'em, but all could be lost if you don't save the files (or versions of the files) to a storage device such as your startup drive, external hard drive, solid-state drive (SSD), or USB thumb drive (a.k.a. USB flash drive).

Another option is to save documents in iCloud, so they're available on all your Apple devices all the time without syncing or doing much of anything beyond saving the file.

When you *save* a file, you're committing a copy to a drive, whether it's a drive connected directly to your Mac, one available over a local area network, a removable disc such as a USB thumb drive or external hard or solid-state drive, or even a drive on a cloud-based server somewhere else, such as iCloud.

Speaking of iCloud, you'll be hearing a lot more about it — and especially the iCloud Drive feature — in Chapter 8 (once you get the hang of saving and opening files from drives or discs).

macOS's Resume feature automatically reopens all windows that were onscreen when you quit the app. So, when you launch the app again, all the windows are reopened in the same position onscreen as when you quit. Best of all, Resume seems to work with *most* (but not all) third-party apps.

Individual programs have offered Auto Save before, but it's been baked into macOS for years. Auto Save automatically saves versions (which you learn more about shortly) of your work as you work, when you pause, and every 5 minutes, whether you need it or not.

Versions are awesome. Every time you Save or Auto Save, a new version of the document is created. For as long as we've had Macs, we've saved unique versions of our files, creating and managing them with the Save As command or by duplicating and renaming them in Finder. Now macOS takes over version control for you by automatically saving versions, as described in the preceding paragraph.

The big advantage is that rather than ending up with a separate file on your hard drive each time you Save As or duplicate and rename a file, Versions saves them all in the same document icon. To access a previous version, select Choose File ⇨ Revert To ⇨ Browse All Versions or choose Enter Time Machine from the Time Machine icon on the menu bar while the document is active onscreen. (See Chapter 24 for more on Time Machine.)

WARNING

That's the good news, but there's also bad news. Although Auto Save and Versions are built right into macOS, not all third-party apps choose to take advantage of these features. So please don't get too comfortable with Auto Save and Versions until you're sure that your applications offer them. Even a decade after the debut of these features in macOS, many third-party apps continue to rely on the old-school Save and Save As commands for versioning. Furthermore, if these features aren't in a third-party app by now (I'm looking at you, Adobe — even Microsoft has Versions now, though they work only if the file is stored on your Microsoft OneDrive), I wouldn't hold my breath waiting for their appearance.

The bottom line is that if the app you're using doesn't have Auto Save and Versions, macOS takes no responsibility for saving files and saving versions of files; it's all up to you. Most (or all) Apple apps that save files — Pages, Keynote, Numbers, and Logic Pro, to name a few — use Auto Save and Versions. I prefer to use apps that support Auto Save and Versions whenever possible.

REMEMBER

In the following sections, I show you how to save your masterpieces. Prevent unnecessary pain in your life by developing good saving habits. I recommend that you save your work (or save a version in apps that support versions)

>> Every few minutes

>> Before you switch to another program

>> Before you print a document

>> Before you stand up

TIP

The keyboard shortcut for Save in almost every Mac program is ⌘+S, and it works with Auto Save and Versions as well as with Save and Save As. Memorize it. See it in your dreams. Train your finger muscles to do it unconsciously. Use it (the keyboard shortcut) or lose it (your unsaved work).

WARNING

If you don't heed this advice — and then the program you're using crashes while switching programs, printing, or sitting idle (the three likeliest times for a crash) — you may lose everything you did since your last save or saved version. The fact that a program crash doesn't bring down the entire system or force a restart is small consolation when you've lost everything you've typed, drawn, copied, pasted, or whatever since the last time you saved.

Stepping through a basic save

This section walks you through the steps you use the first time you save a document. The process is the same whether your app supports Auto Save and Versions or not. It's only after the initial save that Auto Save and Versions come into play.

REMEMBER

In a few sections of this book, I ask you not only to read the instructions while sitting in front of your Mac but also to perform each step of the instructions as described. This section is one of them. If you read it and follow along, I can pretty much guarantee that it'll make sense. If you read it somewhere other than at your Mac, it could be a mite confusing.

Saving a file works pretty much the same way in any application you use to create documents. For this example, I use the macOS word-processing application, TextEdit, but the process will be similar in Microsoft Word, Adobe Photoshop, Apple Keynote, or any other application.

TIP

If you're going to follow along as I recommend, please launch the TextEdit program now (it's in your Applications folder), click the New Document button or choose File⇨New, and type a few words on the Untitled page that appears after you launch it.

DOES IT HAVE AUTO SAVE AND VERSIONS OR NOT?

It can be hard to discern at a glance whether an app uses the Auto Save and Versions features.

The first way to discern if an app supports Auto Save and Versions is whether the app has a Save As or Duplicate command in its File menu. Programs with a Save As command are old-school and don't support the modern Auto Save and Versions features. Programs with a Duplicate command have usually been updated with support for Auto Save and Versions. (Interestingly, the shortcut for Duplicate and Save As is almost always the same: ⌘+Shift+S.)

The next way is to discern whether the app has Rename and Move To commands in its File menu. If it doesn't, it's old-school; if it does, it's Auto Save- and Versions-savvy.

The easiest way to tell, however, is to look at the title bar of a document. If it displays a little v to the right of the document's name when you hover your cursor over it (as shown on top of the figure here) and a pop-up window appears if you click the triangle, the app supports Auto Save and Versions. (You read more about the options in the pop-up window later in this chapter.)

Click the little v

Everything I've said so far in this chapter applies to every app that saves files, with or without Auto Save and Versions. But I'd be remiss if I didn't reiterate that saving a file with Auto Save and Versions has one additional effect: It creates a new version of the file that you can access with Time Machine. To obtain that kind of functionality in apps without Auto Save and Versions, you'll need to use Save As to create a new version of the file periodically if you want to be able to roll back to an earlier version.

One last thing: Using Save As to create new versions uses more disk space (possibly much more) than using Auto Save and Versions and adds files on your drive — one file for each Save As versus one file for unlimited Versions. For example, after using Save As 11 times, you'll end up with 12 files on your drive; with Auto Save and Versions you'd still have 11 versions, but they're all contained in a single file.

Now that we're both on the same page (literally and figuratively), here's how saving a file works. When you choose to save a file for the first time (choose File ⇨ Save or press ⌘+S), a Save sheet appears in front of the document that you're saving, as shown in Figure 7-4. I call this a *basic* Save sheet (as opposed to an *expanded* Save sheet, which I get to in a moment):

1. **In the Save As field, type a name for your file.**

When a Save sheet appears for the first time, the Save As field is active and displays the name of the document. The document name (usually Untitled) is selected; when you begin typing, the name disappears and is replaced by the name you type.

Disclosure button

Where menu

FIGURE 7-4:
A basic Save sheet looks a lot like this.

2. **If the Where pop-up menu lists the location where you want to save your file, choose that location and proceed to Step 5. If not, click the disclosure icon (labeled in Figure 7-4).**

You can choose from a short list of folders and volumes listed in the basic Save sheet's Where pop-up menu (which are the same devices and favorites you see in the sidebar of Finder windows). Or, if you click the disclosure icon on the right of the Save As field, the sheet expands so that you can navigate folders just as you do in Finder: by opening them to see their contents.

WARNING

If you click the Save button in Figure 7-4, your file will be saved to iCloud Drive, Apple's free online storage service (see Chapter 8). Or you can choose another location from the Where menu before you click Save, and save the file elsewhere.

If you switch to expanded view (shown in Figure 7-5) by clicking the disclosure icon, a standard Save sheet appears so you can save your file in any folder you like.

Note that the Where menu in the expanded Save sheet in Figure 7-5 doesn't have a Favorites section, but instead displays the path to the folder in which the file will be saved (Documents). I think that the Where menu should be the same in both basic and expanded Save sheets, as it was before macOS 10.5 Leopard. It seems more confusing to have the contents of this menu change based on whether the Save sheet is expanded or not. I've called it to your attention so it won't confuse you.

For what it's worth, Favorites are still available in an expanded Save sheet, but instead of being in the Where menu, they're in the sidebar.

TIP

Switch between the basic and expanded Save sheets a few times by clicking the disclosure icon. Make sure that you see and understand the difference between what you see in the Where menu in a basic Save sheet and what you see in the Where menu in an expanded Save sheet. All the steps that follow assume you're using the expanded Save sheet.

3. **To make it easier to find the folder you want to save your file into, choose among views by clicking the View icon and making your choices from its drop-down menu.**

The View icon's drop-down menu, shown in Figure 7-5, allows you to choose the view that works best for you.

In Icons view, you double-click a folder to open it. List view offers disclosure triangles for folders and drives, so single-click the disclosure triangles of folders to see their contents. In Columns view, you click an item on the left to see its contents on the right, just as you do in a column-view Finder window.

You can also use the Forward and Back icons or the sidebar, both available only in an expanded Save dialog, to conveniently navigate your drive. Many of these navigation aids work just like the ones in Finder; see Chapter 4 for more details. You can enlarge the Save sheet to see more the same way you enlarge a Finder window: Drag an edge or corner of the sheet.

TIP

If you can't find the folder in which you want to save your document, type the folder name in the Search box. It works just like the Search box in a Finder window, as described in Chapters 4 and 8. You don't even have to press Return; the Save sheet updates itself to show you only items that match the characters as you typed them.

View button and drop-down menu   Where menu

FIGURE 7-5:
An expanded
Save sheet looks
similar to this one
(shown in List
view).

4. **Select the folder where you want to save your file in the Where pop-up menu or the sidebar.**

5. **If you want to create a new subfolder of the selected folder to save your file in, click the New Folder button or icon (labeled in Figure 7-6), give the new folder a name, and then save your file in it.**

   In Figure 7-6, I selected an existing folder named Novels. You can tell that it's selected because its name is displayed in the Where menu and highlighted below that in the first column.

   The selected folder is where your file will be saved.

   REMEMBER

   The keyboard shortcut for New Folder is Shift+⌘+N, regardless of whether you're in a Save sheet or Finder. If I want to create a folder inside the Novels folder in Figure 7-6, I could click the New Folder button or press the shortcut.

6. **In the File Format pop-up menu (which says Rich Text Document in Figure 7-6), make sure the format selected is the one you want.**

   Double-check the Where pop-up menu one last time to make sure that the correct folder is selected.

7. **Click the Save button to save the file to the active folder.**

   If you click Save, the file appears in the folder you selected. If you change your mind about saving this file, clicking Cancel dismisses the Save sheet without saving anything anywhere. In other words, the Cancel button returns things to the way they were before you displayed the Save sheet.

New Folder buttons

FIGURE 7-6:
Saving a file in the
Novels folder
(which is in the
Documents
folder).

After you save a file for the first time, choosing File ➪ Save or pressing ⌘+S won't bring up a Save sheet. Instead, what happens next depends on whether the app supports macOS's Auto Save and Versions. If the app *doesn't* support Auto Save and Versions, Save and its shortcut (⌘+S) merely resave your document in the same location and with the same name. If you want to save a unique version with a different name, you have to choose the Save As command and save the file under a new name.

If the app *does* support Auto Save and Versions, however, the upcoming section, "Save As versus Duplicate: Different names for the same result," explains how things work.

When you use apps that don't support Auto Save and Versions, I beg you to get into the habit of pressing ⌘+S often. It can't hurt — and just might save your bacon someday.

One last thing: In Figures 7-4, 7-5, and 7-6, I used the Save sheet for TextEdit as an example. In programs other than TextEdit, the Save sheet might contain additional options, fewer options, or different options, and therefore might look slightly different. The File Format menu, for example, is a feature specific to TextEdit; it might not appear in other applications' Save sheets. Don't worry. The Save sheet always *works* the same way, no matter what options it offers.

Save As versus Duplicate: Different names for the same result

The two commands File ⇨ Duplicate and File ⇨ Save As serve the same purpose and achieve the same result. The difference is that you'll find File ⇨ Duplicate in apps that support Versions and Auto Save, and File ⇨ Save As in apps that don't. They're different names for achieving the same result: saving a file that's already been saved with a different name.

Before I get into the details, you may be wondering *why* you would want to save an existing file with a different name. So here's a good (albeit kind of rude) example: Suppose that you have two cousins, Kate and Nancy. You write Kate a long, chatty letter and save this document with the name Letter to Kate. Later, you decide that you want to send almost the same letter to Nancy, but you want to change a few things. So you change the part about your date last night and replace all references to Kate's husband, Kevin, with references to Nancy's husband, Norman. (Aren't computers grand?)

So you make all these changes in Letter to Kate, but you haven't resaved this document yet — and although the document on your screen is actually a letter to Nancy, its filename is still Letter to Kate. Think of what would happen if you were to save it now without using the Save As feature: Letter to Kate reflects the changes that you just made. (The stuff in the letter meant for Kate is blown away, replaced by the stuff that you just wrote to Nancy.) Thus the filename Letter to Kate is inaccurate. Even worse, you no longer have a copy of the original letter you sent to Kate! The solution? Just use Save As or Duplicate to rename this file Letter to Nancy by choosing File ⇨ Save As or File ⇨ Duplicate.

If you opt for Save As: A Save sheet appears, in which you can type a different filename in the Save As field. You can also navigate to another folder, if you like, and save the newly named version of the file there. Now you have two distinct files: Letter to Kate and Letter to Nancy. Both contain the stuff they should, but both started life from the same file.

If you choose Duplicate: The title bar of the document becomes editable so you can change its name without even seeing a Save sheet. (Refer to the figure in the earlier sidebar, "Does it have Auto Save and Versions or not?") By default it has the same name as the original with the word *copy* appended. Change its name or don't, and then press Return, and the duplicated file will be saved in the same folder as the original. Or, if you want to save the newly renamed file in a different location, choose File ⇨ Move To or click the little v to the right of the document's name, and select a different location in the Where menu.

Now that you understand what Save As or Duplicate are all about, here's an easier way to get the same result: Before you start, duplicate the document in Finder (choose File⇨Duplicate or press ⌘+D). Rename the copy and open it. This way, when you have finished making changes, you don't have to remember to choose Save As; you can just perform your habitual Save. This approach also protects you from accidentally saving part of the letter to Nancy without changing the file's name first (which you're likely to do if you're following my advice about saving often). So when you decide that you're going to reuse a document, choose Save As (or duplicate and rename the file) *before* you begin working on it, just to be safe.

TIP

For those who, like yours truly, prefer to use Save As, just press the Option key before you click the File menu and Duplicate magically transmogrifies into Save As. Sweet!

Versions gives you the benefits of Save As without any action on your part, but many programs still lack support for Auto Save and Versions nearly a decade after their introduction. And, in fact, some Apple apps, as well as most third-party apps, still use the Save As technique, and I expect that to be the status quo for quite some time. But because most of Apple's offerings (TextEdit, Pages, Numbers, Keynote, and more) use Auto Save and Versions, I'd be remiss if I glossed over Apple's current way of doing things.

REMEMBER

One last thing: If the app you're using supports Versions, it creates a snapshot called a *version* automatically as you work, when you pause, every 5 minutes, and every time you choose File⇨Save (⌘+S). Choose File⇨Revert To⇨Browse All Versions or click the Time Machine icon in the dock while the document is active onscreen. (See Chapter 24 for more on Time Machine.) Either way, Time Machine displays versions of the document side-by-side, as shown in Figure 7-7.

FIGURE 7-7:
Browse All Versions lets you compare all versions and revert to an earlier version.

Open, Sez Me

You can open any icon in Finder — whether it's a file or a folder — in at least six ways. (Okay, there are at least *seven* ways, but one of them belongs to aliases, which I discuss in great detail back in Chapter 4.) Anyway, here are the ways:

» Click the icon once to select it and choose File ➪ Open.

» Double-click the icon.

  If the icon doesn't open, you double-clicked too slowly. You can test (and adjust) your mouse's sensitivity to double-click speed in the Mouse (or Trackpad) System Preferences pane, which you can access by launching the System Preferences application (from the Applications folder, the dock, or the menu) and then clicking the Mouse (or Trackpad) icon.

» Select the icon and then press either ⌘+O or ⌘+↓.

» Right-click or Control-click it and then choose Open from the contextual menu.

» If the icon is a document, drag it onto the application icon (or the dock icon of an application) that can open that type of document.

» If the icon is a document, right-click or Control-click it and choose an application from the Open With submenu of the contextual menu.

You can also open any document icon from within an application, of course. Here's how that works:

» **Just launch your favorite program, and choose File ➪ Open (or press the shortcut ⌘+O, which works in most Mac programs).**

  An Open dialog appears, like the one shown in Figure 7-8.

  When you use a program's Open dialog, only files that the program knows how to open appear enabled (in black rather than light gray) in the file list. In effect, the program filters out the files it can't open, so you barely see them in the Open dialog. This method of selectively displaying certain items in Open dialogs is a feature of most applications. Therefore, when you're using TextEdit, its Open dialog dims all files it can't open, like the Carbon Copy Cloner application in the Novels folder in Figure 7-8. Pretty neat, eh?

  For what it's worth, TextEdit can open text, Rich Text Format, Microsoft Word, Microsoft Excel, and some picture files.

TIP

» **In the dialog, simply navigate to the file you want to open (using the same techniques you use in a Save sheet).**

Click a favorite folder in the sidebar or use Spotlight (see Chapter 10) if you can't remember where the file resides.

» **Select your file and click the Open button.**

FIGURE 7-8:
The Open dialog using Column view.

For what it's worth, some applications allow you to select multiple files in their Open dialogs by holding down either Shift (for contiguous selections) or ⌘ (for noncontiguous selections). If you need to open several files, it's worth a try; the worst thing that could happen is that it won't work and you'll have to open the items one at a time.

Some programs, including Microsoft Word and Adobe Photoshop, have a Show or Format menu in their Open dialogs. This menu lets you specify the type(s) of files you want to see as available in the Open dialog. You can often open a file that appears dimmed by choosing All Documents from the Show or Format menu (in those applications with Open dialogs that offer such a menu).

With drag-and-drop

Mac drag-and-drop is usually all about dragging text and graphics from one place to another. But there's another angle to drag-and-drop — one that has to do with files and icons.

You can open a document by dragging its icon onto the icon of the proper application. You can open a document created with Microsoft Word, for example, by dragging the document icon onto the Microsoft Word application icon in the Applications folder, an alias of the Word icon, or Word's dock icon. The Word icon highlights, and the document launches. Usually, of course, it's easier to double-click a document's icon to open it; the proper application opens automatically when you do — or at least, it does most of the time. Which reminds me . . . .

With a Quick Look

The Quick Look window, shown in Figure 7-9, can display the contents of many types of files.

FIGURE 7-9:
The Quick Look window showing the contents of an image file.

To use the Quick Look command to peek at the contents of most files in Open dialogs, right-click or Control-click the file and choose Quick Look, or use its easy-to-remember shortcut: Press the spacebar or ⌘+Y. Whichever way, you'll soon see the contents of that file in a floating window without launching another application.

TIP

Chapter 10 contains more information about Quick Look.

When your Mac can't open a file

If you try to open a file, but macOS can't find a program to open that file, macOS prompts you with an alert window. I tried to open a very old (1993) file created on a long-defunct Psion Series 3 handheld PDA (a file so old that most of you have probably never seen the .wrd file extension), shown in Figure 7-10.

Click Cancel to abort the attempt to open the file, or click the Choose Application or Search App Store button to select another application to open this file.

If you click the Choose Application button, a dialog appears (conveniently opened to your Applications folder). Applications that macOS doesn't think can be used to open the file are dimmed. For a wider choice of applications, choose All Applications (instead of Recommended Applications) from the Enable pop-up menu.

FIGURE 7-10:
Oops! macOS
helps you find the
correct
application.

REMEMBER

You can't open every file with every program. If you try to open an MP3 (audio) file with Microsoft Excel (a spreadsheet), for example, it just won't work; you get an error message or a screen full of gibberish. Sometimes, you just have to keep trying until you find the right program; at other times, you don't have a program that can open the file.

TIP

When in doubt, use a search engine to read about the file extension. You'll usually find out more than you need to know about what application(s) create files with that extension.

With the application of your choice

I don't know about you, but people send me files all the time that were created by applications I don't use . . . or at least that I don't use for that document type. macOS lets you specify the application in which you want to open a document in the future when you double-click it. More than that, you can specify that you want all documents of that type to open with the specified application. "Where is this magic bullet hidden?" you ask. Right there in the file's Info window.

Assigning a file type to an application

Suppose that you want all .jpg files that usually open in Preview to open instead in Affinity Photo, a more capable third-party image-editing program. Here's what to do:

1. **Click one of the files in Finder.**

2. **Choose File ⇨ Get Info (⌘+I).**

   Or right-click, Control-click, or tap with two fingers on the file and then select Get Info from the contextual shortcut menu.

3. **In the Info window, click the gray triangle to disclose the Open With pane.**

4. **From the pop-up menu, choose an application that macOS believes will open this document type.**

   In Figure 7-11, I'm choosing Affinity Photo. Now Affinity Photo opens when I open this file (instead of the default application, Preview).

5. **(Optional) If you click the Change All button at the bottom of the Open With pane, as shown in Figure 7-11, you make Affinity Photo the new default application for all .jpg files that would otherwise be opened in Preview.**

   Notice the handy alert that appears when you click the Change All button and how nicely it explains what will happen if you click Continue.

FIGURE 7-11:
Changing the application that opens this document and all others like it (that is, .jpg files).

Opening a file with an application other than the default

TIP

Here's one more technique that works great when you want to open a document with a program other than its default. Just drag the file onto the application's icon or alias icon or dock icon, and presto — the file opens in the application.

If I were to double-click an MP3 file, for example, the file usually would open in Music (and, by default, would be copied into my Music library). But I frequently want to audition (listen to) MP3 files with QuickTime Player, so they're not automatically added to my Music library. Dragging the MP3 file onto QuickTime

Player's icon in the Applications folder or its dock icon (if it's on the dock) solves this conundrum quickly and easily.

WARNING

If the icon doesn't highlight and you release the mouse button anyway, the file ends up in the same folder as the application with the icon that didn't highlight. If that happens, just choose Edit⇨Undo (or press ⌘+Z), and the mislaid file magically returns to where it was before you dropped it. Just remember — don't do anything else after you drop the file, or Undo might not work. If Undo doesn't work, you must move the file back to its original location manually.

TIP

Only applications that *might* be able to open the file should highlight when you drag the file on them. That doesn't mean the document will be usable — just that the application can *open* it. Suffice it to say that macOS is usually smart enough to figure out which applications on your hard drive can open what documents — and to offer you a choice.

One last thing: If all you want to do is open a file with an application other than its default (and not change anything for the future), the techniques I just described work fine, but an even easier way is to right-click the file and choose another app from the contextual menu, as shown in Figure 7-12.

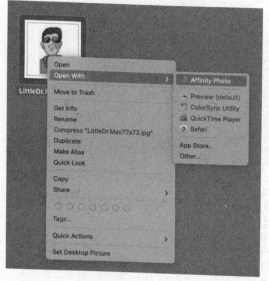

FIGURE 7-12:
To open a file with an app other than its default, right-click and choose the app you desire.

TIP

You can also change the default application to open *this* file by pressing Option after you right-click the file, which causes the Open With command to magically transform into Always Open With. Alas, you can't change the default application for *all* files of this type (.jpg in Figures 7-11 and 7-12); for that, you'll have to visit the Info window.

Chapter **8**

File and Folder Management Made Easy

Y ou'll eventually accumulate a lot of files on your disk(s): tens, hundreds, thousands, even millions of files. I have well over a million files on my startup disk, with more than 50,000 of them in my Home folder alone.

In Chapter 7, you can read about Finder and opening and saving files. In this chapter, it's time to take a look at how to organize all those files so you can find them when you need them.

Organizing Your Stuff in Folders

I won't pretend to be able to organize your Mac for you. Organizing your files is as personal as your taste in music; you develop your own style with the Mac. But after you know how to open and save documents when you're using applications, these sections provide food for thought — some ideas about how I organize things — and some suggestions that can make organization easier for you, regardless of how you choose to do it.

The upcoming sections look at the difference between a file and a folder; show you how to set up nested folders; and cover how some special folder features work. After you have a good handle on these things, you'll almost certainly be a savvier — and better organized — macOS user.

Files versus folders

When I speak of a *file*, I'm talking about what's connected to any icon except a folder or disk icon. A file can be a document, an application, an alias of a file or an application, a dictionary, a font, or any other icon that *isn't* a folder or disk. The main distinction is that you can't put something *in* most file icons.

TECHNICAL STUFF

The exceptions are icons that represent macOS packages. A *package* is an icon that acts like a file but isn't. Examples of icons that are really packages include many software installers and applications, as well as documents saved by some programs (such as Keynote, GarageBand, Pages, or TextEdit files saved in its .rtfd format). When you open an icon that represents a package in the usual way (double-click, choose File⇨Open, press ⌘+O, and so on), the program or document opens. If you want to see the contents of an icon that represents a package, right-click or Control-click the icon and choose Show Package Contents from the contextual menu. If you see an item by that name, you know that the icon is a package; if you don't see Show Package Contents on the contextual menu, the icon represents a file, not a package.

When I talk about *folders,* I'm talking about things that work like manila folders in the real world. Their icons look like folders, like the one in the margin to the left; they can contain files or other folders, called *subfolders.* You can put any icon — any file or folder — inside a folder.

WARNING

Here's an exception: If you try to put a disk icon in a folder, all you get is an alias to the disk *unless* you hold down the Option key. Remember that you can't put a disk icon in a folder that exists on the disk itself. In other words, you can copy a disk icon only to a *different disk*; you can never copy a disk icon to a folder that resides on that disk. For more about aliases, flip to Chapter 4.

TIP

File icons can look like practically anything. If the icon doesn't look like a folder, package, or one of the numerous disk icons, you can be pretty sure that it's a file.

Organizing your stuff with subfolders

As I mention earlier in this chapter, you can put folders inside other folders to organize your icons. A folder nested inside another folder is a *subfolder.*

You can create subfolders according to whatever system makes sense to you — but why reinvent the wheel? Here are some organizational topic ideas and naming examples for subfolders:

>> **By type of document:** Word-Processing Documents, Spreadsheet Documents, Graphics Documents

>> **By date:** Documents May–June, Documents Spring 2017

>> **By content:** Memos, Outgoing Letters, Expense Reports

>> **By project:** Project X, Project Y, Project Z

When you notice your folders swelling and starting to get messy (that is, filling with tons of files), subdivide them again by using a combination of these methods that makes sense to you. Suppose that you start by subdividing your Documents folder into multiple subfolders. Later, when those folders begin to get full, you can subdivide them even further, as shown in Figure 8-1.

FIGURE 8-1: Before (left) and after (right) organizing the Books and Novels folders with subfolders.

My point (yes, I do have one!): Allow your folder structure to be organic, growing as you need it to grow. Let it happen. Don't let any single folder get so full that it's a hassle to deal with. Create new subfolders when things start to get crowded. (I explain how to create folders in the next section.)

TIP

If you want to monkey around with some subfolders, a good place to start is the Documents folder, which is inside your Home folder (that is, the Documents folder is a *subfolder* of your Home folder).

If you use a particular folder a great deal, drag it to the right side of your dock, or make an alias of it and move the alias from the Documents folder to your Home folder or to your desktop (for more info on aliases, see Chapter 4) to make the folder easier to access. Or drag the folder (or its alias) to the sidebar, so it's always available, including in Open dialogs and Save sheets.

If you write a lot of letters, keep an alias to your Correspondence folder in your Home folder, on the dock, on your desktop, or in the sidebar for quick access. (By the way, there's no reason why you can't have a folder appear in all four places, if you like. That's what aliases are for, right?)

TIP

If you create your own subfolders in the Documents folder, you can click that folder on the dock to reveal them, as shown in Figure 8-2. I show you how to customize the dock in Chapter 3.

FIGURE 8-2: It's super-convenient to have your Documents folder on the dock.

TIP

It's even more convenient if you choose to view the Documents folder as a list, as described in Chapter 3 and shown in Figure 8-2.

Creating new folders

So, you think that Apple has already given you enough folders? Can't imagine why you'd need more? Think of creating new folders the same way you'd think of labeling a new folder at work for a specific project. New folders help you keep your files organized, enabling you to reorganize them just the way you want. Creating folders is quite simple.

To create a new folder, just follow these steps:

1. Decide which window you want the new folder to appear in — and then make sure that window is active.

If you want to create a new folder right on the desktop, make sure that *no* window is active or that you're working in your Home/Desktop folder window. You can make a window active by clicking it, and you can make the desktop active if you have windows onscreen by clicking the desktop itself.

2. Choose File ⇨ New Folder (or press Shift+⌘+N).

A new, untitled folder appears in the active window with its name box already highlighted, ready for you to type a new name for it.

3. Type a name for your folder.

If you accidentally click anywhere before you type a name for the folder, the name box is no longer highlighted. To highlight it again, select the icon (single-click it) and press Return once. Now you can type its new name.

Give your folders relevant names. Folders with nebulous titles like Stuff, Untitled, or sfdghb will make it that much harder to find a file or folder six months from now.

For folders and files that you might share with users of non-Mac computers, here's the rule for maximum compatibility: Use no punctuation and no Option-key characters in the folder name. Periods, slashes, backslashes, and colons in particular can be reserved for use by other operating systems. When I say Option-key characters, I'm talking about special-purpose ones, such as ™ (Option+2), ® (Option+R), ¢ (Option+4), and even © (Option+G).

Navigating with spring-loaded folders

A *spring-loaded folder* pops open when you drag something onto it without releasing the mouse button. Spring-loaded folders work with all folder or disk icons in all views and in the sidebar. Because you just got the short course on folders, subfolders, and various ways to organize your stuff, you're ready for your introduction to one of my favorite ways to get around my disks, folders, and subfolders.

Here's how spring-loaded folders work:

1. **Select any icon except a disk icon.**

The folder highlights to indicate that it's selected.

2. **Drag the selected icon onto any folder or disk icon — but don't release the mouse button.**

I call this *hovering* because you're doing just that: hovering the cursor over a folder or disk icon without releasing the button.

In a second or two, the highlighted folder or disk flashes twice and then springs open, right under the cursor.

Press the spacebar if you want the folder to spring open immediately.

TIP

3. **After the folder springs open, perform any of these handy operations:**

- Continue to traverse your folder structure this way. Subfolders continue to pop open until you release the mouse button.

- If you release the mouse button, the icon you've been dragging is dropped into the active folder at the time. That window remains open — but all the windows you traversed clean up after themselves by closing automatically, leaving your window clean and uncluttered.

- If you want to cancel a spring-loaded folder, drag the cursor away from the folder icon or outside the boundaries of the sprung window. The folder pops shut.

After you get used to spring-loaded folders, you'll wonder how you ever got along without them. They work in all four views, and they work with icons in the sidebar or dock. Give 'em a try, and you'll be hooked. And don't forget to slap the spacebar to spring folders open instantly.

Smart folders

As the late Steve Jobs was fond of saying near the end of his keynotes, "There is one more thing," and when it comes to folders, that one last thing is the smart folder.

A *smart folder* lets you save search criteria and have them work in the background to display the results in real time. In other words, a smart folder is updated continuously, so it displays all the files on your computer that match the search criteria at the moment.

So, for example, I created a smart folder that gathers all files with Dr. Mac in their name that were created after 1/1/2020, as shown in Figure 8-3. Or you can create a smart folder that displays graphics files, but only the ones bigger (or smaller) than a specified file size. Then all those files appear in one convenient smart folder.

FIGURE 8-3: A smart folder that displays files created after 1/1/2020 with names that contain the phrase *Dr. Mac*.

The possibilities are endless. Because smart folders use alias-like technology to display items, the actual files reside in only one location: the folder where you originally put them. True to their name, smart folders don't gather the files themselves in a separate place; rather, they gather *aliases* of files, leaving the originals right where you stashed them. Neat!

Also, because Spotlight (discussed in Chapter 10) is built deep into the bowels of the macOS file system and kernel, smart folders are updated in real time and so are always current, even after you add or delete files on your hard drive since creating the smart folder.

Smart folders are so useful that Apple provides four ways to create one. The following steps show you how:

1. Start your smart folder by using any of the following methods:

   - Choose File ➪ New Smart Folder.

   - Choose File ➪ Find.

- Press ⌘+F.

- Type at least one character in the Search box of a Finder window.

WARNING

If you have Recents selected in the sidebar, you can't use the last method, because Recents is a smart folder itself — one with a weird icon, but a smart folder nonetheless.

2. **Refine the criteria for your search by clicking the + button to add a criterion or the – button to delete one.**

3. **When you're satisfied and ready to gather your criteria into a smart folder, click the Save button below the Search box.**

   A sheet drops down.

4. **Choose where you want to save your folder.**

   Although the Save sheet is displayed, you can add the smart folder to the sidebar by selecting the Add to Sidebar check box.

TIP

5. **When you're finished editing criteria, click the Save button to save the folder with its criteria.**

After you create your smart folder, you can save it anywhere on any hard drive and use it like any other folder.

If you want to *change* the criteria for a smart folder you created, right-click or Control-click the smart folder in the sidebar and choose Show Search Criteria.

When you're finished changing the criteria, click the Save button to resave your folder. Don't worry — if you try to close a smart folder that you modify without saving your changes, macOS politely asks whether you want to save this smart folder and warns that if you don't save, the changes you made will be lost. You may be asked whether you want to replace the previous smart folder of the same name; usually, you do.

Smart folders (with the exception of the sidebar's Recents, which has its own weird little icon) display a little gear icon, making them easy to tell apart from regular folders, such as the Dr. Mac 2020 smart folder icon shown in the sidebar in Figure 8-3.

Smart folders can save you a lot of time and effort, so if you haven't played with them much (or at all) yet, be sure to give 'em a try.

Shuffling Files and Folders

Sometimes, keeping files and folders organized means moving them from one place to another. At other times, you want to copy them, rename them, or compress them to send to a friend. These sections explain all those things and more.

TIP

All the techniques that I discuss in the following sections work at least as well for windows that use List, Column, or Gallery view as they do for windows that use Icon view. I use Icon view in the figures in this section only because it's the best view for pictures to show you what's going on. For what it's worth, I find moving and copying files much easier in windows that use List or Column view.

Moving files and folders

You can move files and folders around within a window to your heart's content — *as long as that window is set to Icon view.* Just click and drag any icon to its new location in the window.

TIP

If the icons won't move, make sure View⇨Arrange By is set to None.

Some people spend hours arranging icons in a window until they're just so. But because using Icon view wastes so much screen space, I avoid using icons in a window.

TIP

You can't move icons around in a window that is displayed in List, Column, or Gallery view, which makes total sense when you think about it. (Well, you can move them to put them in a different folder in List, Column, or Gallery view, but that's not moving them around, really.) And you can't move icons around in a window under the spell of the Arrange By command.

As you probably expect from Apple by now, you have choices for how you move one file or folder into another folder. You can use these techniques to move any icon (folder, document, alias, or program icon) into folders or onto other disks:

>> **Drag an icon onto a folder icon.** Drag the icon for one folder (or file) onto the icon for another folder (or disk) and then release when the second icon is highlighted, as shown in Figure 8-4, top. The first folder will then be inside the second folder. Put another way, the first folder is now a subfolder of the second folder. This technique works regardless of whether the second folder's window is open.

REMEMBER

If you *don't* release when the second folder is highlighted, the folder will spring open, allowing you to see its contents *before* committing to moving the icon into it (by releasing the button).

» **Drag an icon into an open folder's window.** Drag the icon for one folder (or file) into the open window for a second folder (or disk), and then release it when the second folder's window is highlighted in yellow, as shown in Figure 8-4 (bottom).

FIGURE 8-4:
Two ways of
putting one folder
into another.

REMEMBER

If you want to move an item from one *disk* to another disk, you can't use the preceding tricks. Your item is copied, not moved. If you want to *move* a file or folder from one disk to another, you have to hold down the ⌘ key when you drag an icon from one disk to another. The little Copying Files window even changes to read Moving Files. Nice touch, eh?

Selecting multiple icons

Sometimes you want to move or copy several items into a single folder. The process is pretty much the same as it is when you copy one file or folder: That is, you just drag the icons to where you want it and drop them there. But you need to select all the items you want before you can drag them en masse to their destination.

If you want to move all the files in a particular folder, simply choose Edit⇨Select All or press ⌘+A. This command selects all icons in the active window, regardless of whether you can see them onscreen. If no window is active, choosing Select All selects every icon on the desktop.

TIP

But what if you want to select only some of the files in the active window or on the desktop? Here's the most convenient method:

1. **To select more than one icon in a folder, do one of the following:**

   - Click once in the folder window (don't click any one icon), and drag the cursor while continuing to hold down the mouse (or trackpad) button. You see an outline of a box (a *selection rectangle*) around the icons while you drag, and all icons within or touching the box become highlighted (the five topmost icons in Figure 8-5).

   - *Click one icon and hold down the Shift key while you click others.* As long as you hold down the Shift key, each new icon that you click is added to the selection. To deselect an icon, click it a second time while still holding down the Shift key.

   - *Click one icon and hold down the ⌘ key while you click others.* The difference between using the Shift and ⌘ keys is that the ⌘ key doesn't select everything between it and the first item selected when your window is in List, Gallery, or Column view. In Icon view, it really doesn't make much difference.

   To deselect an icon, click it while still holding down the ⌘ key.

2. **After you select the icons, click one of them (clicking anywhere else deselects the icons) and drag them to the location where you want to move them (or Option-drag to copy them).**

WARNING

Be careful with multiple selections, especially when you drag icons to the Trash. You can easily — and accidentally — select more than one icon, so watch out that you don't accidentally put the wrong icon in the Trash by not paying close attention. (I detail how the Trash icon works later in this chapter.)

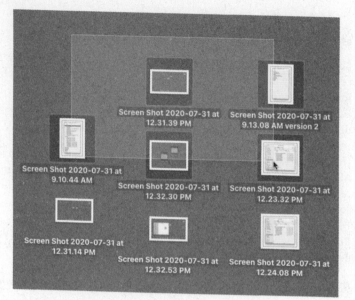

FIGURE 8-5:
All icons that the
selection
rectangle touches
are selected.

Playing the icon name game: Renaming icons

Icon, icon, bo-bicon, banana-fanna fo-ficon. Betcha can change the name of any old icon! Well, that's not entirely true . . . .

TECHNICAL STUFF

If an icon is locked or busy (the application is currently open), or if you don't have the owner's permission to rename that icon (see Chapter 18 for details about permissions), you can't rename it. Similarly, you should never rename certain reserved icons (such as the Library, System, and Desktop folders).

To rename an icon, you can either click the icon's name directly (don't click the icon itself because that selects the icon) or click the icon and press Return once.

Either way, the icon's name is selected and surrounded with a box, and you can type a new name, as shown in Figure 8-6. In addition, the cursor changes from a pointer to a text-editing I-beam. An I-beam cursor is the Mac's way of telling you that you can type now. At this point, if you click the I-beam cursor anywhere in the name box, you can edit the icon's original name. If you don't click the I-beam cursor in the name box but just begin typing, the icon's original name is replaced by what you type.

FIGURE 8-6:
Change an icon's
name by typing
over the old one.

untitled folder

Name I just typed over
untitled folder

If you've never changed an icon's name, give it a try. And don't forget: If you click the icon itself, the icon is selected, and you won't be able to change its name. If you do accidentally select the icon, just press Return once to edit the name of the icon.

WARNING

Don't change the name of a folder that contains open files because it might screw up the saving process and possibly cause data loss. So don't do that, okay?

Renaming multiple icons at once

To rename a group of files, first select them all, and then right-click anywhere in your selection and choose Rename x Items (where x is the number of files selected) from the pop-up menu. A sheet appears with options for adding or replacing text in the existing filename, or creating a custom format with indexes, counters, and dates before or after whatever new filename you choose.

TIP

One last thing: If you have two or more icons you want to move to a new folder, select the items and choose File⇨New Folder with Selection, press ⌘+Control+N, or right-click or Control-click one of the selected items and choose New Folder with Selection. All three techniques will create a new folder, move the selected icons into it, and select the name of the new folder (which will be New Folder with Items) so you can type its new name immediately.

Compressing files

TIP

If you're going to send files as an email enclosure, creating a compressed archive of the files first and sending the archive instead of the originals usually saves you time sending the files and saves the recipient time downloading them. To create this compressed archive, simply select the file(s) or folder(s) and then choose File⇨Compress. The name of the document or folder you're compressing appears after the word Compress in the menu, so if you were compressing a file called Foo. doc, the File menu command would read Compress Foo.doc. This creates a compressed .zip file out of your selection. The compressed file is smaller than the original — sometimes by quite a bit. Double-click a compressed (.zip) file to decompress it.

Getting rid of icons

To get rid of an icon — any icon — merely drag it onto the Trash icon in your dock.

REMEMBER

Trashing an alias gets rid of only the alias, not the parent file. But trashing a document, a folder, or an application icon puts it in the Trash, where it *will* be deleted permanently the next time you empty the Trash. The Finder menu offers a couple of commands that help you manage the Trash:

>> **Finder ⇨ Empty Trash:** This command deletes all items in the Trash from your hard drive, period.

WARNING

I'll probably say this more than once: *Use this command with a modicum of caution.* After a file is dragged into the Trash and the Trash is emptied, the file is gone, gone, gone unless you have Time Machine or other backup. (Okay, maybe ProSoft Engineering's Data Rescue or some other third-party utility can bring it back, but I wouldn't bet the farm on it.)

TIP

If you put something in the Trash by accident, you can almost always return it from whence it came: Just click the Trash icon in the dock to open its window, right- or Control-click the icon you want to return, and choose Put Back in the shortcut menu.

You can also invoke the magical Undo command by choosing Edit⇨Undo or by pressing ⌘+Z. The accidentally trashed file returns to its original location. Usually. Unfortunately, Undo doesn't work every time — and it remembers only the very last action that you performed when it does work — so don't rely on it too much. (The right- or Control-click trick, however, works every time.)

The Incredible iCloud Drive

iCloud has been around in various forms for years, but iCloud Drive is the current incarnation for taking advantage of Apple's remote storage service.

iCloud Drive stores files of any type in iCloud. It's built into Big Sur and works like any other folder on your Mac. In other words, you can drag documents of any type into it, organize them with folders and tags (see Chapter 4) if you care to, and find them with Spotlight (see Chapter 10).

The best part is that the files are available not only on your Mac but also on your iPhone, iPad, or Windows PC as well. That's the good news. The bad news is that if you need more than 5GB of storage space, it's going to cost you. You get up to 5GB at no cost; if you need more it's 99 cents per month for 50GB, $2.99 per month for 200GB, or $9.99 per month for 2TB.

For what it's worth, iCloud was much more expensive not so long ago: $40 per year for 25GB, or $100 per year for 55GB. Compare that to the current pricing of $12 per year for 50GB or $36 per year for 200GB. Kudos to Apple for making iCloud Drive not just convenient but also (more) affordable.

On the other hand, it would be nice if it were even more affordable (hint, hint).

Although iCloud Drive should be enabled by default, if yours isn't (you don't see it in the sidebar), launch System Preferences (⌘⇨ System Preferences), click the Apple ID icon, and then enable the check box for iCloud Drive.

If you still don't see iCloud Drive in your sidebar, open Finder Preferences (Finder⇨ Finder Preferences), click the sidebar icon, and then enable the check box to Show iCloud Drive in the sidebar.

You can choose to store the contents of your desktop and Documents folders in iCloud rather than on your startup disk. The upside is that files in those folders are available to all your Macs (assuming you have more than one), on your iDevices, and via the iCloud website. The downside is that you may have to have Internet access to access those files.

If storing your Desktop and Documents folders in the cloud appeals to you, click the Options button next to iCloud Drive in the iCloud System Preferences Pane and enable the check box for Desktop & Documents Folders.

Chapter **9**

Comprehending the macOS Clipboard

Before you start copying files, let me introduce you to the Clipboard. The *Clipboard* is a holding area for the last thing that you selected, and then cut or copied. That copied item can be text, a picture, a portion of a picture, an object in a drawing program, a column of numbers in a spreadsheet, any icon (except a drive icon), or just about anything else that can be selected.

Put another way, the Clipboard is your Mac's temporary storage area.

Introducing the Clipboard

Most of the time, the Clipboard works quietly in the background, but if you want to know what it currently contains, the Clipboard will reveal itself if you choose Edit ➪ Show Clipboard.

This command summons the Clipboard window, shown in Figure 9-1, which displays the type of item (such as text, an image, or sound) on the Clipboard, as well as either the item itself or a message letting you know that the item on the Clipboard can't be displayed.

Clipboard contents: TIFF image

FIGURE 9-1:
The Show
Clipboard
command
displays whatever
is on the
Clipboard if
it can.

As a storage area, the Clipboard's contents are temporary. *Very* temporary. When you cut or copy an item, that item remains on the Clipboard only until you cut or copy something else, logout, restart, or crash. When you cut or copy something else, the new item replaces the Clipboard's contents, and the newcomer remains on the Clipboard until you cut or copy something else (or logout, restart, or crash). And so it goes.

WARNING

Whatever is on the Clipboard heads straight for oblivion if you crash, lose power, log out, or shut down your Mac, so don't count on it too heavily or for too long.

If you want to preserve something on the Clipboard after you cut or copy something else, crash, lose power, log out, or shut down, paste it into a note in your Notes app.

TIP

Myriad third-party clipboard enhancers remember the last 100 things (or more) that you copy or cut to the Clipboard. These utilities also preserve their contents if you crash, lose power, log out, or shut down. My favorites are CopyClip from FIPLAB (free) and its more powerful successor, CopyClip 2 ($7.99), both available from the Mac App Store (see Chapter 23).

**TECHNICAL
STUFF**

The Clipboard commands on the Edit menu are enabled only when they can be used. If the selected item can be cut or copied, the Cut and Copy commands in the Edit menu are enabled (black). If the selected item can't be cut or copied, the commands are unavailable and are dimmed (gray). If the Clipboard is empty or the current document can't accept what's on the Clipboard, the Paste command is dimmed. And when nothing is selected, the Cut, Copy, and Paste commands are dimmed (as in Figure 9-1).

One more thing: Icons can't be cut; they can only be copied (and pasted). So when an icon is selected, the Cut command is always gray.

Last but not least, if you don't see the Show Clipboard command in the Edit menu, chances are, an application other than Finder is active. Just activate Finder first and you'll see the Show Clipboard command in its Edit menu.

Copying Files and Folders

One way to copy icons from one place to another is to use the Clipboard. When a file or folder icon is selected, choose Edit⇨Copy (or use its shortcut, ⌘+C) to copy the selected icon to the Clipboard. Note that this doesn't delete the selected item; it just makes a copy of it on the Clipboard. To paste the copied icon in another location, navigate to that other location and then choose Edit⇨Paste (or use its shortcut, ⌘+V).

Other methods of copying icons from one place to another include these:

WARNING

>> **Drag the icon from one folder onto the icon of another folder while holding down the Option key.** Release the mouse button and Option key when the second folder is highlighted. This technique works regardless of whether the second folder's window is open.

If you don't hold down the Option key, you *move* the icon to a new location rather than *copy* it, as I explain a little later in this section.

When you copy something by dragging and dropping it with the Option key held down, the cursor changes to include a little plus sign (+) next to the arrow, as shown in the margin. Neat!

>> **Drag an icon into the open window for another folder while holding down the Option key.** Drag the icon for the file or folder that you want to copy into the open window for a second folder (or other hard drive or removable media, such as a USB flash drive).

>> **Choose File⇨Duplicate (⌘+D) or right-click or Control-click the file or folder that you want to duplicate; then choose Duplicate from the contextual menu that appears.** This makes a copy of the selected icon, adds the word *copy* to its name, and then places the copy in the same window as the original icon. You can use the Duplicate command on any icon except a disk icon.

You can't duplicate an entire disk onto itself. But you can copy an entire disk (call it Disk 1) to any other actual, physical, separate disk (call it Disk 2) as long as Disk 2 has enough space available. Just hold down Option and drag Disk 1 onto Disk 2's icon. The contents of Disk 1 are copied to Disk 2 and appear on Disk 2 in a folder named Disk 1.

WARNING

If Disk 1 is a *startup disk* (macOS has been installed on the disk and it can start your Mac), Disk 2 will contain the same files but will not be a bootable startup disk (that is, it can't start a Mac). Also, some files may not be copied properly due to macOS permissions issues (see Chapter 18 for the story on permissions).

You can cut an icon's name, but you can't cut the icon itself; you may only copy an icon.

There are two ways to achieve the same effect as cutting an icon:

» Select the icon, copy it to the Clipboard, paste it in its new location, and then move the original icon to the Trash.

» Use the secret shortcut to move the icon via Copy and Paste. The secret is that you press the Option key before clicking the Edit menu. When you do, the Paste command transmogrifies into Move Item Here, providing the functional equivalent of cutting and pasting the icon. You can even use a keyboard shortcut — ⌘+Option+V — to move items from one location to another. Cool, eh?

If you're wondering why anyone would ever want to copy a file, trust me: Someday, you will. Suppose that you have a file called *Long Letter to Mom* in a folder called Old Correspondence. You figure that Mom has forgotten that letter by now, and you want to send it again. But before you do, you want to change the date and delete the reference to Clarence, her pit bull, who is no longer with us. So now you need to put a copy of *Long Letter to Mom* in your Current Correspondence folder. This technique yields the same result as making a copy of a file by using Save As, which I describe in Chapter 7.

WARNING

When you copy a file, it's wise to change the name of the copied file after you paste it. See, having more than one file on your hard drive with the same name isn't such a good idea, even if the files are in different folders. Trust me — having 12 files all named *Expense Report* or 15 files named *Consulting Invoice* is confusing no matter how well organized your folder structure is.

TIP

Add distinguishing words or dates to the names of files and folders you copy, such as *Expense Report Q3 2018* or **Working Smarter for Mac Users** *Consulting Invoice 4-4-2018.*

You can have lots of files with the same name *on the same disk* (although, as I mention earlier, it's probably not a good idea). But your Mac won't let you have more than one file with the same name and extension (.txt, .jpg, .doc) *in the same folder.*

Pasting from the Clipboard

As I mention earlier in this chapter, to place the icon that's on the Clipboard someplace new, click where you want the item to go, and choose Edit⇨Paste or use the keyboard shortcut ⌘+V to paste what you've copied or cut.

REMEMBER

Pasting doesn't purge the contents of the Clipboard. In fact, an item stays on the Clipboard until you cut or copy another item, restart, shut down, log out, or crash. This means that you can paste the same item over and over and over again, which can come in handy at times.

Almost all programs have an Edit menu and use the Macintosh Clipboard, which means you can usually cut or copy something from a document in one program and paste it into a document in another program.

Usually.

Big Sur's Universal Clipboard

The Universal Clipboard lets you copy or cut an item on one device (say, your Mac), and then paste it on another device (say, your iPhone or iPad). Because it performs this magic using iCloud, the requirements are as follows:

>> Wi-Fi and Bluetooth must both be enabled.

>> Both devices must have Handoff enabled. (It's in System Preferences ⇨ General on your Mac and Settings ⇨ General ⇨ Handoff on your iOS device.)

>> Both devices must be logged into the same iCloud account.

>> The devices must be within a few feet of each other.

When these conditions are met, Universal Clipboard just works. If you cut or copy something on one device, you can paste it on another device for approximately 2 minutes after you cut or copy it; after a couple of minutes, however, all bets are off.

If Universal Clipboard doesn't work for you, check the Apple website (www.apple.com/osx/continuity) to make sure both devices meet the system requirements. If both are supported and you still can't make Universal Clipboard work, try turning off Handoff on both devices, wait a minute or two, and then turn it back on. You might also try logging out of iCloud on both devices, restarting them, and then logging back into iCloud on both. Finally, some older Macs have issues with Continuity features such as Handoff and Universal Clipboard even though they meet the specifications.

One more thing before we move on: Big Sur (like Catalina and Mojave before it) lets you use your iPhone or iPad camera (or camera roll) to add photos to documents on your Mac and to scan documents to your Mac. Look for the Import from iPhone or iPad command in the File menu (and shortcut menu, right- or Control-click) of many apps. You discover more about this awesome Big Sur feature in Chapter 23.

3 Getting Things Done

IN THIS PART . . .

Be more productive with Big Sur's suite of time- and effort-saving tools.

Keep your life organized with Calendar, Reminders, and Notes.

Master Siri — Siri-ously.

Go places with Maps.

Meet the many iOS apps that are now Mac apps, too!

Chapter **10**

Five Terrific Time-Saving Tools

I n this chapter, I show you the ins and outs of five terrific time-saving tools: Quick Look, Spotlight, Mission Control, Control Center, and Launchpad. Each is designed to let you use your Mac better, faster, and more elegantly. Yes, you can use your mouse and click your way to any file or folder on any drive, but these features are built into Big Sur for your convenience.

At the risk of repeating myself, Apple frequently provides more than one way to accomplish a task in macOS, so there's duplication and overlap among and between the tools in this chapter and tools I discuss elsewhere in this book. Don't worry. Take what you need, and leave the rest. Most users love Quick Look, but some never use it. Some people love Spotlight; others rarely invoke it. Mission Control is amazingly helpful, especially on laptops with small screens, but quite a few users find it inconsistent and confusing and don't care for it at all.

My advice: Try all the tools and techniques in this chapter at least a few times before you decide whether you want or need them. The good news is that unlike many Mac users, you will at least know what these five useful tools are about and how to use them if you choose to.

With a Quick Look

The Quick Look command displays the contents of the selected file in a floating window. The key point is that it's built into Big Sur, so you can see what's in a file without double-clicking (to open) it and without launching an application.

This feature is handy when you want to peek at the contents of a file without having to open it.

To take a Quick Look yourself, select an icon and do any of the following:

» Choose File ⇨ Quick Look.

» Right-click or Control-click the file's icon and choose Quick Look from its contextual menu.

» Choose Quick Look from the Action icon/menu on the toolbar.

» Use one of its two keyboard shortcuts: ⌘+Y or the easiest shortcut ever, just press the spacebar while an icon is selected.

One of my favorite ways to use Quick Look is with a folder full of images, such as the one shown in Figure 10-1.

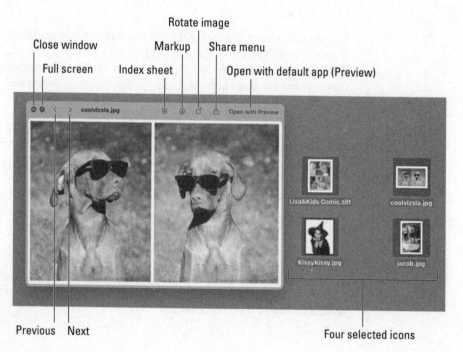

FIGURE 10-1: The Quick Look window (right) displaying an image from one of the four selected icons in a folder full of pictures (left).

TIP

While the Quick Look window is open you can select different icons in the Finder window — use the arrow keys to select the next or previous icon — and see their contents in the Quick Look window!

The bad news is that although Quick Look works with many types of files — Microsoft Office, Apple iWork, plain-text, PDF, TIFF, GIF, JPEG, PNG, and most types of audio and video files — it doesn't work with *all* files. You'll know it doesn't work if Quick Look shows you a big document, folder, or application icon instead of the contents of that file.

If you select multiple items before you invoke Quick Look, as I did before snapping Figure 10-1, three icons appear at the top of the Quick Look window near the left side: Previous, Next, and Index Sheet. With these controls, you can view all selected items at the same time as an *index sheet* or view them one at a time by clicking the Next or Previous icons.

The outline around the image at the top left indicates that the pointer is hovering over that image (Jacob.jpg); if I were to click, that image would fill the window, and the icons shown at the top of the Quick Look window in Figure 10-1 would reappear.

REMEMBER

You can invoke Markup from the Quick Look window. Just click the Markup icon and the Markup tools appear. (Markup is described in loving detail in Chapter 5.)

Share and share alike with the Share menu

If you use an Apple iDevice, you're surely familiar with the rectangular icon with an arrow escaping from it, as shown in the margin and in the toolbar in Figure 10-1. That's the Share menu, and it has as many as seven options (depending on the type of file you selected):

» **Mail:** Launches the Mail app and attaches the selected file to a blank message, ready for you to address and send.

» **Messages:** Launches the Messages app and puts the selected file in an outgoing message, ready for you to address and send. You become well acquainted with the Messages app in Chapter 17.

» **AirDrop:** Sends the selected file to other Mac users or iDevice users. As long as you're on the same Wi-Fi network, your file transfer takes but a single click (or a single tap on iDevices).

» **Notes:** Sends the selected file to the Notes app, where you can add it to an existing note or create a note for it. (You discover the Notes app in Chapter 11.)

>> **Add to Photos:** Adds the selected item to the All Photos album in the Photos app.

>> **More:** Big Sur's extensible architecture lets you add other services (such as Vimeo or LinkedIn) and apps (such as Photos or Aperture) to your Share menu. To manage these extensions, choose More from the Share menu. Alternatively, you can launch the System Preferences application, click the Extensions icon, and then click the Share Menu item on the left side of the window.

Slide into Slideshow (full-screen) mode

Quick Look really shines in its Slideshow (full-screen) mode, which you can start with any of these techniques:

>> Hold down Option and choose File ⇨ Slideshow.

>> Press ⌘+Option+Y.

>> If your file is already open in the Quick Look window, click the full-screen icon, as labeled in Figure 10-1 and shown here in the margin.

When you're in Slideshow mode, a completely different set of controls appears onscreen automatically, as shown in Figure 10-2.

FIGURE 10-2:
The Slideshow controls appear automatically in full-screen Slideshow mode.

Previous Play Next Index Share Exit full screen

Close Quick Look

The Slideshow controls disappear after a few seconds of inactivity; if you don't see them when you need them, just wiggle the pointer anywhere on screen, and they'll magically reappear.

TIP

To exit Slideshow (full-screen) mode, press Esc or click the Exit Full Screen icon to return to the Quick Look window or the Close Quick Look icon to both exit Slideshow mode and quit Quick Look.

When you're finished with the Quick Look window, click the X icon in the top-left corner (refer to Figure 10-1). If you're in full-screen mode, click the X icon in the control bar, as shown in Figure 10-2, or press ⌘+Y, which works in either mode.

Spotlight on Finding Files and Folders Faster

Even if you follow every single bit of advice provided in this chapter, a time will come when you won't be able to find a file or folder even though you know for certain that it's somewhere on your hard drive. Fortunately, Big Sur includes a fabulous search technology called Spotlight, which can help you find almost anything on any mounted disk in seconds. Spotlight can search for

>> Files

>> Folders

>> Text inside documents

>> Files and folders by their metadata (creation date, modification date, kind, size, and so on)

Spotlight finds what you're looking for and then organizes its results logically, all in the blink of an eye (on most Macs).

Spotlight is both a technology and a feature. The technology is pervasive throughout Big Sur, and is the underlying power behind the Search boxes in many Apple applications and utilities such as Mail, Contacts, System Preferences, and Finder. You can also use it by clicking the Spotlight menu — the little magnifying glass in your menu bar. Finally, you can reuse Spotlight searches in the future by turning them into smart folders (which I explain in Chapter 8).

Finding files and folders has never been faster or easier than it is in Big Sur. So in the following sections, I look at the two separate but related ways that Spotlight helps you find files, folders, and even text inside document files and on the web: the Search box in the toolbar of Finder windows and the main Spotlight menu.

Using the Find command

With its power provided by Spotlight, this isn't your father's old search.

The following steps walk you through all the features:

1. Choose File ⇨ Find or press ⌘+F to begin a new search or click in the Search box of any open window.

If you want to conduct a search limited to a specific folder (and its subfolders), open that folder first, and then click its Search box or press ⌘+F.

You can then search for files by clicking This Mac (all files) or the active window's name, if there is one. If no windows are open, the desktop is used by default, as shown in Figure 10-3.

FIGURE 10-3:
Type one
character in the
Search box, and
the magic begins.

2. **In the Search box, type a single character.**

   I typed the letter *a,* and the window starts displaying the results, as shown in Figure 10-3.

   At the same time, a menu drops down below your pointer to offer search suggestions, such as Filenames, Kinds, and Sent By, as shown in Figure 10-3, as well as others such as Dates or Downloaded From (not shown).

   Select an item from the menu to narrow the scope of your search. Or type additional characters: The more you type, the fewer matches and suggestions you'll see.

   Spotlight's default behavior is to search files' contents if it can (and it can search the text inside files created by many popular applications).

TIP

Third-party Spotlight plug-ins are available that let you search the contents of file types not supported by Big Sur, including old WordPerfect and QuarkXPress files and many others. Search the Internet for *Spotlight plug-ins,* and you'll find plug-ins for dozens of popular apps.

If you know all or part of the file's name, you can limit your search to filenames (that is, exclude text in files and search only for files by name). Just choose Name Matches: (it's *a* in Figure 10-3) from the drop-down menu.

3. **When you find the file or folder, you can open any item in the window by double-clicking it.**

Keep these points in mind when you perform a search:

» You have a choice of where to search. This Mac is selected in Figure 10-3 and 10-4.

» You can choose additional search criteria — such as the kind (Folder in Figure 10-4) and the date the file or folder was last opened (Within Last 120 Days in the figure) — as well as other attributes, including Modification Date, Creation Date, Keywords, Label, File Contents, and File Size.

» To add another criterion, simply click the + button on the right side of the window.

» To save a search for reuse in the future, click the Save button on the upper-right side of the window.

FIGURE 10-4: Search your entire Mac or a specific folder (and its subfolders) and then narrow your search using one or more criteria.

Searching "This M...			Q Big Sur
Search: **This Mac** "Desktop"			Save
Kind ⌄ is Folder ⌄			
Last opened date ⌄ is within last ⌄ 120 days ⌄			
Name ^	Kind	Date Last Opened	
macOS Big Sur For Dummies	Folder	Today at 12:11 PM	
macOS Big Sur For Dummies research	Folder	Today at 12:11 PM	

Favorites
- AirDrop
- Recents
- Desktop
- Documents
- Applications
- Downloads
- Dr. Mac 2020

iCloud
- iCloud Drive

Locations
- Bob's MacBook Air
- Big Sur

2 items

TIP

Try choosing different options from the window's Arrange menu — Name, Kind, Date Last Opened, and so on — to see the search results presented in different ways.

So there you have it — fast searches made easy in Finder. But you can access the power of Spotlight in many ways, and the Search box in the toolbar of Finder windows is merely one of them.

Using the Spotlight menu and its keyboard shortcut

Another way to search for files and folders is to use the Spotlight menu itself — the magnifying-glass icon at the far-right end of your menu bar. Click the icon or use the keyboard shortcut ⌘+spacebar to open the Spotlight Search box. Now type a character, word, or series of words in the Search box begins your search.

Spotlight floats elegantly in the middle of your screen, as shown in Figure 10-5.

Check out the previews (*Bigsurcalifornia.org* in Figure 10-5), which is a nice touch. Also note that results may be culled from external sources, including Wikipedia, the iTunes Store, and Maps (in addition to results from files your hard drive).

FIGURE 10-5: This is Spotlight in Big Sur searching for *Big Sur*.

TIP

Memorize and use the super-convenient and easy-to-remember keyboard shortcut for opening the Spotlight Search box, which is ⌘+spacebar by default. If you don't find ⌘+spacebar appealing as a shortcut, you can change it to whatever you like in the Spotlight System Preferences pane.

Spotlight is more than just a menu and a Search box; it also uses a technology that's pervasive throughout macOS and apps, including (but certainly not limited to) Mail and Contacts. The reason why it's so spectacularly speedy is that it indexes your files when your Mac is idle. The upshot is that Spotlight knows file locations and contents soon after a file is created or modified.

REMEMBER

One last thing: The Search field in Finder windows finds items only on your hard drive. To include results from the Internet, you have to use the Spotlight floating window via its menu icon or keyboard shortcut.

The bottom line is that regardless of which method you choose to invoke it — the Search box in a Finder window or the new floating Spotlight window — using Spotlight saves you time and effort.

Blast Off with Mission Control

Mission Control shows you big icons representing all open applications including full-screen apps, or all open document windows for the active application, presenting them in an organized and unified view. Before you see how it works, look at Figure 10-6, which shows the Mission Control System Preferences pane, where you turn specific Mission Control features on and off and assign keyboard or mouse shortcuts to them.

FIGURE 10-6: The Mission Control System Preferences pane.

The Mission Control pane: It's painless

The top part of the pane contains four check boxes: Automatically Rearrange Spaces Based on Most Recent Use; When Switching to an Application, Switch to a Space with Open Windows for the Application; Group Windows by Application; and Displays Have Separate Spaces. These long-winded check boxes will all start to make sense shortly; for now, just know that they do what their lengthy names imply. You should experiment with the settings, turning them on and off, to see which way you prefer them.

Moving right along, the three pop-up menus govern keyboard and mouse shortcuts for Mission Control. The pop-up menus let you specify the trigger for each of the three Mission Control features with a keystroke or mouse button. The default keyboard shortcuts appear in upcoming text, but yours may differ; to change them, click the appropriate pop-up menu and make a new selection.

TIP

Hold down the ⌘, Option, Control, or Shift key (or any combination thereof) when you choose an item from any of the shortcut menus to add modifier keys to the shortcuts you create. So, for example, if you were to hold down ⌘+Shift when you select F11 from a pop-up menu, the keyboard shortcut for that feature would be ⌘+Shift+F11.

Finally, most Apple keyboards made since April 2007 also include a dedicated Mission Control shortcut key (on the F3 or F4 key). If you see a tiny picture that looks like the Mission Control icon (shown in the margin) on your F3 or F4 key, you can use them in addition to the other shortcuts discussed in this section.

A picture is worth a thousand words, so check out Figures 10-7 and 10-8 as you read about each feature.

>> To see Mission Control, which displays all open windows in all open applications, as shown in Figure 10-7, press Control+↑ (up arrow).

FIGURE 10-7:
After invoking
Mission Control
(Control+↑).

>> To see all open windows belonging to the current application (TextEdit in Figure 10-8), press Control+↓ (down arrow).

FIGURE 10-8:
After invoking Application Windows (Control+↓) when TextEdit was active.

>> If you hover your cursor over a window on a Mission Control screen, a blue border appears around the item you're hovering over (a TextEdit document entitled *The Cod-Father: Part II* — in both Figures 10-7 and 10-8).

If you press the spacebar while a mini-window is highlighted, you'll see an overlay with a preview of the window's contents, which is especially helpful when a window is partially obscured by another window.

>> To hide all open windows so you can see icons on the desktop, press F11 or Fn+F11.

Note that when you're using Mission Control, windows appear as reduced-size thumbnails. Identifying information — either the program or window name — appears when you hover the pointer over a thumbnail (Mission Control) or below it (Application Windows), making it easier to discern what each item contains. When you click any of these small windows, Mission Control deactivates, and the window you clicked becomes the active window.

One last thing: If you use a trackpad, check out the More Gestures tab in the Trackpad System Preferences pane, where you can enable a three- or four-fingered swipe upward to invoke Mission Control.

Hot corners are hot stuff!

In the bottom-left corner of the Mission Control System Preferences pane is a Hot Corners button, which lets you designate any or all of the corners of your screen as hot spots to trigger Mission Control, Launchpad, Screen Saver, Display Sleep, or Lock Screen. Click the menu for a corner, and select the feature you want associated with that corner. Then, whenever you move your pointer onto that corner and leave it there for a second or two, the feature executes.

Hot corners have been part of Mac OS since time immemorial and are still as useful as ever. For example, I like to set the top-right corner to start my screen saver and the bottom-right corner to disable it.

Mission Control is enabled by default, but you can disable any or all of its features by turning off its trigger: Just choose the minus sign from a pop-up menu instead of a keyboard shortcut.

Hold down the ⌘, Option, Control, or Shift key (or any combination thereof) when you choose an item from any of the Active Screen Corner menus to add modifier keys to the hot corners you create. So, for example, if you were to hold down ⌘+Shift when you select Mission Control as the shortcut assigned to the top-left corner, you'd have to press ⌘ and Shift and move the pointer to the top-left corner to trigger it. Or if you were to hold down Shift when you select Application Windows from the pop-up menu, you'd have to hold down Shift when you move the pointer to the top-left corner to invoke the command. If you don't press a modifier key when you select an item from a hot corner menu, merely moving the pointer to that corner will invoke the command.

Trackpad users have the option of invoking Mission Control with a three-finger (or four-finger) swipe up. If that appeals to you, enable it in the Trackpad System Preferences pane's More Gestures tab.

Mission Control's Spaces from 30,000 feet (an overview)

If Mission Control lets you manage your windows in real time, its spaces let you manage windows by organizing them in groups called *desktops*, and switch from desktop to desktop with a keystroke or trackpad gesture.

In earlier versions of macOS, what are now called desktops were called *spaces*. Mission Control, improbably, uses the words *spaces* and *desktops* more or less interchangeably, so as you see in Figure 10-9, my three spaces are named Desktop 1,

Desktop 2, and Desktop 3. I think it's dumb, and I'm going to continue to call a space a space regardless of what Mission Control labels them (because calling them desktops would be even more confusing).

FIGURE 10-9:
Mission Control
showing
off my four
spaces (named
Desktop 1, 2, 3,
and Music).

Think of a space as being a single screen, set up just the way you like it, with its windows arranged just the way you like them. When you use spaces, only two kinds of windows are shown in the space you're using: windows from applications associated with the active space and windows from applications launched while that space is active.

By the way, apps running in full-screen mode are automatically considered a space of their own, which bears the name of the app (Music in Figure 10-9) rather than Desktop x.

If you find yourself spending too much time moving and resizing windows onscreen, consider setting up spaces for specific tasks. You might have one space dedicated to a specific project, another for web surfing, and a third for email, each with all its windows arranged just the way you like them.

Take, for example, the four spaces shown in Figure 10-9. I have one for writing (Desktop 1), one for web surfing (Desktop 2), one for my calendar (Desktop 3), and one for music, each with its windows arranged exactly as I like 'em (which is "big enough to read easily").

Moving right along, you manage your spaces with Mission Control, which provides an overview of what's running on your Mac, including all your spaces and all open windows. In a nutshell, this dynamic duo makes it easier than ever to manage and maintain the mélange of Finder and application windows that conspire to clutter and eventually consume your screen.

To see spaces in action, press the Mission Control key (Control+↑ by default). If you have a trackpad, you can also swipe upward using three fingers to see Mission Control, which will look something like Figure 10-9 based on the four spaces just described.

TIP

Try this: Hover your cursor over the name of a desktop and a thumbnail image of all of your spaces appears like magic (as shown in Figure 10-9).

To add a new space, first enter Mission Control; then move the pointer to the top-right corner of the screen and click the Add (+) button. Note that if you have your dock on the right side of the screen, you have to move your pointer to the top-left corner for the + to appear.

You can use this technique to add as many spaces as you like. When you're finished using Mission Control, you can

>> Click a space at the top of the screen to switch to it.

or

>> Press the Mission Control key, press the Esc key, or swipe upward with three or four fingers to return to the space you were using when you entered Mission Control.

REMEMBER

The three-finger gesture requires a Magic Mouse, Magic Trackpad, or laptop with a buttonless trackpad.

TIP

If you're using a notebook Mac, I implore you to learn to use gestures with Mission Control. Visit the Trackpad System Preferences pane's More Gestures tab and make sure you've enabled three- or four-finger swipes. I love swiping between Mission Control spaces like the ones in Figure 10-9. Swipe, and I've got my writing setup; swipe again, and I've got Safari; swipe again, and I have Calendar; and finally, one more swipe to see the Music app. Try it — I think you'll like swiping to switch spaces (desktops) as much as I do.

One last thing: macOS Big Sur takes full advantage of multiple displays no matter how many displays are connected to your Mac. So, for example, you can work in Finder's desktop on one display and use a full screen app on another. And finally, each display has its own exclusive set of Mission Control spaces associated with it.

If you use multiple monitors (like I do), you can drag and drop a space (desktop) from one display to another. Try it — it's way cool!

Getting around in space(s)

The preceding section shows you one way to move from one space to another — enter Mission Control, and click the space you want to use. You can also navigate spaces in the following ways:

>> Press the Control key and ← (left-arrow key) or → (right-arrow key) to move to the previous or next space.

>> Swipe left or right with three fingers to move to the next or previous space.

You can enable or disable these keyboard shortcuts in the Shortcuts tab of the Keyboard System Preferences pane.

There will be times when you want to move a window from one space to another. Do one of the following:

>> Drag a window to the top of the screen; when Mission Control appears, drag it onto a different space (desktop).

>> Press and hold down the mouse button on the window you want to move while pressing the Control key and the left-arrow key (←) to move the window to the space on the left of the current space or the right-arrow key (→) to move the window to the space on the right of the current space.

>> Start in the space that has the window you want to move. Enter Mission Control, press Control and drag the window to the thumbnail of the appropriate space at the top of the screen. When you release the mouse button, the window will move to that space.

Finally, should you want to delete one or more spaces, simply enter Mission Control, and move the pointer over the space. A Delete icon — an X that should look familiar if you use the an iPhone, iPad, or iPod touch — appears in its top-left corner. Click it to delete that space.

Deleting a space doesn't delete or quit any applications or close any documents. Applications and windows in a deleted space move to the first (or only) space called desktop (the one *without* a numeric suffix).

The bottom line is that spaces can be particularly useful for those with a smaller display. And it can be even more useful for users with more than one display.

REMEMBER

Using Mission Control can be an acquired taste, so even if you have a small screen or multiple screens, you may not care for it at first. My advice: Try it for a while, and if you decide that you hate it, turn its triggers off (by selecting the minus sign) and be done with it.

Taking Control of Essential Settings

NEW

Big Sur introduced a feature long beloved by iPhone and iPad users, namely, Control Center. By default, Control Center lets you quickly manage Wi-Fi, Bluetooth, AirDrop, and other settings without opening System Preferences.

To access Control Center, click its icon in the menu bar, as shown on the left in Figure 10-10 (and in the margin). To see the options for each control, click the control or, for Display and Sound, click the little icon to the right of the slider. The options for Wi-Fi are shown in Figure 10-10, right.

FIGURE 10-10:
The default
Control Center
(left), and its Wi-Fi
controls (right).

To add additional controls to Control Center, open System Preferences and click the Dock & Menu Bar icon. Here you can add Accessibility Shortcuts, Battery, and Fast User Switching to Control Center as well as manage other menu bar icons. If the control already appears in Control Center, it may be faster to click it in Control Center and drag it to the menu bar, which works for most controls.

In Figure 10-11, I added (left to right) Battery, Music, Bluetooth, Keyboard Brightness, AirDrop, and Wi-Fi icons to the left of the Control Center icon in my menu bar. The Dock & Menu Bar System Preferences pane is displayed, with Battery selected in the sidebar. I like direct access to most of those controls, so their icons live permanently in my menu bar, which means I don't have much use for Control Center. Still, I suppose it's a convenient way to have fewer icons in your menu bar.

FIGURE 10-11: Add or delete Control Center or menu bar items in the Dock & Menu Bar System Preferences pane.

Launchpad: The Place for Applications

Launchpad presents all the applications in your Applications folder in a view that looks like the home screen of any iOS device (that is, iPhone, iPad, or iPod touch). In fact, if you use one of these devices, I suspect that you could skip everything that follows about Launchpad, because it works almost exactly like the home screen on an iPhone or other iDevice.

 Click the Launchpad dock icon (shown in the margin). It fills your screen with big, beautiful application icons, as shown in Figure 10-12.

FIGURE 10-12:
Launchpad, in all its glory.

TECHNICAL STUFF

I changed my desktop picture from plain gray to the default Big Sur picture for Figure 10-12. The photo is actually in focus; the background's nifty blur effect happens only when Launchpad is active. Sure, it's just eye candy, but it's *elegant* eye candy.

If your Launchpad has more than one page of apps, you'll see dots (two in Figure 10-12) near the bottom of the screen. To switch pages, click a gray dot; press ⌘ + right arrow (→) or ⌘+left-arrow (←) to move to the next or previous page, respectively; or click anywhere (except on an icon) and flick left or right. Trackpad users can also use a three-finger swipe left or right to move from page to page.

To launch an app, just click its icon. In a heartbeat, Launchpad disappears, and the app replaces it on your screen.

Launchpad is configurable, just like home screens on iDevices. As you're about to see, you can rearrange app icons on a page, move them from one page to another, organize them in folders, and delete them. Say it all together now: "Just like on iDevices."

For those who are unfamiliar with iOS or devices that run it, here's how these things work on your Mac:

>> **To find an app:** Type the first few characters of its name in the Search box at the top of the screen.

>> **To rearrange app icons:** Click and drag the app to its new location.

>> **To move apps to the next or previous page:** Click and drag the app to the left or right edge of the screen. When the next page of apps appears, drag the app to its new location on that page.

>> **To add an app to your dock:** Click and drag the app onto the left side of the dock.

>> **To create a folder for apps:** Drag one app's icon on top of another app's icon to create a folder (such as Other in Figure 10-10).

>> **To add an app to a folder:** Drag the app onto that folder to add it.

>> **To move an app out of a folder:** Click the folder to open it and drag the app out of the folder to a new location.

>> **To change a folder's name:** Click to open the folder, click the current name, and then type a new name.

>> **To uninstall apps:** Click an app's icon, but don't release the mouse button until all the icons begin to wiggle. Apps that can be uninstalled display a Delete icon (X); click to uninstall the app.

>> **To stop the wiggling:** Press Esc.

TIP

Many Apple apps don't have a Delete icon because they're integral pieces of macOS Big Sur and can't be removed.

Finally, you may notice that some items from the Applications and Utilities folders on your startup disk are in a folder named Other in Launchpad. Why? Which apps and for what reason? Nobody knows. It's been like that for as long as I can remember, but the logic behind it remains a mystery.

Chapter **11**

Organizing Your Life

When you install macOS Big Sur, the folks at Apple generously include applications that can help simplify and organize your everyday affairs — Calendar, Reminders, and Notes (to name three you discover in this chapter).

In fact, macOS Big Sur comes with a folder full of applications — software you can use to do everything from surfing the Internet to capturing an image of your Mac's screen to playing QuickTime movies to performing numeric calculations.

Technically, most of these applications aren't even part of macOS. Rather, the vast majority of them are what are known as *bundled* apps — programs that come with the operating system but are unrelated to its function. Readers (bless them) tend to complain when I skip bundled applications, so I mention almost all of them in this book.

But in this chapter, you get a look at only the applications that help you organize your everyday life — appointments, to-do items, and notes — and how to keep them in sync with your other Macs and iDevices.

The applications discussed in this chapter are stored in (where else?) the Applications folder, which you can get to in four ways:

>> Click the Applications folder in the sidebar of any Finder window.

>> Choose Go ➪ Applications from Finder.

>> Press ⌘+Shift+A in Finder.

>> Click the Launchpad icon on the dock to see all the applications installed on this Mac (refer to Chapter 10).

TIP

Other bundled apps you might be especially interested in include Safari (Chapter 15), Contacts (Chapter 16), Mail (Chapter 17), Music (Chapter 19), a whole handful of multimedia applications that enable you to play video and more on your Mac, including Preview, which lets you view and annotate PDF and other image files (Chapter 20), and TextEdit (Chapter 21).

Keeping Track with Calendar

Calendar is a wonderful program that provides multiple appointment calendars with alerts. More precisely, you can have multiple color-coded calendars; several types of visual, audible, and emailed alerts; repeating events; and more. You can publish your calendar(s) on the web for others to view (which requires an iCloud account or other WebDAV server), and you can subscribe to calendars published by other Calendar users.

In the sections that follow, I share some of the features I find most useful.

Navigating Calendar views

Calendar lets you display the main Calendar window just the way you like it:

>> **You can view your calendar by the day, week, month, or year.** Figure 11-1 shows a weekly view. To select a view, click the Day, Week, Month, or Year button at the top.

>> **To move back or forward,** click the arrow buttons on either side of the Today button (upper right). You see the previous or next week in Week view, yesterday or tomorrow in day view, and so on.

>> **To go to today's date,** click the Today button.

» **To add a new calendar,** choose File ➪ New Calendar or use its keyboard shortcut, ⌘+Option+N.

Show/hide Calendar sidebar

Show/hide invitations

Create Quick Event

Views

Search

Today button

FIGURE 11-1:
The Calendar main window displaying the view I prefer: Week view.

Calendar sidebar

Event info for selected event

Selected event

Events

You can find all these items, most of which have shortcuts, in the Calendar application's View menu, which offers almost total control of what you see and how you navigate.

TIP

If you want to master Calendar, it would behoove you to spend some time experimenting with these views and with their navigation commands and options.

Creating calendars

If you refer to Figure 11-1, you see a list of my calendars in the top-left corner: Bob's Appointments, Family, Bob's Deadlines, Bob's Travel, Lisa@Work, and so on. The check boxes turn the visibility of a calendar on (selected) and off (deselected).

To create a calendar in Calendar, follow these steps:

1. **Choose File ➪ New Calendar.**

If you have more than one account enabled (in Calendar ➪ Preferences ➪ Accounts or the Internet Accounts System Preferences pane), choose File ➪ New Calendar ➪ iCloud (or whichever account you want to use for this calendar).

A new calendar named Untitled is created and added to the appropriate account in the sidebar.

2. **To give your calendar a name, select Untitled and type a new name.**

3. **(Optional) To color-code the entries for this calendar, right-click or Control-click it in the sidebar to select a color from its shortcut menu.**

TIP

In my humble opinion, Custom Color is the coolest choice because it lets you select from thousands of colors — including the lovely dusky rose hue I use for my Bob's Appointments and Bob's Reminders calendars.

TIP

If you have an iCloud account, you can publish your calendars and invite others to subscribe to them by right- or Control-clicking the iCloud calendar in the list and choosing Sharing Settings. Type their email address in the Shared With field, and then click Done. Each invitee receives an email asking him or her to Join your calendar. This is what my wife and I do. Each of us maintains and publishes his or her own calendar and joins the other's. That way, we can see at a glance who's doing what and when they're doing it. This is by far the slickest solution we've found.

Deleting a calendar

To delete a calendar, select it in the list and press ⌘+Delete. An alert will appear to ask if you're sure.

This alert has a useful button, Merge, which provides an opportunity to merge the calendar with another rather than just blowing it (and all the events it contains) away.

Click Merge to select another calendar to merge this one with, click Delete to delete it, or click Cancel to do neither. Note that you can't merge calendars you subscribe to such as Found in Apps, Birthdays, US Holidays, and others — you can only turn them off.

⚠️
WARNING

When you delete a calendar, all the events and reminder items in that calendar are also deleted. Although you *can* undo a deleted calendar (choose Edit ➪ Undo or press ⌘+Z), you must do so before you quit Calendar. If you quit Calendar without undoing a calendar deletion, everything on that calendar (or calendars) will be gone forever (unless, of course, you have Time Machine or another backup, as I explain in Chapter 24).

WARNING

If you sync your calendars with iCloud or another cloud-based service, deleting the calendar will delete it from all your devices.

Creating and managing events

The heart of Calendar is the event. To create a new one, follow these steps:

1. **Choose File ⇨ New Event, press ⌘+N, double-click a date or time on the calendar in any view, or drag up or down anywhere on a date in Week or Day view.**

TIP

   If you double-click or click and drag on the day of the event, you can skip Step 2, and you don't need to specify the date in Step 3.

   Alternatively, try the Create Quick Event (+) icon. It's smart enough to interpret commands such as "Family Movie 7–10PM Thursday" and create a new event on the proper day and time, as shown in Figure 11-2.

2. **If the event doesn't appear in the proper place, just click it and drag it wherever you like.**

3. **To edit an event, select it and choose Edit ⇨ Edit Event, press ⌘+E, or double-click it to open its event bubble, as shown in Figure 11-2.**

   All the items can be edited. For example, click the date or time to change it. The other items — Repeat, Travel Time, and Alerts — are pop-up menus. The Alert menu is popped up in Figure 11-2. The green square in the upper-right corner of the event bubble is a pop-up menu that lets you select a different calendar for this event.

TIP

   The Travel Time item lets you add travel time to and from an event (and blocks out that time on your calendar) while preserving the event's start and end times.

4. **When you're satisfied with all of the event's items, press Return or click anywhere outside the event bubble.**

TIP

If you prefer working in a little window rather than the event bubble, check out the Edit ⇨ Show Inspector command (⌘+Option+I), which displays the selected event in a window. Click a different event on a calendar, and that event's info instantly fills the Inspector window. Try it; you might like it.

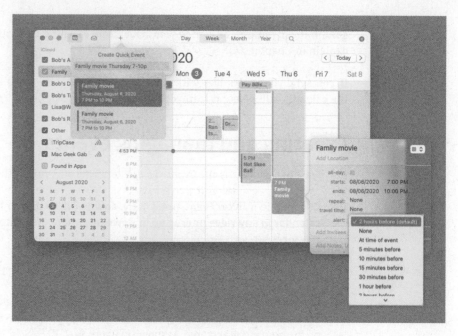

FIGURE 11-2:
Creating a Quick Event (upper left) and the resulting event bubble (lower right) for this three-hour event on my Family calendar.

TECHNICAL STUFF

What's the difference between the Get Info and Inspector windows? The Inspector window changes contextually and displays information about the currently selected event. Get Info windows, on the other hand, display info for a specific event. Put another way, a Get Info window displays the info for a specific event, and you can have as many Get Info windows on the screen as you like. There's only one Inspector window, though, and it displays info for whichever event is currently selected.

Inviting others to attend an event

To invite other people to your event, open the Contacts app or the Calendar Address panel (Window ⇨ Contacts) and drag the contacts onto the event in Calendar. Alternatively, you can type the first few letters of the name in the Invitees field for an event, and names that match magically appear. In Figure 11-3, I typed the letters *Stan L*, and Calendar offered me a choice of my two contacts with names that start with *Stan L* — Stan LeVitus and Stan Lee. Sweet! (If you're unfamiliar with Contacts, flip to Chapter 17 for details.)

After you add one or more invitees, click the Send button to invite them to the event. If the invitees have a compatible calendar application (Calendar, its predecessor iCal, Microsoft Outlook, and most calendar programs on most platforms), they can open the enclosure (included with your invitation email), which adds the event to Calendar with Accept, Decline, and Maybe buttons. All they have to do is click the appropriate button, and you receive an email informing you of their decision along with an enclosure that adds their response to the event in Calendar. Nice, eh?

FIGURE 11-3:
Invite people to
your event.

It doesn't always work with some third-party mail programs, but the majority of people use either Apple Mail, Google Calendar, or Microsoft Outlook, which do the right thing with Calendar invitations.

If the invitee doesn't have a compatible calendar app (or doesn't open the enclosure that was included with the email invitation), he or she has to respond the old-fashioned way: by replying to your email, texting, or calling you on the telephone.

Setting an alert

What's the point of putting an event on your calendar if you forget it? If you set an alert, Calendar won't let you forget. To set an alert, click None (just to the right of the word *alert)* in the Event info window or Inspector. Now choose a time for the alert from the menu (shown in Figure 11-2) or choose Custom for more options. I find the custom Email alerts so useful that I use them for almost every event I create.

You can have as many alerts as you like for each event. When you add the first alert to an event, a +-in-a-circle will appear to its right when you hover the cursor over the alert pop-up menu; click the + to create a second (or third or fifteenth) alert.

To remove an alert, click the pop-up menu to the right of the word *alert* and choose None from the pop-up menu.

TIP

You can choose separate default alerts for Events, All Day Events, and Birthdays in Calendar Preferences. Choose Calendar ⇨ Preferences or press ⌘+ (type the comma), and then click the Alerts tab at the top of the window.

All the features mentioned so far are wonderful, but my favorite Calendar feature is the alert. I rarely miss an important event anymore; Calendar reminds me of them with time to spare. Better still, I sync events and alerts among my Mac and iPhone and iPad. So, when I create an event or alert on any device, within a few minutes — through the magic of iCloud — it appears on the other devices.

Reminders: Protection Against Forgetting

Reminders help you stay organized. Unlike an event, a reminder item isn't necessarily associated with a particular day or time (although it can be). Furthermore, reminders can be associated with a location, which is handier on an iDevice than on a Mac, but a great feature if you have such a device. Finally, reminders can have a priority level of low, medium, high, or none.

If you have an iDevice and sync with iCloud, Microsoft Exchange, or Office 365, your reminders will appear simultaneously on all your Apple devices — other Macs, iPhones, iPads, and iPod touches — which means you should never miss a reminder. Just set a reminder on your Mac or any iDevice, and you'll never forget anything.

Getting started with Reminders

Before you create or manage your own reminders, you should know a couple of things, starting with the concept of lists. Reminders includes a list called Reminders by default. You can delete or rename it if you like, and you can create additional lists if you care to by choosing File ⇨ New List, pressing ⌘+Shift + N, or clicking the Add List icon (+) at the bottom of the window.

I like to have a bunch of lists with names such as Sooner, Later, and Out and About. And Reminders creates a separate section for completed items when you click the circle before each reminder's name to indicate a task is done, like *A completed reminder* and *Another completed reminder* in Figure 11-4.

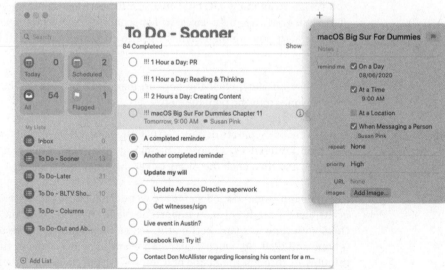

FIGURE 11-4: When a list (To Do - Sooner) is selected in the sidebar, its reminders are displayed on the right.

After you select the circle for an item, the item is moved to the completed list. To see completed items, click Show near the upper-right corner of the window, choose View⇨ Show Completed, or press ⌘+Shift+H. When shown, completed items appear at the end of the list below uncompleted items.

The aforementioned Show commands change to Hide when completed items are showing; click Hide, choose View⇨ Hide Completed, or press ⌘+Shift+H again.

Here are more helpful techniques for working with lists:

>> **To rename a list:** Right- or Control-click the list, choose Rename from the contextual menu, type the new name, and press Return when you're done. Or select the list, press Return, type the new name, and then press Return again when you're done.

>> **To display a list in a separate window:** Double-click the list name; right- or Control-click the list, and choose Open List in New Window from the contextual menu; choose Window ⇨ Open in New Window; or press ⌘+Return.

>> **To show or hide the sidebar:** Choose View ⇨ Show/Hide Sidebar or press ⌘+Option+S.

TIP

You don't have to have more than one list. You don't even have to change the default list name (Reminders). That being said, I like having Reminders organized into separate To-Do lists. The point is that you can make a bunch of lists or dump everything into a single list; just use lists to organize your reminders so they make sense to you.

Finally, the four boxes near the top of the sidebar — Today, Scheduled, All, and Flagged — are preconfigured smart lists. To hide a smart list, choose View⇨ Show Smart List⇨ and then select the smart list to remove its check mark and hide it. Or right- or Control-click the smart list and choose Hide.

To do or not to do: Setting reminders

The preceding sections tell you pretty much everything about reminders except how to create one, so it's time to find out how to create a reminder. It couldn't be easier: Just choose File ⇨ New Reminder; press ⌘+N; click the + at the top-right corner of the Reminders window; or click the first blank line in a list and begin typing.

Ah, but there's much more to a reminder, including:

>> Reminding you at a specific time on a specific date (as shown in Figure 11-4)

>> Repeatedly reminding you at a specified interval

>> Reminding you at a specific location (as shown in Figure 11-5)

FIGURE 11-5:
Location-based
reminders are
super handy.

If you have an iPhone, location-based reminders are the best. Give them a try, and I'm sure you'll be as hooked as I am. As you can see in Figure 11-5, the next time I am near HEB (our local grocery store), I'll receive an alert notification from Reminders that says *Get bacon.* That's sweet!

Reminders can also have a priority and notes. To access these features, you need to Show Info for the reminder by choosing View ⇨ Show Info; pressing ⌘+I; clicking the little *i* that appears on the right side of the reminder (hover your cursor over the right side of the reminder if you don't see it); or double-click a blank spot on the reminder.

To change the order of reminders in a list, choose View ⇨ Sort By and then choose Due Date, Priority, Creation Date, or Title. Or choose Manual and control the item order yourself by clicking a blank spot on any reminder and then dragging it to its new position.

Also, reminders can have subtasks (such as the two subtasks below the *Update my Will* reminder in Figure 11-4: *Update Advance Directive paperwork* and *Get witnesses/ sign.* To create a subtask, choose View⇨ Indent Reminder or press ⌘ +]; to promote a subtask, choose View⇨Outdent Reminder or press ⌘ + [. If the subtask is below the wrong reminder, click a blank spot on the subtask and drag it where you want it. You can show or hide all subtasks by choosing View⇨Show/Hide All Subtasks or by pressing ⌘+E (show) or ⌘+Shift+E (hide).

Sharing lists and assigning reminders

Although list sharing has been in Reminders for a while, assigning reminders to people you share lists with is a new thing in Big Sur. Because you can assign a reminder only to someone you've shared a list with, you'll look at sharing lists first.

To share a list, right- or Control-click the list and choose Share List, or click the list to select it and then choose File⇨Share List. A sheet appears with options for Mail, Messages, AirDrop, and Copy Link. However you choose to share the list, the recipient will get a link that adds the list to his or her reminders, synchronizing changes in (almost) real time.

I share a shopping list called Groceries with my wife. That way, either of us can pull out our iPhone and see what's on the Groceries list in Reminders. We mark items we buy as Completed, which is also synced in near real-time. It's convenient, handy, and easy to set up.

NEW

After you've shared a list, you can assign its reminders to anyone with whom you've shared the list. To assign a reminder, right- or Control-click the reminder and then choose Assign⇨*person's name,* or click the reminder to select it and then choose Edit⇨Assign⇨*person's name.*

One more thing: You can view your Reminders in any web browser on any device by logging into www.icloud.com and clicking Reminders. You'll see the same lists and reminders that you see on your Macs and iDevices. You can't share lists or assign reminders (at this time), but you can manage existing reminders or create ones at icloud.com, which can be handy when you're stuck somewhere without your Apple devices.

Everything You Need to Know about Notification Center

The item in Figure 11-6 should look familiar to those of you who use an iPhone, iPad, or iPod touch — it's Big Sur's rendition of Notification Center.

FIGURE 11-6:
Calendar and Screen Time alert banners (top), Notification Center's Up Next widget (middle), with a Reminders widget (lower left) and Weather widget (lower right).

Notification Center manages and displays alerts from any app that supports Apple's notifications protocol. You can show or hide Notification Center by either clicking the clock icon in your menu bar or by swiping from the right edge of your trackpad to the left with two fingers.

Tweaking Notification settings

You manage which apps display notifications in the Notifications System Preferences pane. Choose ➪ System Preferences or click the System Preferences icon in the dock, and then click the Notifications icon.

On the left side of the Notification Center System Preferences pane, you'll find a list of all installed apps that support notifications. To specify the settings for an app, click it once in the list to select it. The selected app offers some or all of the following options:

>> **To turn off notifications for the app:** Deselect the Allow Notifications From on/off switch near the top of the window.

TIP

>> **To specify the alert style for the app:** Click the Alert Style you prefer: None, Banners, or Alerts. Alerts remain onscreen until you dismiss them; banners appear in the upper-right corner for a few seconds before fading away.

To make a banner reappear after it fades away, just click the clock in your menu bar or use the two-fingered trackpad swipe as just described.

>> **To see notifications for this app on the Lock Screen:** Enable the Show Notifications on Lock Screen check box.

>> **To see notifications for this app in Notification Center:** Enable the Show in Notification Center check box.

>> **To see the number of new notifications for the app on its dock icon:** Select the Badge App Icon check box.

>> **To hear a sound when receiving notifications:** Select the Play Sound for Notifications check box.

>> **To display a preview for this app's notifications:** Choose Always (the default), When Unlocked, or Never in the Show Previews pop-up menu.

>> **To change how apps are grouped in Notification Center:** Click the Notification Grouping pop-up menu and choose Off, By App, or Automatic (which groups them by time with the most recent notifications first).

One more Notification Center item worth mentioning is Do Not Disturb, the first item in the list on the left side of your Notifications System Preferences pane.

TIP

If you don't see Do Not Disturb, make sure you've scrolled all the way up to the top of the list.

Enable the Do Not Disturb switch to temporarily silence alerts and banners during the specified hours. To specify the hours in which Do Not Disturb is in effect, choose ◆ ⇨ System Preferences or click the System Preferences icon in the dock and then click the Notifications icon. Or click the little gear at the bottom-right of Notification Center, which is a shortcut that opens the Notifications Preferences pane instantly. Either way, click the first item in the list, Do Not Disturb, to turn on Do Not Disturb automatically, with check boxes to enable the following:

>> Turn on Do Not Disturb automatically between the hours of *x* and *x*.

>> Turn on Do Not Disturb when the display is sleeping.

>> Turn on Do Not Disturb when the screen is locked.

>> Turn on Do Not Disturb when mirroring to TVs and projectors.

In addition, two check boxes allow for specific exceptions when Do Not Disturb is turned on:

>> Allow calls from everyone.

>> Allow repeated calls.

If you allow repeated calls, a second call from the same person within three minutes will not be silenced.

You can also enable Do Not Disturb manually by clicking the Control Center icon on the menu bar and then clicking Do Not Disturb. A list of options appears with four choices—For 1 Hour, Until This Evening, Until Tomorrow, and Always On. Click your choice to enable it.

Widget management 101

To manage the Widgets displayed in Notification Center, click the clock icon to display Notification Center, and then click the Edit Widgets button at its bottom.

A list of widgets available in Notification Center appears on the left side of the screen (as shown in Figure 11-7), with details displayed in the middle. Note that most widgets offer three sizes—Small, Medium (selected), and Large, as represented by the three little buttons (S, M, L) below the Up Next calendar widget. Small widgets display less information than Medium widgets; Medium widgets display less info than Large widgets; and not all widgets come in all sizes. I suggest trying all sizes of widgets you prefer to determine which size works best given your work style and screen size.

To add a widget to Notification Center, start by clicking a size button (if available), and then double-clicking the widget.

To move a widget to a different spot, click and drag it (on the right side of the screen) to its new location.

Finally, many widgets offer additional options, such as the Reminder list or Calendar it will display, the zip code (for weather forecasts), and stock symbols it will display. To access such options, click the widget on the right side of the screen. If options are available, the widget will spin around to display them on its backside, as shown in Figure 11-8 for the Weather widget. When you've finished working with a widget's options, click Done.

Finally, to rearrange widgets, click a widget on the right side of the Edit Widgets screen and drag it to its new location.

FIGURE 11-7:
The Edit Widgets screen with all available widgets on the left (and middle) and your current widget lineup on the right.

Forecast
Weather

Done

See the current weather conditions and forecast for a location.

Location   Austin

FIGURE 11-8:
The backside of the Weather widget lets you specify a location for your forecasts.

Data provided by The Weather Channel

When you're happy with your widget lineup and arrangement, click the Done button.

Using Notification Center

Now, here's a quick rundown of ways you can use Notification Center:

>> **To respond to a notification:** Click the banner or alert before it disappears. Or open Notification Center, and then click the notification to launch its app.

   If you hover the pointer over banners, you may see additional options such as the ability to reply to an email or message without launching Mail or Messages. Give it a try!

TIP

>> **To repeat a notification in nine minutes:** Click its Snooze button.

>> **To close all notifications for an app:** Hover the pointer over a notification. If the app has more than one notification, the little X in its upper-left corner (which would close only this notification) transmogrifies into Clear All. Click Clear All to close all notifications from that app.

Use Notes for Making Notes

Notes is an electronic notepad for your Mac. A note is a convenient place to jot quick notes, recipes, phone numbers, or whatever. Some notes are shown in Figure 11-9.

To create a new note, choose File ➪ New Note; press ⌘+N; or click the button with the little square and pencil in the toolbar.

Notes is supremely flexible; here are just a few things you can do:

TIP

>> **Double-click a note to open it in its own window** so you can drag it around onscreen by its title bar.

After opening a note in its own window, if you want the note to float in front of other windows so it's always visible, choose Window ➪ Float on Top.

>> **Change text** to any font, color, size, and style by selecting it and using the myriad of tools in the Format menu and Style icon (Aa).

>> **Search for a word or phrase** in any note by typing your query in the Search box.

>> **Create bulleted, numbered, or dashed lists** by selecting the text and choosing Format ➪ Font ➪ Lists. (Ingredients is a bulleted list, and Directions is a numbered list in Figure 11-9.)

>> **Create folders** (Notes and Imported Notes in Figure 11-9) to organize your notes by choosing File ➪ New Folder, pressing ⌘+Shift+N, or clicking the New Folder button at the bottom of the Folder list.

WARNING

The Notes window must be selected to create a folder. If a note in a window is active, the New Folder command will be unavailable. So click the main Notes window if the New Folder command is grayed out. Or click the New Note icon in the toolbar, which is enabled even when working with a note in a separate window.

FIGURE 11-9:
Notes is for making notes on your Mac.

REMEMBER

Folders in the Notes application are exclusive to Notes. In other words, the folders described in the following bullets aren't folders in Finder. You won't find them on your hard drive; they live only in the Notes app (and iCloud or other Internet accounts if you've enabled them). And also remember that folders are optional. If you don't have a ton of notes, keeping them all in a single folder and using the Search box to filter them may work for you.

>> **Show or hide the Folders list** by choosing View ⇨ Show/Hide Folders or pressing ⌘+Option+S.

>> **Show only notes in a folder** by clicking the folder name in the Folders list, or click All iCloud to see all your notes.

>> **Automatically sync notes with your iDevice by using iCloud or other Internet Accounts** by choosing Notes ⇨ Accounts, which will open the Internet Accounts System Preferences pane; then click the appropriate Internet account — such as Office 365 or Gmail — and enable its check box to sync Notes.

>> **Send the contents of a note via the Mail or Messages app** by choosing File ⇨ Share or clicking the Share icon.

>> **Print a note** by choosing File ⇨ Print or pressing ⌘+P.

TIP

Whatever you type in a note is saved automatically as you type it, so Notes has no Save, Save As, or Duplicate commands.

Moving right along, here are more useful features in Notes:

>> You can drag and drop photos, PDFs, videos, and other files into any note.

>> The Attachments browser displays every external file you've dragged into every note in a single place, making it easier to find things. Choose View ⇨ Show/Hide Attachments Browser or use its keyboard shortcut ⌘+3 to see the Attachments Browser in action.

>> Use the Share menu in apps such as Safari and Maps to add content to Notes.

>> You can add checklists (in addition to bulleted, numbered, and dashed lists) by clicking the Checklist icon in the toolbar, by choosing Format ⇨ Checklist, or by using the shortcut ⌘+Shift+L.

And here are three more features you may find useful when creating notes:

>> You can add a table to any note by choosing Format ⇨ Table, by using its keyboard shortcut, ⌘+Option+T, or by clicking the Table icon in the toolbar.

>> You can format text as a title, heading, or body by choosing Format ⇨ Title, Heading, or Body or using their keyboard shortcuts ⌘+Shift+T, ⌘+Shift+H, or ⌘+Shift+B, respectively, as shown in Figure 11-10.

>> Notes appear in the list in chronological order with the most recently created note on top. You can pin a note to the top of the list, where it remains until you unpin it. To pin or unpin a note, click it once to select it and then choose File ⇨ Pin Note (or Unpin Note). Or right- or Control-click the note in the list and choose Pin Note (or Unpin Note).

You can also share your notes with others and allow them to edit them. Here's how it works: Click the Add People icon in the toolbar and choose how you'd like to send your invitation: Mail, Messages, Link, or AirDrop.

This is text formatted as TITLE.
This is text formatted as HEADING.
This is text formatted as BODY.

FIGURE 11-10:
Text in a note
formatted as title,
heading, and
body.

If the person you invite is also running Big Sur (or Catalina or Mojave), she'll see the note in her copy of Notes; if she's running any other operating system, the note will open in the iCloud website for editing. When she's done, you'll see her edits in Notes on your Mac (and other devices) within a few minutes.

Other Notes goodies include a spell checker, spoken notes, text substitutions (such as smart quotes and smart dashes), and transformations (such as Make Upper or Lowercase). You can find all these options on the Edit menu.

One more thing: Don't forget that you can use your iDevice as a camera or scanner by using Continuity Camera. (Chapter 23 has the details.)

You now know everything you need to know to use and enjoy Big Sur's Notes app!

Tracking Productivity with Screen Time

We can all use a break from our digital devices, and Apple's solution is Screen Time. Although Screen Time includes the parental controls that used to appear in the Parental Controls System Preferences pane, this new feature is about policing your own behavior as well as the behavior of others in your family (if you so desire).

If you have an iDevice, you're probably familiar with Screen Time, which provides insight into how you spend your time on your iPhone or other iDevices, including which apps you used and websites you visited and for how long you. On the Mac, Screen Time is a System Preferences pane (choose ⇨ System Preferences or click the System Preferences Dock icon).

Today's date appears at the top of the pane by default. Use the arrows on either side of the Today button near the upper-right corner to view days before or after the day being displayed, or click the Today button to return to your stats for today. If you have other devices using Screen Time, you'll see a pop-up menu at the bottom of the window; click it and choose what you see in Screen Time: All Devices or any individual device.

And if you're using Family Sharing, click your name below your picture to set Screen Time options for other family members.

All action takes place in the seven tabs in the sidebar on the left, namely:

>> **App Usage:** Displays details about the apps you used and how long you used them.

>> **Notifications:** Displays the number of notifications you received on this day and the time you received them.

>> **Pickups:** Shows you how many times you picked up your devices.

>> **Downtime:** Sets a schedule for times when only apps you have specifically allowed during downtime are available. A reminder appears 5 minutes before downtime starts.

>> **App Limits:** Sets time limits for apps and app categories.

>> **Always Allowed:** Enables the check box for apps you want to remain available during downtime.

>> **Content & Privacy:** Replaces the Parental Controls options in earlier versions of macOS. Enable or disable content by type, Apple online store, or specific app, as well as allow or disallow passcode changes, account changes, and other options for which you may want to restrict changes.

Finally, the Options button at the bottom of the sidebar offers two choices. Share Across Devices enables reporting for this Mac to be shared with your other devices. Screen Time Passcode lets you secure your Screen Time settings with a passcode and allow more time when limits expire.

» **Working with Siri**

» **Making Siri your very own**

Chapter **12**

Are You Siri-ous?

f you aren't familiar with Siri, Apple's intelligent digital assistant, you will be after reading this chapter. Although Siri made her first appearance on the iPhone 4s back in 2011 and has appeared on iPads, iPod touches, and even Apple TVs, it's been available on the Mac only since 2016. (It first appeared in macOS Sierra.)

Siri is designed to help you get things done using your voice, and the Mac incarnation does it with aplomb. Big Sur's rendition of Siri offers new capabilities designed specifically for your Mac, which means you can search for information, find files, send messages, and much, much more using only your voice.

NEW

According to Apple, Big Sur's new and improved Siri helps you find answers to more questions using information from across the web. To be honest, I haven't noticed much difference, but don't let that stop you from integrating Siri into your workflow. If you haven't tried Siri, you should. And if you're already a Siri fan, the latest rendition works the same as before.

Finally, Siri is optimized to work well with your Mac's built-in microphone, so you don't have to buy or connect a mic. That said, I think Siri (along with Dictation and Voice Control) works better with a wired or wireless headset, as I explain in Chapter 23.

What Siri Can Do for You

Before we get to the "how," let's look at what, exactly, Siri can do for you. Here's a short list of some cool things you can ask Siri to do:

>> **"Open the Microsoft Word document I worked on yesterday."**

>> **"Remind me to take the pizza out of the oven in 14 minutes."**

>> **"Add a meeting to my calendar at 11 a.m. tomorrow with Dr. Spock."**

>> **"Call Jacob LeVitus with FaceTime."**

>> **"Play songs by The Beatles."** This one works only if you have songs by The Beatles in your iTunes Library or subscribe to Apple Music, of course.

>> **"Call me 'Your Highness.'"** Replace "Your Highness" with, "Sir," "Madam," or anything else you like; Siri will refer to you by that name forevermore.

>> **"Who am I?"** If you forget who you are, Siri will remind you, as shown in Figure 12-1.

>> **"Call my wife on her cellphone."**

>> **"What song is this?"** If you've ever used Shazam to identify songs, Siri uses its technology. So, like the Shazam app, it can identify millions of songs after a brief listen.

>> **"Send a message to Lisa to reschedule dinner tomorrow."**

>> **"Find an ATM near here."**

>> **"Send an email to Jack Black that says, 'You rock.'"**

>> **"Show me pictures I took in Florence Italy"** or **"Show me all the pictures I took on Thanksgiving."**

>> **"What is the Dow at?"**

>> **"Send a tweet: 'Going on vacation. Smiley-face.'"** Siri will replace "Smiley-face" with a smiley-face emoji in the tweet.

>> **"I need directions to House of Blues."**

>> **"Who was the 19th president of the United States?"**

>> **"How many calories are in a blueberry muffin?"**

>> **"Wake me up at 8:30 in the morning."**

>> **"Who is pitching for the Yankees tonight?"**

>> **"Who won the Academy Award for Best Actor in 2003?"**

>> **"What is trending on Twitter?"**

TIP

Click the little question mark in a circle in the lower-left corner of Siri's speech bubbles to see more things you can ask, as shown in Figure 12-1.

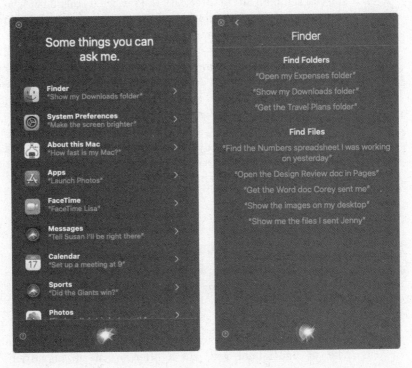

FIGURE 12-1: Tap any topic (left) for more suggestions (right).

Siri is relatively intelligent and understands many things in context. So, for example, if you ask, "Will I need an umbrella this weekend?" Siri will grok that you're looking for a weather forecast. Siri is also smart about using your personal information, so you can say, "Remind me to call Mom at 8 p.m." When the time comes, Siri will offer a list of your mom's phone numbers. And if Siri can't determine who "Mom" is, she'll ask you — and then, in the future, Siri will remember your mother.

You can also ask things such as, "What's the traffic like around here?" or "Where can I get cheap gas around here?" Siri knows where, precisely, "here" is based on your Mac's current location.

Now that you've had a glimpse of the kinds of things Siri will do for you, let's dive in and take a look at how to actually *use* Siri.

Working with Siri

You can summon Siri in three easy ways: Click its menu bar icon or its icon in the Applications folder (and shown in the margin), or use its keyboard shortcut: Press and hold down ⌘+spacebar.

TIP

If you pressed and held down ⌘+spacebar and Spotlight appeared instead of Siri, you didn't press and hold down long enough. Keep both keys pressed for two or three seconds and Siri will be at your beck and call. Pressing and releasing them any faster summons Spotlight, not Siri.

Moving right along, when you've summoned Siri, a bubble will appear near the top-right corner of your screen, and Siri asks its favorite question: "What can I help you with?" as shown in Figure 12-2.

FIGURE 12-2:
Speak now or Siri will bug you . . . .

At this juncture, you need to start talking to your Mac. If you don't, or if Siri can't hear or understand you, she'll offer a list of suggestions, as shown in Figure 12-1.

REMEMBER

You can always click the little question mark in a circle in the lower-left corner of Siri's speech bubbles to see the list.

That's really all there is to it. Just remember two things: how to invoke Siri, and how to ask it a question or give it a command. That's all. Well, that's all except for one last thing: how to customize Siri to your liking.

Making Siri Your Own

Using Siri couldn't be easier: You summon it, ask or tell it to do something, and then wait for that something to be done. But you can invoke several tweaks that can help make Siri sound and behave the way you prefer.

You manage Siri in its System Preferences pane (⌘⇨System Preferences⇨Siri).

You can't change much, but here's what you can customize and how to do it:

>> **Enable Ask Siri check box:** Deselect the box to disable Siri (it's selected/enabled by default).

>> **Keyboard Shortcut menu:** If you don't care for the default ⌘+spacebar keyboard shortcut, this menu lets you change it to anything you like.

>> **Language menu:** Use this menu to select the language Siri will speak and understand from a long list — including nine varieties of English; four varieties each of Chinese, French, and Spanish; and dozens of others.

TIP

Siri is known to have difficulty understanding people with distinct accents. If it has trouble understanding you, look in the Languages menu for a different version of the language. It couldn't hurt, and it might just help.

>> **Siri Voice menu:** Select the gender and nationality of your Siri. You can choose a female or male to speak with an American, an Australian, a British, an Irish, or a South African accent.

>> **Voice Feedback radio buttons:** These buttons allow you to enable or disable voice feedback. Do you want to hear Siri's dulcet tones? Click the On button. Do you prefer that Siri keep its mouth shut and just type its replies? If so, click the Off button.

>> **Delete Siri & Dictation History button:** If you say something you shouldn't have said and want to eradicate any record of it, click this button.

>> **Show Siri in Menu Bar check box:** This option does what you'd expect — it allows you to disable Siri's menu bar icon, which is enabled by default.

And that's pretty much all you need to know to use and customize Siri in Big Sur.

TIP

I'd like to mention two more things before we move on:

>> Siri requires an active Internet connection. If you aren't connected to the Internet, you can't use Siri.

>> Although I mentioned that Siri isn't great with heavily accented voices, I forgot to tell you that it's just as bad at recognizing your words when your environment is noisy. If Siri misunderstands you frequently and changing languages didn't help, try moving your face closer to your Mac and speaking in the direction of its microphone. Or try using a headset or other higher-quality microphone; most third-party headsets and microphones work better with Siri than the built-in mic on your Mac.

Chapter **13**

Maps Are Where It's At

 f you know how to use the Maps app on your iPhone, iPad, or iPod touch, you already know most of what you need to know to use Maps on your Mac.

As for the rest of you — the ones without iOS devices — I'll have you up to speed RealSoonNow™.

Finding Your Current Location with Maps

I'll start with something supremely simple yet extremely useful: determining your current location. At the risk of sounding like a self-help guru, here's how to find yourself. Launch the Maps application from the dock, Launchpad, or Applications folder, and then click the Current Location icon, which is a little arrowhead (shown in the margin) and found on the toolbar at the top of the window.

Your location is indicated by a blue dot. I clicked the arrowhead in the toolbar, and the blue dot displayed my location, as shown in Figure 13-1.

REMEMBER

If you tap or drag the map, your Mac continues to update your location but won't re-center the blue marker — meaning that the blue dot can scroll (or zoom) off the screen. If that happens, click the Current Location icon again to center the map on your current location again.

FIGURE 13-1:
I am here.

Of course, this and many other Maps features rely on an active Internet connection and having Location Services enabled (System Preferences⇨Security & Privacy⇨Privacy tab).

Use the − and + icons in the lower-right corner (or the scroll control on your mouse or trackpad) to zoom in and out on the map.

TIP

Finding a Person, Place, or Thing

To find a person, place, or thing with Maps, choose Edit⇨Find, press ⌘+F, or click in the Search field in the center of the toolbar (where it says Search for a Place or Address), and then type what you're looking for. You can search for addresses, zip codes, intersections, towns, landmarks, and businesses by category and by name, or combinations, such as *New York, NY 10022, pizza 60645,* or *Texas State Capitol.*

If the letters you type match names stored in your Mac (or iDevice) Contacts app (see Chapter 16), the matching contacts appear in a list below the Search field. Click a name to see a map of that contact's location. The Maps app is smart about it, too, displaying only the names of contacts that have a street address.

TIP

If you don't find a match in the list, press Return, and with any luck, a map will appear within a few seconds. If you search for a single location, it's marked with a single bubble. If you search for a category (*BBQ Lockhart TX,* for example), you may see multiple bubbles, one for each matching location (4 BBQ joints in Lockhart, TX), as shown in Figure 13-2.

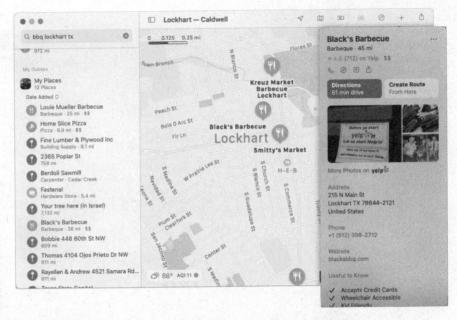

FIGURE 13-2:
Bubbles indicate matching locations; click a bubble to see its details.

TIP

You can search for all sorts of things, including intersections, neighborhoods, landmarks, restaurants, and businesses. Furthermore, you can combine several items, such as pizza and a zip code. The Maps app is adept at interpreting search terms and finding the right place. After you use the app a few times, you'll be as addicted as I am.

To find out more, click a name in the list below the Search field or click a pin. An overlay with details appears (refer to Figure 13-2).

This handy little info window sometimes contains reviews or photos or both (neither is visible in Figure 13-2), so scroll through the overlay to read reviews or view pictures.

Views, Zooms, and Pans

The preceding section talks about how to find just about anything with Maps, and the following section shows ways to use what you find. But before doing that, I want to take a little detour and explore how you can work with Maps.

Click the View icon on the toolbar to choose Default, Transit, or Satellite view (see Figure 13-3), all of which can be viewed also in 3D. Just FYI, Figure 13-1 shows Satellite view in 2D; Figure 13-2 shows Default view in 2D; Figure 13-3 shows Transit view in 2D; and Figure 13-4 shows Satellite view in 3D.

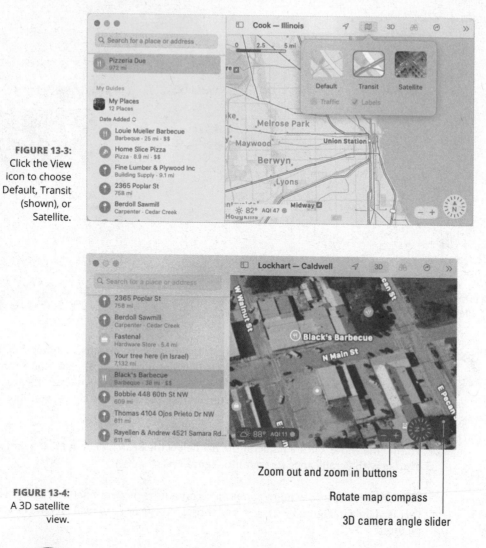

FIGURE 13-3:
Click the View icon to choose Default, Transit (shown), or Satellite.

FIGURE 13-4:
A 3D satellite view.

Zoom out and zoom in buttons

Rotate map compass

3D camera angle slider

WARNING

3D

3D maps aren't available in every area. It appears that the more populated the area, the more likely it is available in 3D.

Speaking of which, to display a 3D map click the 3D icon in the toolbar (shown in the margin), choose View⇨Show 3D Map, or press Shift+⌘+1. You may have to zoom in for the map to appear in 3D.

Moving right along, these tools are available in all views, in 2D or 3D:

>> **To zoom in:** Choose View ⇨ Zoom In or press ⌘++ (plus sign). If you have a trackpad, you can also expand (spread two fingers) to zoom in (just like on an iPhone).

>> **To zoom out:** Choose View ⇨ Zoom Out or press ⌘+− (minus sign). If you have a trackpad, you can also pinch to zoom out (just like on an iPhone).

If you have a scroll-wheel mouse, you can use the wheel to zoom in and out.

You can also click the tiny + (zoom in) and − (zoom out) icons in the lower-right corner of the window.

>> **To scroll:** Hold down the mouse or trackpad button and drag left, right, up, or down. If you have a trackpad, drag using two fingers.

If you click and then fling your mouse in any direction (or flick with two fingers on a trackpad), you'll "fly over" the ground below. It's usually not useful, but it's fun and looks cool.

>> **To rotate the map:** Click the compass in the lower-right corner and drag.

Finally, to adjust the camera angle in 3D views, press the Option key before you click and drag on the map (Option+drag with two fingers on a trackpad), or click and drag on the little slider in the lower-right corner (shown in Figure 13-4).

Maps and Contacts

Maps and Contacts (see Chapter 16) go together like peanut butter and jelly. For example, if you want to see a map of a contact's street address, type a few letters of the contact's name in the Search field and click the name in the list that automatically appears.

If you're in the Contacts app, it's even easier: Hover your pointer over a street address and click the little blue pin that appears to its right, as shown in Figure 13-5. Maps will then open with a pin at the address.

After you find a location by typing an address in Maps, you can add that location to your contacts.

First, click the location's bubble on the map. Then, either click the ellipsis in the upper-right corner of the Info sheet and choose Create New Contact or scroll to the bottom of the Info sheet and click Create New Contact near the bottom of the sheet.

FIGURE 13-5:
Click the little
blue pin to see
this address in
Maps.

You can also get driving directions to and from most locations, including a contact's address, to most other locations, including another contact's address. You see how to do that in the "Smart Map Tricks" section, later in the chapter.

Time-saving Map Tools: Favorites, Guides, and Recents

The Maps app offers three tools in its sidebar that can save you from having to type the same locations over and over.

Favorites

Favorites in the Maps app, like favorites in Safari, lets you return to a location without typing a single character. To make a location a favorite, click its bubble on the map, and then either click the ellipsis in the upper-right corner of the Info sheet and choose Add to Favorites or scroll to the bottom of the Info sheet and click the Add to Favorites button.

You can also add a favorite by clicking the little + that appears to the right of the word Favorites. The little chevron that also appears when you hover your cursor over Favorites is a disclosure triangle. Click it and you'll see either all or none of your favorites.

After you add a favorite, you can recall it at any time.

TIP

The first items you should add as favorites are your home address and work address. You use these addresses all the time with Maps, so you might as well add them now to avoid typing them over and over.

Here's how to manage your favorites:

>> **To move a favorite up or down in the Favorites list:** Click and drag the favorite upward to move it higher in the list or downward to move it lower in the list.

>> **To delete a favorite from the Favorites list:** Right- or Control-click the favorite and choose Delete from the pop-up menu.

Guides

NEW

Guides are collections of places that you can create and share with others. A few big cities such as San Francisco, New York, London, and Los Angeles will have guides created by "brands you trust" (at least according to Apple).

The cool thing about guides is that they update automatically, so if you share them with others, their guide will update if you add or delete locations from it.

To create a guide, hover your cursor over the word Guides and click the little + that appears to its right. A new guide named New Guide appears. Right- or Control-click your new guide to do the following:

>> **Edit the guide.** Changes the name of this guide, add or change its photo, or delete it.

>> **Add a new place.** Opens an overlay where you can search for a place or choose one from your Recents list by clicking its + button.

>> **Duplicate the guide.** Creates a copy of this guide.

>> **Open the guide in a new tab or window.** Does what it says.

>> **Share.** A submenu that provides the standard share options — Mail, Messages, AirDrop, Notes, and Reminders.

>> **Send the guide to a device.** A submenu that lists all Apple devices nearby; select one to send this guide to it.

And there you have all you need to know to create and share Big Sur's new guides.

Recents

The Maps app automatically remembers every location you've searched for in its Recents list (unless you've cleared it, as described next). Click Recents to see your recent searches; click the item's name to see it on the map.

To clear the Recents list, scroll down if necessary until you see Clear Recents at the bottom of the list.

To clear a single location from your Recents list, right- or Control-click it and choose Delete.

Smart Map Tricks

The Maps app has more tricks up its sleeve. This section lists a few nifty features you may find useful.

Get route maps and driving directions

You can get route maps and driving directions to any location from any other location in a couple of ways:

>> **If a bubble is already on the screen:** Click it, and then click the Directions button on its Info sheet Click in the My Location field to choose where the directions begin.

>> **When you're looking at a map screen:** Click the Directions button on the toolbar (shown in the margin). The Directions overlay appears with Start and End fields at the top. When you click in either field, a drop-down list appears with your current location and a few recent locations. If you don't see what you need, type a few letters and choose the location in the list that appears. To swap the starting and ending locations, click the little swirly arrow to the right of the Start and End fields.

If you need to change the start or end location, click the little x-in-a-circle to the right of its name to erase it and try again.

When the start and end fields have been filled, press Tab or Return and step-by-step directions appear in an overlay, as shown in Figure 13-6.

Maps will often suggest several routes. The suggestions appear on the map with the selected route in darker blue (the 37-minute route is selected in Figure 13-6). The alternate routes are shown on the map in lighter blue, and cartoon balloons that tell you how long it will take (42 or 43 minutes, respectively). Click a cartoon balloon or alternate route in the list to select it. The selected route always appears in dark blue; alternate routes always appear in a lighter shade of blue.

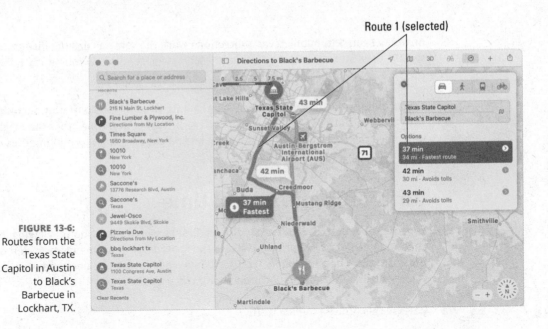

FIGURE 13-6:
Routes from the Texas State Capitol in Austin to Black's Barbecue in Lockhart, TX.

Click a blue line or cartoon balloon to select a route, as in Figure 13-6, where the first (and fastest) route is selected.

Click the chevron to the right of a route to see step-by-step directions for it.

After you've selected your route, you can print the directions (File ➪ Print or ⌘+P), share them (File ➪ Share), or send them to any nearby Apple device (File ➪ Send to Device).

When you're finished with the step-by-step directions, click the Directions button to close the Directions sidebar.

Get walking directions

For step-by-step directions for walking, click the Walk icon above the Start and End fields. Walking directions generally look a lot like driving directions except for your travel time.

Get directions for public transportation

Big Sur's Maps app offers directions for using public transportation in more cities than ever. That's the good news. The bad news is that unless you live in a relatively large city, it may be a while (and possibly a long while, depending on the size of your city) before such directions are available for your hometown.

As far as I can tell, public transit directions work the same as driving directions; specify your start and end points and Maps suggests several routes via public transit.

TIP

If you zoom in far enough you can see the entrances to transportation facilities such as train stations. Also, to see the effect of leaving at a time other than right now, click the Leave Soon drop-down menu and choose 30, 60, or 120 minutes or Custom to specify another time.

Get traffic info in real time

You can find out the traffic conditions for whatever map you're viewing by choosing View ⇨ Show Traffic or clicking the Show drop-down menu lower-left on the map and choosing Show Traffic. When you do this, major roadways are color-coded to inform you of the current traffic speed.

TIP

Reverse this process to hide traffic.

Here's the key to those colors: Orange means 25 to 50 miles per hour; red means under 25; and no color means no data is available at this time.

WARNING

Traffic info isn't available in every location, but the only way to find out is to give it a try. If color codes don't appear, assume that traffic information doesn't work for that particular location.

Flyovers and look arounds

Certain cities and landmarks include cool additional features such as 3D flyover tours and *look around,* which you can use to explore select cities in an interactive 3D experience, panning 360° and moving smoothly through streets.

Flyovers

To try a flyover, first search for a city or landmark by name and select it; if a 3D flyover tour is available for it, you'll see the Flyover Tour button on its Info sheet, as shown in Figure 13-7. Click the button to watch the flyover tour; click the little x-in-a-circle at the bottom of the window to end the tour.

FIGURE 13-7:
Click the Flyover
Tour button to
watch the 3D
flyover tour of the
Statue of Liberty.

Look arounds

Look arounds are rare but interesting when you find them. You can start a look around by clicking the Look Around icon in the toolbar. The map screen changes to look around view, where you can click to move (or look) in any direction, as shown in Figure 13-8. If the Look Around icon is light gray and nothing happens when you click it, a look around doesn't exist for that location.

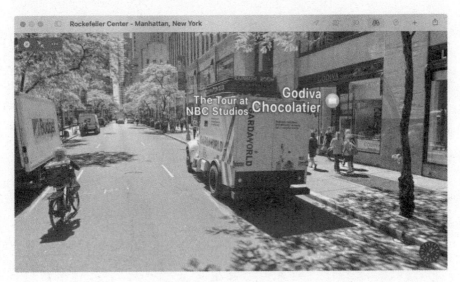

FIGURE 13-8:
A look around
view near
Rockefeller
Center in
Manhattan.

Do more on the Info sheet

As I explain earlier in this chapter, after clicking a location's bubble you can get directions to or from that location, add the location to your favorites or contacts, or create a new contact from it. But you can do three more things with a location from its Info sheet:

>> Click the phone number to call it.

>> Click the email address to launch the Mail app and send an email to it.

>> Click the URL to launch Safari and view its website.

And that, my friends, should be all you need to know to get you anywhere you want to go with Maps.

Chapter **14**

Apps Born in iOS

This chapter covers four apps that have been around on the iPhone and iPad for years, but only made their debut on the Mac a couple of years back (macOS Mojave). They should be familiar to anyone who uses an iOS device:

» Stocks lets you monitor information about specific stocks and the market in general.

» News gathers stories from myriad publications in one convenient place.

» Voice Memos lets you record (what else?) memos with your voice.

» Home lets you control your HomeKit-enabled smart devices such as lights, thermostats, and locks.

None of the four is earthshattering as a Mac app, but all can be useful if you need what they provide. More Mac apps that started out as iOS apps are coming up in Chapters 19 and 20. For now, just dive right in with Stocks.

Taking Stock of the Market with Stocks

If you're familiar with the Stocks app from your iDevices, you're in for a treat because the Big Sur Stocks app features an all-new design that makes it easy to view stock quotes, interactive charts, and top business news (from Apple News, which is covered in the next section).

When you launch Stocks for the first time, it's populated with a default set of quotes and indexes that Apple thinks you might appreciate, as shown in Figure 14-1. Note that if you have an Apple ID and have selected securities in the Stocks app prior to Big Sur, your selections will appear instead.

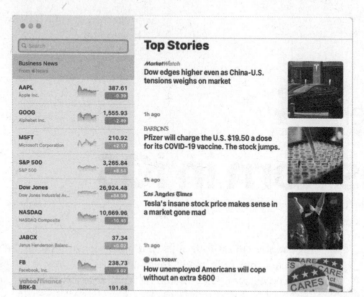

FIGURE 14-1:
The Stocks app comes stocked with a handful of securities and indexes chosen by Apple.

The default stocks, funds, and indexes are listed in the sidebar on the left; news items appear in the pane on the right. Figure 14-1 shows only a handful of stocks and news items; scroll down either pane to see more.

When you open the Stocks app, it displays the latest price for the listed stocks, with two provisos:

>> The quotes are provided in near-real time.

>> The quotes are updated only if your Mac can connect to the Internet.

Your stocks also appear by default in Notification Center. If you don't see stocks in yours, click the Edit Widgets button at the bottom of Notification Center to add the Stocks app. (Flip back to Chapter 11 if you don't remember how to add widgets.)

Adding and deleting stocks, funds, and indexes

Your chance of owning the exact group of stocks, funds, and indexes displayed by default is slim, so this section shows you how to add your own stocks, funds, or indexes and delete any or all default ones.

Here's how to add a stock, a fund, or an index:

1. **In the Search field in the top-left corner of the Stocks window, type the name of a stock, fund, or index you want to add.**

    As you type, the list updates with companies, indexes, and funds that match what you've typed so far, with items already in your watchlist appearing in a separate section, as shown for AAPL and APLT in Figure 14-2.

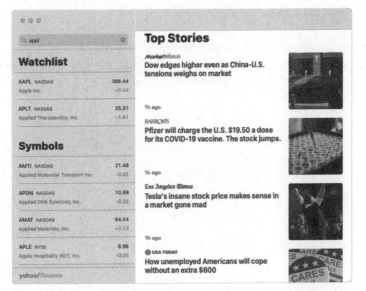

FIGURE 14-2:
The search list updates as you type, and items already in your watchlist (APPL and APLT here) appear in a separate section.

2. **Do one of the following:**

    -   *Right- or Control-click the stock, fund, or index you want to add and choose Add Symbol.*

    -   *Click the stock, fund, or index and then click the Add to Watchlist button, near the top-right corner of the stocks window.*

3. **When you've finished adding stocks, funds, and indexes, click < (Back) above the Search field to return to your watchlist.**

To delete a stock, fund, or index: Right- or Control-Click the item and choose Remove from Watchlist.

That's all there is to adding and deleting stocks.

TIP

To change the order of the items on your watchlist, click and hold down on the item and drag it up or down to its new place in the list.

Details, details, details

To see the details for an item, click it; the right side of the window will offer additional information on the item. The interactive chart described in the next section appears at the top of the pane. Scroll down for additional news; click More Data from Yahoo! for even more additional news.

Charting a course

In Figure 14-3, check out the bunch of numbers and letters above the chart, namely 1D, 1W, 1M, 3M, 6M, 1Y, 2Y, 5Y, 10Y, and ALL. They stand for 1 day, 1 week, 1 month, 3 months, 6 months, 1 year, and 2, 5, 10, and all recorded years, respectively.

FIGURE 14-3: The Stocks screen.

Click one and the chart is updated to reflect that period of time. (In Figure 14-3, 6M is selected.)

You can do the two other very cool things with charts:

>> Hover your cursor over the chart to see the value for that day.

>> Click and drag to see the difference in values between two days.

By default, the Stocks app displays the change in a stock's price in dollars. You can instead see the change expressed as a percentage or as the stock's market capitalization. Just choose Price Change, Percentage Change, or Market Cap from the View menu.

While the View menu is open, check out its other Stocks-related commands:

>> Refresh (⌘+R)

>> Back (⌘+[)

>> Next Story

>> Previous Story

>> Actual Size (⌘+Shift+0)

>> Zoom In (⌘+plus sign)

>> Zoom Out (⌘+minus sign)

>> Enter Full Screen (⌘+Control+F)

And that's about all you need to know to enjoy and be educated by Big Sur's Stocks app.

Read All about It in News

The Apple News app gathers articles, images, and videos you might be interested in and displays them in a visually appealing fashion. Participating publishers include ESPN, *The New York Times,* Hearst (publisher of the newspaper I write for, the *Houston Chronicle*), Time, Inc., CNN, Condé Nast, Bloomberg, and many more.

What are your interests?

You can customize what appears in your News app by choosing File ⇨ Discover Channels & Topics.

When the Follow Your Favorites screen appears, scroll down and click the little red plus sign for each source you want to follow in the News app. When you click, a red checkmark in a circle appears to indicate that you're following this source (such as NPR and Axios in Figure 14-4).

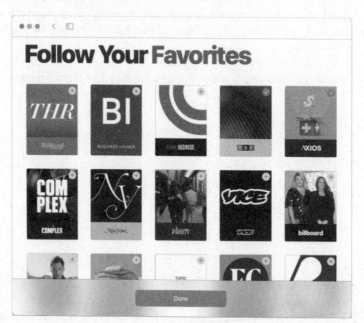

FIGURE 14-4:
The Follow Your Favorites screen with NPR and Axios selected to follow.

Click the item again and the check mark turns back into a small red plus (like all items but NPR and Axios in Figure 14-4) to indicate that you're not following this source.

When you've clicked all the sources you want to follow, click Done and they'll appear in the Following section of your sidebar.

To remove an item from the sidebar's Following section, either:

>> Select the item and choose File ⇨ Unfollow Channel.

>> Select the item and press ⌘+Shift+L.

>> Right- or Control-click the item and choose Unfollow Channel.

How News works

News creates a customized real-time newsfeed based on the sources you're following, highlighting stories it expects you to be interested in. The more you read, the better its suggestions become, or at least that's what Apple says.

Click a story to read it; click < (Back) above the sidebar to return to the main News screen. Or use the handy commands and shortcuts in the View menu, including the following:

>> Check for New Stories (⌘ + R)

>> Next Story

>> Previous Story

>> Actual Size (⌘ + 0)

>> Zoom In (⌘ + plus sign)

>> Zoom Out (⌘ + minus sign)

Managing your news

In addition to the useful commands in the View menu, the News app's File menu also offers myriad commands that help you manage your news.

For example, to help News find stories you'll enjoy, choose File ⇨ Suggest More Stories Like This (⌘ + L) if you love the story you're reading, choose File ⇨ Suggest Fewer Stories Like This (⌘ + D) if you don't love it, or choose File ⇨ Save Story (⌘ + S) to save the story for future reading. You'll find your saved stories in the Saved Stories section near the bottom of the sidebar.

TIP

The History section in the sidebar can help you find that story you read the other day and now want to share.

Finally, check out the other commands in the File menu, which can help fine-tune what you see in News, including the following:

>> Follow Channel (⌘ + Shift + L)

>> Block Channel (⌘ + Shift + D)

>> Manage Notifications & Email

>> Manage Blocked Channels and Topics

>> Manage Subscriptions

In 2019, Apple began offering a subscription news service called News+, which offers access to hundreds of newspapers and magazines for $9.99 a month. Click News+ in the sidebar for more information or to begin a free one-month trial.

And that's about all you need to know to customize and enjoy news in the News app.

Recording Memos with Voice Memos

The third addition from iOS is called Voice Memos, a simple one-trick-pony of an app that lets you record, play back, and share short audio recordings.

Consider all the times you'd find it useful to have an audio recorder in your MacBook — perhaps when you're attending a lecture or interviewing an important source (a big deal for writers). Or maybe you just want to record a quick reminder ("Pick up milk after work"). Well, you're in luck. Big Sur includes the same built-in digital voice recorder you know and love on your iPhone (and other iDevices).

Recording a voice memo

Launch Voice Memos and you'll see a simple window with a sidebar that sports your previous recordings (if you have them) and a big red button.

TIP

Recordings use your Mac's built-in microphone by default. If you prefer to use a different microphone, select it in the Sound System Preferences pane's Input tab before you begin recording. To adjust the recording level, visit the Sound System Preferences pane's Input tab and adjust the Input Volume slider.

To record a voice memo, click the big red button. The waveform that moves across the screen as Voice Memo detects sounds helps you gauge the recording level and a timer on the screen indicates the length of your recording session (12.38 in Figure 14-5).

If you want to pause the recording, click the red Pause icon (lower left in Figure 14-5). The Pause icon then becomes the Resume icon; click it to resume your recording, or click Done to finish and save the recording.

FIGURE 14-5:
You can pause at
any time, then
click Resume or
Done.

Listening to a voice memo

After you capture your thoughts or musings, you'll probably want to play them back. To do so, just click the voice memo you want to hear, and then click the triangular Play icon to listen.

TIP

You can drag the playhead (the vertical blue line in the middle of the waveform) to move forward or back in the memo.

Naming a voice memo

When a memo is added to your list of recordings, it shows up with the date and length of the recording and the uninspiring title *New Recording.* You could have named it something else at that point, but if you didn't, you may have a tough time remembering which recording was made for which purpose. Fortunately, you can easily create a custom title after the fact:

1. **Click any Voice Memo in the sidebar.**

2. **Double-click the name Apple assigned (New Recording 1, New Recording 2, and so on).**

3. **Type your own name for the voice memo.**

   Professor Snookins on Biology, for example.

That's it. Your recording is duly identified.

Trimming a voice memo

Maybe the professor you were recording rambled on and on. Fortunately, it's easy to trim the audio. To do so, first click a recording and then choose Edit ⇨ Trim Recording.

Now, drag the start marker, end marker, or both to determine the portion of the audio you want to keep. See Figure 14-6.

FIGURE 14-6: Drag the start and end markers to trim the recording.

To conclude the process, click the Trim button — but before you do, I recommend that you preview your edit by clicking the Play icon. Then if you're happy, click the Trim button.

If you make a mistake, choose Edit ⇨ Undo immediately to restore the audio you trimmed.

You may want to share a Voice Memo with others. No problem. Just click a Voice Memo to select it, and then click the share icon (shown in the margin). You then have the option to email the memo or send it in a message. Or you can share it instantly with Mac or iDevice users via AirDrop (covered in Chapter 4), or add it to the Notes app.

When you have no further use for a recording, you can remove it from the Voice Memos app by selecting it and pressing Delete (or Backspace).

TIP

To see all your voice memos on all your Apple devices:

›› On your Mac: Open System Preferences, click Apple ID, click iCloud in the sidebar, click the iCloud Drive Options button, and enable Voice Memos in the list of apps.

›› On your iOS or iPadOS device: Tap Settings ➪ *your name here* ➪ iCloud, and then enable Voice Memos.

Controlling Lights, Locks, and More with Home

The Home app is all about controlling from your Mac smart *HomeKit* accessories such as smart door locks, lightbulbs, thermostats, garage-door openers, and other devices that lend themselves to being smartened and controlled remotely.

The good news is that with Big Sur's Home app you can turn lights on and off, lock and unlock doors, and do much more, right from your Mac, as long as the accessories are compatible with HomeKit, Apple's framework for controlling smart devices around your house, and are connected to the same Wi-Fi network as your Mac.

For remote control over the Internet, you'll need a device to act as a hub — an Apple TV, an iPad, or a HomePod speaker — which will allow you to control devices over the Internet using a Mac (or iDevice).

Before you get too excited, if you're not already using the Home app on your iDevice, you'll need to start now because you *still* can't add new HomeKit accessories with the Mac Home app. Unless or until you add your HomeKit-enabled accessories to the Home app on an iPhone or iPad, you're out of luck.

If you do have devices you've added to the Home app on your iDevice, you can use the Home app on your Mac to turn them on or off. You can also create or edit *scenes*, which let you control multiple devices simultaneously, such as all the lights in the office.

Finally, you can also create or edit *automations*, which control devices or scenes based on the time of day or location of a device (usually an iPhone).

4

Getting Along with Others

IN THIS PART . . .

Get the Internet working on your Mac (and find out what to do with it after that).

See how to surf the Internet with Safari.

Make imaginatively named apps such as Mail, Contacts, and Messages work for you.

Share files and more.

Chapter **15**

(Inter)Networking

These days, networking online is easier than finding a log to fall off: You simply use the Internet to connect your Mac to a wealth of information residing on computers around the world. Luckily for you, macOS Big Sur has the best and most comprehensive Internet tools ever shipped with a Mac operating system.

macOS offers built-in Internet connectivity right out of the box. macOS Big Sur comes with the following:

» Apple's Safari web browser, which you use to navigate the web, download remote files, and more.

» The FaceTime app for video chats with other Mac or iDevice users.

» The Messages app, used for instant messaging and live online chatting (text). Messages works with other Messages users and people using Google, Yahoo!, AOL, Jabber (an open-source chatting protocol), or Bonjour (which discovers other users on your local area network). It also includes audio and video chatting, screen sharing, and file transfers.

» The Mail application (for email).

In this chapter and the two that follow, I cover the top things most people use the Internet for: surfing the web and video and audio chatting. You discover Safari and FaceTime in this chapter, Contacts in Chapter 16, and Mail and Messages in Chapter 17.

But before I can talk about any of those things, I first have to walk you through configuring your Internet connection, given that none of these apps work well without it. The good news is that after you finish making the connection, you can play with your Internet-enabled applications to your heart's content.

And here's more good news: If you're already able to surf the web, send and receive email, or send and receive text messages, you're connected and could skip many (if not most) of the steps in the "Getting Connected to the Internet" section. However, I suggest that you don't skip that section, even if your Internet already works perfectly, because it offers a number of useful tips and techniques. (Do you know what Locations are? Or why you might want to use them?)

Onward!

Getting Connected to the Internet

Before you can use (or surf) the Internet, you need to connect to the Internet. If you're a typical home user, you need three things to surf the Internet:

>> **A connection to the Internet,** such as a cable modem, digital subscriber line (DSL) modem, or a satellite Internet service (referred to generically as your *Internet box*).

REMEMBER

If you use technology other than DSL, cable, or satellite to connect your computer to the Internet, your network administrator (the person you run to at work when something goes wrong with your computer) or ISP (Internet service provider) might have to help you set up your Mac because setting up those other configurations is (sigh) beyond the scope of this book.

>> **An account with an ISP** (Internet service provider), such as AT&T or Comcast.

TIP

The technical reviewer for previous editions of this book reminded me that these days, that's not necessarily true. All you really need is free Wi-Fi, which is available almost everywhere — in stores, restaurants, parks, libraries, and other places — and a free email account from Apple's iCloud, Microsoft's Outlook.com, Google's Gmail, or Yahoo! Mail.

>> **A Mac,** preferably one running macOS 11 Big Sur.

You might need to tweak a few settings, as I explain in the upcoming section "Plugging in your Internet-connection settings."

After you set up each of these components, you can launch and use Safari, Mail, Messages, and any other Internet applications.

Your Internet service provider and you

You may have to select a company to provide you access to the Internet: an ISP. The prices and services that ISPs offer vary, often from minute to minute. Keep the following in mind when choosing an ISP:

>> **If your connection comes from a cable or telephone company, your ISP is probably that company.** In effect, the choice of ISP is pretty much made for you when you decide on cable or DSL service.

>> **Broadband access to the Internet starts at around $25 or $30 per month.** If your service provider asks for considerably more than that, find out why.

Higher-throughput packages for cable or fiber connections might run you twice that, but they may not be available in your area. To wit: The only Internet package available from AT&T at my address in Austin, Texas, today is $50/month for speeds up to 50Mbps and 1TB of data, plus an additional $10 for each 50GB over 1TB (up to a maximum $100 a month) and a $10/month equipment fee.

For example AT&T's best deal at my address sucks (as does AT&T itself, but that's a story for another day). Luckily, at least one other ISP serves my neighborhood — Spectrum (a cable TV provider). I pay around $80 a month for the fastest Internet connection available at my address, which is 400Mbps (download) and 20Mbps (upload) with unlimited data. And if I bundled Spectrum cable TV or Internet telephone services (which I don't), I would get a small discount on my Internet access.

If you think you're paying too much for Internet service or you don't like your current provider, by all means do your homework and determine what other options are available in your neighborhood.

TIP

Because most Mac users like things to be easy, macOS includes a cool feature in its Setup Assistant to help you find and configure an account with an ISP. When you installed macOS Big Sur (assuming that you did and that it didn't come preinstalled on your Mac), Setup Assistant may have asked you a bunch of questions about your Internet connection and set up everything for you.

If you didn't have an Internet connection (an ISP) at that time, you may need to configure the Network System Preferences pane yourself. Chances are you'll be good to go as soon as you connect the cable, but in the event it doesn't just work, these settings could be something you'll have to hash out with your ISP.

If you have questions or problems not answered by this book, your ISP should be able to assist you. And if your ISP can't help, it's probably time to try a different ISP (if you can).

Plugging in your Internet-connection settings

If you didn't set up your Internet connection when you installed macOS, you need to open System Preferences (from the Applications folder, the dock, Launchpad, or the menu) and click the Network button. The Network pane offers options for connecting your Mac to the Internet or to a network. Setting up your Internet connection in the Network System Preferences pane is beyond the purview of this book, so the easiest way to do it is to search for *network setup* in Mac Help (Help ⇨ Search).

WARNING

If you're part of a large office network, check with your system administrator before you change anything in this pane. If you ignore this advice, you run the risk of losing your network connection completely.

TIP

If your Mac asks you a question you can't answer during setup, ask your ISP (or search its online help if you can) or contact your network administrator for the answer. I can't possibly tell you how in this book because there are just too many possible configurations, and each depends on your particular ISP and service.

That said, here's a brief rundown on the most common things you may need to know to set up a network connection:

» **TCP/IP:** TCP/IP is the language of the Internet. You may be asked to specify things such as your IP address, domain name servers, and search domains.

» **PPP or PPPoE:** These acronyms stand for *Point-to-Point Protocol* and *Point-to-Point Protocol over Ethernet.* Which one you see depends on what service you're using to connect. These protocols are used less today, but some cable and DSL modems still use PPPoE.

» **Proxies:** If you're on a large network or your Mac is behind a firewall, you may need to specify one or more proxy servers. If so, your network administrator or ISP can help you with configuration. (Most home users will never need to touch this tab.) Some ISPs require you to specify proxy servers; if you need to do so, ask your ISP what to do.

If you use your Mac in more than one place, you can set up a separate configuration for each location and choose it from the Location menu. A *location*, in this context, consists of all settings in all items in the Network System Preferences pane.

TIP

My technical editor for a previous edition reminded me that you probably don't need to create separate locations these days. My MacBook Pro just works. I may have to choose a Wi-Fi network and provide a password the first time I visit a hotel, cafe, or office; after that, my Mac remembers everything so the next time I'm at that hotel, cafe, or office, it just works.

After you have this entire pane configured the way that you like, follow these steps to create separate locations:

1. **Pull down the Location menu and choose Edit Locations.**

2. **Click + at the bottom of the Locations list.**

   A new, untitled Location appears in the list.

3. **Type a descriptive name for the new location, such as AirPort at Starbucks or Ethernet at Joe's Office.**

4. **Click Done, and then click Apply.**

   From now on, you can change all your network settings at the same time by choosing the appropriate location from the Location pop-up menu.

If, on the other hand, your Mac has a single network or Internet connection (as most home users have), just leave the Location menu set to Automatic and be done with it.

REMEMBER

And while this may be beyond the purview of this book, I'd like to remind you to use only wireless networks that you know and trust, especially in public places such as hotels and airports, and consider using a virtual private network (VPN) when you're out and about as an alternative to free public Wi-Fi (which is often less secure than a VPN).

Finally, if you have any reservations about using public Wi-Fi, use your mobile phone's hotspot feature (if available — not all carriers and plans include it) instead of public Wi-Fi. Why? Because cellular networks encrypt all traffic, making them more secure than Wi-Fi networks.

Also look for *https* (not *http*) at the beginning of URLs to ensure your wireless connection is encrypted (more secure).

Browsing the Web with Safari

With your Internet connection set up, you're ready to browse the web. In the following sections, I concentrate on browsing the web with Safari because it's the web browser installed with macOS Big Sur.

TIP

If you don't care for Safari, check out Firefox or Chrome, which are both free browsers and have features you won't find in Safari. It never hurts to have a spare in case Safari has issues with a particular website.

To begin, just open your web browser. No problem. As usual, there's more than one way. You can launch Safari by any of these methods:

» Single-click the Safari icon on the dock or Launchpad (look for the big blue compass that looks like a stopwatch, as shown in the margin).

» Double-click the Safari icon in your Applications folder.

» Single-click a URL link in an email, an iMessage, or a document.

» Double-click a URL link document (a .webloc file) in Finder.

The first time you launch Safari, you see a generic Favorites page, as shown in Figure 15-1. In the sections that follow, I show you the highlights of using Safari, starting at the top of its window.

FIGURE 15-1:
Safari first displays a generic Favorites page.

Note that if you're upgrading from an earlier version of macOS, Safari will open to the same page it opened to before you upgraded.

TIP

You can choose what appears in new Safari windows and tabs by choosing Safari⇨Preferences and clicking the General tab at the top of the Preferences window.

NEW

You can also customize your start page by clicking the little settings icon in the lower-right corner of the start page (shown in Figure 15-1 and in the margin) to enable or disable sections on your start page, including Favorites, Frequently Visited, Privacy Report, Siri Suggestions, Reading List, iCloud Tabs, and Background Image.

Enable or disable an item by selecting or clearing its check box. In Figure 15-1, you can see (from top to bottom): Favorites, Privacy Report, Reading List, and iCloud Tabs (from my other Mac, named *MacBook The Knife XIII*).

TIP

If you have more than one Apple device near your Mac, hover the pointer over the current device's name (*MacBook The Knife XIII* in Figure 15-1), and then click the little up and down arrow icon that appears on its right to see the open Safari tabs from a different device (*Bob's iPhone X* or *iPad Pro* in Figure 15-1).

Owning your toolbar

The Safari toolbar, at the top of every Safari window, consists of a narrow row of icons and the Search or Enter Website Name field. The icons do pretty much what their names imply. From left to right, they are

NEW

>> **Show/Hide Sidebar:** Click to see your favorites or Reading list in the sidebar; click it again to hide the sidebar.

>> **Back/Forward:** When you open a page and move to a second page (or third or fourth), Back takes you to previously visited pages. Remember that you need to go back before the Forward icon will work.

>> **Privacy Report:** Click to see an overlay with a brief privacy report; click the little *i*-in-a-circle on the overlay to see a more comprehensive report.

>> **Search or Enter Website Name:** This field, to the right of the Show Sidebar button, is where you type web addresses, or URLs (Uniform Resource Locators) that you want to visit. Just type one, and press Return to surf to that site.

To the right of the Search or Enter Website Name field are three more icons. Keep reading.

>> **Share:** When you find a page of interest or a page you know you'll want to remember, click this icon (which is actually a drop-down menu) to tell Safari to remember it for you in Big Sur's cool Reading list or as a bookmark — two topics I explore further a little later in this chapter. Or send a link to it via Mail or Messages, both covered in Chapter 17, or post it on Facebook or tweet it on Twitter.

>> **Create a New Tab (+):** Click to create a tab.

>> **Show/Hide Tab Overview:** Click the Show/Hide Tab Overview icon to see previews of all your open tabs (which you learn about shortly). If you have other Macs or iDevices, you'll also see the open tabs in Safari on other devices that have Safari enabled in iCloud. This feature is so handy you can also find it in the View menu, where you'll also spy its handy keyboard shortcut, ⌘+Shift+\.

Safari also offers pinned tabs, which persist in the tab bar until you unpin them, even after quitting and reopening Safari. To pin a tab, choose Window⇨Pin Tab or right- or Control-click the tab and choose Pin Tab from the contextual menu. To unpin a tab you've pinned previously, reverse the process and choose Window⇨Unpin Tab or right- or Control-click the pinned tab and choose Unpin Tab.

NEW

Want to preview an inactive tab? Hover the pointer over that tab and a small preview appears below it.

But wait — there's more. To add other useful icons to your toolbar, choose View⇨Customize Toolbar (or right-click anywhere on the toolbar and choose Customize Toolbar from the contextual menu). The Customize Toolbar sheet drops down, and you can drag items into or out of the toolbar to create a custom set of icons. In Figure 15-2, for example, I added four new icons to my toolbar (left to right): Grammarly, Honey, Send to Downie, and 1Password — placed between the Forward icon and Privacy Report icon.

FIGURE 15-2: The Customize Toolbar sheet and my customized toolbar.

Below the Search or Enter Website Name field is the Favorites bar, which is populated by default with icons for web pages that Apple thinks you might enjoy, including Apple, Yahoo!, Google Maps, YouTube, and Wikipedia.

TIP

If you don't see your Favorites bar, choose View⇨Show Favorites Bar or press ⌘+Shift+B.

I've replaced all the default icons on my Safari Favorites bar with folders that are drop-down menus, as denoted by the little chevron after their names, as shown in Figure 15-3.

FIGURE 15-3:
All the icons in my Favorites bar are actually drop-down menus.

TIP

Adding bookmarks to and deleting bookmarks from the Favorites bar (and sidebar) is described in the next section.

One last thing: Favorites and bookmarks are not exactly the same in Big Sur. Favorites is a folder of bookmarks that appear in the Favorites bar and Favorites page. Not all bookmarks are Favorites, but all Favorites are bookmarks. Which makes total sense when you think about it.

And perhaps to confuse matters even further, you can change what you see in the Favorites page (but not the Favorites bar) via a setting in the Safari Preferences General pane. It can be a trifle confusing at first, but you'll get used to it.

Using the Safari sidebar

Click the Sidebar icon on the toolbar to show or hide the Safari sidebar, which has two tabs — Bookmarks and Reading List— which I explore in this section.

Bookmarking your favorite pages

When you find a web page you want to remember and return to, you *bookmark* it. Here's how it works:

1. **Choose Bookmarks⇨Add Bookmark, press ⌘ + D, or click the Share icon and choose Add Bookmark.**

2. **Choose where to store the bookmark from the pop-up menu, as shown in Figure 15-4.**

   By default, Safari puts them in the Favorites folder.

FIGURE 15-4:
Creating a
bookmark.

3. **Rename the bookmark or use the name provided by Safari.**

   I accepted the name Safari suggested, so now this page will appear in the Favorites bar as Working Smarter for Mac Users.

4. **(Optional) Add a brief description if you like.**

   I typed "my website!"

5. **Click the Add button to save the bookmark.**

Finding your bookmarks in the sidebar

To return to a bookmarked page, click it in the Favorites bar, choose Bookmarks⇨Show Bookmarks, press ⌘+Option+B, or click the Show Sidebar icon (shown in margin) to see all your bookmarks in the sidebar, as shown in Figure 15-5.

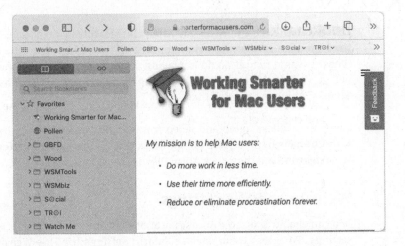

FIGURE 15-5:
The sidebar in all its glory.

If you add the bookmark to the Favorites folder (as shown), it automatically appears in the Favorites bar. If you add the bookmark outside the Favorites folder in the sidebar, it will not appear in the Favorites bar but will be available at the bottom of the Bookmarks menu and in the Bookmarks sidebar.

Open bookmarked pages in the sidebar by clicking them once. View the contents of a folder (such as Favorites, GBFD, Wood, WSMTools, and WSMbiz in Figure 15-5) by single-clicking the folder name in the list. Figure 15-5 shows, in particular, the contents of the Favorites bar folder with the contents of the WSMbiz subfolder expanded.

To organize your Bookmarks window or place bookmarks by dragging them to the Safari Favorites bar or the Bookmarks sidebar. If you drag a folder of bookmarks to the Favorites folder (or directly onto the Favorites bar itself), the result is a drop-down menu (refer to Figure 15-3).

To delete a bookmark, right- or Control+click it and choose Delete.

TIP

⌘+click a folder in the Bookmarks window or Favorites bar to simultaneously open all the bookmarks it contains.

While we're on the subject of favorites, you've probably noticed this handy behavior by now, but it's worth mentioning: When you click in the empty Search or Enter Website Name field, a sheet drops down, displaying your favorites. The sheet is replaced by a list of search results and suggestions as soon as you type the first character. Understandably, the sheet doesn't appear if the current page is Favorites or Top Sites. But it's a convenient feature I'd be remiss not to mention.

Last but not least, one of my favorite Safari features (introduced in El Capitan) is the little blue speaker icon that appears on the right side of the Search or Enter Website Name field if audio is playing on any page. Click the speaker and Safari will go silent even if the audio is coming from an inactive tab or a hidden window. Thanks, Apple; we needed that.

Safari now blocks audio and video from playing automatically by default. If you want to enable it for all sites or specific sites, choose Safari⇨Preferences, click the Websites tab, and then click Auto-Play in the sidebar on the left.

Website-specific settings

You can enable or disable Auto-Play another way — with Safari's website-specific settings. To access them, choose Safari⇨Settings for This Website. Or right- or Control-click the site's URL in the Enter Website Name field and choose Settings for This Website.

In addition to the aforementioned auto-play, other website-specific options you can set follow:

>> Use Reader view when available.

>> Enable/disable content blockers.

>> Set page zoom.

>> Ask permission to use the camera, microphone, or your location.

>> Auto-Play: Allow All Auto-Play; Stop Media with Sound; or Never Auto-Play.

>> Pop-up Windows: Block and Notify; Block; or Allow.

What's on your Reading list?

The Reading list serves as a repository for pages or links you want to read but don't want to read right now. It's a lot like a bookmark but easier to create on the fly, which makes the Reading list perfect for sites or links you don't need to keep forever (that's what bookmarks are for).

To see your Reading list, click the Show Sidebar icon and then click the Reading List tab (shown in the margin).

To add the page you're viewing to your Reading list, hover your cursor over the left side of the Search or Enter Website Name field and then click the +-in-a-circle. (You can also use the keyboard shortcut ⌘+Shift+D or click the Share icon and choose Add to Reading List from its menu.)

To add a link to your Reading list without visiting the page, just press the Shift key before you click that link. It's fast and easy, and it works even if the sidebar is closed. Or you can right- or Control-click the link and choose Add to Reading List from the contextual menu.

Right-click any item in your Reading list for additional options, as shown in Figure 15-6.

To delete an item from the Reading list, right- or Control-click the item and then choose Remove Item. To remove all items from the Reading list, right- or Control-click any item and then choose Clear All Items.

TIP

If you have other Macs or iDevices, you can sync your Reading list among your devices by enabling Safari in the iCloud System Preferences pane.

Reader view

Finally, if an icon like the one shown in the margin appears at the left edge of the Search or Enter Website Name field, click it to show the Reader view for the current page. Click the icon again to exit Reader view. Reader view reformats the page for easier reading while hiding ads, navigation, and other distractions. The icon appears only if the current page can be shown in Reader view.

Searching with Google

Looking for something on the Internet? Check out Google, the fantastic search engine that's totally integrated with Safari to help you hunt down just about anything on the Internet in no time.

Don't care for Google? Choose Safari ➪ Preferences, click the Search tab, and choose a different one, as long as you prefer Yahoo!, Bing, or DuckDuckGo (a privacy-friendly search engine that, unlike Google, doesn't track your searches or collect information about your search habits).

In this section, you discover how to use Google to search the Internet and find almost anything, as well as how to get help with Google when all else fails.

To search the Internet with Google, follow these steps:

1. In the Search or Enter Website Name field, type the beginning of a word or phrase.

As you type, Safari offers a list of suggestions and recent searches, as shown in Figure 15-7. Note that I had typed only *vizsla pi* when Safari offered this list.

2. **Click one of the list items; finish typing the word or phrase, or use the arrow keys to select a list item; and then press Return to start the search.**

   Google almost immediately offers your search results, as shown in Figure 15-6.

3. **Click one of the result links.**

   Click an item in the list to be taken instantly to that page.

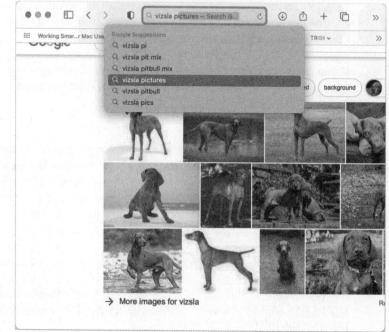

FIGURE 15-6:
A Google search for pictures of Vizsla dogs.

If the fish you catch on your first try aren't what you want, use different bait:

>> **If a particular result isn't just what you're looking for:** Click the Back icon and try another result link.

>> **If Google offers too many results that aren't just right:**

   a. *Click the Settings link near the top of the results page and choose Advanced Search.* Advanced searches refine your search with a multitude of options, some of which are shown in Figure 15-7. I am refining my search for pictures of Vizsla dogs that are cute or puppies and not ugly, senior, or old.

   b. *Click the Advanced Search button (not visible in Figure 15-7).* A refined results page quickly appears. As before, click a result link to visit that page. If it's not just what you're looking for, click the Back icon, and try a different result link.

FIGURE 15-7:
Running a Google
advanced search.

By the way, the little double-chevron icons on the right side of the toolbar and Favorites bar (shown in the margin) indicate that the window is too narrow to display all the tools or bookmarks. Click the chevron, and a menu shows you the previously hidden choices, as shown in Figure 15-7. In this figure, the toolbar overflow menu (not shown) would display the hidden toolbar icons; the Favorites bar overflow menu (shown) displays the seven hidden items (three folders and four bookmarks).

That's pretty much all you need to know to have a great time searching the web with Google.

Protect yourself from malice (and ads)

There are a couple of privacy-related settings in Safari — Prevent Cross-Site Tracking and Block All Cookies — both found in Safari Preferences' Privacy tab. Enabling the former periodically deletes tracking data from third-party sites; enabling the latter submits a request not to track you when you visit a website. It's up to each individual website to actually *honor* the request. Sadly, not all websites do.

While you're viewing the Privacy tab, enable the check box for Apple Pay and Apple Card if you want to use them to make purchases on the web — and avoid typing or look up card numbers, expiration dates, and CCV codes.

Checking out Help Center

Safari has a lot more features, and I could write an entire chapter about using Safari, but one of the rules we *Dummies* authors must follow is that our books can't run 1,000 pages.

So I'm going to give you the next best thing: Open Help Center (by choosing Help ⇨ Safari Help). A special Safari Help window appears; you can search for any Safari-related topic or solution to any Safari-related problem right there.

Audio and Video Calls with FaceTime

FaceTime works beautifully for Mac-to-Mac audio or video calls. And, because it's a single-purpose application, many users (including my mom) find it easier and less intimidating to set up and use than Messages or Skype.

By the way, there's no Windows version of FaceTime at the moment, so you'll have to use a third-party solution such as Skype or Zoom for cross-platform video chats with your less fortunate PC-using brethren (or sisteren).

TIP

A feature known as Wi-Fi Calling lets you use your Mac to make and receive voice calls via your iPhone with the FaceTime app on your Mac. When enabled, you can make or receive phone calls using your Mac's microphone and speakers (as long as your iPhone is nearby). It's easy and trouble-free if your wireless carrier supports it; you'll find the details at https://support.apple.com/en-us/HT203032.

For now, to get started, launch FaceTime from your Applications folder, Launchpad, or dock. The main (only) FaceTime window appears, as shown in Figure 15-8. The right side of the window shows what your Mac's camera is seeing (which happens to be me in Figure 15-8).

I clicked the camera icon next to my wife's name to initiate a call from my Mac to my wife's iPad (or iPhone or Mac). She answered on her iPad; what we each saw is shown in Figure 15-9.

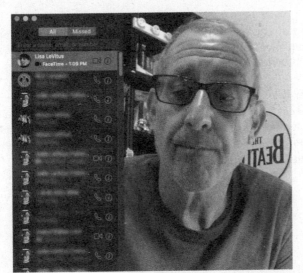

FIGURE 15-8:
The FaceTime
window, ready to
make a call.

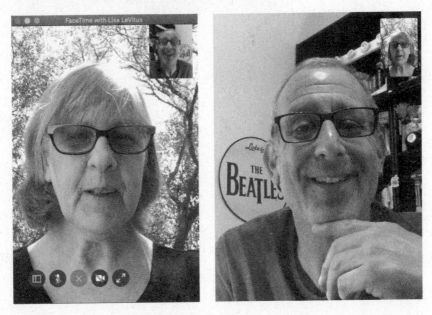

FIGURE 15-9:
A FaceTime call:
What I saw on my
Mac screen (left)
and what Lisa
saw on her iPad
screen (right).

TIP

FaceTime uses Contacts (covered in Chapter 16), so if you have friends or family
who have an iPhone 4 or later, iPad 2 or later, iPad mini, iPod touch (fourth generation or later), or a Mac, just type their name in the field in the top-left corner,
and then click the camera or phone icon to initiate a video or audio chat.

If you're running Mojave V10.14.3 or later (which includes Big Sur), you can also host Group FaceTime chats with up to 32 friends. At least Apple says you're supposed to be able to host multi-person chats.

I've never been able to get it to work, but feel free to give it a try. In theory, you start a video chat with someone, and then click the little video camera icon next to another contact's name in the sidebar. You should be able to add up to 31 other people, but I've never been able to get it to work more than one person at a time, so good luck.

» Managing your contacts

» Syncing your contacts with other devices

Chapter **16**

Dealing with People

I n this chapter and the next, you discover a trio of programs that work beautifully together and make managing your contacts, email, and messages (chats) a breeze. You're about to find out how these eponymous programs — Contacts in this chapter, and Mail and Messages in Chapter 17 — work, and how to use them individually and as a team.

REMEMBER

I cover a lot of material in not a lot of space in these two chapters, so if you want to find out something about Contacts, Mail, or Messages that I don't cover, remember the capable assistance you can find in Help ⇨ Contacts Help (or Mail Help, or Messages Help).

Collecting Your Contacts

Contacts stores and manages information about your family, friends, companies, and any other entity you want to keep in touch with. It works seamlessly with the Mail, Messages, and Maps applications, enabling you to quickly look up phone numbers or email addresses when you're ready to communicate with someone.

In fact, Contacts works with several applications, both on and beyond your Mac, including the following:

> » Use it with FaceTime (covered in Chapter 15) to video chat with friends and family.

>> Use it with Calendar (covered in Chapter 11) to display your contacts by choosing Window ⇨ Contacts. You can then drag any person in your contacts from the Address Panel to any date and time on the calendar, and a special meeting event is created automatically by Calendar. The event even has a Send Invitation button; if you click it, it launches Mail and sends the person an invitation to this meeting. Very cool stuff.

>> The Contacts application can also work with any other application whose programmers choose to make the connection or with any device that's compatible with Contacts. For example, BusyContacts ($49.99 in the Mac App Store) exchanges data with Contacts seamlessly, so changes made in Contacts appear in BusyContacts (and vice versa) almost immediately.

>> Contacts is available also in most programs that have a Share icon or menu so you can share with your contacts via whichever method is appropriate, usually their phone number, email, or iCloud.com or Me.com address (for an iMessage).

>> If you use iCloud, you can choose to sync contacts with devices that include (but are not limited to) other Macs, iPhones, iPads, and iPod touches. And you can also sync contacts via Google, Microsoft Exchange, Microsoft Office 365, or any combination.

In the following sections, you find out the best ways to fill Contacts with your own contacts and how to keep those contacts organized.

Adding contacts

Follow these steps to create an entry in Contacts:

1. **Launch the Contacts application by double-clicking its icon in the Applications folder, clicking its dock icon, or clicking its Launchpad icon.**

   The Contacts window appears. The first time you open Contacts, you see two cards: Apple Computer and the one with whatever personal identification information you supplied when you created your account.

2. **To create an entry, click the + button at the bottom left of any Contact card and choose New Contact from the drop-down menu.**

   An untitled address card appears. The First name text field is initially selected.

3. **In the First text field, type the person's first name.**

   Here, I typed *Bob "Dr. Mac."*

4. Press Tab.

Your cursor should now be in the Last text field.

TIP

You can always move from one field to the next by pressing Tab. In fact, this shortcut works in almost all Mac programs with fields. (Move to the previous field by pressing Shift+Tab.)

5. Type the last name for the person you're adding to your Contacts.

Here, I typed *LeVitus*. Continue this process, filling in the rest of the fields shown in Figure 16-1.

TIP

If you don't see the field you need, click the + icon at the bottom of the card and choose More Field to add a field.

6. When you've finished entering information, click the Done button to exit editing mode.

The contact I created with this step appears in Figure 16-1.

TIP

The little triangles (actually up and down arrows) between the labels and their content fields in Figure 16-1 are pop-up menus that offer alternative labels for the field. For example, if you were to click the arrows next to the word Child, you would be able to choose Father, Parent, Brother, Sister, and so on to replace the label Child.

To add more info about any Contacts entry, click the name in the list on the left (Bob "Dr. Mac" LeVitus in Figure 16-1). Click the Edit button at the bottom of the Contacts window, make your changes, and click Done.

Repeat these steps for everyone you want to keep in touch with.

FIGURE 16-1:
My address card
displayed in the
Contacts window.

Importing contacts from other programs

If your contacts are on another Mac or an iDevice, or stored by Google or Microsoft, you won't need to import your contacts. Just enable the appropriate account in the Internet Accounts System Preferences pane, and enable syncing for contacts.

Those who have contacts in another program (such as FileMaker Pro or ACT) might be able to import them into Contacts, which can import contacts in vCard, LDIF, or text file format.

The first thing is to export the data from the other program in one of these formats.

TIP

I always export the file to the desktop, so that the file is easy to find in the next step.

Then, back in the Contacts app, choose File ⇨ Import, select the exported data file in the Open File dialog, and then click the Open button.

Creating a basic group

Now let me explain how to organize your contacts into groups. Why would you want to organize your contacts into groups? The main reason, at least for me, is practical: I can send email with a single click to everyone in a group that I've defined. For example, when it's time to send out a press release, I can simply send it to my Press/PR group, shooting the email off to all 68 people I have in that group. And when I want to send an email to all the parents of kids on my son's indoor football team, I merely address it to my Flag Football Parents group, and all 12 families in that group receive it.

Here's how to create a group and add contacts to it:

1. **Launch the Contacts application by double-clicking its icon in the Applications folder or clicking its dock icon.**

2. **Create the new group by choosing File ⇨ New Group, pressing ⌘+Shift+N, or clicking the + icon at the bottom of the window and choosing New Group.**

   An untitled Group appears in the Group column with Untitled Group highlighted.

3. **Type a descriptive name for this group and then press Return.**

   I named mine Family.

4. **Click All Contacts on the left side of the window to show all your contacts on the right side.**

5. **Click the contacts you want in the group from the contacts list.**

   To select more than one contact, hold down the ⌘ key when clicking the contacts.

TIP

   You can use the Search field at the top of the window to find a contact or contacts, and then drag them onto the group to add them, as shown in Figure 16-2.

6. **Drag the selected contact names onto the group, as shown in Figure 16-2.**

   Contacts considerately displays the number of contacts you're dragging, which happens to be five in this instance.

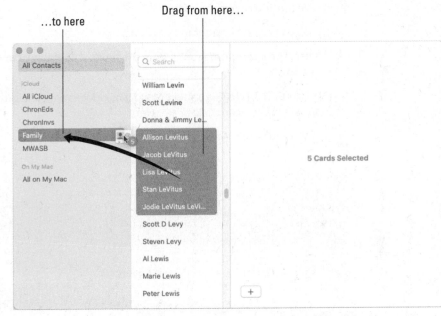

...to here

Drag from here...

FIGURE 16-2:
Adding five
contacts to the
Family group.

TIP

Another way to create a group is to select contacts by clicking, ⌘-clicking, or Shift-clicking contacts and then choosing File ➪ New Group from Selection.

Setting up a smart group (based on contact criteria)

A second type of group — a smart group — might be even more useful to you because it gathers contacts in your Contacts based on criteria you specify. For example, say I create a group that automatically selects Apple staff members who have email addresses that end in @apple.com.

REMEMBER

The big advantage of using a smart group instead of a regular group is that when I add, say, a new Apple contact, that contact automatically becomes a member of the Apple smart group with no further action on my part. And if you delete a card or modify it so the contact no longer matches the smart group criteria, the contact is removed from the group automatically.

To create a smart group, follow these steps:

1. **Choose File ⇨ New Smart Group or press ⌘+Option+N.**

   A Smart Group sheet appears in front of the Contacts window, as shown in Figure 16-3.

2. **Give the smart group a name.**

   I named mine @Apple.com.

3. **Select the appropriate items from the menus: Company, Contains, Email, and so on.**

   In Figure 16-3, I created a smart group that includes any contact that contains *Apple* in the company field or *@apple.com* in any email field.

4. **When you're happy with the criteria specified, click OK.**

FIGURE 16-3:
Creating a smart group.

Deleting a group or smart group

To delete a group or a smart group from your Contacts, click to select it, and then press Delete or choose Edit ⇨ Delete Group.

Sync + Contacts = your contacts everywhere

If you're not syncing contacts with iCloud, Google, or Microsoft Exchange/Office 360 (I discuss syncing calendars and reminders with iCloud in Chapter 11; you're on your own with Google or Microsoft), your contacts will be stored locally on your hard drive. iCloud, Google, and Microsoft users, on the other hand, can choose to store their contacts locally or in iCloud, Google's cloud, or Microsoft's cloud. The difference is if you store your contacts in the cloud, you can sync all your devices so they all display the same information. In other words, if you add a contact to your iPhone, you'll see it on your Mac in the Contacts app within a few minutes. Conversely, if you add a contact on your Mac, within a few minutes, it magically appears in the Contacts app on your iDevice.

Here is how to enable cloud syncing for Contacts:

1. **Choose System Preferences from the menu (or click its dock icon or double-click its icon in the Applications folder).**

   The System Preferences window appears.

2. **Click the Internet Accounts icon.**

   The Internet Accounts pane appears.

3. **In the list on the left, if you see the account you want to use for syncing contacts, click it and skip to Step 5.**

4. **At the bottom of the window, click the + icon, and then on the right side of the window click the name of the provider you want to sync with (iCloud, Exchange, Google, and so on).**

   Provide your user name and password and follow the prompts to add the account.

5. **In the list on the left, click iCloud (or Exchange or Google or other).**

6. **In the list on the right, select the check box for Contacts.**

   If you previously enabled contact syncing with a service provider, reenabling it is even easier: Click its name in the list on the left, and then select the check box for Contacts in the list on the right.

TIP

If you use iCloud, there's no reason to store contacts locally, that is, On My Mac. And, in fact, if you use iCloud, you won't even see an On My Mac section in the Groups list. My advice is that if you do see both sections (On My Mac and iCloud) in the Groups list, copy the contacts stored in On My Mac to iCloud by clicking All on My Mac in the Groups list, selecting all its contacts (Edit ⇨ Select All or ⌘+A), and dragging them onto the iCloud group. Now click the iCloud group and confirm that the contacts you just dragged are visible, and then delete the contacts in the On My Mac group (select all contacts and then choose Edit ⇨ Delete Cards). Finally, click iCloud and look for duplicate contacts by choosing Card ⇨ Look for Duplicates. If any duplicates are found, you're invited to either delete one (if they're the same) or merge them (if one is different).

Now you'll see the same contacts on all your devices. More precisely, you'll see them on devices that are signed in to the same Apple ID as your Mac and have iCloud Contacts syncing enabled.

Chapter **17**

Communicating with Mail and Messages

Y ou can see how to use Contacts and Maps to find people and places in Chapters 16 and 13, respectively. In this chapter, I take a look at two more terrific programs — Mail and Messages — that work with Contacts to make managing your email and messages (chats) a breeze.

Sending and Receiving Email with Mail

TIP

I cover a lot of material in not a lot of space in this chapter, so if there's something you want to find out about Mail or Messages that I don't cover, don't forget about the wonderful assistance you can find in Help⇨Mail Help (or Messages Help).

Mail is a program for sending, receiving, and organizing your email. Mail is fast and easy to use, too. Click the Mail icon on the dock or Launchpad or double-click the Mail icon in the Applications folder to launch Mail. The Mail icon looks like an envelope, as shown in the margin.

You can use other applications to read email. The App Store has dozens of other mail readers, and most versions of Microsoft Office include Outlook. And most email services, including Google's Gmail and Apple's iCloud (to name a couple), offer a web-based interface you can use in a pinch. You can continue to use any or all of these options for your email if you like, but when you're using your Mac, the easiest and best mail reader around (meaning the best one on your hard drive by default) is almost certainly Mail. And of course, you can't beat the price; it's free!

Setting up Mail

If this is your first time launching Mail, you need to set up your email account(s) before you can proceed. A set of Choose a Mail Account Provider screens appears automatically. Just follow the instructions on each screen, fill in the fields as requested, and keep clicking the Continue button until you're finished.

TIP

If you don't know what to type in one or more of these fields, contact your ISP (Internet service provider) or mail provider for assistance.

After you set up one or more email accounts, you see a Welcome message asking whether you'd like to see what's new in Mail. If you click Yes, Help Viewer launches and shows you the What's New in Mail page; the Mail main window, which looks like Figure 17-1, appears in the background. Or if you click No, the Mail main window appears as the active window immediately.

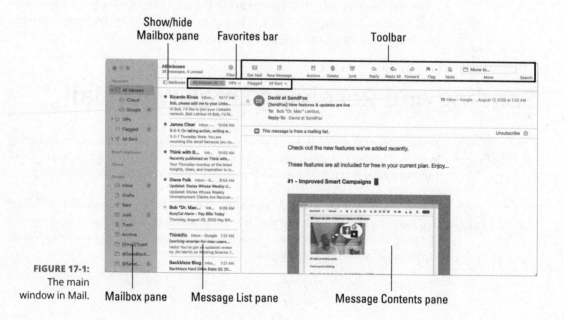

FIGURE 17-1:
The main window in Mail.

Show/hide Mailbox pane   Favorites bar   Toolbar

Mailbox pane   Message List pane   Message Contents pane

TECHNICAL
STUFF

The Mail main window is called a *viewer window* or *message viewer window*. You can have more than one of them on your screen, if you like; just choose File➪New Viewer Window or press ⌘+Option+N.

A quick overview of the toolbar

Before you go any further, look at Figure 17-1, which shows the 11 handy icons and a Search field on the viewer window's toolbar by default:

>> **Get Mail:** Checks for new email.

>> **New Message:** Creates a new, blank email message.

>> **Archive:** Archives selected message or messages.

>> **Delete:** Deletes selected message or messages.

TIP

To select more than one message in the list, hold down the ⌘ key when you click the second and subsequent messages.

>> **Junk:** Marks the selected message or messages as junk mail.

Mail has built-in junk-mail filtering that can be enabled or disabled in Mail Preferences. (Choose Mail➪Preferences and click the Junk Mail icon on the toolbar.) If you receive a piece of *spam* (junk mail), select it and click the Junk icon to help train the Mail junk-mail filter. If a selected message has been marked as junk mail, the icon changes to read Not Junk.

TIP

For more info on junk-mail filtering, click the question mark icon in the Junk Mail pane of the Mail Preferences window.

>> **Reply:** Creates a reply to the sender only.

>> **Reply All:** Creates a reply to the sender and everyone who was sent the original message.

>> **Forward:** Creates a copy of this message you can send to someone other than the sender or other recipients.

>> **Flag/Unflag:** From this drop-down menu, you can mark or unmark one or more messages with any of seven colored flags, which you can specify in searches and smart mailboxes (as you discover shortly).

>> **Mute:** Clicking this icon (or choosing Message➪Mute, or using the keyboard shortcut Control+Shift+M) turns off notifications for new messages in the selected message thread.

>> **Move:** This drop-down menu moves the selected messages to the folder of your choice.

Finally, the Search field on the toolbar finds a word or phrase in any item stored in Mail. When you begin typing, a drop-down menu appears (refer to Figure 17-2) so you can narrow the search to people or subjects matching your search phrase. I searched for items with *working* in all mailboxes, which reveals 12,021 items.

Note that you can also click the buttons on the Favorites bar to limit your search to specific mailboxes — All Inboxes, VIPs, Flagged, and All Sent in Figure 17-2.

TIP

If you see little numbers next to the mailbox buttons on the Favorites bar or Mailbox pane, they indicate the number of unread messages in that mailbox. A message is considered read after you click it.

Searching in Mail should be familiar because it works the same way as searching in Finder. So, for example, if you want to save a search as a smart mailbox (Mail's version of a smart folder in Finder), click the Save Search icon on the toolbar (visible in Figure 17-2).

Mail populates the Favorites bar with mailboxes it expects you to use often, namely Inbox, VIPs, Sent, and Flagged, as shown in Figure 17-2. Add your own mailboxes by dragging them from the Mailbox pane to the Favorites bar.

FIGURE 17-2:
Searching all mailboxes for messages containing *working*.

Composing a new message

Here's how to create an email message:

1. **Choose File⇨New Message, click the New Message icon on the toolbar, or press ⌘+N.**

   A new window appears. This is where you compose your email message, as shown in Figure 17-3.

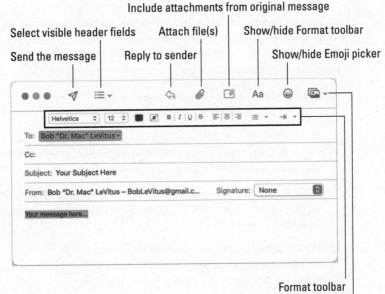

Select visible header fields · Attach file(s) · Show/hide Format toolbar

Include attachments from original message

Send the message · Reply to sender · Show/hide Emoji picker

Format toolbar

Show/hide Photo browser

FIGURE 17-3:
Composing an email message.

2. **Click in the To field, and type someone's email address.**

   Use my address (BigSur4Dummies@boblevitus.com) if you don't know anyone else to send mail to.

   TIP

   If the recipient is in your Contacts, just type a few letters, and Mail's intelligent autocomplete function matches it up with names in your Contacts database. When the list appears, you can choose an item by either clicking it or using the arrow keys to select it and then pressing Return.

3. **Press the Tab key twice and type a subject for this message in the Subject text field.**

   I typed *Your Subject Here* in Figure 17-3.

4. **Click in the main message portion of the window, and type your message there.**

   I typed *Your message here . . .* in Figure 17-3.

5. **When you're finished writing your message, click the Send button to send the email immediately, or close it to save it in the Drafts mailbox so you can work on it later.**

   TIP

   If you save your message to the Drafts mailbox (perhaps so you can write more later on), you can send it when you're ready by opening the Drafts mailbox, double-clicking the message, and then clicking the Send button.

Just for the record, here's what the icons on the toolbar in Figure 17-3 are all about:

>> **Send:** Duh. Sends the message.

>> **Header Fields:** This drop-down menu lets you add header fields — BCC, Reply-To, and Priority — to this message.

   If you want a BCC or Reply-To field in every new message you create, choose View⇨BCC Address Field or View⇨Reply-To Field (or use their keyboard shortcuts: ⌘+Option+B and ⌘+Option+R, respectively).

>> **Reply to Sender:** Lets you reply to the sender directly from the message window. It's inactive in Figure 17-3 because this is a new message and there is no sender to reply to.

>> **Attach:** Opens a standard Open File sheet so you can choose a file or files to enclose with this message. To enclose multiple files, hold down the ⌘ key while you click each file you want to enclose.

   If the recipients of this message use Windows, you probably want to click the Options button and select the Send Windows-Friendly Attachments check box, which appears at the bottom of the Open File sheet (if it's not already selected).

TIP

   I recommend that you select it even if you don't think you have Windows-using recipients because there's no downside for Mac or iOS users.

>> **Include Attachments from Original Message:** This icon includes any files that were attached to the message you're replying to or forwarding. It's inactive in Figure 17-3 because this is a new message, not a reply.

>> **Format Toolbar:** Shows or hides the Format toolbar, which is displayed (between the toolbar and the To field) in Figure 17-3.

>> **Show/Hide Emoji Picker:** Opens the Emoji picker; double-click an emoji to add it at the insertion point.

>> **Photo Browser:** Opens the Photo Browser panel, which displays the images in your photo library and lets you drag and drop them into a mail message.

Sending email from the Contacts app

TIP

You don't even have to open the Contacts app to send an email to a contact or group contained in your Contacts. In the preceding section, you see how Mail finds contacts (or groups) for you without launching Contacts. But if you already have Contacts open, the following technique for sending email to a contact or group is probably most convenient.

To create a blank email message to a contact, click and hold down on the field label next to the desired email address, and choose Send Email from the pop-up menu that appears, as shown for the Other label in Figure 17-4. Or move the pointer over an email address and then click the blue envelope icon that appears to the right of its name, as shown for my Work address in Figure 17-4.

FIGURE 17-4:
Sending email to
a contact is as
easy as clicking.

The Mail program becomes active, and a blank email message addressed to the selected contact appears on your screen. Just type your email as you normally would.

As you can see in Figure 17-4, in addition to sending an email, the pop-up menu next to email addresses lets you do the following:

>> Send an email.

>> Send a message (see the "Communicating with Messages" section, later in this chapter).

>> Send your vCard (see the following Tip) to this email address.

>> Search for this email address in documents on your Mac using Spotlight (see Chapter 10).

TIP

The information for each contact can be sent to others in an industry-standard file format known as a *vCard* (virtual business card). Choosing Send My Card works the same as Send Email, but instead of starting with a totally blank email message, the message starts with your vCard enclosed. When the recipient opens the vCard file, all your contact information will be added to his or her Contacts (or other contact manager in Windows).

Checking your mail

How do you check and open your mail? Easy. Just click the Get Mail icon at the top of the main Mail window (refer to Figure 17-1) or press ⌘+Shift+N.

>> **To read a new message,** select it. Its contents appear in the Message Content pane.

>> **To delete a selected message,** click the Delete icon on the toolbar or press Delete (or Backspace) on your keyboard.

You can delete a message in one other way if you have a trackpad. Swipe with two fingers from right to left a little bit and the Trash icon appears. Now you can click the Trash icon or continue your swipe to the left a bit farther. Either way, the message will disappear into Mail's Trash folder.

>> **To retrieve a message you accidentally deleted,** click Trash on the left and drag the message to the Inbox or another mailbox.

TIP

>> **To configure Mail to send and check for your mail every *x* minutes,** choose Mail ➪ Preferences and click the General icon at the top of the window. Click the Check for New Mail pop-up menu and make a selection — Automatically; every 1, 5, 15, 30, or 60 minutes; or Manually. The default is to check for new mail automatically, which means every few minutes. If you don't want Mail to do that, choose Manually.

>> **To add a sender to Contacts:** When someone who isn't already in your Contacts sends you an email message, simply choose Message ➪ Add Sender to Contacts.

Adding a sender to your Contacts has an additional benefit: It guards future messages from that person against being mistaken for junk mail. If a sender appears in your Contacts, his or her messages will never be mistakenly marked as junk mail. In other words, your Contacts is a white list for the spam filter. See the next section in this chapter for how to deal with spam.

TIP

When you receive an email containing details for an event, such as a flight or a dinner reservation, or even an invitation that says something like, *Let's have a beer at 6,* a smart suggestion appears between the message's header and body, so you can add the event to Calendar with just a click if you so desire.

Dealing with spam

Speaking of junk mail . . .. Although email is a wonderful thing, some people out there try to spoil it. They are *spammers*, and they're lowlifes who share their lists among themselves — and before you know it, your email inbox is flooded with get-rich-quick schemes, advertisements for pornographic websites and chat rooms, pills and powders that claim to perform miracles, and plenty of the more traditional buy-this-now junk mail.

Fortunately, Mail comes with a pretty darn good junk mail filter that analyzes incoming message subjects, senders, and contents to determine which ones are likely to contain bulk or junk mail. When you open Mail for the first time, it's running in its training mode, which is how Mail learns to differentiate between what it considers junk mail and what you consider junk mail; all it needs is your input. Mail identifies messages it thinks are junk, but if you disagree with its decisions, here's what you do:

>> Click the Not Junk icon on the toolbar for any message that *isn't* junk mail.

>> Conversely, if a piece of junk mail slips past Mail's filters and ends up in the Inbox, select the message and click the Junk icon on the toolbar.

After a few days (or weeks, depending on your mail volume), Mail should be getting it right almost all the time. When you reach that point, choose Move It to the Junk Mailbox on the Junk Mail tab of Mail's Preferences dialog. Now Mail starts moving junk mail automatically out of your Inbox and into a Junk mailbox, where you can scan the items quickly and trash them when you're ready.

If you prefer to use your email provider or third-party spam filters, you can turn off junk mail processing in Mail by disabling it on the Junk Mail tab of Mail's Preferences dialog. Or use both.

Mailboxes smart and plain

After reading mail, you can either delete it or file it in a mailbox. The following sections take a closer look at the two types of mailboxes you have at your disposal — plain and smart.

Plain old mailboxes

Plain mailboxes are just like folders in Finder; you create them and name them, and they're empty until you put something in them. They even look like folders in the Mailboxes sidebar in Mail. You use mailboxes to organize any messages you want to save.

Here are three ways to create a plain mailbox:

>> Choose Mailbox ➪ New Mailbox.

>> Click the + that appears to the right of top-level Mailboxes in the mailbox pane. If you don't see the +, it will magically appear if you hover your cursor over mailbox name (such as iCloud or Gmail).

>> Right-click or Control-click in the Mailboxes sidebar and choose New Mailbox from the shortcut menu.

Whichever way you choose, the next thing that happens is that a sheet drops down with a Location pop-up menu and a field for you to type the name you want to give this mailbox. Choose On My Mac from the Location menu to store your filed messages locally, on your hard drive; or choose iCloud or another email provider to store filed messages remotely, on the mail server.

TIP

Choosing iCloud or your email provider means messages you move to that mailbox will be stored remotely. If you access your email from more than one device, I recommend you create all your mailboxes on the email server so they'll be available to you no matter where you are or what device you're using to check your mail.

Finally, name the mailbox anything you like and click OK, and the mailbox is created in the Mailboxes sidebar.

If you right- or Control-click a mailbox and choose New Mailbox, the Location menu in the sheet will show the name of the mailbox you clicked. So, if you were to click OK now, the new mailbox would be a sub-mailbox of the mailbox you clicked. *Sub-mailboxes* — mailboxes inside other mailboxes — are a useful feature if you care to further subdivide your message storage system.

In Figure 17-5, the MyArchive mailbox has 12 sub-mailboxes — from BLTV Show to Udemy — and the 10 mailboxes between them are all sub-mailboxes of MyArchive.

TIP

Note how the top of the window tells you that 12 mailboxes are selected, with 1,562 messages displayed. That happens to be the total number of messages in the dozen highlighted mailboxes. Coincidence? I think not.

You can also drag and drop a mailbox or mailboxes from the top level of the list into another mailbox to make *them* sub-mailboxes. If you drag a mailbox into a sub-mailbox, it becomes a sub-sub-mailbox.

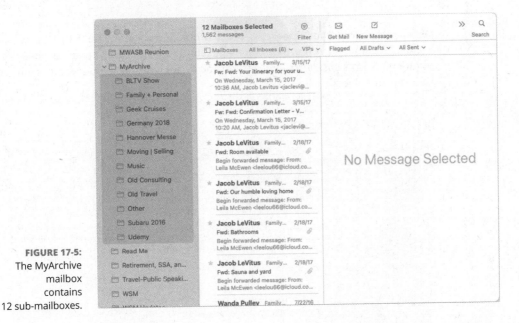

FIGURE 17-5:
The MyArchive
mailbox
contains
12 sub-mailboxes.

To delete a mailbox (and its sub-mailboxes if it has any), do one of the following:

>> Click it to select it and then choose Mailbox➪Delete Mailbox.

>> Right-click or Control-click the mailbox, and choose Delete Mailbox.

Intelligent smart mailboxes

A smart mailbox is Mail's version of Finder's smart folder. In a nutshell, *smart mailboxes* are mailboxes that display the results of a search. The messages you see in a smart mailbox are *virtual;* they aren't really in the smart mailbox itself. Instead, the smart mailbox displays a list of messages stored in other mailboxes that match whatever criteria you defined for that smart mailbox. Like smart folders in Finder, smart mailboxes are updated automatically when new messages that meet the criteria are received.

To create a smart mailbox:

>> Choose Mailbox➪New Smart Mailbox.

>> Click the +-in-a-circle on the right side of the Smart Mailboxes header in the Mailboxes pane.

Whichever method you choose, a sheet drops down with a field for the smart mailbox's name, plus some pop-up menus, buttons, and check boxes, as shown in Figure 17-6. This smart mailbox gathers messages with the words *Big Sur* in either the body or subject.

FIGURE 17-6:
Set criteria for a smart mailbox.

Name your smart mailbox, determine its criteria (by using the pop-up menus, plus and minus buttons, and check boxes), and then click OK. The smart mailbox appears in the Mailboxes sidebar with a little gear to denote that it's smart. You can see the Smart Big Sur smart mailbox in the Mailboxes pane in Figure 17-6. Note that it has a gear to its left (plain mailboxes don't).

I use a smart mailbox that holds every mail message to or from my wife and children in one place. And I use another to see all my Dummies email in a single place. Since they don't use up any additional disk space, smart mailboxes are a great way to organize mail, automatically making it easier to find a message with no effort on your part (after you set them up).

Changing your preferences

Mail's preferences (Mail ⇨ Preferences or ⌘+,) are more than you might expect from the name. The Mail Preferences window is the control center for Mail, where you can do the following:

>> **Create and delete email accounts.**

>> **Determine which fonts and colors are used for your messages.**

>> **Decide whether to download and save attachments (such as pictures).**

>> **Decide whether to send formatted mail or plain text.**

>> **Decide whether to turn on the spell checker.** The default is to check spelling as you type, which many people (myself included) find annoying.

>> **Decide whether to have an automatic signature appended to your messages.**

>> **Establish rules to process mail that you receive.**

The first five items are up to you to decide. The last two are the most important features of the Preferences window — namely, automatically adding your signature(s) to outgoing messages and inbound-mail processing rules.

Sign here, please

If you're like me, you'd rather not type your entire signature every time you send an email message, and you don't have to with Mail. If you create canned signatures, you can use them in outgoing messages without typing a single character.

Here's how it works:

1. **Choose Mail ⇨ Preferences or press ⌘+, (comma).**

2. **On the Preferences dialog's toolbar, click the Signatures icon.**

3. **In the left column, click the name of the mail account for which you want to create this signature.**

    I clicked iCloud.

4. **To create a new, blank signature, click the little + sign at the bottom of the middle column.**

5. **Type a descriptive name for this signature to replace the default name Signature #1.**

    My new default name is *BL Long*.

6. **In the right column, type the signature exactly as you want it to appear in outgoing messages.**

    I typed *All the best, Bob "Dr. Mac" LeVitus – Technology Columnist. . .* and so on in Figure 17-7.

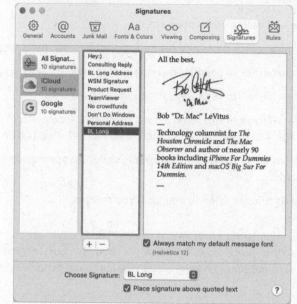

FIGURE 17-7:
My newly created
BL Long
signature.

7. **(Optional) Drag a scanned image of your signature to the appropriate place in your document.**

I dragged it between *All the best* and *Bob "Dr. Mac" LeVitus*.

8. **Drag the name you assigned this signature to the mail account you're using it with.**

I dragged BL Long to iCloud.

If you have more than one signature, you can select the one you want to use as the default: Choose the account in the column on the left, and then choose the signature from the Choose Signature pop-up menu.

TIP

If you have more than one signature, another cool thing happens. The Signature pop-up menu appears in new messages and replies, so you can choose a signature other than the default for this message.

Mail rules rule

If you really want to tap the power of Mail, you need to set *rules*. With some cool rules, you can automatically tag messages with a color; file them in a specific mailbox; reply to, forward, or redirect the messages automatically (handy when you're going to be away for a while); automatically reply to messages; and *kill-file* messages (just delete them without even bothering to look at them — what better fate for mail from people you hate?).

There's no way I can do rules justice in a page or so, but here's a quick look at how to create one. In broad terms, you create a condition and then an action. In this example, I create a filter named Message From LeVitus, with the action to sound a funky alert, as shown in Figure 17-8.

FIGURE 17-8:
Setting a rule.

Here are the steps:

1. **Choose Mail⇨Preferences.**

2. **Click the Rules icon on the toolbar of the Preferences dialog.**

3. **Click the Add Rule button.**

4. **In the Description field, type a description.**

   I typed *Message From LeVitus*.

5. **Click the first pop-up menu (which says Any in Figure 17-8) to determine when to apply this rule.**

   The options are Any or All. I chose Any, which is the default. Note that my choice in this menu doesn't matter for this rule, which only has one condition.

6. **Click the first pop-up menu in the Conditions section to define the condition.**

I chose From in Figure 17-8 but there are myriad other options, including Date Sent, Date Received, Sender Is or Isn't in My Contacts, and Sender Is or Isn't a Member of a Group. I implore you to explore them at your leisure.

7. **Click the second pop-up menu in the Conditions section (Contains in Figure 17-8) and make a selection.**

Your choices are Contains, Does Not Contain, Begins With, Ends With, or Is Equal To.

8. **In the field on the right side of the Conditions section, type a word or phrase.**

I typed *LeVitus,* so my condition reads: From Contains LeVitus.

9. **Click the first pop-up menu in the Actions section (Play Sound in Figure 17-8).**

Look at your options in this pop-up menu (too numerous to mention) and choose one.

10. **Click the second pop-up menu in the Actions section (Funky in Figure 17-8) to specify the sound you'll hear when this action is triggered.**

11. **Click OK.**

Mail asks whether you want to apply your rule(s) to the selected mailboxes.

12. **Choose Apply if you want Mail to run this rule on the selected mailboxes, or choose Don't Apply if you don't.**

And that's how you build a rule. From this point forward, every time you get a message from someone named LeVitus, you hear the Funky sound.

TIP

Note the little – (minus) and + (plus) buttons to the right of the conditions and actions. Use + to add more conditions or actions and – to delete a condition or action. If you have multiple conditions, you can choose Any or All from the pop-up menu above them, which executes this rule when either any condition is met or all conditions are met. All the actions you create are always executed when this rule is triggered.

Take a (Quick) look and (Slide) show me some photos

One last cool feature, and you're finished with Mail. That cool feature is Quick Look, which includes a slick Slideshow option. If you press and hold down on the paper clip icon (shown in Figure 17-9) and choose Quick Look from the resulting drop-down menu, a new window appears showing one of the enclosed pictures, as shown lower right in Figure 17-9.

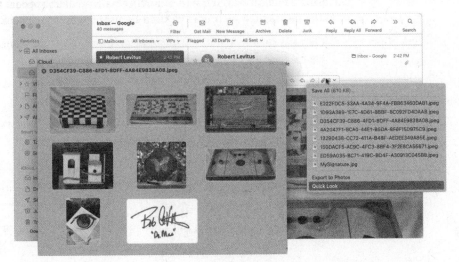

FIGURE 17-9:
Using Quick Look.

If you don't see a paperclip, hover your cursor over the line between the message header and the message body and the paper clip will magically appear. Or click the image in the message body so it is highlighted, and then press the spacebar to take a Quick Look.

To close the Quick Look window, click the little X in its top-left corner or press the spacebar.

Markup and Mail Drop

Last but not by any means least, two more excellent Mail features: Markup and Mail Drop.

Markup

Markup lets you annotate images or PDF documents. When you're composing a message that has an image or a PDF you've attached or dragged in, hover the pointer over the picture and a little chevron (v) appears in its upper-right corner. Click it to use the Markup tools on this image.

Details on using Markup appear in Chapter 5.

Mail Drop

Mail Drop, on the other hand, is an elegant solution for large email attachments. If you enclose files or a folder full of files in a message and Mail thinks the enclosure(s) might be too big to send via email, an alert appears when you try to send the message. A picture is worth a thousand words, so check out my alert in Figure 17-10.

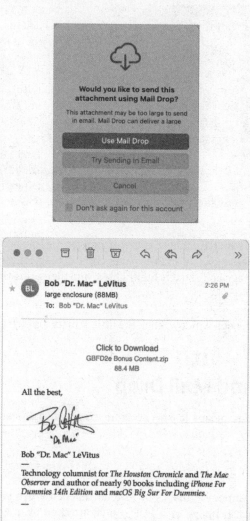

FIGURE 17-10: Choose Use Mail Drop in the alert box (top), and your recipient sees this message (bottom).

If I opt for Try Sending in Email, Mail will go ahead and try to send my message even though the file is 88.4MB. Chances are pretty good, though, that the mail server I send the message through will bounce it back to me for being too large. But if I choose Use Mail Drop, which uses iCloud, the enclosure's size can be huge and the message still won't bounce. If I go this route, the recipient will receive a link to download the files from iCloud, as shown on the bottom in Figure 17-10.

Mail Drop should be enabled by default. If it's not, choose Mail⇨Preferences and click the Accounts icon at the top of the window. Then click the account you want to use it with, click the Account Information tab, and select its Send Large Attachments Mail Drop check box.

Mail didn't receive a lot of love this year, but it has a handful of minor but useful new features. My favorite is the new Unsubscribe button. When you receive an email from a mailing list, just click the Unsubscribe button (between the header and the body of the message) and it's done.

You'll also find a toolbar icon (a bell with a slash) to mute the selected conversation. Clicking this icon (or choosing Message⇨Mute, or using the keyboard shortcut Control+Shift+M) will turn off notifications for new messages in this thread.

Finally, you can now block a sender by right- or Control-clicking a sender's name and choosing Block Sender from the pop-up menu. You'll then see This Message Is from a Blocked Sender, along with a Preferences button. Click the button to specify how you want your blocked mail handled: marked as blocked but left in your inbox or moved directly to the Trash.

Communicating with Messages

Instant messaging (IM) enables interactive communication among users all over the world. Messages gives you immediate access to all the other users of AIM, Google Talk, and iCloud. All you need are their screen names, and you're set to go.

 To get started, launch Messages from your Applications folder, Launchpad, or the dock.

What the heck is an iMessage?

iMessage is Apple's inter-device messaging protocol. That means you can send unlimited iMessages to anyone with an iPhone, iPad, or iPod touch running iOS 5 (or later) or a Mac running Mountain Lion (OS X 10.8) or later.

Think of it as MMS messaging, similar to what you find on smartphones, but you can send and receive messages from your Mac. Better still, an iMessage can include photos, audio recordings, videos, locations, and contacts in addition, of course, to text. And if you have more than one iOS device or Mac, iMessage keeps all your conversations going across all of them. You can also get delivery receipts letting you know your messages went through. You'll know it's been read, too, if your friend has enabled read receipts.

If you have an iPhone 4 or newer, the Continuity feature allows all SMS and MMS text messages you send and receive on your iPhone via your wireless carrier's messaging system to appear also in the Messages app on your Mac, iPad, and iPod touch almost simultaneously — even if the person you're messaging doesn't have an iPhone. Better yet, you can reply from whichever device is closest to you, regardless of what kind of cellphone the person has.

For this to happen, all devices need to be using the same Apple ID for Messages on all devices, and Enable Messages in iCloud must be enabled (Messages⇨Preferences⇨iMessage tab).

TIP

You can start a new iMessage also by clicking a phone number in Safari, Contacts, or Calendar.

Chit-chatting with Messages

Your chats can be one to one, or they can be group bull sessions. Messages is integrated with Contacts, so you don't have to enter your buddies' information twice. It also communicates directly with the Mail application. Here's all the essential info you need to get started:

>> **To start a text chat,** open Messages, click the New Chat icon next to the Search field (shown in the margin) and then either begin typing a contact's name in the To field or click the little plus-in-a-circle to see a list of contacts with its own search field.

If you've already shared a message with someone, click his or her name in the list on the left to send a new message or use the Search field to find your chat with that person.

After you've chosen a recipient, type your text in the iMessage field at the bottom of the window and press Return or Enter to send it.

In Figure 17-11, I clicked my wife's name in the list on the left and saw a message that she left home without her driver's license. I asked if that was going to be a problem. She replied "No" and asked me if it was on the table, to which I replied "Yes."

In a chat, each participant's text appears in a different color and orientation; my words are in blue bubbles with white text on the right; her words are in gray bubbles with black text on the left.

FIGURE 17-11:
A chat between my wife and me.

>> **To start a group text chat,** click the new Chat icon, and add each person you want to include as described above.

When you finish adding names to the To field, type and send your message as just described and everyone in the To field will receive it. From then on, everyone will see every message from every participant.

Click Details at the top right, and you can use your iPhone (if it's nearby) to call someone by clicking the phone icon next to the person's name. You can also choose Do Not Disturb for this conversation to mute notifications for this conversation only, which is great if one or more participants is a serial texter. Finally, click Leave This Conversation if you want to, well, leave this conversation permanently.

>> **To attach a picture to a person in your Contacts:** Copy a picture of the person to the Clipboard in your favorite graphics application (Preview, for example). Now open Contacts, and display the card for the person you want to add a picture to. Click the empty picture box at the top of the card, and paste the picture from the Clipboard. You should now see that picture on the Contacts card and also when you chat in Messages with the person. Neat!

If you already attached a picture to a contact in Contacts, that picture will appear automatically when you chat.

TIP

>> **To transfer a file or files,** just drag the icon(s) to the iMessage field (where you type your messages), and then press Return. The file zips across the ether. This is a convenient way to share photos or documents without resorting to file sharing or email.

When you drag an image file onto the Messages window's message box, you see an oversize semitransparent preview, letting you know you're sure you're sending the right image and not something totally embarrassing. Way to go, Big Sur.

You could also choose Conversations⇨Send File or press ⌘+Option+F and then select the file(s) from a standard Open File sheet, but the drag-and-drop method is faster and easier.

>> **To send a voice message,** click the sound wave to the right of the iMessage field and begin talking. When you're finished, click the red Record icon and then click Cancel or Send.

>> **To start a FaceTime video or audio call,** select the person you want to call in the list on the left, and then choose Conversations⇨FaceTime Video or Conversations⇨FaceTime Audio.

>> **To share your Mac screen with a contact** (or ask a contact to share his or her Mac screen with you), choose Conversations⇨Invite to Share My Screen or Conversations⇨Ask to Share Screen.

TIP

This semi-hidden feature is awesome for providing technical support to other Mac users. I use it all the time to help my family with their Mac issues. Solving a Mac problem is much easier when I can see the person's Mac screen and control it remotely.

>> **To search for a person, a word, a phrase, or an image,** begin typing in the Search field or press ⌘+F.

NEW

>> **To pin a conversation to the top of the list,** right- or Control-click the conversation and choose Pin. To unpin a pinned conversation, right- or Control-click and choose Unpin.

NEW

>> **To add message effects (balloons, confetti, lasers, fireworks, and more), create a memoji, use memoji stickers, or search for images on the Internet,** click the Applications icon (A) on the left side of the iMessage field.

>> **To send an email from Messages,** just select a conversation in the list and choose Conversations⇨Send Email (or press ⌘+Option+E). Mail launches (if it's not already open) and addresses a new message to the selected buddy, ready for you to begin typing.

Chapter **18**

Sharing Your Mac and Liking It

Have you ever wanted to grab a file from your Mac while you were halfway around the world, around the corner, or in the next room? If so, I have good news for you: It's not difficult with macOS (believe it or not) even though computer networking in general has a well-deserved reputation for being complicated and nerve-wracking. The truth is that you won't encounter anything scary or complicated about sharing files, folders, and disks (and printers, for that matter) among computers as long as the computers are Macs. And even if some of the computers are running Windows, Big Sur even makes that (almost) painless.

Your Macintosh includes everything that you need to share files and printers, except the printers and the cables (and maybe a router). So here's the deal: You supply the hardware, and this chapter supplies the rest.

The first sections of this chapter provide an overview and tell you everything you need to know to set up new user accounts and share files successfully. I don't show you how to actually share a file, folder, or disk until the "Connecting to a Shared Disk or Folder on a Remote Mac" section, later in this chapter. Trust me, there's a method to my madness. If you try to share files without doing all the required prep work, the whole mess becomes confusing and complicated pretty fast — kind of like networking PCs.

One last thing: If you're the only one who uses your Mac, you don't intend to share it or its files with anyone else, and you never intend to access your Mac from another computer in a different location, you can safely skip this chapter.

Introducing Networks and File Sharing

Big Sur's file sharing enables you to use files, folders, and disks from other Macs on a network — including the Internet — as easily as though they were on your own local hard drive. If you have more than one computer, file sharing is a blessing.

Before diving in and sharing, allow me to introduce a few necessary terms:

>> **Network:** For the purposes of this chapter, a *network* is two or more Macs connected by Ethernet cables, wireless networking (Apple refers to this as AirPort or Wi-Fi), or FireWire cables (rarely seen anymore).

>> **Ethernet:** This network protocol and cabling scheme lets you connect two or more computers so they can share files, disks, printers, or whatever.

>> **Ethernet port:** This is where you plug an Ethernet cable into your Mac (as long as your Mac has one — not all Macs do).

Be careful to match the cable to its specific jack. On your Mac and printer, the Ethernet ports look a lot like a phone jack, and the connectors on each end of an Ethernet cable look a lot like phone cable connectors — but they aren't the same. Ethernet cables are typically thicker, and the connectors (RJ-45 connectors) are a bit larger than the RJ-11 connectors that you use with telephones. (See examples of both types of ports in the margin.) Standard phone cables fit (very loosely) into Ethernet ports, but you shouldn't try that, either; they'll probably fall out with the slightest vibration. It's unlikely that such a mistake will cause damage, but it won't work and will be frustrating.

If your Mac didn't include an Ethernet port but you'd like one, you can find Thunderbolt and USB adapters that will let you have your cake (and an Ethernet port) and eat it too (plug an Ethernet cable into a Thunderbolt or USB port).

» **Local devices:** Such devices are connected directly to your computers, such as hard or optical drives. Your internal SSD or hard drive, for example, are local devices.

» **Remote devices:** You access (share) these devices over the network. The hard drive of a computer in the next room, for example, is a remote device.

» **Protocols:** These are the languages that networks speak. When you read or hear about networks, you're likely to hear the words *Bonjour, Ethernet, SMB,* and *TCP/IP* bandied about with great regularity. These are all *protocols*. Macs can speak several different protocols, but every device (Mac or printer) on a network needs to speak the same protocol at the same time to communicate.

REMEMBER

Support for the TCP/IP protocol is built into every Mac, and macOS Big Sur includes all the software you need to set up a TCP/IP network. The hardware you provide consists of Ethernet cables and a hub (if you have more than two computers) or Wi-Fi provided by a wireless router. Here, I'm using the term *hub* generically; its more powerful networking cousins, switches and routers, also work for this purpose.

Portrait of home office networking

A typical Mac home office network consists of two Macintoshes, a wireless Wi-Fi router (or other type of Ethernet hub, switch, or router), and a network printer. Check out Figure 18-1 to see the configuration of a simple network. In the figure, the black lines between the devices are Ethernet cables; the rectangular device with those cables going into it is an Ethernet hub, switch, or router. (I tell you more about cables and such devices in the section "Three ways to build a network," later in this chapter.) You need enough Ethernet cable to run among all your devices.

TIP

With the setup shown in Figure 18-1, either Mac can use the other Mac's files, and both Macs can print to the same printer. If you have a broadband Internet connection, you can also connect the cable or DSL modem to the hub or switch or router so all Mac users on the network can share the Internet connection.

TECHNICAL STUFF

A network can — and often does — have dozens or hundreds of users. Whether your network has two nodes (machines) or two thousand, the principles and techniques in this chapter apply.

FIGURE 18-1:
Two Macs and a
printer make up a
simple Mac
network.

Mac   Mac

Ethernet router, switch, or hub

Printer

FILE SHARING MADE EASY WITH AIRDROP

Perhaps all you want to do is share an occasional file (not necessarily a printer or a home Internet connection or a folder of music files or pictures). In that case, check out AirDrop (available on all Macs built in the past few years), which uses Bonjour, Apple's proprietary zero-configuration network protocol. It's a big part of the secret sauce in macOS that makes Mac networking so simple.

Here's how it works: If two devices speak Bonjour, you don't have to do any configuration other than possibly turning on the sharing capability (and holding them near each other), as I explain in "Setting Up File Sharing," later in this chapter. Bonjour queries the other available networked devices to see what services they support and then configures the connections for you automatically. Sweet!

It gets even better if you're using macOS 10.7 Lion or later (which I suspect most of you are), because you can use the nifty sharing feature called AirDrop. It appears in your Finder window sidebar and locates all other AirDrop-capable Macs on your local wireless network.

And it's better still if you're using macOS 10.10 Yosemite or later, because in these versions, AirDrop can also locate and share files with AirDrop-capable iPhones, iPads, and iPod touches. Sweeter!

The only caveats are that AirDrop uses both Bluetooth and Wi-Fi, and users must enable AirDrop from Control Center on iDevices or by selecting it in the sidebar on a Mac's Finder window. On a Mac, you see AirDrop in the Finder window, as shown in the figure here.

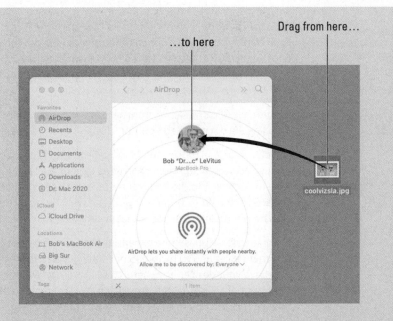

To send a file (or multiple files and/or folders) to the other Mac or iDevice, just drag it (or them) onto the other Mac's or iDevice's icon as shown. AirDrop displays a dialog on the other Mac asking whether the user wants to accept delivery; if so, the items are transferred immediately to the Downloads folder on the Mac. If you're sending to an iDevice, its user gets an alert asking whether to accept the file, and then is asked what app to open it in using a familiar Share sheet-like interface.

When you close the AirDrop window, you're no longer visible to other AirDrop users.

Three ways to build a network

In this chapter, I assume you're working on a small network, the kind typically found in a home or small business. If you're part of a megamonstrous corporate network, and you have questions about your particular network, talk to the PIC (*person in charge,* also known as your *network administrator*). In other words, if you're trying to build a meganetwork, you're going to need a book a lot thicker and harder to understand than this one.

The following list gives you three common ways to build a modern small home or office network:

>> **Wi-Fi:** All Macs come equipped with Wi-Fi; if you have an AirPort, AirPort Extreme, Time Capsule, or any other Wi-Fi router, you don't need cables at all.

For what it's worth, you can use most third-party Wi-Fi routers, which is a good thing since Apple stopped producing AirPort products, including Time Capsule, early in 2018. You can still find them and they still work, but I advise against buying one now because they are no longer in production and may or may not work with future versions of macOS.

For the sake of convenience, from here on I'm going to refer to wireless routers — including the discontinued Apple products — generically as Wi-Fi routers.

Just plug in a Wi-Fi router, and Macs can communicate with one another. If you use an Ethernet printer (connected to your Mac by Ethernet cable), you have to connect it to the Wi-Fi router before you can print from your wireless Macs. Both the Wi-Fi router and printer have Ethernet ports, so you can use an Ethernet cable (more about that in a minute) to make the connection.

Although this setup is more expensive than connecting everything with Ethernet cables and a cheap hub or router, it's also more flexible because you can move your devices anywhere. (Well, almost anywhere; you're limited to a maximum of 150 to 200 feet from each Wi-Fi router, and that's assuming that nothing is in the way to block your signal. Your mileage may vary.) That said, Ethernet is usually significantly faster than Wi-Fi.

TIP

I've been using wireless printers for years. If you have a Wi-Fi network available, many inexpensive printers (and expensive ones, too) now offer wireless printing, which means you can stash your printer in a closet or another room if you care to.

>> **Traditional Ethernet:** Most desktop Macs still have an Ethernet port, while most laptops don't. If you need an Ethernet port for a Mac that doesn't have one, you can buy an inexpensive Ethernet-to-USB dongle (adapter).

To connect Ethernet-equipped Macs to a wired network, you need Ethernet cables for each Mac and a little device called a *hub, switch,* or *router,* which acts as the center of a wheel; the cables to computers and printers are the spokes.

A typical Ethernet router includes two to eight Ethernet ports. You plug the router into an electrical outlet and then connect Ethernet cables from each of your Macs and printers (from their Ethernet ports) to the router. *Voilà* — instant network. These gadgets are pretty cheap, starting at around $30; cables start at a few bucks, increasing in price with the length and quality.

>> **Small Ethernet:** If you have only two devices to network (two Macs, or a Mac and an Ethernet printer, in most cases), you can use an Ethernet cable to connect them directly to each other via the Ethernet ports. You can purchase an Ethernet cable at your local electronics store. Plug one end of the Ethernet cable into one device and the other end into the other device.

If you use an Apple AirPort Extreme Wi-Fi router or Time Capsule, you may not need a hub, switch, or router because these devices incorporate small routers with three Ethernet ports. Either one is all you need unless you have more than three Ethernet devices to connect. If that's the case, you'll need to add a hub, switch, or router with additional Ethernet ports to accommodate them all (in addition to your AirPort or Time Capsule).

TIP

If you have a cable modem or digital subscriber line (DSL) as your Internet connection, you might need a router or switch instead of a (cheaper-but-going-out-of-fashion) hub. Routers and switches are similar to hubs but cost more and have additional features that you may or may not need. Your ISP can tell you whether you need one and what they recommend.

Last, but not least, if your Mac doesn't have an Ethernet port built-in but you wish it did, pick up an inexpensive Ethernet-to-USB adapter for less than $20 at Amazon.com or your favorite tech store.

Setting Up File Sharing

Before you get into the nitty-gritty of sharing files, you must complete a few housekeeping tasks, such as enabling the appropriate type of file sharing. Follow these steps to do so:

1. **Choose ⇨ System Preferences and then click the Sharing icon.**

   The Sharing System Preferences pane appears. The first word of the long username of the first admin account created on this computer appears in the Computer Name field by default, followed by the type of Mac (for example, Bob's MacBook Air).

2. **If you want to change the name of your computer from whatever Big Sur decided to call it to something more personal, do that now in the Computer Name text field at the top of the Sharing pane.**

   In Figure 18-2, you can see that I renamed mine *Bob's MacBook Air*. You can name yours anything you like.

3. **Enable the check box for File Sharing, as shown in Figure 18-2.**

   Now other users on your network can access files and folders on your computer, as you see later in this chapter.

   By default, only one folder in your Home folder is shared, and that folder is your Public folder. If you want to access files or folders on this computer while you're using another computer on the network, you can so long as you first provide your username and password. Everyone else on the network can see only your Public folder.

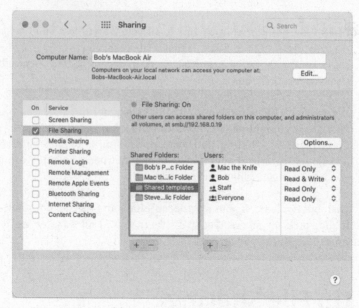

FIGURE 18-2:
Turning file
sharing on
and off.

WARNING

These are the safest settings. Unless you have good reason to tinker with them, you should probably not change anything here. That said, if you feel you must change these settings, you find out how to do so in the next section of this chapter.

4. **(Optional) If you want remote users to upload and download files to and from this computer, make sure that File Sharing is selected in the sidebar. Then click the Options button, and select the Share Files and Folders Using SMB check box.**

   Doing so gives users on the Internet but not on your local area network (LAN) an alternative to file sharing by allowing any client program that uses Server Message Block (Samba, or SMB) protocol.

   If you want to enable Windows or Linux users — or users of other operating systems — to share files with you, the SMB check box must be selected.

   Select the On check box (in the leftmost column) for each account you want to enable to use these protocols to access your Mac, providing the password when prompted.

5. **Click the Done button when you're done, and then proceed to the following section to continue setting up your network.**

Access and Permissions: Who Can Do What

After you set up file sharing (as I explain in the preceding section), your next step on the path to sharing files on a network is telling your Mac who is allowed to see and access specific folders. Fortunately, this happens to be what I cover in the following sections.

Users and groups and guests

Mac file sharing (and indeed, macOS as well) is based on the concept of users. You can share items — such as drives or folders — with no users, one user, or many users, depending on your needs.

Before you can understand how file sharing works, you need to grok the terminology. So here are brief descriptions of users, administrators, groups, and guests:

>> **Users:** People who share folders and drives (or your Mac) are *users*. A user's access to items on your local hard drive is entirely at your discretion. You can configure your Mac so only you can access its folders and drives, or so only one other person or group — or everyone — can share its folders and drives.

When you first set up your Mac, you created your first user. This user automatically has administrative powers, such as adding more users, changing preferences, and having the clearance to see all folders on the hard drive.

REMEMBER

For the purposes of this book, I assume that some users for whom you create identities will be not folks who sit at your Mac but those who connect to it only from remote locations when they need to give or get files. But you could allow such a user to use the same name and password to log in while sitting at your desk.

TECHNICAL STUFF

For most intents and purposes, a remote user and a local user are the same. Here's why: After you create an account for a user, that user can log in to your Mac while sitting in your chair in your office, from anywhere on your local area network via Ethernet or Wi-Fi, or from anywhere in the world via the Internet — as long as that person has an Administrator, Standard, or Sharing account on your Mac.

>> **Administrative users:** Although a complete discussion of the special permissions that a user with administrator permissions has on a Mac running macOS is far beyond the scope of this book, note two important things:

● The first user created (usually when you install macOS for the first time) is automatically granted administrator (admin) powers.

- Only an administrator account can create users, delete some (but not all) files from folders that aren't in his or her Home folder, lock and unlock System Preferences panes, and do a bunch of other stuff. If you try something and it doesn't work, make sure you're logged in as an administrator or can provide an administrator username and password when prompted.

TIP

You can give any user administrator permissions by selecting that user's account in the Users & Groups System Preferences pane and selecting the Allow User to Administer This Computer check box. You can select this check box when you're creating the user account or anytime thereafter.

>> **Groups:** As you may recall, macOS is based on the UNIX operating system and *Groups* are the Unix-level designations for privilege consolidation. For example, there are groups named Staff and Everyone (as well as a bunch of others). A user can be a member of multiple groups. For example, your main account is in the Staff, Admin, and Everyone groups (and others, too). Don't worry — you find out more about groups shortly.

>> **Guests:** Two kinds of guests exist. The first kind lets your friends log into your Mac while sitting at your desk without user accounts or passwords. But they have no access to your data. When they log out, all information and files in the guest user account's Home folder are deleted automatically.

TIP

If you want this kind of guest user account, you need to enable the account in the Users & Groups System Preferences pane. To do so, click Guest User account in the list of accounts on the left and select the Allow Guests to Log In to This Computer check box.

The second kind of guest is people who access Public folders on your Mac via file sharing over your LAN or the Internet. They don't need usernames or passwords. If they're on your LAN, they can see and use your Public folder(s), unless you or the Public folder's owner has altered the permissions. If they're on the Internet and know your IP address, they can see and use your Public folder(s) if you don't have a firewall blocking such access. Public folders are all that guests can access, luckily. You don't have to do anything to enable this type of guest user account.

Creating users

Before users can share folders and drives (or have their own accounts on your computer, for that matter), they must have an account on your Mac. You can create two different kinds of accounts for them — a user account or a sharing only account.

>> **When you create a user account** for a person (I call that person and account *User 1*), the account has its own Home folder (called — what else? — User 1), which is filled with User 1's files. Nobody but User 1 can access files in this Home folder unless, of course, User 1 has provided someone the account name and password.

>> **When you create a sharing only account** for a person (I call that person and account *Sharing 1*), the person using that account doesn't have a Home folder and can't access other users' Home folders. Sharing 1 can access only the Public folders inside all the Home folders on that Mac.

You can create a new *user* account only in the Users & Groups System Preferences pane. You can create a new *sharing only* account in either the Users & Groups or Sharing System Preferences panes.

REMEMBER

Anyone can remotely access files or folders in your Public folder(s) over a LAN or the Internet. But if you want them to be able to access folders or files other than those in the Public folder(s) on your Mac, they need either a user account or a sharing only account.

When you add (create) a user, you need to tell your Mac who this person is. This is also the time to set passwords and administrative powers for this new user. Here's the drill:

1. **Choose ⇨ System Preferences (or click the System Preferences icon on the dock), click the Users & Groups icon, and then make sure that the Password tab is selected.**

The Users & Groups System Preferences pane appears. In this pane (shown in Figure 18-3), you can see the name of the first user (Bob) and the administrative control that this user is allowed.

REMEMBER

The first user created (usually at the same time you installed macOS or turned on a brand-new Mac) always has administrator permissions. This is why the Allow User to Administer This Computer check box is selected but the option is dimmed in Figure 18-3. (The first user created is *always* an admin.)

2. **Click the + button below the list of users.**

A sheet appears in which you enter the new user's information.

REMEMBER

If the + button is dimmed, here's how you get it functioning: Click the lock (at bottom left), supply an administrator name and password in the resulting dialog, and then click OK.

3. **Choose Standard from the New Account menu.**

FIGURE 18-3:
The Users &
Groups System
Preferences pane
is where you
manage user
accounts on
the Mac.

4. **In the Full Name text box, type the full name of a user you want to add.**

In the Account Name text box, your Mac inserts a suggested account name (formerly known as the *short name*). Check out Figure 18-4 to see both.

In Figure 18-4, I added Steve Wozniak as a user, typing his full name in the Full Name field. You don't really need to type the user's full name, but I do so in this example to show you the difference between a full name and an account name.

FIGURE 18-4:
Name the new
user, and your
Mac suggests a
shortened name
and password.

5. Press the Tab key to move to the next field.

macOS suggests an abbreviated version of the name in the Account Name field.

Because he's not the only Steve who matters around here, I changed the account name suggested by macOS (stevewozniak) to TheWoz, which is shorter. (In other words, I typed TheWoz in the Account Name field, replacing the suggested stevewozniak.) The name of each user's folder (in the Users folder) is taken from the account name that you enter when you create a user.

TIP

Users can connect to your Mac (or log in from their own Macs, for that matter) by using the account name, rather than having to type their full names. The account name is also used in environments in which usernames can't have spaces and are limited to eight or fewer characters. Although macOS Big Sur allows longer usernames (but no spaces), you might be better off keeping your account name shorter than eight characters, just in case.

6. Tab to the Password field and enter an initial password for this user.

The small, square icon with the key to the right of the Password field, when clicked, displays the Password Assistant. You can use the Password Assistant, as seen to the right of the New Account sheet in Figure 18-4, to help you generate a password that will be hard for a cracking program to guess.

TIP

To make your password even harder to guess or crack, choose Random or FIPS-181–compliant from the Password Assistant's Type pop-up menu. It will also make it harder for you to remember, so make sure you either memorize it or store it in a safe place.

7. Press the Tab key to move your pointer to the Verify text field.

8. In the Verify text box, type the password again to verify it.

9. (Optional) To help remember a password, type something in the Password Hint text box to jog the user's memory.

TIP

If a user forgets her password and asks for a hint, the text that you type in the Password Hint field pops up, ideally causing the user to exclaim, "Oh, yeah . . . *now* I remember!" A password hint should be something simple enough to jog the user's memory but not so simple that an unauthorized person can guess. Perhaps something like "Your first teddy bear's name backward" would be a good hint. And, of course, you should never include the password in the hint.

10. Click the Create User button to create the account.

The sheet disappears, and the new user now appears in the Users & Groups System Preferences pane's Users list.

11. **(Optional) Click the account picture and choose a different one.**

TIP

macOS suggests a picture from its default collection for each account, but you can select a different one from the sheet that appears when you click the account picture. Or choose Camera in the sheet and take a photo with an attached or built-in camera.

Changing a user

If circumstances dictate a change to a user's picture, administrator privileges, or parental control options, do the following:

>> **Change a user's picture:** Click the user you want to modify, click his or her picture, and select a replacement. Click Done when you're done.

>> **Grant a user administrator privileges:** Click the user you want to modify and then click the Allow User to Administer This Computer check box.

>> **Enable a user's parental controls:** Click the user you want to modify, and then click the Enable Parental Control check box (more on this in a moment).

Removing a user

To delete a user — in effect, to deny that user access to your Mac — select the user you want to delete in the list of accounts and click the – (minus) button. A sheet appears, offering three choices:

>> **Save the Home Folder in a Disk Image** saves a disk image of the user's Home folder in a folder named Deleted Users (which it creates inside the Users folder).

>> **Don't Change the Home Folder** removes the user from the Users & Groups System Preferences pane and login screen but leaves that user's Home folder in the Users folder. *(Deleted)* is appended to the folder's name, so if I had selected this option in the previous example, Steve Wozniak's Home folder would be renamed *Steve (Deleted)*.

>> **Delete the Home Folder** does what it says. You have the option of a secure erase (the contents get overwritten multiple times) if you select this option.

WARNING

Be certain you really want to kiss that Home folder goodbye, because after you delete it there's no way to get it back.

REMEMBER

To remove a user from your Mac, you must be logged in using an account that has administrator permissions. And you can't remove the first user ever created on this Mac.

macOS knows best: Folders shared by default

When you add users in the Users & Groups System Preferences pane as I describe earlier, macOS automatically does two things behind the scenes to facilitate file sharing: It creates a set of folders, and it makes some of them available for sharing.

Each time you add a standard, administrator, or sharing-only user, macOS creates a Home folder hierarchy for that user on the Mac. The user can create more folders (if necessary) and also add, remove, or move anything inside these folders. Even if you create a user account solely to allow him or her to exchange files with you, your Mac automatically creates a Home folder for that user. Unless you, as the owner of your Mac, give permission, the user can't see inside or use folders outside the Home folder (which has the user's name), with only three exceptions: the Shared folder in the Users folder, the top level of other user account folders; the Public folders in every user's folder; and the Shared folder within the Users folder. A description of the latter follows:

>> **Public:** A Public folder is located inside each user's Home folder. That folder is set up to be accessible (shared) by any user who can log in to the Mac. Furthermore, any user can log in (as a guest) and copy things out of this folder as long as she knows your Mac's IP address, even if she doesn't have an account on this Mac at all. Files put into the Public folder can be opened or copied freely.

WARNING

It's not hard for someone to obtain your IP address. For example, when you visit most web pages, your IP address is saved to that site's log file. So be careful what you put in your Public folder. Protecting your data is also a fine reason to employ a firewall. Big Sur has an excellent software implementation available via the Firewall tab in Security & Privacy System Preferences (see Chapter 24), and most routers include a hardware firewall.

Inside each user's Public folder is a Drop Box folder. As the name implies, this folder is where others can drop a file or folder for you. Only the owner can open the Drop Box to see what's inside — or to move or copy the files that are in it. Imagine a street-corner mailbox: After you drop your letter in, it's gone, and you can't get it back out.

A popular cloud-based storage service is called Dropbox. The Drop Box folder in your Public folder has nothing to do with that Dropbox service beyond having a similar name.

>> **Shared:** In addition to a Public folder for each user, macOS creates one Shared folder on every Mac for all users of this Mac. The Shared folder *isn't* available to guests, but it is available to all users who have an account on this

Mac. You find the Shared folder within the Users folder (the same folder where you find folders for each user). The Shared folder is the right place to put stuff that everyone with an account on this Mac might want to use. (Check out my introduction to the Mac OS Big Sur folder structure in Chapter 8.)

Sharing a folder or disk by setting permissions

As you might expect, permissions control who can use a given folder or any disk (or partition) other than the startup disk.

TECHNICAL STUFF

Why can't you share the startup disk? Because macOS won't let you. Why not? Because the startup disk contains the operating system and other stuff that nobody else should have access to.

REMEMBER

Throughout the rest of this chapter, whenever I talk about *sharing a folder*, I also mean *sharing disks and disk partitions other than your startup disk* (which, when you think of it, are nothing more than big folders anyway). Why am I telling you this? Because it's awkward to keep typing *a folder or any disk (or partition) other than your startup disk*. So anything that I say about sharing a folder also applies to sharing any disk (or partition) other than your startup disk. Got it?

You can set permissions for

>> The folder's owner

>> A subset of all the people who have accounts on the Mac (a group)

>> People who have the Mac's address, whether they have an account or not (guests)

To help you get a better handle on these relationships, a closer look at permissions, owners, and groups is coming right up.

Contemplating permissions

When you consider who can use which folders, three distinct kinds of users exist on the network. I describe each of them in this section. Then, in the "Useful settings for permissions" section, later in this chapter, I show you how to share folders with each type of user. Here's a quick introduction to the different user types:

>> **Owner:** The *owner* of a folder or disk can change the permissions to that folder or disk at any time. The name you enter when you log in to your

Mac — or the name of your Home folder — is the default owner of Shared folders and drives on that machine. Ownership can be given away (more on that in the "Useful settings for permissions" section, later in this chapter). Even if you own the Mac, you can't change permissions for a folder on it that belongs to another user (unless you get Unix-y and do so as root). The owner must be logged in to change permissions on his folders.

macOS is the owner of many folders outside the Users folder. If macOS owns it, you can see that "system" is its owner if you select the folder and choose File ⇨ Get Info (or press ⌘+I).

Folders that aren't in the User directories generally belong to system; it's almost always a bad idea to change the permissions on any folder owned by system.

WARNING

If you *must* change permissions on a file or folder, select its icon and choose File ⇨ Get Info (⌘+I) and then change the settings in the Sharing & Permissions section at the bottom of the resulting Get Info window. I urge you not to change permission settings if you're not absolutely sure of what you're doing and why. And by all means think twice before deciding to apply changes to all the items in a folder or disk; change permissions on the contents of the wrong folder and you could end up with a mess.

>> **Group:** In Unix systems, all users belong to one or more *groups.* The group that includes everyone who has an account with administrator permissions on your Mac is called Admin. Everyone in the Admin group has access to Shared and Public folders over the network, as well as to any folder that the Admin group has been granted access to by the folder's owner.

For the purpose of assigning permissions, you can create your own groups the same way you create a user account: Open the Users & Groups System Preferences pane, click the little plus sign, choose Group from the New Account pop-up menu, type the name of the group, and then click the Create Group button.

The group appears in the list of users on the left, and eligible accounts appear with check boxes on the right, as shown in Figure 18-5.

>> **Everyone:** This category is an easy way to set permissions for everyone with an account on your Mac at the same time. Unlike the Admin group, which includes only users with administrative permissions, this one includes, well, everyone (everyone with an account on this Mac, that is).

REMEMBER

If you want people without an account on this Mac to have access to a file or folder, that file or folder needs to go in your Public folder, where the people you want to see it can log in as guests.

FIGURE 18-5:
This group, The
Outsiders,
contains the Mac
the Knife and
Miss Kitty
accounts.

Sharing a folder

Suppose you have a folder you want to share, but it has slightly different rules than those set up for the Public folder, for the Drop Box folder in the Public folder, or for your personal folders. These rules are *permissions,* and they tell you how much access someone has to your stuff.

Actually, the rules governing Shared and Public folders are permissions, too, but they're set up for you when macOS is installed.

TIP

I suggest that you share only those folders located in your Home folder (or a folder within it). Because of the way Unix works, the Unix permissions of the enclosing folder can prevent access to a folder for which you *do* have permissions. Trust me, if you share only the folders in your Home folder, you'll never go wrong. If you don't take this advice, you could wind up having folders that other users can't access, even though you gave them the appropriate permissions.

By the way, you can set permissions for folders in your Public folder (like the Drop Box folder) that are different from those for the rest of the parent folder.

REMEMBER

I said this before, but it bears repeating: Whenever I talk about *sharing a folder,* I also mean sharing disks — and disk partitions other than your startup disk (which you just can't share, period). So don't forget that anything I say about sharing a folder also applies to sharing any disk (or partition) other than your startup disk. Although you can't explicitly share your startup disk, anyone with administrator access can mount it for sharing from across the network (or Internet).

To share a folder with another user, follow these steps:

1. **Choose ⌘ ⇨ System Preferences (or click the System Preferences icon on the dock).**

   The System Preferences window appears.

2. **In the System Preferences window, click the Sharing icon.**

   The Sharing System Preferences pane appears.

3. **Click File Sharing in the list of services on the left.**

   The lists of Shared folders and their users appear on the right, as shown in Figure 18-6.

FIGURE 18-6:
Changing the privileges of the Recipes folder for the group Everyone.

4. **Click the + (plus) button under the Shared Folders list or drag the folder from Finder onto the Shared Folders list to add the folder you want to share (Recipes in Figure 18-6).**

   If you select the Shared Folder check box in a folder's Get Info window, that folder already appears in the list of Shared Folders, so you won't have to bother with Step 4.

   Alas, although selecting the Shared Folder check box in a folder's Get Info window causes it to appear in the Sharing System Preferences pane's Shared Folders list, you still have to complete the steps that follow to assign that folder's users and privileges.

WARNING

5. **Click the + (plus) button under the Users column to add a user or group if the user or group you want isn't already showing in the Users column.**

6. **Click the double-headed arrow to the right of a user or group name and change its privileges.**

   I'm changing the permission for Everyone from Read Only to Read & Write (refer to Figure 18-6). You can choose among three types of access (in addition to no access) for each user or group, as shown in Table 18-1. If you're the folder's owner (or have administrator access), you can click the padlock icon and change the owner or group or both for the file or folder.

TABLE 18-1   **Privileges**

Permission	What It Allows
Read and write	A user with read and write access can see, add, delete, move, and edit files just as though they were stored on her own computer.
Read only	A read only user can see and use files that are stored in a Shared folder but can't add, delete, move, or edit them.
Write only (Drop Box)	Users can add files to this folder but can't see what's in it. The user must have read access to the folder containing a write only folder.
No access	With no permissions, a user can neither see nor use your Shared folders or drives.

Useful settings for permissions

The following sections show you some of the most common ways that you can combine permissions for a folder. You'll probably find one option that fits the way you work and the people you want to share with.

REMEMBER

Owner permissions — Bob (single silhouette) in the example in Figure 18-7 — must be at least as expansive as Group permissions (double silhouette; Staff in the figure), and Group permissions must be at least as expansive as Everyone's permissions (triple silhouette; Everyone in the figure). So to set the Everyone privilege to read and write, the Group and Owner privileges must also be set to read and write.

TIP

In the following examples, I show how to set permissions in the Sharing System Preferences pane. Another way to set permissions is by selecting an icon in Finder and choosing File ⇨ Get Info (⌘+I) and then changing the settings in the Sharing & Permissions section at the bottom of the resulting Get Info window. The two methods are pretty much interchangeable, so you can use whichever is more convenient:

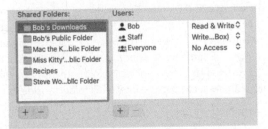

FIGURE 18-7:
Allow everyone
access,
if you want.

>> **Allow everyone access:** In Figure 18-7, I configure settings that allow everyone on a network to access the Bob's Downloads folder. Everyone can open, read, and change the contents of this Shared folder. Do this by choosing Read & Write for Others from the pop-up menu to the right of the user's name in the Sharing System Preferences pane or the folder's Get Info window.

>> **Allow nobody but yourself access:** The settings shown in Figure 18-8 reflect appropriate settings that allow owner-only access to the Bob's Downloads folder. No one but me can see or use the contents of this folder. Members of the Staff group can drop files and folders into this folder (see the later bullet "Allow others to deposit files and folders without giving them access: A drop box"). Use the pop-up menus to choose Write Only (Drop Box) as the Staff privilege and No Access as the Everyone privilege.

FIGURE 18-8:
Allow access for
no one but the
folder's owner.

>> **Allow all administrative users of this Mac access:** Check out Figure 18-9 to see settings that allow the group Staff (in addition to the owner, Bob) access to see, use, or change the contents of the Bob's Downloads folder. Use the pop-up menu to choose Read & Write for the Staff privilege.

>> **Allow others to deposit files and folders without giving them access: A drop box:** The settings in Figure 18-10 enable people to drop their own files or folders in the Bob's Downloads folder without being able to see or use the contents of the Shared folder. After a file or folder is deposited in a drop folder, the dropper can't retrieve it because he or she doesn't have permission to see the items in the drop folder.

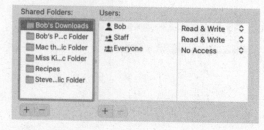

>> **Read-only bulletin boards:** If you want everyone to be able to open and read the files and folders in this Shared folder — but not to modify them — choose Read Only from the pop-up menus for Group and Others. If you do this, however, only the owner can make changes to files in this folder.

>> **One more privilege:** The Apply to Enclosed Items icon (click the gear at the bottom of the Sharing and Permissions section of a Get Info window in Finder) does exactly what its name implies. This feature (which is available only in Get Info windows and doesn't appear in the Sharing System Preferences pane) is a fast way to assign the same permissions to many subfolders at the same time. After you set permissions for the enclosing folder the way you like them, click this icon to give these same permissions to all folders inside it.

Be careful — there is no Undo for this action.

WARNING

What is true of Get Info windows is also true of their Inspector window variant. Show Inspector replaces Get Info on the File menu when the Option key is pressed (also Option+⌘+I).

Unsharing a folder

To unshare a folder that you own, change the permissions for every user and group to No Access. When you do, nobody but you has access to that folder. If you're not sure how to do this, see the "Sharing a folder" and "Useful settings for permissions" sections, earlier in this chapter.

Connecting to a Shared Disk or Folder on a Remote Mac

After you set up sharing and assign permissions, you can access folders remotely from another computer. (Just make sure first that you have the correct administrative permissions to it.)

TIP

File sharing must be activated on the Mac where the shared files/folders reside; it doesn't have to be activated on the Mac that's accessing the files/folders. When file sharing is turned off, you can still use that Mac to access a remote Shared folder on another machine as long as its owner has granted you enough permissions and has file sharing enabled. If file sharing is turned off on your Mac, others won't be able to access your folders, even if you've assigned permissions to them previously.

TIP

If you're going to share files, and you leave your Mac on and unattended for a long time, logging out before you leave it is a very good idea. This prevents anyone who just walks up to your Mac from seeing your files, email, applications, or anything else that's yours — unless you've given that person a user account that has permissions for your files. If you don't want to log out, at least consider requiring that your password be entered when waking from sleep or dismissing the screen saver (General tab of Security & Privacy System Preferences).

Move along now and see how to access your Home folder from a remote Mac — a supercool feature that's bound to get more popular as the Internet continues to mature.

REMEMBER

The following steps assume that you have an account on the remote Mac, which means you have your own Home folder on that Mac.

To connect to a Shared folder on a Mac other than the one you're currently on, follow these steps:

1. **Make sure that you're already set up as a user on the computer that you want to log in to (LisaMBP in Figure 18-11).**

   If you need to know how to create a new user, see the "Creating users" section, earlier in the chapter.

2. **On the computer that you're logging in from (my MacBook Air in this example), click Network in the sidebar's Locations section.**

   If you don't see anything below the Locations header, click the Locations header to expand its contents.

   All available shared servers appear. (Two are visible in the sidebar in Figure 18-11 — Big Sur and Bob's MacBook Air.)

FIGURE 18-11:
I am connected
to LisaMBP
as a guest.

3. **If the computer you want doesn't appear in the Locations section, click Network (also in the Locations section), and then double-click the icon of the remote Mac that you want to access.**

   At this point, you're connected to the remote Mac as a guest, as shown in Figure 18-11.

4. **Click the Connect As button.**

   The Connect dialog appears. The name of the person logged in and using this Mac automatically appears in the Name field (my account name, bob, in Figure 18-12).

   If that's not your username on the Mac you're trying to access, type the username in the Name field.

   TIP

   If you select the Remember This Password in My Keychain check box in the Connect dialog, macOS remembers your password for you the next time you connect to this server. Sweet!

FIGURE 18-12:
The Connect
dialog needs my
password.

5. **Select the Guest radio button if you don't have an account on the remote computer and then click Connect; if you're logging in as a user, skip to Step 6.**

TIP

Pressing ⌘+G is the same as selecting the Guest radio button, and pressing ⌘ + R is the same as selecting the Registered User radio button.

6. **Type your password and click the Connect button.**

After you connect as a registered user, you see your Home folder (bob in Figure 18-13) and everyone else's Public folders.

REMEMBER

File sharing must be active on LisaMBP (the Mac I'm accessing remotely in the example). If file sharing weren't active on LisaMBP, its name wouldn't appear in the Locations section of the sidebar, and I wouldn't be able to connect to it. But file sharing doesn't have to be active on the computer *you're* using (my MacBook Pro in this example) to give you access to the remote computer and make this trick work.

When you access your Home folder on a remote Mac, as I did in this example, you see an icon with the short name of your Home folder on that Mac (bob in Figure 18-14) on the desktop of the Mac you're using (unless you've deselected Connected Servers in Finder's General Preferences pane, under Show These Items on the Desktop).

LisaMBP

Connected as: boblevitus@mac.com [Share Screen...] [Disconnect]

bob   Bob's Public Folder   Lisa LeVitus's Public Folder

Desktop
Documents
Applications
Downloads
Dr. Mac 2020

iCloud
iCloud Drive

Locations
Bob's MacBook...
Big Sur
LisaMBP
Network

Tags
Important
Done
Warm (Do Soo...
weird

FIGURE 18-13: Connecting to LisaMBP as Bob LeVitus (bob).

7. **When you finish using the remote Mac, disconnect by using one of these methods:**

- Drag the shared-volume icon (bob in Figure 18-14) to the Eject icon on the dock.

FIGURE 18-14:
Accessing my Home folder on LisaMBP remotely.

Eject icon   Shared volume icon

- Right-click or Control-click the shared volume icon and choose Eject from the contextual menu that appears.

- Select the shared volume icon and choose File ⇨ Eject.

- Select the shared volume icon and press ⌘ + E.

- In a Finder window sidebar, click the little Eject symbol to the right of the remote computer's name (LisaMBP in Figure 18-14).

  When a disk or volume is selected (highlighted), the Trash icon turns into a little arrow, which represents eject. Nice touch, eh?

TIP

- If you've finished working for the day, and you don't leave your Mac on 24/7 (as most folks do), choose ⇨ Shut Down or Log Out. Shutting down or logging out automatically disconnects you from shared disks or folders. (Shut Down also turns off your Mac.)

Changing Your Password

You can change your password at any time. Changing your password is a good idea if you're concerned about security — for example, if there's a chance your password has been discovered by someone else.

You can change the password for your account on your own Mac, or you can change the password you use to connect to your account on a remote Mac. I show you how to do both in the following sections.

Changing your account password on your Mac

To change the password on your own Mac, just follow these steps:

1. **Choose ⇨ System Preferences, or double-click its icon in your Applications folder and click the Users & Groups icon.**

   The Users & Groups System Preferences pane appears.

2. **In the list on the left, select your account.**

   Your account information appears in the area on the right.

3. **Click the Change Password button.**

   A sheet drops down.

4. **In the Old Password field, type your current password.**

   This demonstrates that you are who you're supposed to be, not someone who just walked up to your unattended Mac.

5. **In the New Password field, type your new password.**

6. **In the Verify field, retype your new password.**

7. **(Optional but recommended) In the Password Hint field, type a hint.**

8. **Click the Change Password button.**

   Assuming that you entered your old password correctly, the sheet disappears.

9. **Close the System Preferences window.**

Changing the password of any account but your own on your Mac

To change a password on your own Mac, just follow these steps:

1. **Choose ⇨ System Preferences or double-click its icon in your Applications folder and click the Users & Groups icon.**

   The Users & Groups System Preferences pane appears.

You may have to click the lock (at bottom left), supply an administrator name and password in the resulting dialog, and then click OK before you can proceed.

2. **In the list on the left, select the account for which you want to change the password.**

   The account information appears in the area on the right.

3. **Click the Reset Password button.**

   A sheet drops down.

4. **In the New Password field, type the new password.**

5. **In the Verify field, retype the new password.**

6. **(Optional but recommended) In the Password Hint field, type a hint.**

   It's a terrible idea to type the password here.

7. **Click the Reset Password button.**

8. **Close the System Preferences window.**

More Types of Sharing

Several more types of sharing exist, and I'd like to at least mention a few in passing. All are found in (where else?) the Sharing System Preferences pane, which you can find by launching the System Preferences application (from the Applications folder, menu, or dock) and clicking the Sharing icon.

Sharing a screen

Here's the sharing that I consider the coolest. Screen Sharing lets you control another Mac on your network from your Mac. In essence, you see the other Mac's screen on *your* Mac — and control it using *your* mouse and keyboard.

To set up Screen Sharing on the Mac you want to control remotely, follow these steps:

1. **Open the Sharing System Preferences pane by launching the System Preferences application (from the Applications folder, the menu, Launchpad, or the dock) and clicking the Sharing icon.**

2. **In the list of services on the left, select the check box for Screen Sharing.**

3. **Select either the All Users or Only These Users radio button.**

4. **If you opt for Only These Users, click the + (plus sign) button and add the user or users you want to allow to control this Mac remotely.**

   Note that the Staff group is included by default.

To take control of your Mac from another Mac, follow these steps:

1. **If the Location section of the sidebar isn't displayed, expand it by clicking the Location header in the sidebar.**

   All available servers appear.

2. **Click the name of the remote Mac you want to control.**

3. **Click the Share Screen button.**

   Depending on whether you selected the All Users or Only These Users radio button, you may have to enter your name and password, and then click the Connect button.

   A window with the name of the remote Mac in its title bar appears. In it, you see the screen of the Mac you're looking to control remotely.

4. **Go ahead and click something.**

   Pull down a menu or open a folder. Isn't that cool? You're controlling a Mac across the room or in another room with your mouse and keyboard!

Sharing the Internet

If your Mac has an Internet connection and another Mac nearby doesn't, you can enable Internet Sharing, and the other Mac can share your Internet connection. The following steps show you how:

1. **Open the Sharing System Preferences pane by launching the System Preferences application (from the Applications folder, the menu, Launchpad, or the dock) and clicking the Sharing icon.**

2. **In the list of services on the left, select the Internet Sharing check box.**

3. **In the Share Your Connection From pop-up menu, choose the connection you want to share.**

   Your choices are Wi-Fi, Bluetooth, FireWire, Ethernet, or Thunderbolt.

4. **Select the check boxes next to connections other computers will use: Wi-Fi, Ethernet, or Built-In FireWire.**

5. **(Optional) Click the Wi-Fi Options button to name, select a wireless channel for, enable encryption for, and/or set a password for your shared network.**

That's all there is to it.

And yet more ways to share

A few more cool ways to share your Mac follow:

>> **Printer/Scanner Sharing:** If you turn on Printer Sharing in the Sharing System Preferences pane, other people on your LAN can use any printer or scanner connected to your computer.

>> **Media Sharing:** Enable this option to allow devices on your network to browse and play downloaded music, movies, and TV shows from your Library.

>> **Scanner Sharing:** Analogous to Printer Sharing, Scanner Sharing allows others on your local network to use scanners connected to your Mac.

>> **Bluetooth Sharing:** If you have a Bluetooth mobile phone or PDA and your Mac has Bluetooth, you can configure many of the default behaviors for transferring files to and from your Mac. A picture is worth a thousand words, so Figure 18-15 shows all the things Bluetooth Sharing lets you configure.

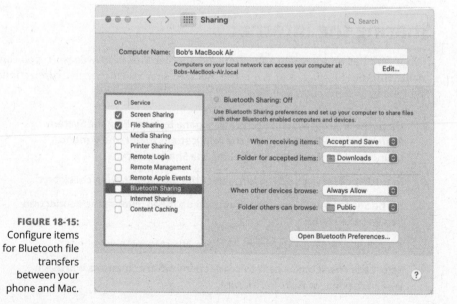

FIGURE 18-15:
Configure items for Bluetooth file transfers between your phone and Mac.

5 Getting Creative

Chapter **19**

The Musical Mac

A long time ago, before the iPod and the iTunes Store were even born, iTunes was a program that stored, managed, and played your MP3 music files. Over the ensuing years, it grew into a bloated monstrosity barely resembling the iTunes we knew and loved. I thought it was so awful I wrote, produced, and released a song called "iTunes Must Die" a couple of years ago. (To snag a free copy, search for *iTunes Must Die free download*.)

Apple finally listened; iTunes died with the release of macOS Catalina and was replaced by three apps: Music, Podcasts, and TV. We look at Music in this chapter, and Podcasts and TV in the next.

Entire books have been dedicated to the app formerly known as iTunes. (I once wrote one called *The Little iTunes Book*, which is now out of print.) So, the best I can do in this chapter is show you a handful of things you really need to know.

Before you can look at Music (formerly iTunes), however, you need to know a few things about the Apple Music and iTunes Match subscription services because what you see in your Music app might be different if you subscribe to one or both.

Apple Music and iTunes Match Rock!

iTunes Match and Apple Music are a pair of subscription music services offered by Apple.

iTunes Match is the older of the two, designed to let you store all your music in iCloud so you can stream songs to any Mac, PC, or iDevice. iTunes Match performs its magic by first determining which songs in your iTunes library are already available in the iTunes iCloud library. Because Apple's vast iCloud repository contains tens of millions of songs, chances are that much of your music is already there. Then iTunes proceeds to upload a copy of every song it *can't* match (which is much faster than uploading your entire Music library). The result is that you can stream any song in your iTunes library on any of your Macs, PCs, or iDevices, regardless of whether the song file has been downloaded to the device. As a bonus, all the music iTunes matches plays back from iCloud at 256Kbps AAC DRM-free quality even if your original copy was lower quality. (You can even download higher-quality versions of those songs to replace your lower bit-rate copies if you want.)

Subscribers can store up to 100,000 songs in iCloud, and songs you purchased from the iTunes Store don't count. Only tracks or albums you specify are stored locally on your devices, saving tons of precious storage space.

At just $24.99 a year, iTunes Match is a bargain for those with extensive collections of music *not* purchased from Apple.

But Apple Music, introduced in early 2015, may be a better (albeit more expensive) option. For $9.99 a month (or $14.99 a month for you and up to five family members), an Apple Music subscription provides instant access to more than 60 million songs on all your devices. Whatever you want to hear is usually just a few clicks away.

Now, here's my favorite part: You can ask Siri to play whatever you want to hear on your Mac, as well as on your iPhone and other iDevices. Following are some of the phrases I like to use:

>> Play popular songs by The Beatles (or another artist).

>> Play *While My Guitar Gently Weeps* by The Beatles (or another song by a different artist).

>> Play *Greetings from Asbury Park, N. J.* by Bruce Springsteen (or another album by another artist).

>> Play some smooth jazz (or almost any other genre).

>> Play the number 1 song on April 1, 1955.

>> Play music you think I'll like.

If you find yourself with a song playing in your head (which some call an ear-worm), just ask Siri to play it, and in seconds the song will be playing in real life. Usually.

One more thing: When asking for an album or song, I've found that it helps if you also name the artist. So, rather than saying, "play Rubber Soul," try saying "play Rubber Soul by The Beatles."

WARNING

It would behoove you to make a complete backup of your Music library before enabling either iTunes Match or Apple Music, just in case. There were reports early in their existence that enabling one or both scrambled the data in some users' iTunes libraries.

Both subscription services require Internet access (of course), but as long as you're connected you can have your entire Music library (iTunes Match) or access to a library of over 60 million songs (Apple Music) on your Mac, iPhone, or other device. You'll never have to worry about filling up your device's storage space with your music.

TIP

And here's a tip for subscribers to either service (one I learned the hard way): Before you travel on a plane or ship, remember to tap the iCloud download button next to any songs, albums, and playlists you want to listen to when Internet access isn't available.

You're entirely welcome.

Introducing Music (the App Formerly Known as iTunes)

To open Music, click its icon on the dock or double-click its icon in the Applications folder. If this is your first time opening Music, a Welcome to Apple Music screen appears, offering a quick tour (also available from the Music Help menu) and an opportunity to see how your data is managed. After you click the Start Listening button, an ad for Apple Music (the subscription service, not the app) appears. Click Try It Free, Already a Subscriber, or Not Now (to dismiss the ad).

The main Music window then appears, as shown in Figure 19-1. The important items are labeled, but I encourage you to click whatever you want on the screen — you won't break anything.

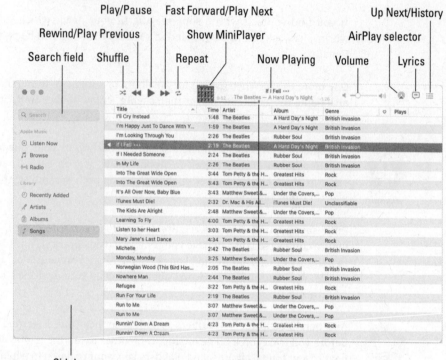

Play/Pause Fast Forward/Play Next Up Next/History
Rewind/Play Previous Show MiniPlayer AirPlay selector
Search field Shuffle Repeat Now Playing Volume Lyrics

FIGURE 19-1:
Dissecting the
Music interface.

Sidebar Playhead

The Music app is pretty straightforward and similar to the old iTunes you knew and loved (or hated). Let me point out some of the more useful items in Figure 19-1 before we move on to doing stuff in Music.

In a nutshell, whatever you select in the sidebar on the left is displayed in the large pane on the right. In Figure 19-1, Songs is selected, so you see a list of songs on the right.

To play a song, double-click it, click it and then click the Play/Pause icon, or click it and choose Controls ⇨ Play.

TIP

The spacebar is the shortcut for Play/Pause. It's way easier and more convenient than the options just listed.

After you've selected a song, you can use the Fast Forward/Play Next, Play/Pause, and Rewind/Play Previous controls to manage its playback.

I'd like you to take note of a few other interface items before we move on to doing stuff in Music:

>> You can use the more manageable MiniPlayer (on the left in Figure 19-2) by clicking the MiniPlayer icon (labeled in Figure 19-1), choosing Window⇨MiniPlayer, or pressing ⌘+Option+M.

The main window is hidden when you invoke the MiniPlayer and returns when you close MiniPlayer by clicking the x in its upper-left corner.

Finally, you can toggle between the main window and MiniPlayer by choosing Window⇨Switch To/From MiniPlayer or by using the shortcut ⌘+Shift+M.

Although MiniPlayer works in any category, it's most useful for listening to audio — music, podcasts, and audiobooks.

FIGURE 19-2:
The Music MiniPlayer window (left) and equalizer (right).

>> Music offers a ten-band graphic equalizer that can make your music (or video) sound significantly better. Just choose Window⇨Equalizer or use the shortcut ⌘+Option+E to invoke it onscreen. You can see the equalizer on the right in Figure 19-2.

>> Don't miss Music's Visualizer, which offers a groovy light show that dances in time to the music (see Figure 19-3). You turn it on by choosing View➪Show Visualizer or pressing ⌘+T. If you like the default Visualizer, also check out Classic Visualizer, which you'll find in the Visualizer submenu. Search the web for *iTunes Visualizer* to find even more.

When you get sick of Visualizer (as you surely will), just choose View➪Hide Visualizer or press ⌘+T again to make it disappear.

FIGURE 19-3:
The psychedelic light show that is Music Visualizer.

TIP

Try this: Choose View➪Enter Full Screen or press ⌘+Control+F while Visualizer is running, and it takes over your entire screen. Click anywhere on the screen to bring the Music window back.

Working with Media

Music is, first and foremost, a music manager and player, so the next thing I examine is how to get your favorite media *into* Music.

Of course, you can acquire media a number of ways, depending on the type of media and where the files reside. For example, you can add song files that you download from websites or receive as enclosures in email messages. Or you can add songs by ripping audio CDs. You can buy music at the iTunes Store (and, to be fair, from many other online vendors, including www.amazon.com and www.audible.com). You can listen to all sorts of music on the Internet radio stations included with Music. Finally, Apple Music subscribers can listen to pretty much any song they can think of.

REMEMBER

To use the iTunes Store, Internet radio, or Apple Music, you must be connected to the Internet.

In the following sections, you discover the various ways to add media — songs, movies, videos, and podcasts — to your Music library, followed by a quick course in listening to Music Internet radio stations.

Adding songs

You can add songs from pretty much any source, and how you add a song to Music depends on where that song comes from. Here are the most common ways people add songs:

>> **Add a song file (such as an MP3 or AAC file) from a disk drive.** Drag the document into the Music window, as shown in Figure 19-4, drag the document onto the Music dock icon, or choose File⇨Import (⌘+O) and choose the file in the Open File dialog. In all three cases, the file is added to your Music library.

...to here   Drag from here...

FIGURE 19-4:
Drag and drop songs to the Music content pane or library to add them to your Music library.

>> **Add songs from a store-bought or homemade audio CD.** Insert the CD, and Music will launch itself and offer a dialog asking whether you want to import the CD to your Music library. Click the Yes button, and the songs on that CD are added to your Music library. If you don't see a dialog when you insert an

audio CD, you can import the songs on that CD by selecting the CD in the sidebar's Devices section and then clicking the Import CD button.

TIP

If your computer is connected to the Internet, Music magically looks up the song title, artist name, album name, song length, and genre for every song on the CD. Note that this works only for store-bought CDs containing somewhat popular music; Music might not be able to find information about an obscure CD by an even more obscure band, even if the disc is store-bought. And in most cases it can't look up information for homemade (home-burned) audio CDs. Finally, it sometimes gets things wrong.

» **Buy your songs from the iTunes Store.** Click the iTunes Store in the sidebar to visit the iTunes Store. If you don't see the iTunes Store in the sidebar, choose Music ⇨ Preferences, click the General tab, and select the Show iTunes Store check box.

From the home page, you can either click a link or type the song title, album title, artist name, keyword, or phrase in the Search field. Press Enter or Return to start the search. When you find an item that interests you, double-click any song to listen to a 30-second preview (or the entire song if you're an Apple Music subscriber) or click the Buy Song or Buy Album button to purchase the song or album, as shown in Figure 19-5.

Search field   Buy album   Buy songs

FIGURE 19-5:
At the iTunes Store, buying music is as easy as clicking the Buy Song or Buy Album button.

>> **Buy your songs from other online vendors.** Amazon (www.amazon.com) has a huge downloadable music store on the web. Its MP3 Downloads section has more than a million songs, with more added every day. The prices at Amazon are often lower than the prices for the same music at the iTunes Store. If you're concerned about audio quality, carefully read the details for each track or album and buy tracks that meet your criteria. For what it's worth, I prefer a bit rate of 160 or higher for both AAC audio files (Apple) and MP3 audio files (Amazon and most of the rest of the universe).

To make a purchase from the iTunes Store, you first have to create an Apple account, if you don't already have one. To do so, just choose Account ⇨ Sign In and then click the Create New Apple ID button in the Sign In dialog. After your account is established, future purchases require just one or two clicks.

Note that iTunes Store purchases made with this Apple account appear automatically on all other Apple devices signed into the same account.

Listening to Radio

Streaming audio is delivered over the Internet in real time. Think of streaming audio as being just like radio but using the Internet rather than the airwaves as its delivery medium.

To listen to Radio, select Radio in the sidebar. The first thing you see, at the top of the screen, are Apple's own live radio stations — Music 1, Music Hits, and Music Country. These stations are on the air worldwide 24 hours a day, 7 days a week offering world-class programming, interviews, and music. To listen to an Apple radio station, just click it.

If you're an Apple Music subscriber, above the three radio stations you'll see a Recently Played section based on music you've played recently. Scroll down and under the Recently Played and Apple radio station sections you'll see additional sections such as We're Loving, Interviews, Hosts, and Artist Shows. Click any item in any section to listen to it.

And that, friends, is pretty much all you need to know to use and enjoy radio stations in Music.

All about Playlists

Playlists are a big deal in Music; they let you manage otherwise unmanageable amounts of media. Playlists let you create subsets of a large collection, such as the 23,000+ songs in my Music library, so it's easier to enjoy exactly the kind of music you want in Music or on your iDevices.

To play with your playlists, click the Music icon near the top left and then click the Playlists tab near the top center.

Music offers two types of playlists:

>> **Regular playlists,** which contain the songs (or videos, podcasts, or radio stations) that you specify by adding them to the playlist.

>> **Smart playlists,** which select songs from your library based on criteria you specify. Furthermore, smart playlists are updated automatically if you add new items to your library that meet the criteria.

All playlists appear in the sidebar on the left side of the Music window.

TIP

If you're an Apple Music subscriber, you can use songs from your personal Music library, as well as the more than 60 million songs available to Apple Music subscribers in your playlists.

Creating a regular playlist

To create a regular playlist, follow these steps:

1. **Choose File ➪ New ➪ Playlist, or press ⌘+N.**

A new playlist named Playlist appears on the right side of the window.

2. **(Optional) The playlist's name, Playlist, is selected and ready to be edited, so you might want to rename it something meaningful by typing a new name for it.**

I typed *A Shiny New Playlist* in Figure 19-6.

TIP

If you decide not to name your playlist now, you can double-click it and type a new name anytime.

...onto the playlist   Drag songs from your library...

FIGURE 19-6:
Adding songs to a
playlist is as easy
as dragging them
onto the playlist.

3. **(Optional) In the Add Description field, type a description of the playlist.**

4. **To add a song or songs to a playlist, click an item in your library and then drag the song or songs onto the playlist's name in the sidebar.**

The playlist (A Shiny New Playlist in Figure 19-6) is highlighted, indicating that it's selected and the song or songs will be added to it when you release the mouse button.

Note that adding a song to a playlist doesn't remove it from the library. And if you delete a song from a playlist, the song isn't deleted from your library. Furthermore, if you delete a playlist from the sidebar, the songs it contains aren't deleted from your library. In other words, think of songs in playlists as being aliases of songs in your library.

5. **To listen to the songs in a playlist, click it in the sidebar to select it, and then click Play to hear all the songs on the list or double-click a specific song to listen to it.**

TIP

If you don't want to drag songs to your playlist one by one, there's an easy way to do it in one fell swoop. First, ⌘-click all the songs you want to include in the play-list. Then choose File ➪ New ➪ Playlist from Selection or use the keyboard shortcut, ⌘+Shift+N.

TIP

You can also use the ⌘-click technique to select and then drag a batch of songs onto an existing playlist.

Finally, you can add any song to a new or existing playlist by right- or Control-clicking it and choosing Add to Playlist.

Filtering your library

If you have a lot of music in your Music library, you might like the Filter field or Column Browser (the latter of which was missing from early releases of the Music app but is back now and better than ever).

Enabling and using the Filter Field

To enable Filter Field, choose View➪ Show Filter Field (or use its keyboard shortcut, ⌘+Option+F). To hide it, choose View➪ Hide Filter Field (or use its keyboard shortcut, ⌘+Option+F.

To use it, type a word or phrase in Filter Field and all items that match that word or phrase appear below. You can type the name of a song, an album, an artist, a genre, or a composer and the results appear instantly as you type.

Enabling and using Column Browser

To enable Column Browser, choose View➪ Column Browser➪ Show Column Browser (or use its keyboard shortcut, ⌘+B). To hide it, choose View➪ Column Browser➪ Hide Column Browser (or use its keyboard shortcut, ⌘+B).

The Column Browser submenu also allows you to choose which categories are displayed. Genres, artists, and albums are displayed by default. Disable or enable the Composers or Groupings columns by selecting them in the Column Browser submenu. A check mark next to a category means it's enabled.

When enabled, Column Browser appears above the main content area. Narrow your search by clicking one or more items in each column.

So, for example, if you sleeted Rock in the first column (Genre by default), and selected The Beatles in the second column (Artist by default), you'd see every Beatles album in every genre in the third (Albums) column.

Column Browser is an easy, visual way to narrow your search. I leave it enabled at all times. Try it! I predict that the bigger your music library, the more you'll like using Column Browser.

Working with smart playlists

To create a *smart playlist* that builds a list based on criteria and updates itself automatically, follow these steps:

1. **Choose File ⇨ New Smart Playlist (⌘+Option+N).**

   The Smart Playlist dialog appears, as shown in Figure 19-7.

	Playlist
☑ Match `music ▾` for `all ▾` of the following rules:	
`Artist ▾` `contains ▾` `Dr. Mac`	⊖ ⊕
`Genre ▾` `contains ▾` `Unclassifiable`	⊖ ⊕
`Time ▾` `is less than ▾` `3:00`	⊖ ⊕
☐ Limit to `25` `items ▾` selected by `random ▾`	
☑ Match only checked items	
☑ Live updating	
?	Cancel · OK

FIGURE 19-7:
Specify the criteria for your smart playlist.

2. **Use the pop-up menus to select the criteria — song or album name, genre, or other attributes — that will build your smart playlist.**

   To add more criteria, click the + button(s) on the far right.

3. **Click OK when you're done.**

   The playlist appears alongside your other playlists in the sidebar. You can tell it's a smart playlist by the gear on its icon. To modify the criteria of a smart playlist after it's been created, click Edit Rules (below the Smart Playlist's name and description) or right-click (or Control-click) the smart playlist in the sidebar and choose Edit Rules.

TIP Right- or Control-click any playlist to see additional options: Play, Shuffle, Play Next, Play Later, Love, Dislike, Open in a New Window, Edit Rules (as mentioned), Burn Playlist to Disc, Copy to Play Order, Duplicate, and Delete.

I use smart playlists for many things. I have one that gathers Beatles songs and songs by individual Beatles; another for songs in my library that have never been played; another for Classical and Jazz (which I find soothing while working); and one that gathers all of Doctor Mac & His All GarageBand Band's greatest hits in one playlist.

Smart playlists are fabulous. Try 'em and I'm pretty sure you'll like 'em.

Burning a playlist to CD

Another use for playlists is for burning audio CDs you can listen to on almost any audio CD player. The only trick is to make sure the total playing time of the songs in the playlist is less than the capacity of the blank CD you're using, which is usually 74 to 80 minutes. Don't forget to account for the gap between tracks, which is two seconds by default. When you have all the songs you want on your CD on the playlist, choose File ⇨ Burn Playlist to Disc. The Burn Settings dialog appears.

Note that although the default type of disc Music burns is an audio CD, it can also burn two other types — MP3 CDs or data CDs (and DVDs):

>> **MP3 CD** is a special format that can be played in many CD audio players and set-top DVD players. The cool thing about an MP3 CD is that rather than holding a mere 74 to 80 minutes of music, it can hold more than 100 songs! The uncool thing about MP3 CDs is that many older audio CD players won't play them.

>> **A data CD or DVD** is nothing more than a disc formatted to be read and mounted by any computer, Mac or Windows.

If you click the Burn button now, you'll get an audio CD. To burn an MP3 CD or Data CD or DVD, select the appropriate radio button in the Burn Settings dialog.

When you're satisfied, click the Burn button. In a few minutes, you'll have an audio CD that contains all the songs on the playlist — and plays the songs in the order in which they appeared on the playlist (unless, of course, you elected to burn a data CD or DVD).

Looking at the Genius playlist

I'd like to draw your attention to one more playlist: Genius.

Who is Genius?

Genius is more of a *what* than an *is:* It's a Music feature that lets you find new music — in your Music library or the iTunes Store — related to a song of your choosing. Or, as Apple puts it: "Genius makes playlists and mixes from songs in your library that go great together. And the Genius selects music from the iTunes Store that you don't already have."

To use Genius, you must (for some unknown reason) have an iTunes Store account, even though the information Genius sends to Apple about your Music library is stored anonymously. No purchase is required, but I still think it's a dumb requirement. However, that's the way it works, so take it or leave it.

Assuming you take it, sign in to your iTunes Store account if you have one (or create one if you don't). After agreeing to the Genius terms of service, Genius gathers info about your Music library, sends the info to Apple, and then (finally) delivers your results. When all of this is done, you can create Genius playlists and peruse Genius suggestions.

How does Genius work?

How? Glad you asked! Select at least one song (or a bunch of songs) in your library or a playlist and then choose File ⇨ New ⇨ Genius Playlist. After a bit of cogitation, Music presents you with a Genius playlist based on the song you clicked, as shown in Figure 19-8.

FIGURE 19-8: Genius suggests songs that go nicely with the song the suggestions are based on.

Or try a Genius shuffle, which is an instant Genius playlist without the playlist. Select a song and then choose Controls ⇨ Genius Shuffle (or press Option+spacebar) and a selection of songs that go great together will play. To see the songs selected by Genius, just click the Up Next/History button in the toolbar (and shown in the margin).

By the way, if you're not a fan of Led Zeppelin and classic British rock, let me assure you that most of the songs in the Thank You Genius playlist in Figure 19-8 do, mostly, "go great together."

That said, the tech editor of some of the previous editions of this book, the late Dennis R. Cohen, said Genius was not so hot with classical music or comedy. And I've noticed that it works better with big names than lesser-known indie artists.

Even so, it's free. So if you don't have issues with all the legal mumbo jumbo, the iTunes Store account, or sending information about your Music library to Apple, give Genius a try.

TIP

One last thing: I'd be remiss not to mention that unlike iTunes, the Music app doesn't sync with your iDevices. These days (that is, in Big Sur), you use Finder to sync your iPhones, iPads, and iPod touches. To learn more about the Music app, I suggest exploring the excellent Music Help which you'll find in the Help menu along with other excellent Help resources, including a list of keyboard shortcuts!

> » Watching movies and TV shows with the TV app

> » Reading books with Books

> » Taking pictures and movies with Photo Booth

> » Importing media — photos and videos — to your Mac with Image Capture

Chapter 20

The Multimedia Mac

M edia content is more than just music (the topic of Chapter 19), and your Mac is ready, willing, and able to handle almost any type of media (with almost any type of content) you can throw at it. Which is why, in addition to the aforementioned iTunes, macOS Big Sur includes applications for viewing and working with media (such as DVD movie discs and QuickTime movie files) as well as graphics in a variety of file formats (including PDF, TIFF, and JPEG).

In this chapter, you look at some bundled applications you can use to work with such media — namely QuickTime Player, TV, Books, Podcasts, Photo Booth, and Preview — followed by a brief section about importing your own media (photos and videos) into your Mac and the Image Capture app.

Playing Movies and Music in QuickTime Player

QuickTime is Apple's technology for digital media creation, delivery, and playback. It's used in myriad ways by programs such as Apple's iMovie, by websites such as YouTube (www.youtube.com), and in training videos delivered on CD or DVD.

QuickTime Player is the macOS application that lets you view QuickTime movies as well as streaming audio and video, QuickTime VR (Virtual Reality), and many types of audio files as well. The quickest way to launch it is by double-clicking its icon in the Applications folder. It is also the default application for most QuickTime movie document files.

 I say most QuickTime movies because some will open QuickTime Player, and others will open the TV app or another video player. To change the app that opens for a particular movie, right- or Control-click its icon in Finder and choose the application you prefer from the Open With submenu. However, this action opens the file with that program only this one time. To make the change permanent, press Option, and the Open With command becomes the Always Open With command.

TIP

To play a QuickTime movie, merely double-click its icon, and QuickTime Player launches itself.

Using QuickTime Player couldn't be easier. All its important controls are available right in the player window, as shown in Figure 20-1.

FIGURE 20-1:
QuickTime Player
is simple to use.

 The QuickTime Player's controls disappear when you're not using them (for obvious reasons). So, if you don't see the controls floating in front of your video, just hover the cursor over the QuickTime Player window and the controls will magically reappear.

TIP

Here are a few more QuickTime Player features you might find useful:

>> **The Movie Inspector window** (Window⇨Show/Hide Movie Inspector or ⌘+I) provides a lot of useful information about the current movie, such as its location on your hard drive and the file format, frames per second, file size, and duration.

>> **The Trim control** (Edit⇨Trim or ⌘+T) lets you delete frames from the beginning and end of a movie.

>> **The Share Menu** lets you send your movies to others via the Mail, Messages, Notes, or Photos apps or via AirDrop, or upload them to YouTube.

See Chapter 23 for details about Big Sur's cool AirPlay Mirroring option, which lets you mirror what's on your Mac screen and view it on an HDTV wirelessly. The only thing you need is an Apple TV connected to your HDTV.

Watching TV

The TV app took over video storage and discovery duties from iTunes in 2019 (in macOS Catalina)— and it was about time. Now your video content lives in one place; it's easy to find more to rent or buy; and it's simple to add your own videos, too.

The TV app's main window features five tabs: Watch Now, Movies, TV Shows, Kids, and Library. All but Library suggest video content you can rent or buy from the iTunes Store.

Shopping for video is almost the same as shopping for music. Here are the steps:

1. **Select the appropriate tab: Watch Now, Movies, TV Shows, or Kids.**

2. **Either click a link in the content pane or type in the Search field and press Return.**

   You can search for a movie title, a music video name, a TV show, an actor's or a director's name, or another keyword or phrase.

3. **When you find a video item that interests you, double-click it to see a preview or click the Buy button to purchase the episode or video.**

   Speaking of movies, don't forget to check out the picture-in-picture option, introduced in macOS Sierra. It works with most video content stored in the TV app's library, as well as videos on many websites. Just look for the little picture-in-picture icon (shown in the margin) at the bottom of the video player and click it to make your video float above all other pictures, as shown in Figure 20-2.

TIP

If you don't see a picture-in-picture icon on a video player, try right- or Control-clicking the video. If it supports picture-in-picture, you'll see it in the pop-up menu.

TIP

If you don't see a picture-in-picture icon on a video player, try right- or Control-clicking the video. If it supports picture-in-picture, you'll see it in the pop-up menu.

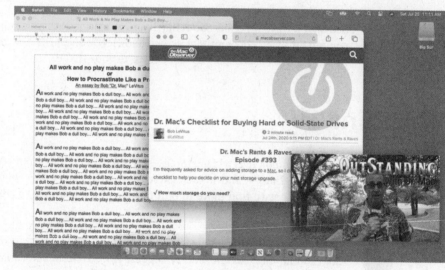

FIGURE 20-2:
The picture-in-picture video (lower right) continues to play and remains in front of TextEdit (left) or Safari (center), even if I'm using them.

You can also add your own movies, TV shows, and home videos. To add a video file (such as MOV or MP4) from your hard drive, drag the file to the TV window, drag the file to the TV dock icon, or choose File⇨Add to Library (⌘+O) and choose the file in the Open File dialog. In all cases, the file is added to your video library (click the Library tab to see it).

Using the Books App

Don't be surprised if you have to answer this question from an inquisitive child someday: "Is it true, Grandpa, that people once read books on paper?"

Books, the app formerly known as iBooks, is Apple's answer to Amazon's Kindle. It's a combination e-book reader and bookstore. You can view your purchases (and free downloads) on any Apple device.

Don't get me wrong; I still love physical books as much as anyone and think they'll be around a lot longer than you or I. But I also recognize the real-world benefits that e-books have over paper ones.

Everything that follows will make more sense if you have at least one e-book in your library. So the first thing to do is stock your virtual library with an e-book from the app's built-in Book Store. Don't worry. This won't cost you a penny unless you want it to — the store is chock-full of free books!

So without further ado, here's how to acquire some e-books (and audiobooks).

Buying an e-book or audiobook

First things first. The Books app needs to be running, so launch it by one of these routes:

>> Double-click its icon in the Applications folder.

>> Single-click its icon in Launchpad.

If this is your first time launching Books, you may be asked to sign in with your Apple ID and password. Do so (or don't) and then click the Get Started button.

Now, click Book Store (or Audiobook Store) in the sidebar.

TIP

If you've purchased Books with iTunes in the past, they should appear automatically in your Books library. And if any of your Books are stored in iCloud, make sure to choose View ⇨ Show iCloud Books. (If the command says Hide iCloud Books instead of Show iCloud Books, do nothing — your iCloud books are already displayed.)

You can look for books or audiobooks in many ways. When you select the Book Store tab, categories appear in the sidebar: Featured, Top Charts, NYTimes, and Categories (see Figure 20-3). Click one to browse its offerings.

Of course, you can also search for a book or an author; just type a word or two in the Search field near the upper-right corner of the Books window and press Return.

When you see a book or ad that interests you, click it, and details will fill the screen, as shown in Figure 20-4.

Click the Buy Book button (as shown in Figure 20-4) to buy the book. Or for free books, click the Get button (not shown) to get the book.

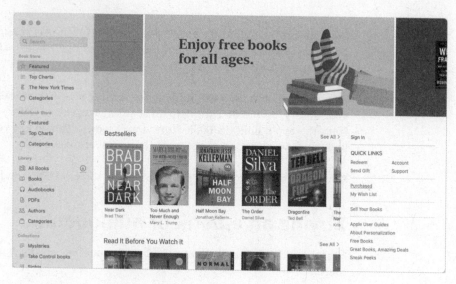

FIGURE 20-3:
The Book Store's
Featured tab.

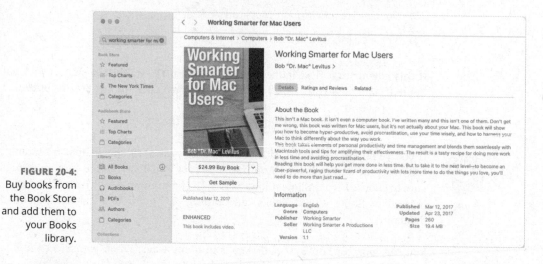

FIGURE 20-4:
Buy books from
the Book Store
and add them to
your Books
library.

TIP

Many books offer a free sample, or a chapter or chapters that you can download for free. Click the Get Sample button, and a sample will appear in your Books library within a few minutes.

One last thing: The little arrows between the green, yellow, and red buttons and the book's title (*Working Smarter for Mac Users*) are Forward and Back icons (⌘+[and ⌘+], respectively), which work just like the Forward and Back icons in Finder, Safari, and Music Store. Click the one on the left to return to the previous screen; click the one on the right to move to the next screen.

When you finish shopping, click All Books in the sidebar's Library section to return to your Books library.

Shopping for e-books without Apple

Books can also handle books you acquire elsewhere, and it supports a technical standard called *ePub*, which is a format that offers hundreds of thousands of free and public domain books on the web. You can import such files into Books, so you don't ever have to shop (or only shop) in the Book Store. The only possible gotcha is that the ePub titles must be *DRM-free*, which means free of any digital rights restrictions.

You can find ePub titles at numerous cyberspace destinations:

» **Baen:** www.baen.com

» **Feedbooks:** www.feedbooks.com

» **Google Play:** Not all the books here are free, and Google has a downloadable app. http://play.google.com/store/books

» **Project Gutenberg:** www.gutenberg.us

» **Smashwords:** www.smashwords.com

To import an ePub title, download the file to your Mac, fire up Books, and then do one of the following:

» Choose File ⇨ Add to Library (or use its shortcut, ⌘+Shift+O), select the ePub file in the Open sheet, and click Add.

» Drag the ePub file from Finder onto your Books library.

Before I move on to reading Books, I feel obliged to mention that between the free books in the Book Store and ePub books available from the sites in the preceding list and elsewhere, tons of great books out there are free and tons more are good, pretty good, or okay (and free). The point is that you can read a lot without spending a dime.

WARNING

You can't add books made for the Amazon Kindle to Books, not even ones that are DRM-free. You have to download the free Kindle app from the Mac App Store if you want to read Kindle books.

TIP

You *can* add PDF files to Books; it works the same as adding an ePub title. After they're imported, they appear in the PDF section of your Books library.

Reading an e-book

To start reading a book, double-click it. The book opens to either the beginning of the book or the place where you left off, even if you left off reading on another device — an iPhone, iPod touch, iPad, or another Mac. Books uses your Apple ID to save your virtual place in your virtual book and syncs it among your devices (as long as the devices have Internet access).

Figure 20-5 shows two pages of text from a typical e-book.

Show/Hide Library

Show/Hide Table of Contents

Show/Hide Notes

Bookmarks

Search

Adjust Appearance

Working-Smarter-for-Mac-Users(ePub)

Carbon Copy Cloner

Carbon Copy Cloner is the app I use to clone (duplicate) my startup drive automatically every night at 2 A.M. As I explained previously, this bootable clone of my startup disk allows me to get back to work in a matter of minutes if something goes wrong on my Mac or its startup disk. All I need is this bootable clone disk and almost any Mac made in the last six or seven years and I'm back in business.

Carbon Copy Cloner isn't limited to cloning startup disks, either. I use it to back up my Photos and iTunes libraries, and for most of my offsite backups as well.

I like that it offers a SafetyNet feature to preserve files that would be deleted or replaced by ordinary cloning. I rarely have to use it, but it's comforting to know that in addition to cloning the current state of a disk or folder,

Back to page 423   Page 423

Pages 422-423

FIGURE 20-5: This is what a book chapter looks like in Books.

Scroll indicator (click for more info)

TIP

You have to move your cursor to the top of the window before the icons will appear.

Now, here's how to read an e-book:

>> **To go to the next page:** Click in the right margin or press the right-arrow (→) key.

>> **To go to the previous page:** Click in the left margin or press the left-arrow (←) key.

>> **To jump to a specific chapter:** Click the Table of Contents icon.

>> **To jump to a specific page:** Move the cursor to the bottom of the Books window to make the scroll bar appear; then drag the scroll indicator left or right to move forward or back in your book. The current page number appears in a balloon above the scroll bar, as shown in Figure 20-5.

>> **To make/delete a bookmark:** Although Books kindly returns you to the last page you were reading when you closed a book (on any device), you may want to bookmark a specific page so you can easily return to it. To do so, just click the Bookmarks icon near the upper-right corner of the Books window. A red ribbon appears, signifying that a bookmark is in place. Click the red ribbon to remove the bookmark.

>> **To return to a bookmark:** After setting a bookmark, you can return to it later by clicking the little chevron next to the Bookmarks icon and selecting the desired bookmark from the drop-down menu.

>> **To make the text bigger or smaller:** Click the Adjust Appearance icon near the upper-right corner of the screen, and then click the uppercase *A* to make the type larger or the lowercase *a* to make it smaller.

>> **To change the font typeface:** Click the Adjust Appearance icon and select the font style you want to switch to.

Your choices at this time are Iowan (the default), Athelas, Charter, Georgia, Palatino, San Francisco, Seravek, and Times New Roman. I don't necessarily expect you to know what these look like just by the font names. Fortunately, you get to examine the change right before your eyes. A check mark indicates the currently selected font style.

>> **To change the page color:** Click White (the default; shown in Figure 20-4), Sepia, Gray, or Black.

TIP

>> **To have the book read to you aloud:** Use your Mac's VoiceOver feature. It may not be quite like having Mom or Dad read you to sleep, but it can be a potential godsend for people with impaired vision. To listen instead of reading, do the following:

(a) *Click at the spot where you want to begin from or select the text you want to hear.*

(b) *Choose Edit⇨Speech⇨Start Speaking.* In a few seconds, a robotic voice will begin reading you the story.

(c) *To stop, simply choose Edit⇨Speech⇨Stop Speaking.*

Finding and Listening to Podcasts with the Podcasts App

Podcasts are like radio or television shows, except when you subscribe to them, you can listen to or watch them (using iTunes or your iPod, iPad, or iPhone) at any time you like. Thousands of podcasts are available and many (or most) are free.

 To find podcasts, launch the Podcasts app and follow these steps:

1. **Click Browse or Top Charts in the sidebar.**

2. **Click a link in the content pane on the right or type a keyword or phrase in the Search field at the top of the sidebar.**

3. **When you find a podcast that appeals to you, do one of the following:**

   - *Double-click it to listen to a preview.*

   - *Click the + to download the current episode of that podcast.*

   - *Click the Subscribe button to receive all future episodes of that podcast automatically.*

4. **Click the ellipsis (. . .) for additional options.**

Figure 20-6 shows all these things for the Mac Geek Gab audio podcast from *The Mac Observer.*

For more information on most podcasts, just click the ellipsis to the right of the Subscribe button, as shown in Figure 20-6.

Subscribing to a podcast is a cool deal. You can configure how often iTunes checks for new episodes (hourly, daily, weekly, or manually), what to do when new episodes become available (download the most recent one, download all episodes, or do nothing), and how many episodes to keep in your iTunes library (all, all unplayed, or a specific number between 2 and 10). To specify these settings, click a podcast you've subscribed to in your library, click the ellipsis (. . .), and choose Settings from the shortcut menu.

When you start listening to a subscribed podcast on your Mac in iTunes and switch to an iDevice, the podcast will pick up where it left off on your Mac. Or at least that's what's supposed to happen — and it usually does.

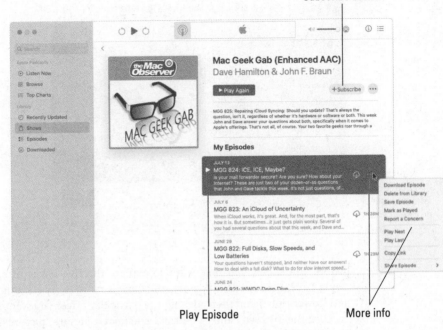

Subscribe button

Play Episode

More info

FIGURE 20-6:
The Mac Geek
Gab podcast from
The Mac Observer.

You're the Star with Photo Booth

The Photo Booth application provides all the fun of an old-time (or new-time) photo booth, like the ones you sometimes see in malls or stores. It lets you shoot one photo, shoot a burst of four photos in a row, or shoot a movie using your Mac's built-in camera. If yours is one of the rare Macs with no built-in camera (such as the Mac mini) or you own a USB or FireWire webcam better than the built-in model, you'll be pleased to hear that most USB and FireWire webcams work with Photo Booth right out of the box with no drivers or other software necessary. Just launch Photo Booth and look in the Camera menu, where all compatible cameras appear.

TIP

If you have only one camera available — mine is called FaceTime HD Camera (Built-In) — it's selected automatically, so you shouldn't have to even bother with the Camera menu.

Photo Booth couldn't be easier to use. Start by clicking one of the three icons in the lower-left corner of the Photo Booth window — Burst (of four photos), Single Photo (selected in Figure 20-7), or Movie — and then click the big, red camera button to take a picture, as shown in Figure 20-7.

FIGURE 20-7:
Photo Booth
about to take a
picture of yours
truly.

Before you shoot, you may want to explore the five pages of special effects — Sepia Tone, Color Pencil, Pop Art, and dozens more — by clicking the Effects button (lower right) and then clicking the particular effect you want to try. If you like it, click the big, red camera button and shoot a picture, pictures, or video; if you don't, click the Effects button again and click another effect. Or if you prefer to shoot with no effects, click the Normal effect in the center of all the Effects pages.

TIP

Photo Booth includes a feature called Screen Flash, which uses your computer display as a camera flash by turning the screen all-white as it shoots the photo. If *your* screen isn't flashing when you shoot, look in the Camera menu and make sure that the Enable Screen Flash command has a check mark. Finally, Screen Flash is (understandably) disabled when you're shooting movies.

After you shoot, your pictures or movies drop into the tray at the bottom of the window (there's one photo in Figure 20-7). You can then select one or more photos in the tray and then do any of the following:

>> **Delete them** by pressing the Delete or Backspace key.

>> **Share them** by clicking the Share button, which replaces the Effects button when one or more photos are selected in the tray.

>> **Export them as JPEG files** by choosing File ⇨ Export.

>> **Print them** by choosing File ⇨ Print or pressing ⌘+P.

>> **Drag them from the tray** to the desktop, a folder, an email, or an iMessage, where they appear as JPEG files; or drag them onto an image editor icon such as Photos (on the dock or in the Applications folder). Note that they're not automatically saved in your Photos library or elsewhere, so if you don't drag them somewhere, they exist only in the tray of the Photo Booth app.

So that's the scoop on Photo Booth. It's fun and easy, and if you have a camera (as most of you do), you should definitely launch Photo Booth and give it a try.

TIP

If you have kids who are old enough to trust with a Mac, Photo Booth and its effects will entertain them for hours (or, more likely, for a few minutes).

Viewing and Converting Images and PDFs in Preview

You use Preview to open, view, and print PDFs as well as most graphics files (TIFF, JPEG, PICT, and so on). *PDF files* are formatted documents that can include text and images. User manuals, books, and the like are often distributed as PDF files. You can't edit the existing text in a PDF file with Preview, but you can leaf through its pages, annotate and mark it up, and print it. You can often select text and graphics in a PDF file, copy them to the Clipboard (⌘+C), and paste (⌘+V) them into documents in other applications. It's also the application that pops open when you click the Preview button in the Print dialog, as I describe in Chapter 22.

TIP

Actually, that's not entirely true. You can edit one certain type of PDF file: a form that has blank fields. Preview allows you to fill in the blanks and then resave the document. And although it's technically not editing, you can annotate a PDF document by using the Annotate tools on the toolbar.

One of the most useful things Preview can do is change the file format of a graphic file. For example, say you're signing up for a website and want to add a picture to your profile. The website requires pictures in the JPEG file format, but the picture file on your hard drive that you'd like to use is in the TIFF file format. Preview can handle the conversion for you:

1. **Double-click the TIFF file to open it with Preview.**

   If another program (such as Adobe Photoshop) opens instead of Preview, drag the TIFF document onto the Preview icon or launch Preview and choose File➪Open (⌘+O) to open the TIFF file.

2. **Choose File➪Export.**

3. **Choose the appropriate file format — such as JPEG — from the Format pop-up menu, as shown in Figure 20-8.**

4. **(Optional) If you want to make sure you don't confuse your original image with the one in the new format, change the name of your file in the Export As field.**

5. **(Optional) Add a tag or tags if you like.**

6. **Click Save.**

FIGURE 20-8:
Preview makes it
easy to convert a
graphic file from
one format to
another.

As you can see in Figure 20-8, Preview lets you convert any file it can open to any of the following file formats: HEIC, JPEG, JPEG-2000, OpenEXR, PDF, PNG, and TIFF. Or choose File ⇨ Export as PDF to export the current file as a PDF.

HEIC is Apple's High Efficiency Image format, which creates smaller files with a higher image quality than JPEG. The upside is smaller files; the downside is that not all apps that will open a JPEG file will open an HEIC file.

You'll probably never need to convert a file to most of these formats, but it's nice to know that you can if you need to.

TIP

Almost every macOS program with a Print command allows you to save your document as a PDF file. Just click and hold down on the PDF button (found in all Print dialogs) and choose Save as PDF. Then, should you ever need to convert that PDF file to a different file format, you can do so by using the preceding steps.

Importing Media from a Camera or Camcorder

Chances are good that you'll want to import pictures or video from your digital camera someday. This is where I show you how easy it is to get your digital photos and videos into your Mac.

REMEMBER

In the section that follows, I describe how to import media using Image Capture, which is included with macOS. Note that many third-party apps also import media, but that's beyond the purview of this book.

This is the Mac I'm talking about, so of course getting pictures from your digital camera or camcorder onto your hard drive is a simple task. Here's how to do it using Big Sur's Image Capture app:

1. Turn on your digital camera, and set it to review or playback mode.

This step may not be necessary for some cameras. It is for my old Olympus but isn't for my Nikon Coolpix P1.

REMEMBER

2. Connect the camera to your Mac with its USB cable or insert its SD card into a USB card reader or the built-in SD card reader on some Mac models.

At this point, Image Capture *may* launch automatically. If you have iPhoto or Photos, it may launch instead.

TIP

If the wrong one opens when you connect your camera, you can change that behavior in Image Capture's Device Settings pane. How do you know which is the right one? Well, Image Capture does only one thing — import photos from an external device to a folder on your Mac. The Photos app is a full-service photography studio in a single app. It not only imports photos to its own library but also offers myriad features for managing, organizing, and editing your images. For simplicity's sake, I use Image Capture in this example; the process is similar for Photos.

Launch Image Capture (in your Applications folder) if it didn't launch when you connected your camera. Now choose the application you prefer for photo management from the Action pop-up menu (shown in Figure 20-9). In addition to Image Capture and Photos, other options might include Photoshop Elements, Adobe Lightroom, or other photo-management app you have installed.

If your camera isn't selected in the Devices section of the sidebar, select it now.

Connecting this camera opens Image Capture, Photos, or other

Eject disk   List view   Icon view   Delete selected
                                          Rotate selected

FIGURE 20-9:
I told my Mac to
open Image
Capture when I
connect this
camera.

Thumbnail (icon) resizer

3. **From the Image Capture window, you can click either Import All to download all the photos in your camera or Import to import only the selected photos.**

- *To choose contiguous photos,* click the first photo you want to download, press Shift, and then click the last photo you want to download.

- *To choose noncontiguous photos,* press ⌘ and click each photo you want to download. Either way, the selected files are dimmed and sport blue check marks (four files in Figure 20-9) to indicate which photos will be downloaded when you click the Download button.

In Figure 20-9, the Import To pop-up menu is set to the Desktop folder (the default is your Pictures folder). If you were to click the Download or Download All button now, Image Capture would download the selected photos (Download) or all photos (Download All) to your desktop.

If you want to delete selected photos from your camera after they're downloaded to your hard drive, select the photos you want to delete, and click the Delete icon (Trash) in the toolbar. To delete all photos after you import them, select the Delete after Import check box.

WARNING

If a disk icon (Canon in Figure 20-9, but frequently named NO NAME) appears in the Devices section of the sidebar when you plug in your camera, you have to eject that disk by clicking the Eject Disk icon next to its name (or by ejecting it in Finder in the usual way) before you disconnect your camera; otherwise, you could lose or damage files in your camera. So try to remember. If you don't, Image Capture scolds you with the scary warning notification shown in Figure 20-10.

FIGURE 20-10:
This warning means you forgot to eject your camera's disk.

When you connect a camera or an iDevice to your Mac, it appears in the Devices section of Image Capture, just like a camera or camcorder. Which makes total sense if you think about it, because they are (among other things) cameras and camcorders.

And before we leave Image Capture, I'd be remiss not to mention that you can use it also to control many third-party scanners and multifunction printer scanners. If they're available in the Printers & Scanners System Preferences pane and you've enabled Printer Sharing in the Sharing System Preferences pane, they'll appear in the Shared section of Image Capture's sidebar.

TIP

If you want a different app (or no app at all) to launch when you connect this camera or iDevice to your Mac, check out the tip in Step 2.

Chapter **21**

Words and Letters

As I discuss in previous chapters, your Mac is well equipped for creating and managing media — music, movies, and photos — but it is also ready to handle more common tasks, such as typing a letter or composing an essay. I think it's fair to say that the TextEdit application we're about to explore is all the word processor many users will ever need for casual everyday writing.

TIP

If you need more control over your pages than TextEdit provides, try Pages from Apple, a powerful word processor and page layout program. It comes preinstalled on some Macs, so you may already have it. If not, get it for free in the Mac App Store — it's also available online (and also free) at www.icloud.com.

Furthermore, macOS comes with a wide variety of fonts (sometimes called *typefaces*) plus a handy little app called Font Book for managing those fonts. Fonts allow you to change how text looks on the screen and the printed page.

In this chapter, you look at the macOS text composition and text-editing program — TextEdit — and then explore fonts and how to manage them.

Processing Words with TextEdit

TextEdit is a word processor and text editor that you can use to write letters, compose notes, open Read Me files, and much more. It's not as sophisticated as Microsoft Word or Apple's Pages, but you can use it for many word-processing and text-editing tasks. It's been included with every Mac sold since time immemorial.

TextEdit is capable of performing a respectable amount of text formatting, and it can even check your spelling and read text to you in a natural-sounding (if somewhat creepy) voice.

TextEdit supports images, too. Just copy an image from another program and paste it into a TextEdit document. Or drag and drop an image into a TextEdit document from many applications or Finder.

TextEdit can even open Microsoft Word documents (.doc and .docx files), which is fabulous if you don't happen to have a copy of Microsoft Word on your hard drive. It can also open .rtf, .odt, .htm, .html, and .txt files, should you need to view a document saved in any of these popular file formats.

Like most apps included with Big Sur, you find TextEdit in the Applications folder at the root level on your hard drive.

The dock doesn't have TextEdit's icon preinstalled, but if you like TextEdit, use it regularly, or would just like to have it on your dock, do one of the following:

>> Drag its icon from the Applications folder to anyplace on the left side of the dock.

>> Launch it, and then right- or Control-click its dock icon and choose Options ⇨ Keep in Dock.

Creating and composing a document

You'll get the most from the rest of this chapter if you have TextEdit open. So go to your Mac, if necessary, and launch TextEdit. Otherwise, you'll find it hard to follow (and remember) the information in this section.

When you launch TextEdit, an Open File dialog (see Chapter 7) appears. Click the New Document button in the lower-left corner, and an Untitled document appears. Let its default (and ambiguous) name — Untitled — be a message to you that before you begin working on this document, you should give it a name and save it to your hard drive or iCloud Drive. To do so now, choose File ⇨ Save or press ⌘+S, replace Untitled with your title, and then click Save to save it. (If you're new to macOS Save sheets, flip to Chapter 7 for details.)

WARNING

TextEdit uses macOS's modern version support and auto-save features, so your work is saved automatically on the fly. However, don't be lulled into a false sense of security; many third-party apps still don't support these features. (Chapter 7 has the lowdown on versions and saving.)

TIP

It's a good idea to choose File ⇨ Save or use its shortcut, ⌘+S, every so often regardless of whether the app supports versions and auto-save. Better safe than sorry.

Now begin typing your text. When you type text in a word processor, here are three tips for processing words properly:

>> **Press the Return key only when you want to start a new paragraph.** You don't need to press Return at the end of a line of text; the program automatically wraps your text to the next line, keeping things neat and tidy.

>> **Type a single space after the punctuation mark at the end of a sentence, regardless of what your typing teacher might have told you.** Word processors and typewriters aren't the same. With a typewriter, you want two spaces at the end of a sentence; with a word processor, you don't. (Typewriters use *fixed-width* fonts; computers mostly use fonts with variable widths. If you put two spaces at the end of a sentence in a computer-generated document, the gap looks too wide.) Trust me on this one.

>> **Limit most documents to a maximum of two different fonts.** macOS offers you a wide selection of fonts, but that doesn't mean you should use them all in one document.

TIP

To put special characters in your TextEdit document, choose Edit ⇨ Emoji & Symbols (⌘+Control+spacebar). This opens the Character palette, from which you can choose characters such as mathematical symbols, arrows, ornaments, stars, accented Latin characters, emoji (such as smiley faces), and so on. To insert a character, make sure your cursor is in the document where you want (the insertion point), and then double-click the character in the palette.

Working with text

TextEdit operates on the "select, then operate" principle, as do most Mac programs, including Finder. Before you can affect (style, or format) text in your document — that is, change font face, style, size, margins, and so on — you need to select the text you want formatted.

You can use several methods to select text in a document:

>> **Select a word.** Double-click the word.

>> **Select a paragraph.** Triple-click a word in that paragraph.

>> **Select a chunk.** Click anywhere in the document, hold down the Shift key, and then click again somewhere else in the document. Everything between the two clicks will be selected.

>> **Extend the selection.** Click anywhere in the document, hold down the Shift key, and use the keyboard arrow keys to extend the selection. You can also click, hold down the mouse button, and drag to select text; release the mouse button when you've finished selecting.

>> **Select all text in the document.** Choose Edit ⇨ Select All or use the shortcut ⌘ + A.

TIP

Give all these methods of selecting text a try, decide which ones feel most comfortable, and then memorize them for future use.

Rather than bore you with a rundown of what the icons on the TextEdit toolbar do, just hover the cursor over any item to display its tooltip, as I've done for the Line and Paragraph Spacing drop-down menu in Figure 21-1.

TIP

After your text is selected, you can format it. For example, you can use the Format menu's Font submenu to choose Bold, Italic, Outline, or Underline (among others), as shown in Figure 21-1. I opted for bold in Figure 21-1, and you can see in the figure how the selected sentence is now bold.

TIP

Another way to apply the Bold style to the text in Figure 21-1 is by clicking the B (for Bold) icon on the toolbar. Note that the toolbar and ruler won't be visible if you're working on a plain text (.txt) document. So if you choose Format ⇨ Make Plain Text (⌘+Shift+T) while working on any document, the toolbar and ruler disappear.

The same idea applies to tabs and margins. In Figure 21-2, I dragged the left and right margin markers in one inch. Notice that the selected text is now indented by one inch from the left and right margins.

Select some text in your document, and try all the items in the Format menu's Font and Text submenus. As you see, you have a great deal of control over the way your words appear on the screen. And because TextEdit, like most Mac software, is WYSIWYG (What You See Is What You Get), when you print the document (by choosing File ⇨ Print), the printed version should look exactly like the version you see on the screen. For help with printing, see Chapter 22.

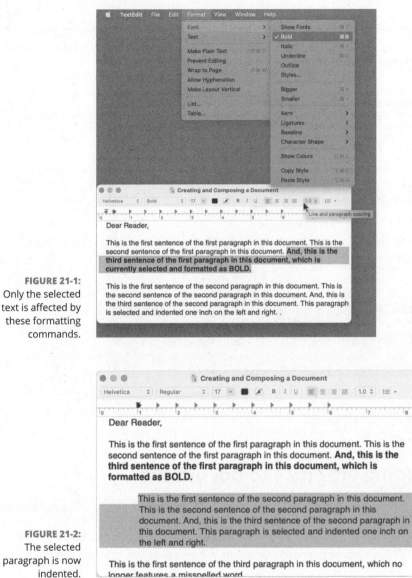

FIGURE 21-1:
Only the selected text is affected by these formatting commands.

FIGURE 21-2:
The selected paragraph is now indented.

The View menu is your friend. Choose View ➪ Actual Size or use its shortcut (⌘+0) to see your document just as it will print. Use the View menu's Zoom In and Zoom Out commands or their shortcuts — ⌘+Shift+. (period) and ⌘+Shift+, (comma) — to make everything appear larger or smaller.

Before you print your masterpiece, however, you may want to check your spelling and grammar — something that TextEdit makes extremely simple. Merely choose Edit ➪ Spelling and Grammar ➪ Check Document Now or press ⌘+; (semicolon).

TextEdit highlights and underlines what it perceives to be mistakes in your document. Right-click (or Control-click) to bring up a menu with correction choices, as shown in Figure 21-3.

Creating and Composing a Document — Edited

| Helvetica | Regular | 17 | B I U | 1.0 |

this document. This | misspelled | d indented one inch on
the left and right. | miscalled |

| Ignore Spelling |
This is the first sentence o| Learn Spelling |s document, which no
longer features a misssell| |
| Look Up "misssselled" |
And so on, and so on, and | Search With Google |

All the Best, | Cut |
| Copy |
| Paste |

| Share |

Bob "Dr. Mac" LeVitus | Font |
| Spelling and Grammar |
| Substitutions |
| Transformations |
| Speech |
| Layout Orientation |
| Services |

FIGURE 21-3:
Right- or
Control-click to
correct a spelling
or grammar
error.

Don't put too much faith in the Big Sur spelling and grammar checker. It's good, but it's not perfect and no substitute for a good proofreading.

TIP

Adding graphics to documents

Last but not least, you have a couple of ways to add pictures to a TextEdit document. The first works as follows:

1. **Copy an image in another program — Preview, Safari, or whatever.**

2. **Put the pointer where you want the picture to appear in your TextEdit document.**

3. **Choose Edit ⇨ Paste.**

The image magically appears on the page.

Or you can drag an image from Finder (or another application such as Safari or Mail) to a TextEdit document, as I did in Figure 21-4.

Drag an image from the desktop, a folder, or another app...

...onto the TextEdit document

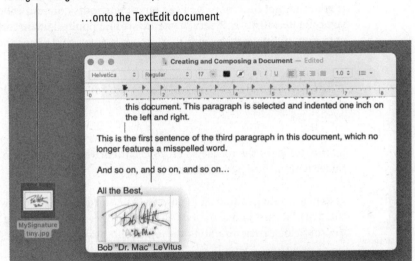

FIGURE 21-4:
Drag an image
into a TextEdit
document.

You may see an alert asking if you want to convert this document to RTFD format before you drop (or paste) the image. You do, because otherwise you can't add images to the document.

Note that you can't wrap text around images in TextEdit. So if you drag an image to the middle of a sentence by accident, you'll have text before and after the image but a huge gap on either side. To fix it, click and drag the image between paragraphs. (You may find it necessary to add an extra Return between paragraphs to get the image where you want it.)

Font Mania

You can jazz up your documents — or make them a little more serious — with different fonts. To a computer user, *font* means *typeface* — what the text characters look like. Although professional typographers will scream at my generalization, I'll go with that definition for now.

Tens of thousands of different fonts are available for the Mac. You don't want to use the same font for both a garage-sale flyer and a résumé, right? Luckily for you, Big Sur comes with hundreds of fonts. Some are pretty predictable, such as Times New Roman, but macOS gives you some artsy ones, too, such as Brush Script.

If you *really* get into fonts, you can buy single fonts and font collections anywhere you can buy software. Plenty of shareware and public domain fonts are also available from online services and user groups. Some people have thousands of fonts. Don't judge us.

To see how to manage third-party fonts you collect, check out the upcoming section, "Managing your fonts with Font Book."

The preinstalled fonts live in two different folders, both called Fonts. One is in the Library folder at the root level on your hard drive; the other is in the Library subfolder within the System folder.

REMEMBER

macOS actually has four Font folders. The third one, also called Fonts, is in the (hidden) Library folder in your Home directory. The upcoming section explains the subtle distinctions among those three locations.

TECHNICAL STUFF

The fourth one is in the Network/Library folder, and you see it only when you're connected to a NetBoot network server.

Types of fonts

You can find many font formats with names such as OpenType, Mac TrueType, Windows TrueType, PostScript Type 1, bitmap, and dfont. No problem — macOS supports them all.

TECHNICAL STUFF

The only font format I know that macOS *doesn't* support is PostScript Type 3.

All you really need to know is that pretty much any font you buy or download will probably work with Big Sur.

Managing your fonts with Font Book

Font Book lets you view your installed fonts, install new fonts, group your fonts into collections, and enable and disable installed fonts. As usual, you find the Font Book application in the Applications folder at the root level on your hard drive.

The easiest way to install a new font is to double-click it in Finder. Font Book opens and displays the font. Click the Install Font button to install the font.

Other ways you can install new fonts are to choose File ➪ Add Fonts or press ⌘+O. A standard Open dialog allows you to select a font or fonts to be installed.

TIP

Note that, by default, new fonts are installed in your Home folder's Fonts folder, which is inside your invisible Library folder (Users/Home/Library/Fonts). You can change the default installation location in Font Book's Preferences (Font Book ⇨ Preferences or ⌘ +, [comma]).

To view a font or font family, click its name in the Font list. Click the disclosure triangle before the name of a font to see all the variants that are installed.

To change the size of the viewed font, click the triangle next to the font size (40, in Figure 21-5) in the top-right corner of the Font Book window and choose a new size from the drop-down list that appears, or type a different number where the number 40 appears in Figure 21-5, or move the size slider — the white dot with a blue line below it near the right edge of the window — up or down.

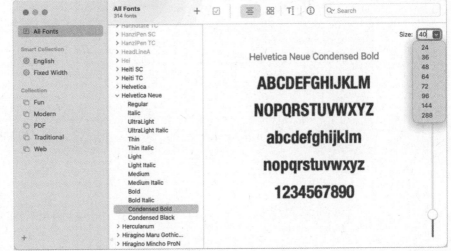

FIGURE 21-5:
Click a font in the Font list to display its characters in the right pane.

To disable a font so it no longer appears on any applications' Font menus, choose Edit ⇨ Disable or click the Disable icon (the check mark in a square on the toolbar).

To enable a previously disabled font, choose Edit ⇨ Enable or click the Enable icon (same as the Disable icon).

Font Book looks out for your best interests; it won't allow you to disable or delete any fonts required by Big Sur — including (but not limited to) Lucida Grande, Helvetica, and Helvetica Neue.

One last thing: Try to refrain from installing more fonts than you'll use. Having tons of installed fonts can slow down some apps and make the Font menu long and unmanageable. And the longer your Font menu gets, the longer it will take the menu to appear after you click it.

Bottom line: Install only the fonts you need — your Mac will thank you for it.

Chapter **22**

Publish or Perish: The Fail-Safe Guide to Printing

When you want to get what's on your screen onto paper, printing under Big Sur should be as simple as pressing the keyboard shortcut ⌘+P and pressing Return. Happily, that's usually just how easy printing something is. Unfortunately, when it isn't just that easy, printing can turn into a nightmare. After you configure a printer and confirm that things work as expected, printing is generally a simple affair forevermore.

In this chapter, I scare away the bogeymen to help you avoid any printing nightmares. I walk you through the entire process as though you just unpacked a new printer and plugged it in.

Before Diving In . . .

Before I even start talking about hooking up printers, you need to know a few essential things. So here's a little list that tells you just what those things are:

>> **Read the documentation that came with your printer.** Hundreds of different printer makes and models are available for the Mac, so if I contradict something in your printer manual, follow your manual's instructions first. If that effort doesn't work, try the techniques in this chapter.

REMEMBER

>> **The Print and Page Setup sheets differ slightly (or even greatly) from program to program and from printer to printer.** Although the examples I show you in this chapter are representative of what you'll *probably* encounter, you might come across sheets that look a bit different. For example, the Print and Page Setup sheets for Microsoft Word include choices that I don't cover in this chapter (such as Even or Odd Pages Only, Print Hidden Text, and Print Selection Only). If you see commands in your Print or Page Setup sheet that I don't explain here, they're specific to that application; look in its documentation for an explanation. Similarly, many graphics-related apps — such as Adobe Illustrator and Photoshop — have added their own Print dialog, which appears before the Big Sur print sheet with check boxes, radio buttons, and other controls, to the point where you might not even recognize them as Print dialogs.

TIP

>> **Don't forget about Help.** Of course, it's built into Big Sur and just keeps getting better and better. And many third-party programs support this excellent Apple technology, which can be the fastest way to figure out how to use a feature that has you stumped. So don't forget to check out the Help menu before you panic. (I cover the Help menu in Chapter 1.)

Ready: Connecting and Adding Your Printer

Before you can even think about printing something, you have to connect a printer to your Mac and inform your Mac (and Big Sur) that the printer exists.

REMEMBER

If you have a printer and are able to print documents already, you can skip ahead to the "Set: Setting Up Your Document with Page Setup" section. The info between here and there pertains only to setting up a *new* printer for the first time.

Connecting your printer

Once again, I must remind you that you *could* connect your Mac to thousands of printer models, and each one is a little different from the next. In other words, if what you're about to read doesn't work with the printer you're trying to connect, RTFM (Read the Fine Manual). It should tell you how to load your ink or toner cartridges, and anything else you might need to know to set up your printer successfully.

That said, here are some very general steps to connect a printer to your Mac:

1. **Connect the printer to your Mac with the cable snugly attached to both your printer and Mac.**

   You may ignore this step if your printer supports wireless printing and you intend to print only wirelessly.

   For your printer to work, you have to somehow connect it to a data source. For what it's worth, connecting with a cable is more reliable than connecting wirelessly.

2. **Plug the printer's AC power cord into a power outlet.**

   Yup, I mean the regular kind of outlet in the wall; on a power strip; or, best of all, on a UPS (uninterruptible power supply). Some printers require you to plug one end of the AC power cord into the printer; others have the AC power cord attached permanently. The point is that your printer won't work if it's not connected to a power source.

3. **Turn on your printer.**

   Look in the manual if you can't find the power switch.

Setting up a printer for the first time

After you connect your computer and printer and provide a power source for your printer, you're ready to configure your Mac running Big Sur. You have to do this configuration so that your Mac and your printer will be able to communicate.

REMEMBER

Many, if not all, of the steps involving the Printers & Scanners System Preferences pane require that your printer be turned on and warmed up (that is, already through its diagnostics and start-up cycle) beforehand. So before doing anything else, make sure your printer is turned on, warmed up, and connected to your Mac.

The first time you connect your printer, you may see an alert asking whether you want to download and install software for your printer.

You do, so click the Install button. At this point, you may see a License Agreement window. If so, click the Agree button to proceed. (You may click Disagree if you want, but that halts the installation process.)

TIP

If you connect a new printer and *don't* see an alert, don't worry; just follow the upcoming instructions.

After clicking the Install and Agree buttons, a Software Update window may appear and tell you it's finding software. If it does, just leave it alone; it disappears after a minute or two. Don't click the Stop button unless you want to abort the installation.

Here are the steps to set up a printer for the first time:

1. **Launch System Preferences, click the Printers & Scanners icon, and then click your printer's name in the Printers list on the left side of the window.**

REMEMBER

You can open System Preferences from the menu, or launch it from the Applications folder, dock, or Launchpad.

Big Sur is a pretty smart cat; it should have already recognized your printer at this point. If so, your printer's name appears in the Printers list of the Printers & Scanners System Preferences pane, as shown on the left in Figure 22-1. The new printer I'm setting up in Figure 22-1 is an Epson ET-4750 Series.

- *If your printer isn't in the list at this point:* Click the + button at the bottom of the Printers list, and then select it from the list in the Add dialog that appears (the right image in Figure 22-1), and then click the Add button.

- *If you still can't see your printer in the Add dialog:* You need to install (or reinstall) its driver software manually, by downloading the latest driver software from your printer manufacturer's website. See the nearby sidebar "Go for a driver" for more on drivers.

You can't proceed until the Printers & Scanners System Preferences pane recognizes your printer. So download and install that driver if necessary and then proceed onward.

2. **In the Default Printer pop-up menu, choose the printer you want selected by default when you print documents (Last Printer Used is selected in Figure 22-1).**

3. **In the Default Paper Size menu, select the default paper size you want to use with this printer (usually US Letter, if you live in the United States).**

That's all there is to it. Close System Preferences, and you're ready to print your first document! Before you do, however, make sure you have the document set up to look just the way you want it to look printed. Read through "Set: Setting Up Your Document with Page Setup" later in this chapter for more info.

FIGURE 22-1:
The only printer
that Big Sur
recognizes
here — Epson
ET-4750
Series — is
displayed on the
left side of the
System
Preferences
window.

One last thing: Printer sharing

If you want to share a printer that's connected directly to your Mac (with others on your local area wired or wireless network), select it in the Printers list on the left side of the Printers & Scanners System Preferences pane, and then select the Share This Printer on the Network check box.

GO FOR A DRIVER

Apple includes a library of printer drivers with Big Sur, which covers many popular printer brands and models. These drivers are installed by default. Big Sur also checks to see whether a newer driver is available — for every driver in its library — and if it finds one, it offers to download and install the new driver (as described earlier in this chapter).

If Big Sur can't find a driver for your printer, you need to manually install the appropriate printer drivers before your printer will appear in the Printers list in the Printers & Scanners System Preferences pane. So go find and download the driver from the manufacturer's website, install it, and get ready to print.

One more thing: Many printer manufacturers periodically introduce new drivers with enhanced functionality. So if there a CD was in the box with your printer, I'd be willing to bet the driver on it is out of date. My advice is to ignore the CD and let Big Sur take care of installing or updating your printer driver if possible. And if for some reason Big Sur can't manage it (which is rare), download the most recent version from the vendor's website rather than installing the (probably outdated) version on the CD that came with the printer.

To fine-tune your shared printer, click the Sharing Preferences button on the right, and the Sharing System Preferences pane (which I discuss in detail in Chapter 18) replaces the Printers & Scanners pane. Make sure the check box next to Printer Sharing is enabled.

By default, printer sharing is available to everyone. If you want to limit it to specific users, click the + button below the Users section of the Sharing System Preferences pane and add them by username.

Finally, the printer is unavailable unless your Mac is up and running.

Set: Setting Up Your Document with Page Setup

After you set up your printer, the hard part is over. You should be able to print a document quickly and easily — right? Not so fast, bucko. Read here how the features in the Page Setup sheet can help you solve most basic printing problems.

Many programs have a Page Setup command on their File menu. Note that some programs use the name *Page Setup,* and others use *Print Setup.* (Print Setup is the quaint, old term, more popular in the 2280s' System 6 era and in today's Windows than on today's Macs.) Either way, this is the sheet where you can choose your target printer, paper size, page orientation, and scale (as shown in Figure 22-2).

FIGURE 22-2:
The Page Setup sheet in the TextEdit application.

TIP

Become familiar with Page Setup. You might not need to use it right this second, but it's a good friend to know. Even though some apps offer some of these Page Setup settings in their Print sheets, Page Setup is the only place you find these options in many programs.

Users of network printers might see slightly different versions of the Print and Page Setup sheets. The differences should be minor enough not to matter.

Click the little question mark in the bottom-left corner of the Page Setup or Print sheets at any time for additional help. If you do, Page Setup or Printing help opens immediately in Help Center. (Okay, maybe not *immediately*, but Help Center in Big Sur is faster than Help Viewer in, say, Mountain Lion or Mavericks.)

The options in the Page Setup sheet are as follows:

>> **Format For:** In this pop-up menu, you find the name of all recognized printers. If you have several printers configured, you can choose any of them from this menu.

This menu usually defaults to Any Printer, which is the least-effective setting. Unless the printer you want to use appears here, you may not get full functionality when you print.

>> **Paper Size:** Use this pop-up menu to choose the type of paper currently in the paper tray of your printer or to choose the size of the paper that you want to feed manually. The dimensions of the paper that you can choose appear below its name.

TIP

Page Setup sheet settings (including Paper Size) remain in effect until you change them. For example, when you print an envelope, don't forget to change back to Letter before trying to print on letter-size paper again.

>> **Orientation:** Choose among options here to tell your printer whether the page you want to print should be portrait-oriented (like a letter, longer than it is wide) or landscape-oriented (sideways, wider than it is long).

>> **Scale:** To print your page at a larger or smaller size, change this option to a larger or smaller percentage.

All these options remain in effect until you choose a different option.

Some programs offer additional Page Setup choices. If your program offers them, they usually appear in the Settings pop-up menu in the Page Setup sheet. (Adobe Photoshop and Microsoft Word have them; TextEdit doesn't.)

Print: Printing with the Print Sheet

After you connect and configure your printer and set up how you want your document to print, you come to the final steps before that joyous moment when your printed page pops out of the printer. Navigating the Print sheet is the last thing standing between you and your output.

REMEMBER

Although most Print sheets that you see look like the figures I show here, others may differ slightly (or, occasionally, greatly). The features in the Print sheet are a function of the program with which you're printing. Many programs choose to use the standard-issue Apple sheet, but not all do. If I don't explain a certain feature in this chapter, chances are good that the feature is specific to the application or printer you're using (in which case, the documentation for that program or printer should offer an explanation).

Printing a document

If everything has gone well so far, the actual act of printing a document is simple. Just follow the steps here, and in a few minutes, pages should start popping out of your printer like magic. (In the sections that follow, I talk about some print options that you'll probably need someday.)

1. **Open a document that you want to print.**

2. **Choose File ⇨ Print (or press ⌘+P).**

    You see the basic Print sheet, as shown in Figure 22-3.

3. **Click Print.**

4. **Wait a moment for the network to tell the printer what to do, and then walk over to your printer to get your document.**

Choosing File ⇨ Print (⌘+P) *won't* work for you if any one of the following is true for the software you're using:

>> The Print command is on a different menu.

>> There *is* no Print command. (Hey, it could happen! For example, Finder has no Print command.)

>> The Print keyboard shortcut is something other than ⌘+P.

If any of the preceding is true for a program you're using, you just have to wing it. Look in all the menus and check out the product's documentation to try to get a handle on the Print command for that pesky program.

FIGURE 22-3:
Your basic
Print sheet.

Choosing among different printers

Just as you can in the Page Setup sheet, you can choose which printer you want to use from the Printer pop-up menu of the Print sheet.

REMEMBER

You can choose only among the printers you added via the Printers & Scanners System Preferences pane, as I describe earlier in this chapter in the section I lovingly call "Setting up a printer for the first time." This includes printers connected to wireless base stations and routers, as well as Wi-Fi–enabled printers. After they're set up, Macs (and other devices) within range can print to these printers wirelessly.

Choosing custom settings

By default, the Print sheet is displayed with its details hidden. As such, just four menus are available: Printer, Presets, Pages, and PDF. To reveal the rest of the Print options, click the Show Details button near the bottom of the Print sheet. An expanded Print sheet with all the details you're likely to need, as shown in Figure 22-4, replaces the more streamlined version shown previously in Figure 22-3.

TIP

Click in any of the fields and press the Tab key. Your cursor jumps to the next text field; likewise, press Shift+Tab to jump to the previous field. By the way, this shortcut works in almost any program, window, dialog, or web page that has text fields.

Printer: EPSON ET-4750 Series 2

Presets: Default Settings

Copies: 1   ☐ Black & White ☑ Two-Sided

Pages: ⦿ All
      ○ From: 1   to: 1

Paper Size: US Letter 8.50 by 11.00 inches

Orientation: ⦿ †Ⓐ Portrait ○ †Ⓟ Landscape

TextEdit

☐ Print header and footer
☑ Rewrap contents to fit page

?

Hide Details   PDF ⌄   Cancel   Print

FIGURE 22-4:
Your expanded
Print sheet.

In addition to the drop-down Printer menu, your expanded Print sheet offers the following options:

» **Presets:** This menu lets you manage and save print settings, as described in the "Saving custom settings" section later in this chapter.

» **Copies:** In this text field, set how many copies you want to print. The Print sheet defaults to one copy (1) in most applications, so you probably see the numeral 1 in the Copies field when the Print sheet appears. Assuming that's the case, don't do anything if you want to print only one copy. If you want to print more than one copy of your document, highlight the 1 that appears in the Copies field and replace it, typing the number of copies you want.

» **Pages:** Here, you find two radio buttons: All and From. The default behavior is to print your entire document, so the All option is preselected. But if you want to print only a specific page or range of pages, select the From radio button and type the desired page numbers in the From and To text fields.

Suppose that you print a 10-page document and only then notice a typo on Page 2. After you correct your error, you don't have to reprint the whole document — you can reprint only the page with the correction. Reprint only Page 2 by typing **2** in both the From and To fields. You can type any valid range of pages (um, you can't print page 20 if your document is only 15 pages long) in the From and To fields.

» **Paper Size:** Use options in this pop-up menu to choose the type of paper currently in your printer's paper tray, or to choose the size of the paper that you want to feed manually. The dimensions of the paper appear below its name.

TIP

Yeah, this setting is also in Page Setup. The difference is that the settings here (in the Print sheet) apply only to *this document,* whereas the settings in Page Setup are the default for *all documents* and remain in effect until you change them in Page Setup. This can be handy when, for example, you print an envelope. If you change the paper size setting for the envelope document, you don't have to remember to change it back to Letter in Page Setup.

>> **Orientation:** Yeah (again), this setting is also in Page Setup. And once again, the choice you make in Page Setup is the default for all pages you print. Keep in mind that the setting you choose here (in the Print sheet) applies only to this document. Choose among options here to tell your printer whether the page you want to print should be portrait or landscape oriented.

The following list describes the features you can find in the unlabeled menu found in the expanded Print sheet (the one that says *TextEdit* in Figure 22-4). In addition to TextEdit, Layout, and other options I cover in a moment, your pop-up menu may offer options such as Media & Quality, Color Options, Special Effects, and Borderless Printing. (Whether you have these options depends on your printer model and its driver as well as the application from which you're printing.) Check out these options if you have 'em; they usually offer useful features:

>> **TextEdit:** The only TextEdit-specific options, as shown in Figure 22-4, are two check boxes. One governs whether to print a header and footer for this document; the other lets you choose to rewrap the contents of the document to fit the page.

TIP

You can see the results of clicking these check boxes in the proxy image of your document on the left half of the sheet.

>> **Layout:** Choose Layout to set the number of pages per printed sheet, the layout direction, and whether you prefer a border. Here are your options for Layout:

REMEMBER

● *Pages per Sheet:* Choose preset numbers from this pop-up menu to set the number of pages that you want to print on each sheet.

Pages appear onscreen smaller than full size if you use this option.

● *Layout Direction:* Choose one of the four icons that govern the way pages are laid out on the printed page.

● *Border:* Your choices from this pop-up menu are None, Single Hairline, Single Thin Line, Double Hairline, and Double Thin Line.

● *Two-Sided:* If your printer supports two-sided (known as *duplex*) printing, the three radio buttons allow you to specify whether you're going to use two-sided printing — and if so, whether you'll be binding (or stapling) along the long or short edge of the paper or creating a booklet.

Two check boxes — Reverse Page Orientation and Flip Horizontally — do just what they say if you enable them.

» **Paper Handling:** Choose Paper Handling if you want to reverse the order in which your pages print or to print only the odd- or even-numbered pages. You can also specify whether the document's paper size is to be used (in which case, you might have lines that break across pages) or whether the output should be scaled to fit the chosen paper size.

» **Cover Page:** Choose Cover Page to add a cover page.

» **Paper Type/Quality:** Choose Paper Type/Quality to specify the type of paper in your printer and the print quality you desire. The choices are Draft, Normal, or Best when you print from TextEdit; other apps may offer other options.

» **Supply Levels:** Choose Supply Levels to see the current ink levels for your printer.

Saving custom settings

After you customize your printer settings just the way you like them, you can save them for future use. Just click the Presets pop-up menu, choose Save Current Settings as Preset, and then provide a name for this preset. From then on, the preset name appears as an option in the Presets pop-up menu. Just choose your saved preset before you print any document, and all the individual settings associated with that preset are restored.

To manage your presets, choose Show Presets from the Print sheet's Presets pop-up menu. This nifty feature displays a list of your presets and their settings and allows you to delete, duplicate, or rename (by double-clicking their current name) your presets.

Preview and PDF Options

To see a preview of what your printed page will look like, choose Open PDF in Preview from the PDF pop-up menu in the bottom-left corner of the expanded Print sheet. When you do so, you see the page or pages that you're about to print displayed by the Preview application.

TIP

As you probably know, Big Sur can save any printable document as a PDF file. To do so, choose Save As PDF in the PDF pop-up menu in every print dialog or sheet.

If you have any doubt about the way a document will look when you print it, check out Preview first. When you're happy with the document preview, just choose File ⇨ Print, press ⌘+P, or click the Print button at the bottom of the Preview window. Or click the Cancel button to return to your application and make changes to the document.

Preview works with the Preview application. With the Preview feature, you can do cool things like these:

>> See all the pages in your document the way they'll be printed, one by one.

>> Zoom in or out to get a different perspective on what you're about to send to the printer (pretty cool!).

>> Rotate the picture 90 degrees to the left or right.

>> Insert (via drag and drop), delete, or reorder pages in Preview's sidebar.

>> Spot errors before you print something. A little up-front inspection can save paper, ink or toner, and frustration.

Click the Show/Hide Edit Toolbar icon (shown in the margin) to reveal a small toolbar with several useful tools.

Check out the Preview program's View menu, where you'll find (among other things), four useful views: Content Only, Thumbnails, Table of Contents, and Contact Sheet, as well as the zoom commands and more.

Also check out Preview's toolbar, from which you can add or delete icons by choosing View ⇨ Customize Toolbar.

And speaking of tools, don't miss the selections in the Tools menu, which let you rotate pages, move forward or backward (through multipage documents), and unleash the awesomeness of Magnifier, shown in Figure 22-5.

FIGURE 22-5:
The Preview app includes this useful Magnifier tool.

TIP

The Magnifier tool is so very darn cool that it has a rare single-key keyboard shortcut. That key is the ` (the grave accent, which shares a key with the tilde); press it to show or hide Magnifier.

One last thing: Big Sur includes the capability to fax a document right from the Print sheet, but it requires a compatible device with a compatible fax modem driver. To find out whether *your* device is compatible, connect the device to your Mac and attempt to add it as a fax modem in the Printers & Scanners System Preferences pane.

6

Care and Feeding

Chapter **23**

Features for the Way You Work

This chapter delves into some macOS Big Sur features that might very well improve the ways you interact with your computer. Unlike the more mainstream applications, System Preferences panes, and utilities that I discuss in Part 1 — Desktop, Finder, Screen Saver, Appearance, Keyboard, Trackpad, Mouse, and such — the items in this chapter are a little more esoteric. In other words, you don't *have* to use any of the tools or technologies I'm about to show you. That said, many of these items can make you more productive and can make using your Mac even better. So I'd like to believe that at least some of you will *want* to use at least a few of the cool features I'm about to introduce.

I begin with three relatively new features (introduced in macOS Mojave): Dark mode, a redesigned Mac App Store, and Continuity Camera, which lets you use your iDevice as a camera or scanner for your Mac.

Finally, a Dark Mode

Have you ever thought that the white background in most windows on your Mac was far too bright? Have you ever fiddled with brightness hoping to take it down a notch? I know I've gone as far as changing the background color of Finder windows to a dark shade of gray (View ⇨ Show View Options), even though it works only on windows using icon view.

In Big Sur, such machinations are a thing of the past. Now it's easy to reduce your screen's brightness by enabling Dark mode. As you can see in Figure 23-1 (top), Dark mode affects the appearance of windows, buttons, menus, and other interface elements.

To choose Dark (or Light) mode, open System Preferences and click General. The first item you see — Appearance — is where you pick your mode.

Or try Auto mode, which switches between dark and light automatically based on the time of day.

TIP

Try changing the accent and highlight colors while in Dark mode — they look slightly different than in Light mode.

And that's all there is to Dark mode. Try using it for a while. I didn't use it much in Mojave (which didn't include Automatic mode) because it was a hassle to switch back and forth manually; since Catalina introduced Dark Mode, I use Auto mode on all my Macs.

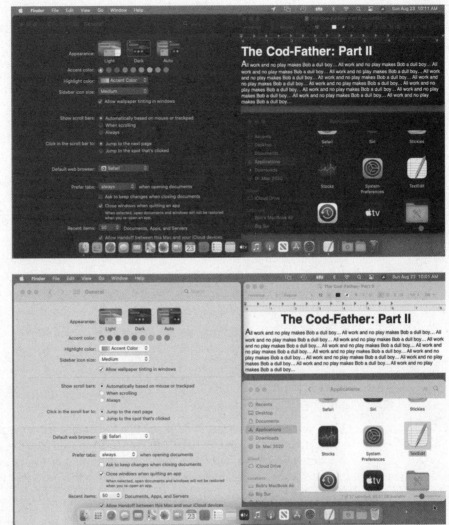

FIGURE 23-1: Three windows, the menu bar, and the dock in Dark mode (top) and Light mode (bottom).

App Shopping, Improved

Introduced in 2011, the Mac App Store is the largest catalog of Mac software in the world. In macOS Big Sur, the App Store continues to evolve, expanding on the clean look introduced in macOS Mojave.

You'll find interesting new apps and recently updated apps in the Discover tab.

The Arcade tab is home to the relatively new Apple Arcade subscription service, which offers more than 100 games with no ads and no additional purchases for a low monthly payment. The best part: One subscription gets you games on all your devices: iPhones, iPads, and even Apple TVs!

The Create tab is chock full of apps for video, audio, photo creation, editing, and more. The Work tab contains productivity apps galore. And in the Play tab you'll discover lots of fun and games.

If you prefer to browse by specific categories, select the Categories tab and choose from nearly two dozen top-level categories, as shown in Figure 23-2.

FIGURE 23-2:
The Categories tab lets you drill down from nearly two dozen categories.

When you click a category, you'll see two recommended apps at the top of the screen, followed by a pair of lists: Top Free and Top Paid. You can see only six apps at a time in each list, but when you hover your pointer over a section, Next and Previous icons appear, looking like giant greater than and less than symbols, as shown in Figure 23-3.

Finally, if any of your installed apps is in need of an update, you'll find them in the appropriately named Updates tab.

Just about everything I tell you in Chapter 19 about the iTunes Store could be said for the App Store. It works pretty much the same, and it uses the same credit card you have on file at the iTunes Store.

TIP

If you see a little number on the App Store icon in your dock, it means that a number of your apps have updates available. Launch the App Store app and click the Updates tab to see the apps with updates awaiting them. Even if you don't see a little number in the App Store's dock icon, it wouldn't hurt to launch the App Store every once in a while to check for updates manually, as the little number sometimes fails to appear in the App Store dock icon.

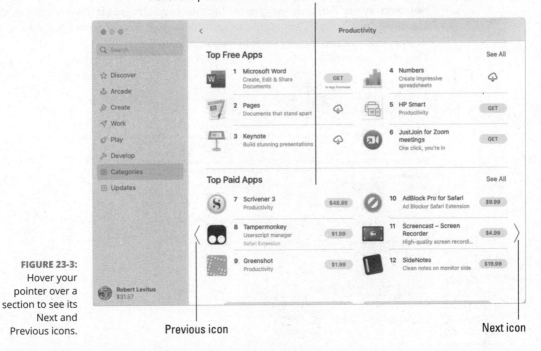

FIGURE 23-3: Hover your pointer over a section to see its Next and Previous icons.

Previous icon

Next icon

Using Your iPhone as Your Mac's Camera or Scanner

Continuity Camera is among Big Sur's coolest and most useful features. It lets you use your iOS device as a camera or scanner for your Mac.

Before you try it, here are the rules:

>> Both devices (Mac and iDevice) must be logged into the same Apple ID.

>> Both devices must be connected to the same Wi-Fi network.

>> Both devices must have Bluetooth enabled.

If you meet those criteria, you can use your iDevice as a camera or scanner and have the resulting photo or scan inserted in your document or saved to the Finder (almost) instantly.

To make the magic happen, just right- or Control-click anywhere an image or scan can be used (Notes, Stickies, TextEdit or Pages documents, and Finder, to name a few).

Not every app or document supports Continuity Camera, but if it's available when you right- or Control-click, you'll see an item called Import from iPhone or iPad in your shortcut menu, as shown in Figure 23-4.

FIGURE 23-4:
If the app supports Continuity Camera, the Import from iPhone or iPad item will appear in the shortcut menu.

Choose the device you want to use if you have more than one nearby. (I had three in Figure 23-4 — two iPhones and an iPad.) Choose Take Photo or Scan Documents.

If you choose Take Photo, the Camera app on your iDevice will launch automatically and you'll see one of two things on your Mac. If you right- or Control-clicked in a document, you'll see an overlay below the insertion point, as shown in Figure 23-5, left. Or if you right- or Control-clicked in Finder, you'll see a dialog, as shown in Figure 23-5, right.

FIGURE 23-5:
What you see after choosing Take Photo in a document (left) or Finder (right).

Take the photo on your iDevice by tapping the shutter release button in the usual fashion. After you snap a shot, a preview appears offering two options: Retake or Use Photo. Tap Retake if you're dissatisfied with the image and want to try again. When you get a shot you're happy with, tap Use Photo and the shot appears in the document at the insertion point or on the desktop almost immediately.

Choosing Scan Documents is similar to taking a photo, with some minor differences. You'll still see an overlay or a dialog on your Mac, but this time it says Scan a Document rather than Take a Photo.

On your iDevice, however, the Camera app works differently. At the top-right corner is a button that toggles between Auto and Manual. In Auto mode, you move the camera up, down, and all around until the yellow box contains the text you want to scan, as shown in Figure 23-6, left.

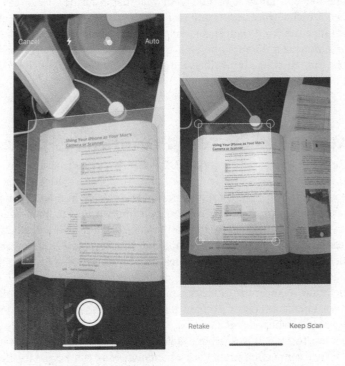

FIGURE 23-6:
Your iDevice captures the page automatically (left); drag the circles to contain the text you want to scan (right).

Or if you tap Auto (which switches the camera to Manual mode), you tap the shutter release button to capture text.

After you've captured a page, a preview of it appears, but in addition to the two buttons at the bottom of the screen — Retake or Keep Scan — a box appears with circles at each of its four corners, as shown in Figure 23-6, right. Drag the circles until the box contains all the text you want to scan, and then tap Keep Scan.

After you tap Keep Scan, the camera reappears with a message: *Ready for Next Scan.* If you have additional pages to scan, continue capturing them as described; when you're finished, tap Save in the lower-right corner.

And that's all there is to using Continuity Camera to take pictures or scan documents with your Mac!

Talking and Listening to Your Mac

Your primary methods for interacting with your Mac are typing and reading text. But there's another way you can commune with your faithful computer: voice.

Whether you know it or not, your Mac has a lot of speech savvy up its sleeve (er . . . up its processors?) and can talk to you as well as listen. Believe it or not, it can type the words you speak and obey your spoken commands. And most of you already have a microphone built into your Mac unless your Mac happens to be a Mac mini or a Mac Pro, which require an external microphone to hear you speak.

In the following sections, you discover how to make your Mac do that and more.

Keyboard System Preferences pane: You talk and your Mac types

Many users don't realize that dictation is available in macOS at no extra cost (and has been for years). In this section, you find out how to harness its power.

First, make sure Dictation is enabled in the Keyboard System Preferences pane's Dictation tab; if it's set to Off, click On.

TIP

Dictation requires an Internet connection unless you enable Voice Control (formerly known as Speech Recognition) in the Accessibility System Preferences pane. Otherwise, when you dictate text, what you say is sent to Apple's servers for conversion to text. If you enable Voice Control, you can use Dictation without an Internet connection after your Mac downloads the necessary files to your Mac. That's the good news. The bad news is that the necessary files are pretty big — a 1.2GB download that could take up to an hour or more depending on the speed of your network connection.

WARNING

Other information, such as your contacts, may also be sent to Apple over the Internet to help your Mac understand what you're saying. If that makes you uncomfortable, you probably shouldn't use the Dictation feature without first enabling Voice Control.

After Dictation is enabled, with or without the Voice Control option, the feature couldn't be easier to use. First, click where you want your words to appear in a document, dialog, web form, or whatever, and then choose Edit ⇨ Start Dictation, or press the Fn key twice in rapid succession.

TIP

If your keyboard doesn't have an Fn key, click the Shortcut pop-up menu in the Keyboard System Preferences pane to change the shortcut to one that works with your keyboard.

When you start Dictation, a little microphone icon appears. The white filling indicates the level (relative loudness) of your voice. Try to keep the white near the middle — not too high and not too low, as shown in Figure 23-7.

FIGURE 23-7:
Volume levels for dictation (left to right): Too soft, just right, and too loud.

When you see the microphone icon, start speaking. After you dictate a few sentences, click Done and let your Mac catch up. When the words appear, you can start Dictation again. Repeat as necessary.

TIP

It might not be a bad idea to save your document after you speak a few sentences or paragraphs; if you don't, the words you dictated since your last Save will be lost if the app or your Mac crashes.

You can insert punctuation by speaking its name, such as "period" or "comma." You can also perform simple formatting by saying "new line" or "new paragraph" to add space between lines.

Here are a few more tips to help you get the best results when you dictate:

>> **Speak in a normal voice at a moderate volume level.** Try to keep the white in the microphone icon about half-full (or half-empty if you're a pessimist).

>> **Avoid background noise.** If you expect to use dictation in a noisy environment or a room with a lot of ambient echo, you should consider using a headset microphone.

TIP

The headset that comes with iPhones and iPod touches is compatible with many Mac models.

>> **Be sure the microphone is not obstructed.** Check your Mac's User Guide for the location of your built-in microphone (if you have one).

>> **Be sure the input volume of an external microphone is sufficient.** If you're using an external microphone and the white meter doesn't respond to your voice, select the microphone in the drop-down menu beneath the microphone in the Dictation tab of the Keyboard System Preferences pane.

Commanding your Mac by voice

Voice Control enables your Mac to recognize and respond to human speech. The only thing you need to use it is a microphone, which most of you have built right into your Mac (unless it's a Mac Mini or Mac Pro as noted previously).

Voice Control lets you issue verbal commands such as "Get my mail!" to your Mac and have it actually get your email. You can also create AppleScripts and Automator workflows (described later in this chapter), and Finder Quick Actions (a feature I cover way back in Chapter 5) and trigger them by voice.

If you've enabled Voice Control, you can use speech commands to instruct your Mac. To see a list of commands your Mac will understand if you speak them, open the Accessibility System Preferences pane, click the Voice Control tab, and then click the Commands button. A sheet appears, in which you can enable or disable the available dictation commands, as shown in Figure 23-8.

FIGURE 23-8:
The Dictation Commands sheet displaying some things your Mac will understand if you say them (properly). Usually.

TIP

If you have a laptop or an iMac, you may get better results from just about any third-party microphone or (better still) a headset with a microphone. The mic built into your Mac is okay, but it's not great. To select a third-party microphone, first connect the mic to your Mac. Then open the Sound System Preferences pane and select it from the list of sound input devices in the Input tab. Below the list is an input volume control (not available with some third-party mics) and a level meter, as shown in Figure 23-9. Adjust the Input Volume so that most of the dots in the Input Level meter darken (9 of 15 in the figure).

FIGURE 23-9:
This is a good level for Voice Control.

REMEMBER

You can also choose an external mic in the drop-down menu below the microphone in the Dictation tab of the Keyboard System Preferences pane. However, you'll need to use the Sound System Preferences pane if you want to adjust your input levels.

To give Voice Control a try, press Fn twice (or whatever shortcut you set earlier) and speak one of the items from the list of Voice Control commands, such as "Open TextEdit." If the command is recognized, it will appear in text above the microphone icon, as shown in Figure 23-10.

FIGURE 23-10:
Open TextEdit above the mic icon means your command was recognized.

This technology is clever and kind of fun, but it can also be frustrating when it doesn't recognize what you say, which occurs too often, if you ask me. And it requires a decent microphone even though the mic built into most Macs works okay. The bottom line is that I've never been able to get Voice Control to work well enough to continue using it beyond a few minutes at best. Still, it's kind of cool (and it's a freebie), and I've heard more than one user profess love for it. Which is why it's included here.

Listening to your Mac read for you

The camera pans back. A voice tells you what you've just seen. And suddenly it all makes sense. Return with me now to those thrilling days of the off-camera narrator . . . . Wouldn't it be nice if your Mac had a narrator to provide a blow-by-blow account of what's happening on your screen?

Or your eyes are tired from a long day staring at the monitor, but you still have a lengthy document to read. Wouldn't it be sweet if you could sit back, close your eyes, and let your Mac read the document to you in a (somewhat) natural voice? Both are possible with macOS Big Sur: the first scenario with VoiceOver, and the second with Text to Speech.

VoiceOver

Big Sur's VoiceOver technology is designed primarily for the visually impaired, but you might find it useful even if your vision is 20/20. VoiceOver not only reads what's on the screen to you but also integrates with your keyboard so you can navigate around the screen until you *hear* the item you're looking for. When you're there, you can use Keyboard Access to select list items, select check boxes and radio buttons, move scroll bars and sliders, resize windows, and so on — all with just a simple key press or two.

To check it out, launch the System Preferences application (from Launchpad, the Applications folder, the menu, or the dock), click the Accessibility icon and then click VoiceOver or press ⌘+Fn+F5 on MacBook models and most Apple keyboards (or try ⌘+F5).

After VoiceOver is enabled, you can turn it on and off in the Accessibility System Preferences pane or by pressing ⌘+Fn+F5 or ⌘+F5.

While VoiceOver is on, your Mac talks to you about what is on your screen. For example, if you click the desktop, your Mac might say something along the lines of "Application, Finder; Column View; selected folder, Desktop, contains 8 items." It's quite slick. Here's another example: When you click a menu or item on a menu, you hear its name spoken at once, and when you close a menu, you hear the words "Closing menu." You even hear the spoken feedback in the Print, Open, and Save (and other) dialogs.

VoiceOver is kind of cool (talking alerts are fun), but having dialogs actually produce spoken text becomes annoying fast for most folks who aren't visually impaired. (Those who are visually impaired, however, rave about VoiceOver and say it lets them do things they couldn't easily do in the past.) In any case, I urge you to check it out. You might like it and find times when you want your Mac to narrate the action onscreen for you.

The VoiceOver Utility

The VoiceOver Utility lets you specify almost every possible option the VoiceOver technology uses. You can adjust its verbosity; specify how it deals with your mouse and keyboard; change its voice, rate, pitch, and/or volume; and more.

You can open the VoiceOver Utility by clicking the Open VoiceOver Utility button in the Accessibility System Preferences pane or in the usual way: by double-clicking its icon (which you find in your Utilities folder).

Of course, you might get the machines-are-taking-over willies when your Mac starts to talk to you or make sounds — but if you give it a try, it could change your mind.

TIP

I wish I had the space to explain further, but I don't. That's the bad news. The good news is that VoiceOver Help is extensive and clear, and it helps you harness all the power of VoiceOver and the VoiceOver Utility.

Text to Speech

The second way your Mac can speak to you is via Text to Speech, which converts onscreen text to spoken words. If you've used Text to Speech in earlier versions of macOS, you'll find that it's pretty much unchanged.

Why might you need Text to Speech? Because sometimes hearing is better than reading. For example, I sometimes use Text to Speech to read aloud to me a column or page I've written before I submit it. If something doesn't sound quite right, I give it another polish before sending it off to my editor.

You can configure this feature in the Accessibility System Preferences pane:

1. Open System Preferences (from Launchpad or the Applications folder, dock, or menu), click the Accessibility icon, and then click Spoken Content in the list on the left.

2. In the System Voice pop-up menu, choose one of the voices to set the voice your Mac uses when it reads to you.

3. Click the Play button to hear a sample of the voice you selected.

4. Use the Speaking Rate slider to speed up or slow down the voice.

5. Click the Play button to hear the voice at its new speed.

I really like Alex, who says, "Most people recognize me by my voice." My second favorite is Fred, who sounds like the Talking Moose and says, "I sure like being inside this fancy computer."

6. (Optional) To make your Mac speak the text in alert boxes and dialogs, select the Speak Announcements check box.

You might hear such alerts as "The application Microsoft Word has quit unexpectedly" or "Paper out or not loaded correctly."

7. (Optional) To make your Mac speak text you've selected in a document, select the Speak Selection check box.

The default keyboard shortcut for Speak Selection is Option+Esc, but you can assign any key combo you like by clicking the Options button and typing a different keyboard shortcut.

8. (Optional) To make your Mac describe whatever is below the pointer, select the Speak Items Under Pointer check box.

9. (Optional) To make your Mac speak whatever you type, select the Speak Typing Feedback check box.

10. (Optional) To explore additional options for the previous four items, click its Options button.

Now, to use Text to Speech to read text to you, copy the text to the Clipboard, launch any app that supports it (I usually choose TextEdit or Pages), paste the text into the empty untitled document, click where you want your Mac to begin reading to you, and then choose Edit ⇨ Speech ⇨ Start Speaking. To make it stop, choose Edit ⇨ Speech ⇨ Stop Speaking.

Another great place Text to Speech is available is in the Safari web browser. It works the same as TextEdit but you don't have to paste — just select the text you want to hear and choose Edit ⇨ Speech ⇨ Start Speaking.

TIP

If you don't care for the sound of the default voice, choose a different one in the Accessibility System Preferences pane. First click Spoken Content in the list on the left, and then choose a new voice from the System Voice drop-down menu or choose Customize to download additional voices.

Automatic Automation

macOS Big Sur offers a pair of technologies — AppleScript and Automator — that makes it easy to automate repetitive actions on your Mac.

AppleScript is "programming for the rest of us." It can record and play back things that you do (if the application was written to allow the recording, such as Finder), such as opening an application or clicking a button. You can use it to record a script for tasks that you often perform, and then have your Mac perform those tasks for you later. You can write your own AppleScripts, use those that come with your Mac, or download still others from the web.

Automator is "programming without writing code." With Automator, you string together prefabricated activities (actions) to automate repetitive or scheduled tasks. How cool is that?

Automation isn't for everyone. Some users can't live without it; others could go their whole lives without ever automating anything. So the following sections are designed to help you figure out how much — or how little — you care about AppleScript and Automator.

Script Editor app: Write and edit AppleScripts

Describing AppleScript to a Mac beginner is a bit like three blind men describing an elephant. One man might describe it as the Mac's built-in automation tool. Another might describe it as an interesting but often-overlooked piece of enabling technology. The third might liken it to a cassette recorder, recording and playing back your actions at the keyboard. A fourth (if there were a fourth in the story) would assure you that it looked like computer code written in a high-level language.

They would all be correct. AppleScript, a built-in Mac automation tool, is a little-known (at least until recently) enabling technology that works like a cassette recorder for programs that support AppleScript recording. And scripts do look like computer programs. (Could that be because they *are* computer programs? Hmm . . . .)

If you're the kind of person who likes to automate as many things as possible, you might just love AppleScript because it's a simple programming language you can use to create programs that give instructions to your Mac and the applications running on your Mac. For example, you can create an AppleScript that launches Mail, checks for new messages, and then quits Mail. The script could even transfer your mail to a folder of your choice. Then there's Automator, which includes a whole lot of preprogrammed actions that make a task like the one just described even easier.

I call AppleScript a time-and-effort enhancer. If you just spend the time and effort it takes to understand it, using AppleScript can save you oodles of time and effort down the road. Therein lies the rub. This stuff is far from simple; entire books have been written on the subject. So it's far beyond the purview of *macOS Big Sur For Dummies*. Still, it's worth finding out about if you'd like to script repetitive actions for future use. To get you started, here are a few quick tips:

» **Script Editor (in the Utilities folder in the Applications folder) is the application you use to create, edit, and view AppleScripts.** Although more information on Script Editor is beyond the scope of this book, it's a lot of fun. And the cool thing is that you can create many AppleScripts without knowing a thing about programming. Just record a series of actions you want to repeat and use Script Editor to save what you recorded as a script. If you save your script as an application (by choosing Format ⇨ Application in the Save sheet), you can run that script by double-clicking its icon.

» **You can put frequently used AppleScripts in the dock or on your desktop for easy access.**

» **Many AppleScripts are designed for use in the toolbar of Finder windows, where you can drag and drop items onto them quickly and easily.**

» **Scripts can enhance your use of many apps, including iTunes, iPhoto, and Finder, to name a few.**

» **Apple provides a script menu extra that you can install on your menu bar in the Script Editor's Preferences window,** along with a number of free scripts to automate common tasks (in the Scripts folder in the root-level Library, or choose Open Example Scripts Folder from the Script Editor's Help menu).

» **If the concept of scripting intrigues you, I suggest that you explore the examples in the Scripts folder (in the root-level Library or choose Open Example Scripts from the Script Editor's Help menu).** Rummage through this folder and when you find a script that looks interesting, double-click it to launch the Script Editor program, where you can examine it more closely.

Automator app: Automate almost anything

Automator does just what you'd expect: It enables you to automate many common tasks on your Mac. If it sounds a little like AppleScript to you (which I discuss in the preceding section), you're not mistaken; the two have a common goal. But this tool is a lot simpler to use, albeit somewhat less flexible, than AppleScript.

For example, in AppleScript, you can have *conditionals* ("if *this* is true, do *that*; otherwise do something else"), but Automator is purely *sequential* ("take *this*, do *that*, then do the next thing, and then . . .").

The big difference is that conditionals allow AppleScripts to take actions involving *decision-making* and *iteration* ("while *this* is true, do *these* things"); Automator workflows can't make decisions or iterate.

The upsides to Automator are that you don't have to know anything about programming, and you don't have to type any archaic code. Instead, if you understand the process you want to automate, you can just drag and drop Automator's prefab actions into place and build a *workflow* (Automator's name for a series of actions).

REMEMBER

You do need to know one thing about programming (or computers), though: *Computers are stupid!* You heard me right — even my top-of-the-line MacBook Pro is dumb as a post. Computers do only what you tell them to do even though they can do it faster and more precisely than you can. But all computers run on the GIGO principle (Garbage In, Garbage Out), so if your instructions are flawed, you're almost certain to get flawed results.

When you launch the Automator application, click the New Document button and the window and sheet shown in Figure 23-11 appear. Choose one of the starting points if you want Automator to assist you in constructing a new workflow; or, choose Workflow to start building a workflow from scratch.

FIGURE 23-11:
Choose Workflow to start a workflow from scratch.

I'm going to choose Quick Action for the sake of this demonstration (you'll see why in a second). When I select Quick Action and click the Choose button, I see the window shown in Figure 23-12.

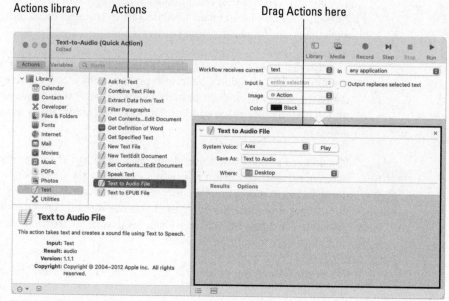

Actions library Actions   Drag Actions here

FIGURE 23-12:
This converts text that I select to an audio file.

The Library pane on the far left contains all the applications Automator knows about that have Actions defined for them. Select an application in the top part of the Library window, and its related actions appear below it. When you select an action, the pane at the bottom of the Library window (Text to Audio File in Figure 23-12) explains what that Action does, what input it expects, and what result it produces. Just drag Actions from the Action list into the window on the right to build your workflow.

This particular Quick Action, which took me less than five minutes of trial and error to perfect, is quite useful. First, I select text from any source — a web page, a Microsoft Word document, an email message, or whatever. Then I choose Services from the Application menu or right- or Control-click and select my newly created Text to Audio Quick Action from the Services menu. My Automator workflow then converts the selected text into an audio file and saves it to the desktop. Then I can have it read to me in iTunes at home or on my iPhone or iPad in the car, on a plane, or just about anywhere. Sweet!

Automator is a useful addition to macOS; it's deep, powerful, and expandable, yet relatively easy to use and master. Do yourself a favor, and spend some time experimenting with ways Automator can save you time and keystrokes. You won't regret it.

TIP

For additional information about AppleScript, Automator, Services, and much more, visit www.macosxautomation.com.

A Few More Useful Goodies

Even more neat and useful technologies are built into Big Sur, but I'm running out of space. So here are, at least in my humble opinion, the best of the rest.

Accessibility System Preferences pane: Make your Mac more accessible

If you've read the chapter to this point, you got a brief glimpse of the Accessibility System Preferences pane when I discussed commanding your Mac by voice. But this System Preferences pane is mostly designed for users with disabilities or who have difficulty handling the keyboard, mouse, or trackpad.

TIP

Select the Show Accessibility Status in Menu Bar check box at the bottom of the window on the left to see the status of all Accessibility Preferences in your menu bar.

The pane has four sections listed on the left — Vision, Hearing, Motor, and General — each of which has one or more subsections.

The Vision section's Display subsection lets you alter the behavior of the screen display. For example, in the Color Filters tab you can choose Grayscale as your filter type, which will desaturate your screen into a *grayscale display* (so it looks kind of like a black-and-white TV).

Or click the Display subsection's Display tab (I know — confusing as heck) and select the check box to Invert Colors, which reverses the colors you see onscreen, as shown in Figure 23-13.

TIP

Click Display in the Vision section on the left and then click the Cursor tab at the top to enable the Shake Mouse Pointer to Locate check box. When enabled, the pointer grows much larger and becomes easier to see whenever you wiggle the mouse back and forth quickly a couple of times. Or drag the Cursor size slider to the right to enlarge the pointer at all times.

The Vision section's Zoom subsection is where you can turn on a terrific feature called *hardware zoom*, which lets you make things on your screen bigger by zooming in on them. To control it by keyboard, select the Use Keyboard Shortcuts to

Zoom check box. Then you can toggle it on and off with the shortcut ⌘+Option+8 and zoom in and out using the shortcuts ⌘+Option+= (equal sign) and ⌘+Option+− (hyphen), respectively. Finally, the More Options button lets you specify minimum and maximum zoom levels, display a preview rectangle when zoomed out, and toggle image smoothing on or off.

FIGURE 23-13:
The Accessibility
System
Preferences
pane with its
colors inverted.

Try this feature even if you're not disabled or challenged in any way; it's actually a great feature for everyone.

You looked at the Vision section's VoiceOver subsection earlier in the chapter.

REMEMBER

I leave it to you, gentle reader, to explore the remaining sections and subsections of the Accessibility System Preferences pane at your leisure. Until then, you might find the following useful:

>> **If you want the screen to flash whenever an alert sound occurs, choose Audio and then select the Flash the Screen When an Alert Sound Occurs check box.**

>> **To treat a *sequence* of modifier keys as a key combination, choose Keyboard and then select the Enable Sticky Keys check box.**

In other words, you don't have to simultaneously hold down ⌘ while pressing another key. For example, with Sticky Keys enabled, you can do a standard keyboard shortcut by pressing ⌘, releasing it, and then pressing the other key. You can select check boxes to tell you (with a beep and/or an onscreen display) what modifier keys have been pressed.

TIP

As useful as Sticky Keys can be, they're really awkward in applications like Adobe Photoshop, Adobe Illustrator, and other applications that toggle a tool's state when you press a modifier key. So if you're a big Photoshop user, you probably don't want Sticky Keys enabled.

>> **To adjust the delay between a keypress and its activation, choose Keyboard and then select the Slow Keys check box.**

Battery and Energy Saver System Preferences panes: For energy conservation and sleep

NEW

The Battery (notebooks) and Energy Saver (desktops) System Preferences panes are where you manage your Mac's energy-saving features.

All Macs are Energy Star–compliant (and have been for years), so the Battery System Preferences pane lets you do things such as turn your Mac off at a specific time or after a specified idle period.

The Battery System Preferences pane (notebooks only)

To get started, open System Preferences and click the Battery icon.

On the left you'll see a list of items specific to your Mac. Click Usage History to see your battery charge levels for the past 24 hours or past 10 days. Click Battery to control your notebook Mac's behavior when it's running on battery power (not plugged in); click Power Adapter to control its behavior when it *is* plugged in.

TIP

Turning off the display is handy if you want your Mac to keep doing what it's doing but you don't need to see its monitor. And if you're a notebook user, turning off the display will preserve your battery.

To wake up your display, merely move your mouse or press any key. Sometimes moving the mouse or a finger on the trackpad won't wake a sleeping Mac but a keystroke will. So try both (or all three) before you give up.

Below the Turn Display Off After slider in the Battery and Power Adapter panes are check boxes for other battery-related settings such as:

>> **Slightly Dim the Display While on Battery Power (Battery pane):** The display dims slightly and uses less power when running on the battery.

- » **Enable Power Nap While on Battery Power (Battery pane):** This option allows your Mac to check for new email, calendar, and other iCloud updates while it's sleeping.

- » **Prevent Computer from Sleeping Automatically When the Display Is Off (Power Adapter pane):** Prevents sleep when the lid is closed and the display is off.

- » **Wake for Network Access (Power Adapter pane):** Enable this option if you want your Mac to wake up automatically for network access.

- » **Enable Power Nap While Plugged into a Power Adapter or Battery (Power Adapter and Battery panes):** This option allows your Mac to back up to Time Machine as well as check for new email, calendar, and other iCloud updates while it's sleeping.

- » **Show Battery Status in the Menu Bar (Power Adapter pane):** This option adds a little battery-status indicator icon and menu.

Finally, to start up, shut down, or put your Mac to sleep at a predetermined time, click the Schedule button and then select the appropriate check box and choose the appropriate options from the pop-up menus.

Energy Saver System Preferences pane (desktops only)

To start, open System Preferences and click the Energy Saver icon. Below the Turn Display Off After slider are check boxes for two energy-related settings:

- » **Prevent Computer from Sleeping Automatically When the Display Is Off (Power Adapter pane):** Prevents sleep when the lid is closed and the display is off.

- » **Wake for Ethernet Network Access (Power Adapter pane):** Enable this option if you want your Mac to wake up automatically for network access.

Bluetooth System Preferences pane: Where Bluetooth lives

Bluetooth is wireless networking for low-bandwidth peripherals, including mice, keyboards, and mobile phones. If your Mac has Bluetooth built in or is equipped with a USB Bluetooth adapter, you can synchronize wirelessly with phones and Palm devices, print wirelessly to Bluetooth printers, and use Bluetooth headsets, mice, and keyboards.

To manage your Mac's Bluetooth features, open the Bluetooth System Preferences pane by choosing ➪ System Preferences and clicking the Bluetooth icon.

Ink System Preferences pane: Visible to pen-input tablet users only

Ink is the macOS built-in handwriting-recognition engine. Sadly, it works only if a third-party drawing tablet with a stylus is connected. Even more sadly, "tablet" in this sense doesn't include your iPad (at least not so far . . .).

To write instead of typing, enable Ink in this pane and you'll be able to handwrite anywhere your Mac accepts typing with the keyboard.

To manage your Mac's Ink features, open the Ink System Preferences pane by choosing ➪ System Preferences and clicking the Ink icon.

TIP

The Ink pane is one you see only if you have one of the pen-input drawing tablets that Ink supports connected to your Mac. Most of the supported drawing tablets come from Wacom (www.wacom.com), with prices starting under $100 for a small wireless stylus and drawing tablet.

Automatic Login in the Users & Groups System Preferences pane: Don't bother with the login screen

Some users don't care for the fact that macOS Big Sur is a multiuser operating system and dislike having to log in when they start up their Mac. For those users, here's a way to disable the login screen:

1. **Open the Users & Groups System Preferences pane, select yourself in the list of users, and click the Login Options button below the list.**

   Click the lock and provide your password first, if necessary.

2. **Choose the account you want to be logged in to automatically from the Automatic Login pop-up menu.**

   To disable the logging-in requirement, you have to be an administrator, and you may need to unlock the Users & Groups System Preferences pane.

WARNING

When you disable logging in, you also affect all the preferences set by other people who use your Mac unless they log out of your account and log into theirs. (Yikes.) So if your desktop pattern, keyboard settings, and so forth are different from those of someone else who uses your Mac, those preferences won't be properly reflected unless each of you has a separate, individual login account. Even if you're not worried about security, consider keeping logging in enabled if any other users have accounts on your machine, or if you don't want just anyone to be able to turn on your Mac and see your personal stuff.

Note that only one account is allowed to use auto-login. If another user wants to use this Mac, you need to choose ⇨ Log Out, press ⌘+Shift+Q, or have Fast User Switching enabled. And if you've disabled automatic login in the Security System Preferences pane, you can't enable it here.

Allow your Apple Watch to unlock your Mac

If you have an Apple Watch, you'll love this. Enable the Allow Your Apple Watch to Unlock Your Mac check box in the Security & Privacy System Preferences pane's General tab, and you can just walk up to your Mac while wearing your unlocked Apple Watch and be automatically logged into your user account without typing your password!

I use it a million times a day and it is sweet!

One last thing: If you don't see the Allow Your Apple Watch to Unlock Your Mac check box in the Security & Privacy System Preferences pane's General tab, your Mac may be too old to support this feature.

Boot Camp Assistant app: Run Windows on your Mac . . . really

Boot Camp is Big Sur's built-in technology that allows you to run Microsoft Windows 10 and (on some Mac models) Windows 7 or 8 on Big Sur–capable Macs. If your Mac meets the following requirements, you can run Windows on your Mac (if you so desire):

>> A Big Sur–capable Mac (of course)

>> A hard drive that isn't already partitioned

>> (Optional) A printer (for printing the instructions)

   It's optional 'cause you could just email them to yourself . . . .

>> A full install copy of Microsoft Windows 8 Home Premium, Professional, or Ultimate edition or Windows 10

REMEMBER

You really do need a *full retail* copy of Windows: one that was purchased in a retail box. If your copy of Windows came with your PC, you probably can't install it in Boot Camp.

To install Windows on your Mac, here are the basic steps:

1. **Launch the Boot Camp Assistant application, which is in your Utilities folder.**

   This step creates a partition on your hard drive for your Windows installation.

2. **Install Windows on the new partition.**

   From now on, you can hold down Option during startup and choose to start up from either the macOS Big Sur disk partition or the new Windows partition.

TIP

If running Windows on your Mac appeals to you, you may want to check out Parallels Desktop (around $80) or VirtualBox (free). Both programs allow you to run Windows — even older versions like XP and Vista — as well as Linux on your Mac without partitioning your hard drive or restarting every time you want to use Windows. In fact, you can run Mac and Windows programs simultaneously with these products.

WARNING

In late 2020, Apple will begin selling Macs with custom Apple processors instead of the Intel processors it's been using for two decades. One of the side effects of this transition is that Boot Camp will not be an option if your Mac runs on Apple silicon. While emulation and virtualization should both be viable, running Windows natively under Boot Camp will not.

One last thing: Apple has a special Boot Camp support page on the web at http://www.apple.com/support/bootcamp/.

AirPlay Mirroring

I would be remiss if I didn't mention the AirPlay Mirroring feature, even though most of you won't be able to use it without first buying an Apple TV.

With AirPlay Mirroring, you can stream whatever is on your Mac (or iOS device) screen wirelessly to your HDTV with a connected Apple TV.

Apple TV couldn't be easier to use. If it's on the same network as your Mac, an option for AirPlay Mirroring will appear in the Displays System Preferences pane. Just enable AirPlay Mirroring, and what is on your Mac screen will appear on your HDTV screen almost instantaneously.

TIP

Enable Show Mirroring Options in the Menu Bar When Available in the Displays System Preferences pane, and a handy menu, shown in Figure 23-14, lets you switch AirPlay Mirroring on and off without the bother of first opening the Displays System Preferences pane.

Screen Mirroring

Bedroom

Den

Display Preferences...

FIGURE 23-14: The AirPlay menu makes life much easier for AirPlay users like me.

The bad news is that many older Macs — including my wife's six-year-old MacBook Pro — don't support mirroring to an Apple TV.

Handoff

The Handoff feature lets you start working on a document, an email, or a message on any Apple device and pick up where you left off on another device. To enable it, open System Preferences, click the General icon, and enable the check box to Allow Handoff between This Mac and Your iCloud Devices.

Now make sure that you're signed into iCloud with the same Apple ID on your Mac and iOS device(s) and that Bluetooth is enabled on all devices.

Handoff works with Apple apps, including Mail, Safari, Maps, Messages, Reminders, Calendar, Contacts, Pages, Numbers, and Keynote, as well as a handful of third-party apps. When another Handoff-enabled device is nearby and using one of these apps, you'll see an icon for it on the right side of the dock, as shown in Figure 23-15.

Messages From iPhone

FIGURE 23-15: My iPhone is nearby and using the Messages app.

If I click that icon (note the tiny phone on it), Messages on my Mac will open and display the message or reply on my iPhone screen.

IN THIS CHAPTER

» Backing up . . . it's easy

» Discovering why you should back up

» Finding out what happens to you if you don't back up

» Keeping your Mac safe from rogue viruses and malicious attacks

» Protecting your data from prying eyes

Chapter **24**

Safety First: Backups and Other Security Issues

lthough Macs are generally reliable beasts, someday your SSD (or hard drive) will die. I promise. They *all* die someday. And if you don't back up *your* drive (or at least back up any files that you can't afford to lose) before that day comes, chances are good those files are gone forever.

In other words, you absolutely, positively, without question *must back up* your files if you don't want to risk losing them. Just as you adopt the Shut Down command and make it a habit before turning off your machine, you must remember to back up important files on your hard drive to another disk or device — and back them up often.

How often is often? That depends on you. How much work can you afford to lose? If your answer is that losing everything you did yesterday would put you out of business, you need to back up hourly or perhaps even continuously. If you would lose only a few unimportant documents if your hard drive died today, you can probably back up less frequently.

D'OH!

And if you do see them again, my friend, it will be only after paying someone such as DriveSavers Data Recovery Service. And even if you pay, there's no guarantee of success.

DriveSavers is the premier recoverer of lost data on hard drives. The people there understand Mac hard drives quite well, do excellent work, and can often recover stuff that nobody else could. (Ask the producers of *The Simpsons* about the almost-lost episodes.) Understandably, DriveSavers charges accordingly.

If you aren't going to back up your data, here are the phone numbers for DriveSavers: 800-440-1904 toll-free or 415-382-2000. You'll probably need them someday (along with a bucketful of cash) if you refuse to believe that you *must* back up and back up often.

Following the comprehensive coverage of backup options, I explain the possible threat to your data from viruses and other icky things, as well as how you can protect against them.

Finally, I cover what you can do to keep other people from looking at your stuff.

WARNING

One last thing: If you turn on FileVault (described later in this chapter) and forget both your login password and your master password, your data is lost forever. Really. Not even DriveSavers or Apple can recover it, so don't forget those passwords, okay?

Backing Up Is (Not) Hard to Do

You can back up your hard drive in basically three ways: the super-painless way with Big Sur's excellent built-in Time Machine, the ugly way using the brute-force method, or the comprehensive way with specialized third-party backup and disk-cloning software. Read on and find out more about all three.

Backing up with Big Sur's excellent Time Machine

Time Machine is an excellent backup system that has become better and more reliable since its introduction more than a decade ago. I say it's a *system* because it consists of two parts: the Time Machine System Preferences pane, shown in Figure 24-1, and the Time Machine application, shown in Figure 24-2.

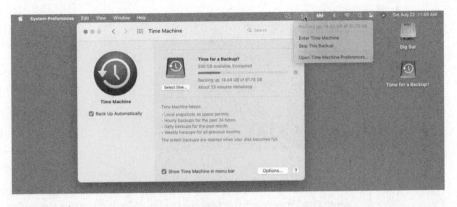

FIGURE 24-1:
The Time
Machine System
Preferences pane
and menu.

FIGURE 24-2:
The Time
Machine
application is
ready to restore a
folder in Finder.

To use Time Machine to back up your data automatically, the first thing you need is another hard drive that's larger than your startup disk. The hard drive can be an external USB 2 or USB 3, or Thunderbolt hard drive, an SSD (if you can afford to use a solid-state drive for backups), or even another internal drive, if your Mac is a Mac mini or Mac Pro.

Moving right along, the first time a new disk suitable for use with Time Machine is connected to your Mac, a notification appears and asks whether you want to use that disk to back up with Time Machine, as shown in Figure 24-3.

Click Set Up in the lower-right corner of the notification. A dialog might ask you to erase the disk first. If so, click Erase. In a few moments the Time Machine System Preferences pane appears with the disk already selected.

FIGURE 24-3:
What you see
when you plug in
a new disk
suitable for use
with Time
Machine.

If that doesn't happen or you want to use a different drive with Time Machine, open the Time Machine System Preferences pane, click the Select Disk button, and then select the hard drive you want to use for your backups. Mine is called Time for a Backup? in Figures 24-1 and 24-3.

Additional consideration

The only other consideration is this: If you have other hard drives connected to your Mac, you should click the Options button to reveal the Exclude These Items from Backups list, which tells Time Machine which volumes (disks) or folders *not* to back up. To add a volume or folder to this exclusion list, click the little + icon; to remove a volume from the list, select the volume and then click the – icon.

If your Mac is a laptop, the Options sheet also offers a check box to enable Time Machine backups when on battery power (disabled by default).

For the record, Time Machine stores your backups for the following lengths of time:

>> Hourly backups for the past 24 hours

>> Daily backups for the past month

>> Weekly backups until your backup disk is full

When your backup disk gets full, the oldest backups on it are deleted and replaced by the newest.

TIP

That's why I recommend that you buy the biggest drive you can afford to use as your backup disk; otherwise Time Machine will be deleting backups all the time rather than archiving them for future use.

When does Time Machine run? Glad you asked! It runs approximately once per hour. If it gets stuck and forgets to run for any reason, use the Backup Now command in the Time Machine menu to get it going again.

TIP

If you enable and set up Time Machine as I just described, you'll never forget to back up your stuff, so just do it.

What does Time Machine back up?

Time Machine backs up your entire hard drive the first time it runs and then backs up files and folders that have been modified since your last backup. That's what backup systems do. But Time Machine does more — it also backs up things such as contacts in your Contacts, pictures in your Photos library, events in your calendars, and emails in your Mail, not to mention its support of versions and locking. About the only thing Time Machine doesn't back up is the content of Home folders other than your own.

Those features — sweet ones, indeed — make Time Machine unlike any other backup system.

How do I restore a file (or a contact, a photo, an event, and so on)?

To restore a file or any other information, follow these steps:

1. **Launch the program that contains the information you want to restore.**

If you want to restore a file, that program is Finder, which (as you know) is always running. So to restore an individual file, you don't need to launch anything; just switch to Finder if it's not the active application. But to restore a contact, a photo, an email message, or an event, for example, you need to launch Contacts, Photos, Mail, or Calendar, respectively.

2. **With the appropriate application running (or the appropriate Finder window open), launch the Time Machine application (refer to Figure 24-2).**

If you selected the Show Time Machine in Menu Bar check box in the Time Machine System Preferences pane (refer to Figure 24-1), you can choose the Enter Time Machine option from the Time Machine menu (also shown in Figure 24-1).

TIP

It will be easier to restore a file in Finder if the folder that the file is in (or was in) is the *active* folder (that is, open and frontmost) when you launch the Time Machine application. Otherwise, you have to navigate to the appropriate folder before you can perform Step 3.

3. **Click one of the bars with dates near the lower-right corner of the screen *or* click the big Forward or Back arrow on the right of the Documents window in Figure 24-2 to choose a backup to restore (Today at 11:47 AM in Figure 24-2).**

TIP

4. **Select the file, folder, Contacts contact, Photos photo, email message, or Calendar event you want to restore.**

5. **Click the Restore button below the window.**

If the file, folder, Contacts contact, Photos photo, email message, or Calendar event exists in the same location today, Time Machine politely inquires as to your wishes, as shown in Figure 24-4.

FIGURE 24-4:
Time Machine
asks what to do
with the file
you're restoring.

The location to which you're restoring "Folder 1" already contains an item with the same name. Do you want to replace it with the one you're restoring?

Keep Original   Keep Both   Replace

TIP

Don't forget that you can search for files or folders in Time Machine by typing a word or phrase in the Search field of the active (frontmost) window.

Backing up by using the manual, brute-force method

If you think you're too cheap to buy a big hard drive, consider this: Amazon.com has numerous 4TB external USB 3 hard drives for under $100. And if you can get by with a 2TB backup drive, prices start at around $60. By the way, these prices go down regularly, so by the time you read this they may be even cheaper.

Face it — a backup disk is a lot cheaper than data recovery (which can run hundreds if not thousands of dollars). So bite the bullet and buy the biggest backup disk you can justify.

If you're still not convinced, you should consider at least backing up important files manually.

You accomplish this by dragging said files a few at a time to another volume — usually another hard drive or solid-state drive, a USB flash drive, or a burned-to-optical media such as a DVD-R or DVD-RW. (If you use an optical disc, don't forget to actually *burn the disc*; merely dragging those files onto the optical disc icon won't do the trick.) By using this method, you're making a copy of each file that you want to protect.

WARNING

Yuck! If doing a manual backup sounds pretty awful, trust me — it is. This method can take a long, long time, you can't really tell if you've copied every file that needs to be backed up, and you can't really copy only the files that have been modified since your last backup.

Almost nobody in his right mind sticks with this method for long.

Note that optical media is slow and costly and USB flash drives are not much better. It would behoove you to spend a few more dollars and purchase a higher-capacity device such as an external hard drive. But if you do, why wouldn't you use it with Time Machine and forget about the inefficient brute-force method?

TIP

Of course, if you're careful to save files only in your Documents folder, as I suggest several times in this book, you can probably get away with backing up only that. Or if you save files in other folders within your Home folder or have any files in your Movies, Music, Pictures, or Sites folders (which often contain files you didn't specifically save in those folders, such as your Photos app pictures and Music app songs), you should probably consider backing up your entire Home folder.

As you read in the following section, backing up your Home folder is even easier if you use special backup software.

Backing up by using commercial backup software

Another way to back up your files is with a third-party backup program. Backup software automates the task of backing up, remembering what's on each backup disc (if your backup uses more than one disc), and backing up only files that have been modified since your last backup.

Furthermore, you can instruct your backup software to back up only a certain folder (Home or Documents) and to ignore the hundreds of megabytes of stuff that make up macOS, all of which you can easily reinstall from your Recovery disk or the Mac App Store.

Your first backup with commercial software might take anywhere from a few minutes to several hours and use one or more optical discs (CD-R, CD-RW, DVD-R, DVD-RW, magneto-optical disc) or non-optical media (such as another hard drive or any kind of tape). Subsequent backups, *incremental backups* in backup software parlance, should take only a few minutes.

TIP

If you do incremental backups with optical discs, be sure to label and number all the discs you use during that operation. Your backup software may prompt you with a message such as *Please insert backup disk 7.* If you haven't labeled your media clearly, you could have a problem figuring out which disc *is* disc 7 or which disc 7 belongs to that particular backup set.

One of the best things about good backup software is that you can set it up to automate your backups and perform them even if you forget. And although Time Machine is a step in the right direction and might be sufficient for your needs, it's not good enough for me. I use a total of five hard drives for backups.

Why You Need Two Sets of Backups

You're a good soldier. You listened to Dr. Mac and you back up regularly. You think you're immune to file loss or damage.

Now picture yourself in the following scenario:

>> You leave the office one day for lunch. When you return, you discover that your office has been burglarized, struck by lightning, flooded, burned to the ground, or buried in earthquake rubble — take your pick.

>> Alas, although you did have a backup, the backup disk was right next to your Mac, which means it was either stolen or destroyed along with your Mac and everything else.

This scenario is unlikely — but it *could* happen, and it does demonstrate why you need multiple backups. If you have several sets of backup disks, and don't keep them all in the same room as your Mac, chances are pretty good that one of the sets will work even if the others are lost, stolen, or destroyed.

TIP

I believe you need at least three sets of backups, with at least one of them stored offsite. I have a full backup that I update monthly in a safe deposit box at my bank. And I use a cloud-based backup service called Backblaze (www.backblaze.com), a second offsite backup for just $6 per month (or $60 per year), which I consider a bargain.

One last thing: If you're religious about storing all your files in the Documents folder or the desktop, you can store your Desktop and Documents folders in iCloud, which counts as another offsite backup (kinda). To do that, launch System Preferences, click Apple ID, click the Options button next to iCloud Drive, and then enable the check box for Desktop & Documents Folders.

Non-Backup Security Concerns

As you probably surmised by now, backing up your files is critical unless you don't mind losing all your data someday. And although backing up is by far your most important security concern, several other things could imperil your data — things such as viruses or other types of malware, including worms, spyware, and intruder attacks. That's the bad news. The good news is that all those things are far more likely to affect Windows users than Mac users. In fact, I'd venture to say that viruses, worms, malware, spyware, and intruder attacks are rarer than hens' teeth for Mac users.

That said, here are a few precautions Mac users should consider, just in case.

About viruses and other malware

A computer *virus* is a nasty little piece of computer code that replicates and spreads from disk to disk. A virus could cause your Mac to misbehave; some viruses can destroy files or erase disks with no warning.

Malware (short for *malicious software*) is software that's hostile, intrusive, annoying, or disruptive. Malware is often designed to gain unauthorized access to your computer or collect personal data (including passwords) without your knowledge or both.

The difference between a virus and other types of malware is that malware doesn't spread by itself. It relies upon trickery, mimicry, and social engineering to induce unsuspecting users to open a malicious file or install a malicious program. So a virus is a type of malware, but not all malware is viral.

You don't hear as much about viruses on the Mac because there have been few since the dawn of the Mac operating system (so many big cats and California landmarks ago). Almost all viruses are specific to an operating system — Mac viruses won't affect Windows users, Windows viruses won't affect Mac users, and so forth. And the vast majority of known viruses affect only (you guessed it) Windows.

The one real exception here is a "gift" from the wonderful world of Microsoft Office (Word and Excel, for example) users: the dreaded *macro viruses* that are spread with Word and Excel documents containing macros written in the Microsoft VBA (Visual Basic for Applications) language. But you're safe even from those if you practice safe computing as I describe (although you can unknowingly pass them along to Windows users).

Much of the viral activity affecting the Mac operating system involved various Windows macro viruses. Sadly, a very real threat known as Flashback appeared in early 2012. It exploited a security flaw in Java and stealthily installed itself on Macs. Soon after its discovery, Apple issued software updates for the Mac operating system that removed the malware and corrected the security flaw. Numerous similar instances have occurred since then, but in every case Apple has patched the operating system before many (or any) users were affected (or infected).

TIP

By default, your Mac automatically checks for software updates every week. To force it to check for updates now, just open the Software Update System Preferences pane. In my humble opinion, it's usually a good idea to install Apple updates sooner rather than later.

Although few truly viral Mac operating system threats have been spotted in the wild so far, most malware is spread via social engineering, which is easy to protect yourself against; here's how:

>> In Safari Preferences General tab, disable the Open Safe Files after Downloading check box.

>> If a suspicious alert or window appears on your screen whilst browsing the Internet, Force Quit your web browser (⌥ ⇨ Force Quit or ⌘+Option+Esc) immediately.

>> If the macOS Installer launches for no apparent reason, *do not click Continue!* Don't install the software, and for heaven's sake, don't type your administrator password.

>> And by all means read the section on Big Sur's Gatekeeper later in this chapter for details on the three different levels of protection it can offer.

>> Don't run *any* installer — the kind built into macOS or the third-party kind — unless you're absolutely certain that it came from a trusted source.

>> Don't use credit or debit cards with unfamiliar vendors or nonsecure websites. (For example, if you don't see http**s** instead of http, or you don't see a little lock icon in the address field of your browser, the site may not be secure.)

REMEMBER

If you use disks that have been inserted into other computers, you need some form of virus-detection software. If you download and use files from the Internet, you need some form of virus detection as well.

You don't have too much to worry about if

>> You download files only from commercial online services, such as CNET or MacUpdate, which are all conscientious about malware.

>> You buy software from only the App Store.

>> You use only commercial software, and never download files from websites with strange names.

You should definitely worry about malicious infection if

>> An unsavory friend told you about a website called PiratedIllegalStolenBootlegSoftware.com, and you actually visited it.

>> You swap disks or USB thumb drives with friends regularly.

>> You shuttle disks or USB thumb drives back and forth to other Macs.

>> You use your disks or USB thumb drives at public computers, photo-printing machines, or other computers likely to have had exposure to many disks.

>> You download files from various and sundry places on the Internet, even ones that don't sound as slimy as PiratedIllegalStolenBootlegSoftware.com.

>> You receive email with attachments (and open them). Note that you can receive malicious software in messages that look like they're from people you know and trust. It's called *spoofing* and it's easily accomplished, so think carefully before opening an attachment and contact the sender if you have any doubt about the message's authenticity.

If you're at risk, do yourself a favor and buy a commercial antivirus program. Or try a free malware scanner such as Malwarebytes or Sophos Home. If you think you might be at risk, scan your drive with one of the free utilities before shelling out any cash. I'm not quite ready to run antivirus software on my Mac full-time, but I do run Malwarebytes occasionally. For the record, it rarely finds anything amiss, and the few so-called malware files it caught were benign. Get it if you need it; don't if you don't.

Firewall: Yea or nay?

According to the macOS built-in *Oxford American Dictionary*, a firewall is

Part of a computer system or network that is designed to block unauthorized access while permitting outward communication.

Using a firewall protects your computer from malicious users on other networks or the Internet and keeps them from gaining access to your Mac.

Unlike older versions of Windows, macOS is difficult to crack. There have been few (if any) reports of outsiders gaining access to Mac computers running macOS.

One reason might be that macOS has a built-in firewall. That's the good news. The bad news is that the firewall is disabled by default, so you'll need to activate it if you want to be better protected against unauthorized network access to your computer.

WARNING

If you use a router with its own firewall (and the router's firewall is enabled), *do not also activate the Big Sur firewall.* Running multiple firewalls can cause serious network issues.

To activate macOS's firewall, follow these steps:

1. **Open the System Preferences application (from the Applications folder, the menu, Launchpad, or the dock).**

2. **Click the Security & Privacy icon and then click the Firewall tab.**

If the lock in the bottom-left corner of the Security & Privacy pane is locked (as it should be), click it, and provide your administrator account name and password.

3. **To turn on the firewall, if it's not already running, click the Turn On Firewall button.**

When you turn it on for the first time, its default setting is Allow All Incoming Connections, which is the least-secure option.

4. **To configure your firewall's settings, click the Firewall Options button.**

5. **For the highest level of protection, select the Block All Incoming Connections and Enable Stealth Mode check boxes.**

6. **Click OK.**

Alas, you probably won't want to keep this setting for long because you won't be able to use awesome macOS features such as Messages and file, screen, printer, and music sharing, to name a few. If (or when) it becomes desirable to allow certain incoming connections from outside computers, enable them in the Sharing System Preferences pane.

The only other issue you're likely to face is when a particular application needs you to allow outside connections to it to function. How would you know? Check the user manual, Read Me file, or application Help. Or you might see an error message that the program can't connect to the Internet. Don't worry — if a program requires you to open your firewall, you can almost certainly find some information in one (or more) of these places.

The solution is to click the little + icon on the left below the list of rules in the Firewall Options window. A standard Open File sheet drops down over the window; select the appropriate program and click the Add button. Your firewall will then allow incoming connections to that particular application evermore.

TIP

You can avoid many trips to the Sharing and Firewall System Preferences panes by enabling the Automatically Allow Built-In Software to Receive Incoming Connections and Automatically Allow Downloaded Signed Software to Receive Incoming Connections check boxes. You'll almost certainly have fewer (if any) issues with apps connecting to the Internet.

Install recommended software updates

I mention this earlier in a short tip, but it bears repeating: By default, your Mac checks with the mothership (Apple) once per week to look for any new or updated software. If there is, your Mac informs you that a new software update is available and asks whether you'd like to install it. In almost all cases, you do. Apple issues software updates to fix newly discovered security concerns, to fix serious bugs in macOS, or to fix bugs in or add functionality to Apple applications. You should update your Apple apps and system software regularly.

You can check for application updates manually by opening the App Store app and displaying its Updates tab. If any updates are available, you'll see them here.

Open the Software Update System Preferences pane to check for system software updates, disable automatic checking, or click its Advanced button to fine-tune both automatic checking and automatic installation.

WARNING

Once in a blue moon, a software update has an unintended side effect; while fixing one problem, it introduces a different problem. This doesn't happen very often because Apple is careful, but if you want to be safe, don't install a software update until you visit Macworld (`www.macworld.com`), The Mac Observer (`www.macobserver.com`), or another authoritative site and look at what they have to say about the update you have in mind. If there are widespread issues with a particular software update, sites like these will have the most comprehensive coverage (and possible work-arounds).

Apps need updates, too. So make a habit of launching the Mac App Store application now and then, clicking the Updates tab, and then updating any apps that require it.

Many third-party programs, including Microsoft Office and most Adobe products, use their own update-checking mechanism. Check and make sure that you have yours enabled. Many third-party apps offer a Check for Updates option in the Help (or other) menu or as a preference in their Preferences window.

One last thing: If you see a little number on the App Store or System Preferences icon in the dock, you have that many updates waiting to be installed. Launch the Mac App Store and click the Updates tab or launch System Preferences and click the Software Update icon.

Protecting Your Data from Prying Eyes

The last kind of security I look at in this chapter is protecting your files from other users on your local area network (LAN) and users with physical access to your Mac. If you don't want anyone messing with your files, check out the security measures in the following sections.

Blocking or limiting connections

The first thing you may want to do is open the Sharing System Preferences pane by launching the System Preferences application (from the Applications folder, ⌘ menu, or dock) and clicking the Sharing icon. Nobody can access your Mac over the network if all the services in the Sharing pane are disabled and your firewall is set to Block All Incoming Connections. See the section "Firewall: Yea or nay?" earlier in this chapter, for details on these settings.

Locking down files with FileVault

If you absolutely, positively don't ever want anyone to be able to access the files in your Home folder without your permission, use FileVault. This app allows you to encrypt your entire disk and protect it with the latest government-approved encryption standard: Advanced Encryption Standard with 128-bit keys (AES-128).

When you turn on FileVault, you're asked to set a master password for the computer. After you do, you or any other administrator can use that master password if you forget your regular account login password.

WARNING

I said it at the beginning of the chapter but it bears repeating: If you turn on File-Vault and forget both your login password and your master password, you can't log in to your account — and your data is lost forever. Really. Not even DriveSavers has a hope of recovering it. So don't forget these passwords, okay?

FileVault is useful primarily if you store sensitive information on your Mac. If you're logged out of your user account and other people access to your Mac, there is no way they can access your data. Period.

Because FileVault encrypts your entire hard drive, some tasks that normally access your disk might be prevented. For one thing, some backup programs (not Time Machine, of course) can choke if FileVault is enabled. Also, if you're not logged in to your user account, other users can't access your Shared folder(s).

REMEMBER

Because FileVault is always encrypting and decrypting files, it can slow older Macs a tiny bit when you add or save new files, and it can take extra time before it lets you log out, restart, or shut down. If your Mac is less than five years old, you'll probably notice little or no delay from enabling FileVault.

To turn on FileVault, follow these steps:

1. **Open the Security & Privacy System Preferences pane.**

2. **Click the FileVault tab.**

3. **To enable FileVault, click the Turn on FileVault button.**

To turn off FileVault, click the Turn Off FileVault button.

One last thing: You have the option of encrypting Time Machine backups (which isn't a bad idea if you're security conscious). Just enable the appropriate check box in the Time Machine System Preferences pane.

Setting other options for security

The General tab of the Security & Privacy System Preferences pane offers several more options that can help keep your data safe. They are as follows:

>> **Change Password:** Click this button to change the password for your user account.

>> **Require Password after Sleep or Screen Saver Begins:** Enable this option if you want your Mac to lock itself up and require a password after the screen saver kicks in or it goes to sleep. It can become a pain in the butt, having to type your password all the time. But if you have nosy co-workers, family members, or other individuals you'd like to keep from rooting around in your stuff, you should probably enable this option.

When enabled, this option offers a pop-up menu that lets you specify how long after sleep or screen saver this password protection should kick in. The options range from immediately to 8 hours.

>> **Show a Message When the Screen Is Locked:** Type the message you want on your screen when it's locked in this text entry box.

>> **Allow Apps Downloaded From:** Last, but certainly not least (at least with regard to the General tab), are two options that can help protect you from downloading and running malicious software by limiting the applications your Mac can run.

TECHNICAL
STUFF

In case you were wondering, Apple calls this feature *Gatekeeper,* though that name doesn't appear in the System Preferences pane.

You have two mutually exclusive options — App Store and App Store and Identified Developers. Select the radio button next to the level of protection you desire, and the other option is automatically deselected.

Here's what they do:

- *App Store:* This option allows you to run only apps you download from the Mac App Store. It's the safest and most restrictive setting.

- *App Store and Identified Developers:* Apple offers a Developer ID program to certified members of the Mac Developers Program. Apple gives them a unique Developer ID, which allows Gatekeeper to verify that their app is not known malware and that it hasn't been tampered with. If an app doesn't have a Developer ID associated with it, Gatekeeper can let you know before you install it.

TIP

- This choice is probably the best for most users. It allows third-party apps from Apple-vetted vendors, including Microsoft, Adobe, and thousands more. It's a lot less restrictive than the Mac App Store option and a lot safer than choosing Anywhere.

Finally, the Privacy tab of the Security & Privacy System Preferences pane has several potentially useful options:

>> **To Enable or Disable Location Services:** Click Location Services on the left, and you'll see a list of apps that are allowed to use your computer's current location. Select or deselect these apps to enable or disable, respectively, their use of Location Services.

>> **To Enable or Disable Other Apps Access to your Contacts, Calendars, and Reminders:** Click Contacts, Calendars, or Reminders in the list on the left and apps with access to their contents will appear on the right. Select or deselect the check box for each app to enable or disable, respectively, its permission to access Contacts, Calendars, or Reminders.

>> **To Enable or Disable Apps Allowed to Control Your Computer:** Click Accessibility in the list on the left, and apps allowed to control your computer appear on the right. Select or deselect the check box for each app to enable or disable, respectively, its permission to control your computer.

>> **To Automatically Send Anonymous Analytics Data to Apple:** Click Analytics in the list on the left and then select the Share Mac Analytics and Share iCloud Analytics check boxes. Details of system crashes, apps that quit unexpectedly, freezes, kernel panics, and issues with iCloud (anonymously) will now be sent to the mothership in Cupertino (Apple's world HQ), where engineers pore over the data and issue software updates to eliminate the bugs. For bonus points, send crash reports to app developers, too, by enabling the Share with App Developers check box.

REMEMBER

Finally, remember the following:

>> Use strong passwords.

>> Don't share your passwords.

>> Don't store passwords in insecure locations (such as on sticky notes on your monitor).

>> Use a password manager (such as Keychain Access or my favorite, 1Password) to store your passwords securely.

>> Don't log in to suspicious or insecure wireless networks.

>> Don't visit suspicious websites or open suspicious emails.

>> If you have any question about authenticity, just don't click!

And that's all you really need to know about security and privacy (or at least enough to make you dangerous).

Chapter **25**

Utility Chest

acOS Big Sur comes with a plethora of useful utilities that make using your computer more pleasant or make you more productive when you use your computer or both. In this chapter, I give you a glimpse of the handful you're most likely to use that are not covered elsewhere in this book.

In the Applications and Utilities Folders

The first item, Calculator, is in your Applications folder (Go⇨Applications; keyboard shortcut: ⌘+Shift+A). All other items in this chapter are in your Utilities folder (Go⇨Utilities; keyboard shortcut: ⌘+Shift+U), which you'll find *inside* your Applications folder.

Calculator

Need to do some quick math? The Calculator application gives you a simple calculator with all the basic number-crunching functions found in a pocket calculator. To use it, you can either click the keys with the mouse or type numbers and operators (math symbols such as +, −, and =) using the number keys on your keyboard (or numeric keypad, if you have one). Calculator also offers a paper tape (Window⇨Show Paper Tape) to track your computations — and, if you want, provide a printed record. It can even speak numbers aloud (Speech⇨Speak Button Pressed and Speech⇨Speak Result).

Check out Calculator in Figure 25-1.

FIGURE 25-1:
Calculator (left),
Convert menu
(middle), and
Paper Tape
(right).

In my humble opinion, the most useful feature in Calculator (after Paper Tape) is the Convert menu — more specifically, the currency-conversion feature. It checks the Internet for the current exchange rate before calculating the conversion for you. That's very cool.

Beyond that, Calculator has three modes: Basic, Scientific, and Programmer. Basic is the default, and you access the other two modes as follows:

>> Pressing ⌘+2 (View⇨Scientific) turns the formerly anemic calculator into a powerful scientific calculator.

>> If you prefer Reverse Polish Notation (RPN), press ⌘+R.

TECHNICAL STUFF

>> Choosing View⇨Programmer (⌘+3) turns Calculator into the programmer's friend, letting you display your data in binary, octal, hexadecimal, ASCII, and Unicode. It also performs programming operations, such as shifts and byte swaps. (If you're a programmer, you know what all that means; if you aren't, it really doesn't matter.)

And that's about all you need to know to use the Calculator like a pro.

TIP

One more thing: Spotlight (and Siri) can perform many basic math calculations and conversions faster than you can launch the Calculator app.

Moving right along, the remaining applications in this section can be found in your Utilities folder (Go⇨Utilities; keyboard shortcut: ⌘+Shift+U).

Activity Monitor

In Unix, the underlying operating system that powers macOS, applications and other things going on behind the scenes are called *processes*. Each application and the operating system itself can run a number of processes at the same time.

In Figure 25-2, you see 420 different processes running, most of them behind the scenes. Note that when this screenshot was taken, I had half a dozen or more programs running, including Finder, Safari, and Activity Monitor itself.

FIGURE 25-2:
The Activity
Monitor window,
two little CPU
monitors, and the
Activity Monitor
dock icon.

To display the two CPU monitor windows on the right side of the Activity Monitor window as shown in Figure 25-2, choose Window⇨CPU Usage (⌘+2) and CPU History (⌘+3).

You also select what appears in the Activity Monitor's dock icon — CPU Usage, CPU History, Network Usage (shown in Figure 25-2), Disk Activity, or the Activity Monitor — by choosing View⇨Dock Icon. All but the Activity Monitor icon appear *live*, meaning that they update every few seconds to reflect the current state of affairs.

Note that you can't display CPU Usage or CPU History in a window and in the dock icon at the same time — those two items can be displayed in the dock or a window, but not both.

To choose how often these updates occur, choose View⇨Update Frequency.

WARNING

Setting Activity Monitor to update more frequently causes it to use more CPU cycles, which can decrease overall performance slightly.

Finally, the bottom portion of the Activity Monitor window displays information for the active tab. Select the CPU, Memory, Energy, Disk, or Network, and the middle and bottom portions of the Activity Monitor window change to reflect that selection.

TECHNICAL STUFF

Because all Macs that can run Big Sur have at least a dual-core processor, you'll see at least two, and possibly four or more, CPUs displayed in Activity Monitor: one for each core.

Geeks and troubleshooters (and even you) can use Activity Monitor to identify what processes are running, which user owns the process, and how much CPU capacity and memory the process is using. You can even use this feature to quit or force-quit a process that you think might be causing problems for you.

WARNING

Messing around in Activity Monitor isn't a good idea for most users. If you're having problems with an application or with macOS, try quitting open applications, force-quitting applications (press ⌘+Option+Esc — the Mac three-finger salute), or logging out and then logging back in again before you start mucking around with killing processes.

Disk Utility

If you're having problems with your hard drive or need to make changes to it, Disk Utility is a good place to start. Start by clicking a disk or volume in the column on the left and then click one of the buttons on the toolbar as described in the following sections.

Volume +/–

The Volume + and Volume – buttons, introduced in Mojave, make it easier than ever to subdivide your hard or solid-state disk into virtual volumes, which look and act like separate disks but are volumes on a single disk.

If you think this sounds a lot like what we used to call *partitioning*, it is. But to understand the difference between a volume and a partition, you first have to understand the difference between APFS and HFS+ by reading the nearby sidebar.

TIP

Although APFS will allow you to create partitions instead of volumes, I can't think of a good reason for you to do so.

One more thing: You can't currently use an APFS volume as a Time Machine backup disk. If you try, Time Machine will complain that the disk's file system is incompatible and ask to erase and reformat it as HFS+.

Partition button

Speaking of partitions, you can use the Partition button to create disk partitions (multiple volumes on a single disk) on disks formatted as HFS+. macOS treats each partition as a separate disk. The Partition button is enabled only when an eligible item is selected in the column on the left.

APFS VERSUS HFS +

In the old days (before Mojave) we used the term *partitioning* to describe creating multiple virtual disks out of a single hard or solid-state drive. But with macOS High Sierra, Apple introduced a new file system called APFS (Apple File System). The old scheme (prior to High Sierra) is HFS+ (Hierarchical File System +). In other words, APFS is the modern replacement for HFS+, though HFS+ is still available in Disk Utility.

According to Apple, when you install macOS High Sierra, Mojave, or Big Sur on a solid-state drive (SSD) or other all-flash storage device, the volume will *automatically* be converted to APFS. However, if the drive is *not* solid-state or flash — a Fusion drive or a traditional hard disk — it will *not* be converted to APFS.

Disk Utility in Big Sur can format most storage devices using either file system. If you need to manually reformat a device, consider these points made in a recent Apple Support article:

- APFS requires macOS High Sierra or later. Earlier versions of the Mac operating system don't mount APFS-formatted volumes.

- APFS is optimized for solid-state drives (SSDs) and other all-flash storage devices.

- Disk Utility tries to detect the type of storage you're formatting, and then shows the appropriate format in the Format menu. If it can't detect the type of storage, it defaults to Mac OS Extended (aka HFS+), which works with all versions of macOS.

(continued)

(continued)

To make a long story short, if you have to format a solid-state drive, use APFS; for all other drive types, use HFS+.

To find out which format (file system) a device is currently using:

1. Select the device in Finder.

2. Choose File ➪ Get Info or press ⌘+I.

3. Check the Format shown in the Get Info window as shown in the following figure.

Partitioning a drive lets you create multiple volumes. A *volume* is a storage space that (from the Mac's point of view) looks and acts just like a hard drive. A *partition* is simply a designated volume on a drive, separate from all other partitions (volumes). You can create any number of partitions, but it's a good idea to limit yourself to no more than a small handful.

By the same token, it's absolutely not necessary to use partitions unless you're running Boot Camp (see Chapter 23). Many users never partition a hard drive and get along just fine. If you do choose to partition, you should probably limit the number of partitions you create. An iMac with a 1TB drive will do just fine as shipped (with a single partition); there's no need to create more.

WARNING

Be careful here. Although some adjustments can be made to partitions without loss of data, not all adjustments can. You'll be warned if what you're about to do will permanently erase your data, but I thought I'd give you fair warning first. And, of course, you should always have a backup (see Chapter 24) before mucking with your disk.

Finally, if you click the Partition button with an APFS disk selected in the sidebar, you'll see an explanation that suggests you might be happier with a volume than with a partition.

First Aid button

If you suspect that something's not quite right with your startup disk (or any other disk connected to your Mac), the First Aid button in Disk Utility should be among your first stops. Use First Aid to verify and (if necessary) repair an ailing drive. To use it, select a volume icon in the list on the left and then click the First Aid button in the upper-left corner of the Disk Utility window. A sheet asks if you'd like to run First Aid on the selected disk; click Run to do it or Cancel to dismiss the sheet. When it's finished, you'll get information about any problems that the software finds.

If the disk you're trying to repair is your startup disk, Disk Utility will warn you that it needs to temporarily lock the boot volume and that other apps will be unresponsive until the operation has completed, as shown in Figure 25-3. Go have a cup of coffee or something — the process takes 15-30 minutes for most disks.

Verifying the startup volume will cause this computer to stop responding.

This may last for several minutes or hours. To avoid this, you can run First Aid while in Recovery.

Cancel   Continue

FIGURE 25-3:
If you try to run First Aid on your startup disk, you'll see this alert before you can continue.

If First Aid doesn't find any problems, you can go on your merry way, secure in the knowledge that that disk is A-okay. If First Aid turns up a problem that it can't fix, it will advise you what to do next. In most cases, that advice is to boot from the Recovery disk (hold down ⌘+R at startup) and run First Aid again.

TIP

You can't use Disk Utility First Aid to fix a CD or DVD, nor can you use it to fix most disk image (.DMG) files. These types of disks are read-only and can't be altered.

Erase button

Use Erase to format (completely erase) any disk except the current startup disk.

WARNING

When you format a disk, you erase all information on it permanently. Formatting can't be undone — so unless you're *absolutely sure* this is what you want, don't do it. Unless you have no use for whatever's currently on the disk, make a complete backup of the disk before you format it. If the data is critical, you should have at least two (or even three) known-to-be-valid backup copies of that disk before you reformat.

After clicking the Erase button, a sheet drops down with a space for you to name the disk you're about to erase and you see a drop-down Format menu so you can choose the disk format.

REMEMBER

Use Mac OS Extended (Journaled) for rotational and hybrid disks, use APFS for solid-state drives.

WARNING

Don't try any of the other options (case-sensitive, encrypted, and other variations) unless you know what you're doing and have a darn good reason. Formatting a disk using many of these options can cause Mac software to misbehave. Don't do it. Only choose Mac OS Extended (Journaled) or APFS — unless you're prepared to spend time troubleshooting when your Mac doesn't work as expected.

Mount/Unmount button

A drive can be connected but not available to your Mac. For example, when you eject a hard drive or SSD, it's still connected to the computer but doesn't appear in Finder. This is called an *unmounted disk*.

The Mount/Unmount button lets you dismount (eject) or mount a connected disk or partition on a disk. For reasons that should be obvious, you can't eject the disk from which you booted.

Info button

Click the Info button to see myriad technical details about the selected disk, including its size, capacity, and free and used space. One last thing: You find out more about Disk Utility (mostly how to use it for troubleshooting) in Chapter 26.

Grapher

Grapher is a venerable piece of eye candy that shows off your CPU's computational power. A quick, visual math instructor, Grapher can graph equations in two or three dimensions and speaks hexadecimal, octal, base ten (decimal), and binary to boot. You can even graph curves, surfaces, inequalities, differential equations, discrete series, and vector and scalar fields . . . whatever that means. (I found all that information in Apple Help.) I have no clue how to use it, but the examples are pretty (see Figure 25-4).

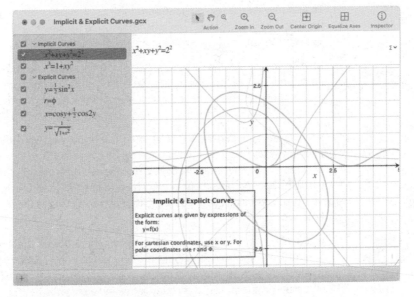

FIGURE 25-4:
Grapher's Implicit & Explicit Curves example.

Keychain Access

A *keychain* is a way to consolidate your passwords — your Mac login password, your email password, and passwords required by any websites. Keychain Access is the application you use to manage those passwords.

Here's how it works: You use a single password to unlock your keychain (which holds your various passwords), and then you don't have to remember all your other passwords. Rest assured that your passwords are secure because only a user who has your keychain password can reach the other password-protected applications.

TIP

The Keychain Access utility is particularly cool if you have multiple email accounts and each one has a different password. Just add them all to your keychain, and you can get all your mail at the same time with one password.

A special master keychain called the Login Keychain is created automatically for every macOS Big Sur user and unlocked automatically when you log into your account.

TIP

Here's how to add passwords to your login keychain:

>> **To add passwords for applications:** If the application supports the keychain, the first time you log in with your username and password, a dialog will ask if you want to add this login to the keychain. Click Yes.

How do you know which programs support the Keychain Access utility? You don't, until you're prompted to save your password in a keychain in that Open dialog, connect window, or so forth. If a program supports Keychain Access, it offers a check box for it in the user ID/password dialog or window.

If that doesn't happen the first time you provide your password, the program doesn't support macOS keychains and you're out of luck. You can add the account details manually (see the next bullet), but they won't be provided automatically when the app requests them — you'll have to open Keychain Access to look them up. The upside is that your passwords are secure as long as they're stored in a keychain.

TIP

If you select the User Names and Passwords check box on the AutoFill tab of Safari's Preferences window (Safari⇨Preferences or ⌘+, [comma]), you don't have to add sites, accounts, or passwords manually. Instead, the first time you visit a site that requires an account name and a password, Safari asks whether you would like to save your password, and then it does so.

>> **To add a website (or other) password to a keychain manually:** If your login credentials aren't being filled in automatically for a website, you can add them manually using the Keychain Access application. Just click the little + (plus) at the top of the main window and type (or copy and paste) the URL of the page in the Keychain Item Name text field. Then type your username in the Account Name field and your password in the Password field, as shown in Figure 25-5. (If you're adding a password for something other than a website, type a descriptive name in the Keychain Item Name field rather than a URL.)

TIP

Click the little key to the right of the password field to use the Password Assistant window, which can help you select a high-quality password.

FIGURE 25-5:
Add a URL to the keychain manually by using Keychain Access.

To use the new URL password, use Safari to open the URL. If the account name and password aren't filled in for you automatically, choose Edit⇨AutoFill Form (⌘+Shift+A) and they will be.

TIP

iCloud Keychain syncing is a great feature that makes keychains even better. Turn it on (System Preferences⇨iCloud), and your Safari passwords will be securely synced to (and from) all your Apple devices, including iPhones and iPads.

WARNING

Just remember that this makes all your passwords available on all your devices. That's handy, but if any of your devices aren't secured with passwords or passcodes or are shared with others, all your passwords could be at risk. Just think about it before you enable iCloud Keychain.

Migration Assistant

Migration Assistant is pretty much a one-trick pony, but that pony is a prizewinner. You use Migration Assistant to transfer your account and other user information from another Mac, another volume on the current Mac, or a Time Machine backup. You need to authenticate as an administrator to use it, but it's a pretty handy way to transfer an entire account without having to re-create your preferences and other settings. When you first installed Big Sur (or when you booted your nice, new Big Sur–based Mac for the first time), the setup utility asked you whether you wanted to transfer your information from another Mac. If you answered in the affirmative, it ran Migration Assistant.

TIP

It's not just for new Big Sur installs. You can launch this one-trick-pony anytime to transfer all or some user accounts, applications, settings, and files from another Mac, PC, or Time Machine backup to this one. You can use it also after replacing a hard drive or reinstalling macOS. Last but not least, Migration Assistant can import user accounts, applications, settings, and files from Windows PCs as well as from Macs.

System Information

System Information (the app formerly known as System Profiler) is a little program that is launched when you click the System Report button in the About This Mac window (⌘⇨About This Mac) or double-click its icon in the Utilities folder inside your Applications folder.

It provides information about your Mac. (What a concept!) If you're curious about arcane questions such as what processor your Mac has or what devices are stashed inside it or are connected to it, give this baby a try. Click various items in the Contents list on the left side of the window, and information about the item appears on the right side of the window. Feel free to poke around this little puppy as much as you like; it's benign and can't hurt anything.

TIP

If you ever have occasion to call for technical support for your Mac, software, or peripherals, you're probably going to be asked to provide information from System Information, so don't get rid of it just because you don't care about this kind of stuff.

Terminal

macOS is based on Unix. If you need proof — or if you actually want to operate your Mac as the Unix machine that it is — Terminal is the place to start.

Because Unix is a command line–based operating system, you use Terminal to type your commands. You can issue commands that show a directory listing, copy and move files, search for filenames or contents, or establish or change passwords. In short, if you know what you're doing, you can do everything on the command line that you can do in macOS. For most folks, that's not a desirable alternative to the windows and icons of the Finder window. But take my word for it; true geeks who are also Mac lovers get all misty-eyed about the combination of a command line *and* a graphical user interface.

WARNING

You can wreak havoc upon your poor operating system with Terminal. You can harm your Big Sur in many ways that just aren't possible using mere windows and icons and clicks. *Before you type a single command in Terminal, think seriously about what I just said.* And if you're not 100 percent certain about the command you just typed, don't even think about pressing Return.

Capturing Your Screen

If you've been a Mac user for a while, you might have noticed that the venerable Screenshot (formerly Grab) app, the app you use to use to manage screen capture features including timed shots and cursor visibility, is no longer in your Utilities folder.

In its place, Big Sur (like Mojave before it) has more and better screen-shooting capabilities than any version of macOS before it. It's now called Screenshot and its functionality is woven into the fabric of Big Sur itself. Furthermore, Screenshot has been updated in several useful ways since it was known as Grab.

I'll tell you about all the newish features and where to find them in just a moment. But I'd be remiss if I didn't point out that all of your old favorite keyboard short-cuts for screen capture — the ones you've known and loved on the Mac since time immemorial — still work the same as always:

To capture the entire screen:

1. Press ⌘+Shift+3.
2. There is no Step 2.

To capture part of the screen:

1. Press ⌘+Shift+4.
2. Move the pointer (crosshair icon) to where you want to start the screenshot.
3. Press the mouse or trackpad button, then drag over the area you want to capture.
4. Release the mouse or trackpad button to capture the selected area.

To cancel, press Esc before you release the mouse button.

To capture a window or the menu bar:

1. **Press ⌘+Shift+4 and then press the spacebar.**

2. **Move the pointer (camera icon) over the area you wish to capture; when it is highlighted, click to capture the selected item.**

To cancel, press Esc before you click.

To capture a menu and its title:

1. **Open the menu to display the menu commands.**

2. **Press ⌘+Shift+4.**

3. **Drag the pointer (crosshair icon) over the entire menu.**

   If you want to exclude the menu's title, press ⌘+Shift+4, press the spacebar, move the pointer (camera icon) over the menu to highlight it, then click.

Big Sur screen-shooting 101

In addition to the old, familiar screenshot shortcuts, Big Sur has another keyboard shortcut that includes everything you can do using the other shortcuts and more.

That fabulous shortcut is ⌘+Shift+5, and you'd be wise to memorize it because, like the other two screenshot keyboard shortcuts, it doesn't appear in any menu or application. If you're going to memorize only one shortcut for screen captures, it should be ⌘+Shift+5, which will open the floating palette of screen-shooting options shown in Figure 25-6.

Cancel (without capturing anything)

Record entire screen (video)

Capture selected portion

Options menu

FIGURE 25-6: Here's what you'll see (more or less) when you press ⌘+Shift+5 in Big Sur.

Capture entire screen

Capture selected window

Record selected portion (video)

To capture your screen as a still image, first click the appropriate icon: Capture Entire Screen, Capture Selected Window, or Capture Selected Portion. When everything is the way you want it, press Enter (or Return) on your keyboard.

What happens next, before the screenshot appears on your desktop (by default), is a relatively new thing (introduced in macOS Mojave). That new thing is a floating thumbnail that appears in the lower-right corner of your screen.

If you do nothing, the floating thumbnail will disappear after a few seconds and the screenshot will appear on the desktop by default. (You learn how to save screenshots elsewhere in the next section.)

But click the floating thumbnail before it goes away and a wonderful new thing happens: A window appears with a bevy of useful tools for modifying images.

These tools are known as Markup — a systemwide set of tools for annotating PDF and image files. I mention Markup briefly in Chapter 17, but the tools aren't restricted to the Mail app — you'll also find them in the Preview app (see Chapter 20), Finder's Quick Look windows (see Chapter 10), in the Preview pane of Finder windows (if enabled), and in Finder shortcut menus. (Details on Markup appear in Chapter 5.)

These same tools also appear if you click the floating thumbnail of a screenshot before it disappears.

These powerful editing tools enable you to annotate screenshots in ways never before possible without a third-party graphics app. Now you can easily add circles, boxes, arrows, and text to your screenshots, image files, and PDFs without even launching an app.

When you've finished annotating and editing your screenshot, click Done in the upper-left corner of the window.

Big Sur screen-shooting options

If you want to change the location where your screenshots are saved, click the Options menu, which is available after you press ⌘+Shift+5. The Options menu also allows you to select a timer of None (the default), 5 seconds, or 10 seconds.

Finally, the Options menu lets you enable or disable the floating thumbnail, show or hide the mouse pointer, and remember the last selection you made (for your next screenshot).

Another set of options appears when you right- or Control-click the floating thumbnail, as shown in Figure 25-7.

FIGURE 25-7: Right- or Control-click the floating thumbnail and choose from these options.

Note that selecting Markup is the same as clicking the floating thumbnail — it opens the Markup window so you can annotate your screenshot.

Big Sur screen recording

Screen recording — movies of your Mac (or iDevice) screens — has been around for a few years on the Mac, but it's been buried in the QuickTime Player app (see Chapter 20). I didn't discuss it in that chapter because this way is so much easier and more convenient. (If you want to make a movie of your iDevice screen, you'll still need to use QuickTime Player.)

Anyway, to make a movie of all or part of your Mac screen, begin by pressing ⌘+Shift+5. Then click either the Record Entire Screen or Record Selected Portion. If you click Record Entire Screen, the recording begins immediately; if you click Record Selected Portion, you need to drag the onscreen handles to select the area you want to record, and then click the Record icon.

To end the recording, click the Stop Recording icon in the menu bar, as shown in Figure 25-8.

FIGURE 25-8:
The Stop Recording icon appears in your menu bar while you're recording the screen.

Stop recording

When the floating thumbnail appears in the lower-right corner of your screen, you can right- or Control-click it for additional options, or do nothing to have the screen recording saved in your default location.

Chapter **26**

Troubleshooting macOS

As a bleeding-edge Mac enthusiast and consultant with more than three decades of Mac troubleshooting experience, I've seen (and resolved) more than my share of Mac troubles. Over those years, I've developed an arsenal of mostly surefire tips and tricks that I believe will help you resolve more than 90 percent of Mac issues without a trip to the repair shop.

Alas, if your hardware is dead, then, sadly, neither you nor I can do anything about it — that's a job for your friendly Mac repairman and your fat checkbook or high-limit credit card. But if your hardware is okay, you have a darn good chance of using the suggestions in this chapter to get your machine up and running.

About Startup Disks and Booting

Although you usually see a stylish Apple logo when you turn on your computer, once in a blue moon, you may instead see a solid blue screen, a solid gray screen, a solid black screen, or something else entirely, as described in the next section.

The point is that your Mac isn't starting up as it should. When this happens, it usually indicates that something bad has happened to your Mac. Sometimes, a hardware component has bitten the dust; other times, macOS itself has somehow been damaged.

Rest assured that these occurrences are uncommon — many Macs and Mac users go an entire lifetime without ever having an issue. But if you ever have a Mac that won't boot, don't despair. Before you declare your Mac terminally ill or worse, try out the advice in this chapter.

Finally, I use the term *hard disk* generically throughout the chapter to refer to hard disks (mechanical with spinning platters) or solid-state disks (electronic with no moving parts).

Finding or creating a startup disk

First things first: When I talk about *booting*, I mean using a particular disk or disk partition as your startup disk.

Big Sur is available only in the Mac App Store as a download. Because you can no longer purchase a bootable installer DVD, the macOS Installer automatically creates a bootable partition named Recovery HD when you install Big Sur on a disk.

TIP

I recommend that you also make a bootable Recovery disk (in addition to the one Big Sur should have created) or a clone of your Mac startup disk. If not, it's something you may wish you had done when your Mac starts acting wonky.

WARNING

Explaining how to create a bootable recovery disk or clone is beyond the purview of this book, but I hope you'll take it upon yourself to search the Internet and figure out how to make one. Start with this Apple Support Article: https://support.apple.com/en-us/HT201372. And bear in mind that you can't start your Mac from a Time Machine backup.

The Recovery HD partition is a good concept, but if your hard disk dies, the Recovery HD partition generally dies with it — which is why *I strongly recommend making a bootable clone of your startup disk as soon as possible,* just in case.

TIP

I use Carbon Copy Cloner (www.bombich.com), a $39.99 app that lets you create a clone of your boot disk with a minimum of fuss. Or you can try SuperDuper! (shareware from www.shirt-pocket.com); just add a hard disk as large as or larger than your boot disk, and you'll be good to go with any of these options.

They call it a prohibitory sign for a reason

When you turn on your Mac, the first thing it does (after the hardware tests) is check for a startup disk that has a viable copy of macOS on it. If your system doesn't find such a disk on your internal hard drive, it begins looking elsewhere — on a FireWire, Thunderbolt, or Universal Serial Bus (USB) disk, a thumb drive, or a DVD.

At this point, your Mac usually finds the (usually internal) hard drive (or SSD), which contains your operating system, and the startup process continues on its merry way with the subtle Apple logo and all the rest. If your Mac can't find a suitable bootable disk you encounter the dreaded prohibitory sign. Think of the prohibitory sign as your Mac's way of saying, "Please provide me a startup disk."

REMEMBER

If you have more than one startup disk attached to your Mac, as many users do, you can choose which one your Mac boots from in the Startup Disk System Preferences pane or by pressing and holding down the Option key when you start up your Mac.

If Apple can figure out a way to put a prohibitory sign on the screen, why the heck can't the software engineers find a way to put the words *I need a startup disk* on the screen as well? The curtness of these icons is one of my pet peeves about the Mac. I know — you're clever and smart (because, of course, you're smart enough to be reading *macOS Big Sur For Dummies*), so *you* know that a prohibitory sign means you should insert a startup disk. But what about everyone else?

If you encounter any of the warning icons shown in Figure 26-1, go through the steps I outline later in this chapter. You can try different options, such as using Disk Utility's First Aid, zapping the parameter RAM (PRAM), and performing a Safe boot. Try them in the order listed, starting with Step 1. Then, if one doesn't work, move on to the next.

You need to restart your computer. Hold down the Power button for several seconds or press the Restart button.

Veuillez redémarrer votre ordinateur. Maintenez la touche de démarrage enfoncée pendant plusieurs secondes ou bien appuyez sur le bouton de réinitialisation.

Sie müssen Ihren Computer neu starten. Halten Sie dazu die Einschalttaste einige Sekunden gedrückt oder drücken Sie die Neustart-Taste.

コンピュータを再起動する必要があります。パワーボタンを数秒間押し続けるか、リセットボタンを押してください。

FIGURE 26-1: Any of these means it's troubleshooting time.

Recovering with Recovery HD

If you see a prohibitory sign (top left in Figure 26-1), spinning-disc cursor (top right), or kernel panic alert (the text in other languages that appears below the other two images) that doesn't go away when you start up your Mac, the first thing to do is attempt to repair hidden damage to your hard drive with the Disk Utility program's First Aid feature.

Step 1: Run First Aid

In most cases, the first logical troubleshooting step is to use the First Aid option in the Disk Utility application.

TECHNICAL STUFF

Every drive has several strangely named components, such as B-trees, extent files, catalog files, and other creatively named invisible files. They're all involved in managing the data on your drives. Disk Utility's First Aid feature checks all those files and repairs the damaged ones.

Because your Mac isn't able to finish the boot process, you'll need to boot from the Recovery partition to perform this repair. So start by rebooting your Mac while pressing ⌘+R, continuing to press them until you see the Apple logo appear. When it does, a window appears offering four buttons: Restore from Time Machine, Reinstall MacOS, Safari, and Disk Utility.

The one you need now is Disk Utility, so click it and then click Continue. When Disk Utility appears:

1. **Click the icon for your boot hard drive, to the left of the Disk Utility window.**

   Your boot drive is the one with macOS and your Home folder on it; mine is called *Big Sur -Data*.

2. **Click the First Aid button in the toolbar.**

   A sheet drops down, asking if you'd like to run First Aid on that disk.

3. **Click the Run button.**

   A sheet drops down informing you that First Aid needs to temporarily lock the boot volume.

4. **Click the Continue button.**

   Your Mac whirs and hums for a few minutes, and another sheet eventually drops down.

5. **(Optional) Click Show Details on the sheet to see (mostly unintelligible) details of what First Aid has done to your disk.**

   It will take anywhere from a few minutes to an hour or more for First Aid to check and repair your disk and allow you to perform Step 7.

6. **Click the Done button.**

7. **Quit Disk Utility.**

   Choose Disk Utility ➪ Quit Disk Utility, press ⌘+Q, or click the red Close Window gumdrop button.

TIP

If First Aid finds damage that it can't fix, a commercial disk-recovery tool, such as Prosoft's Drive Genius *may* be able to repair the damage. And even if First Aid gave your Mac a clean bill of health, you may want to run a third-party utility anyway, just to have a second opinion.

WARNING

Make sure you're running a current version; older versions may not be compatible with macOS Big Sur (or APFS) and could make things worse.

If everything checks out with First Aid but you still get the prohibitory sign after you restart, proceed to the next section to try a dance called booting into Safe mode.

Step 2: Safe boot into Safe mode

Booting your Mac in Safe mode may help you resolve your startup issue by not loading nonessential (and non–macOS) software at boot time. You do it by holding down the Shift key during startup.

If your Mac is set up so you don't have to log in, keep pressing the Shift key during startup until Finder loads completely. If you do log in to your Mac, type your password as usual — but before clicking the Log In button, press the Shift key again and hold it down until Finder loads completely.

You know you held the Shift key long enough if your Login Items don't load (assuming that you have Login Items; you can designate them in the Users & Groups System Preferences pane, although some programs create them for you).

TECHNICAL STUFF

Booting in Safe mode does three things to help you with troubleshooting:

» It forces a directory check of the startup (boot) volume.

» It loads only required kernel extensions (some of the items in /System/Library/ Extensions).

>> It runs only Apple-installed essential startup items (some of the items in /Library/StartupItems and /System/Library/StartupItems). Note that the Startup Items in the Library folders are different from the Login Items in the Users & Groups System Preferences pane. Startup Items run at boot time before the login window even appears; Login Items don't run until after you log into your user account.

Taken together, these changes often work around issues caused by software or directory damage on the startup volume.

WARNING

Some features may not work in Safe mode. Among them are DVD Player, capturing video (in iMovie or other video-editing software), using AirPort, and using some audio input or output devices. Use Safe mode only when you need to troubleshoot a startup issue, and reboot in normal mode as soon as possible.

If your Mac boots in Safe mode, you may be able to determine what's causing the issue by moving the contents of your Preferences folder (in Home/Library, which you can make visible by pressing the Option key when opening the Go menu) to the desktop temporarily or by disabling Login Items (in the Users & Groups System Preferences pane). If either of these things resolves the issue, you can put preferences files back in Home/Library/Preferences a few at a time, or you can reenable login items one at a time until you figure out which preferences file or login item is causing your problems. If your Mac still has problems, see the following section.

Step 3: Zapping the PRAM/NVRAM

Sometimes your Mac's parameter RAM (PRAM) or non-volatile RAM (NVRAM) becomes scrambled and needs to be reset. Both of these are small pieces of memory that aren't erased or forgotten when you shut down. They keep track of things such as the following:

>> Time zone setting

>> Startup volume choice

>> Speaker volume

>> Any recent kernel panic information

>> DVD region setting

To reset (a process often called *zapping*) your PRAM/NVRAM, restart your Mac and press ⌘+Option+P+R (that's four keys — good luck; it's okay to use your nose) until your Mac restarts itself. It's kind of like a hiccup. You might see the spinning-disc pointer for a minute or two while your Mac thinks about it . . . then the icon disappears, and your Mac chimes again (unless your Mac is one of the recent models, which, sadly, are chimeless) and restarts. Most power users believe you should zap it more than once, letting it chime two, three, or even four times before releasing the keys and allowing the startup process to proceed.

Now restart your Mac without holding down any keys. If the PRAM/NVRAM zap didn't fix your Mac, move on to the section "Step 4: Reinstalling macOS."

REMEMBER

Your chosen startup disk, time zone, and sound volume may be reset to their default values when you zap your PRAM. So after zapping, open the System Preferences application to reselect your usual startup disk and time zone, and set the sound volume the way you like it if necessary.

Step 4: Reinstalling macOS

I present the procedure to reinstall the system software as a second-to-last resort when your Mac won't boot correctly because it takes the longest and is the biggest hassle. Apple has a nifty technical note on reinstallation at `https://support.apple.com/en-us/HT204904`.

Follow the instructions, taking care *not* to erase your disk before you reinstall macOS. As long as you do not erase the disk before you reinstall, you won't lose a drop of data. This procedure just installs a fresh copy of Big Sur — it doesn't affect your files, settings, or anything else.

Step 5: Things to try before taking your Mac in for repair

TIP

To get your Mac up and running again, you can try any of the following:

>> **Call the tech-support hotline.** Before you drag it down to the shop, try calling 1-800-SOS-APPL, the Apple Tech Support hotline. The service representatives there may be able to suggest something else that you can try. If your Mac is still under warranty, it's even free.

>> **Ask a local user group for help.** Another thing you might consider is contacting your local Mac user group. You can find a group of Mac users near you by visiting Apple's User Group web pages at www.apple.com/usergroups.

WARNING

>> **Check whether you have RAM issues.** Here's a common problem: If you have problems immediately after installing RAM — or any new hardware, for that matter — double-check that the RAM chips are properly seated in their sockets and that cables are securely inserted into ports.

Don't forget to shut down your Mac first. With the power off and your Mac unplugged, remove and reinsert the RAM chips to make sure they're seated properly.

If you still have problems, remove the RAM chips temporarily and see whether the problem still exists.

Follow the installation instructions that came with the RAM chips or the ones in the booklet that came with your Mac.

WARNING

First discharge any static spark, either by using an antistatic strap (available from most RAM sellers) or by touching an appropriate surface (such as the power-supply case inside your Mac) *before you handle RAM chips.*

Some Macs, notably newer iMacs and most notebook models, don't have upgradeable RAM. So before you open your Mac, check online to see whether its RAM is upgradeable.

If none of my suggestions works for you, and you're still seeing anything you shouldn't when you start up your Mac, you have big trouble. You could have any one of the following problems:

>> Your hard drive is dead.

>> You have some other type of hardware failure.

>> All your startup disks are defective (unlikely).

The bottom line: If you still can't start up normally after trying all the cures I list in this chapter, you almost certainly need to have your Mac serviced by a qualified technician.

If Your Mac Crashes at Startup

Startup crashes are another bad thing that can happen to your Mac. These crashes can be more of a hassle to resolve than prohibitory sign problems, but they are rarely fatal.

You know that a *crash* has happened when you see a Quit Unexpectedly dialog, a frozen cursor, a frozen screen, or any other disabling event. A *startup crash* happens when your system shows a crash symptom any time between the moment you flick the power key or switch (or restarting) and the moment you have full use of the desktop.

Try all the steps in the previous sections *before* you panic. The easiest way to fix startup crashes (in most cases) is to just reinstall macOS from the Recovery HD partition. Again, Apple details this procedure at great length online, at https://support.apple.com/en-us/HT204904.

If you're still unsuccessful after that point, read the "Step 5: Things to try before taking your Mac in for repair" section.

Optimizing Storage

Optimize Storage provides assistance if your startup disk gets close to being full.

Here's why it's in the troubleshooting chapter, in case you're wondering: Your Mac will slow to a crawl as your startup disk gets close to full. If your startup disk is more than 90 percent filled, you'll begin to experience slowness and jerkiness. And as the drive approaches 100 percent fullness, things grow even slower and jerkier.

Optimize Storage aims to help you out as your disk fills up by scanning for duplicates, old email attachments, and downloads so you can delete them or move them to the cloud. But you should read what follows even if your disk isn't approaching fullness right now, because Optimize Storage offers several options that may keep your disk from ever getting too full.

To check it out, choose ➪ About This Mac, click the Storage tab at the top of the window, and then click the Manage button.

Optimize Storage includes four tools, as shown in Figure 26-2:

>> **Store in iCloud:** Store all your files in iCloud to save space, keeping only recently opened files on your Mac when storage space is needed.

WARNING

This option could be convenient, but it's going to chew through your 5GB of free iCloud storage in no time. With additional iCloud storage currently selling for $0.99 a month (50GB), $3.99 a month (200GB), or $9.99 a month (2TB), it could be costly as well as convenient.

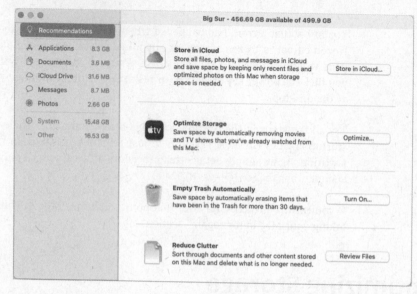

FIGURE 26-2:
If your disk is getting full, use one or more of these Optimize Storage tools.

>> **Optimize Storage:** Remove from your Mac movies and TV shows you've already watched.

>> **Erase Trash Automatically:** Automatically empty files that have been in the Trash for 30 days.

>> **Reduce Clutter:** Review and delete older documents, which are broken down by category — Documents, Messages, Music, Trash, and TV — along the left side of the window.

The bottom line is that you don't want your startup disk anywhere close to 100 percent full, and the Optimize Storage features provide four useful ways for you to stay on top of and avert trouble before it even occurs.

7

The Part of Tens

Find ways to speed up a pokey Mac.

Get a list of awesome Mac websites worthy of your attention.

Chapter 27

Ten Ways to Speed Up Your Mac Experience

This chapter is for speed demons only. At some time in their Mac lives, most users have wished that their machines would work faster — even if their Macs have multiple cores or processors. I can't help you make your processors any faster, but here's where I cover some ways to make your Mac at least *seem* faster. Better still, at least some of these tips won't cost you one red cent.

The ten tips that follow have been finely tuned over the course of this book's many editions, often in response to suggestions by readers or editors. If you think you have a great way to speed up your Mac, please send it to me at Big Sur4Dummies@boblevitus.com. If it's awesome, I may include it in the next edition of this book (and give you full credit for thinking of it, of course)!

Use Those Keyboard Shortcuts

Keyboard shortcuts (see Table 27-1 for a nice little list of the most useful ones) can make navigating your Mac a much faster experience compared with constantly using the mouse, offering these benefits:

>> If you use keyboard shortcuts, your hands stay focused on the keyboard, reducing the amount of time that you remove your hand from the keyboard to fiddle with the mouse or trackpad.

TABLE 27-1   **Great Keyboard Shortcuts**

Keyboard Shortcut	Name	What It Does
⌘+O	Open	Opens the selected item.
⌘+. (period)	Cancel	Cancels the current operation in many programs, including Finder. The Esc key often does the same thing as Cancel.
⌘+P	Print	Brings up a dialog that enables you to print the active window's contents. (See Chapter 22 for info on printing.)
⌘+X	Cut	Cuts whatever you select and places it on the Clipboard. (I cover the Clipboard in Chapter 9.)
⌘+C	Copy	Copies whatever you select and places it on the Clipboard.
⌘+V	Paste	Pastes the contents of the Clipboard at your cursor's location.
⌘+F	Find	Displays a Searching window in Finder; displays a Find dialog in most other programs.
⌘+A	Select All	Selects the entire contents of the active window in many programs, including Finder.
⌘+Z	Undo	Undoes the last thing you did in many programs, including Finder.
⌘+Shift+Z	Redo	Redoes the last thing you undid in many programs, including Finder.
⌘+Shift+?	Help	Displays the Mac Help window in Finder; usually the shortcut to summon Help in other programs.
⌘+Q	Quit	Perhaps the most useful keyboard shortcut of all. Quits the current application (but not Finder because it's always running).
⌘+Shift+Q	Log Out	Logs out the current user. The login window appears onscreen until a user logs in.
⌘+Delete	Move to Trash	Moves the selected item to the Trash.
⌘+Shift+Delete	Empty Trash	Empties the Trash.

>> If you memorize keyboard shortcuts with your head, your fingers will memorize them, too.

>> The more keyboard shortcuts you use, the faster you can do what you're doing.

Trust me when I say that using the keyboard shortcuts for commands you use often can save you a ton of effort and hours upon hours of time.

TIP

Make a list of keyboard shortcuts you want to memorize, and tape it to your monitor until your brain and fingers memorize them. (Or just make a photocopy of Table 27-1!)

Improve Your Typing Skills

One way to make your Mac seem faster is to move your fingers faster. The quicker you finish a task, the quicker you're on to something else. Keyboard shortcuts are nifty tools, but improving your typing speed and accuracy *will* save you even more time. As a bonus, the more your typing skills improve, the less time you'll spend correcting errors. So you'll finish everything even faster!

TIP

The speed and accuracy that you gain have another bonus: When you're a touch typist, your fingers fly even faster when you use those nifty keyboard shortcuts. (I list a gaggle of these in the preceding section, in Table 27-1.)

The best and easiest way I know to improve your keyboarding skills is a typing training app for your Mac such as Ten Thumbs Typing Tutor ($25.95 at www.tenthumbstypingtutor.com), any of the myriad typing-instruction apps in the Mac App Store (search for *typing*), or a free typing-instruction website such as TypingTest (free at www.typingtest.com).

Change Your Resolution

A setting that you can change to potentially improve your Mac's performance is the resolution of your monitor. Most modern monitors and video cards (or onboard video circuitry, depending on which Mac model you use) can display multiple degrees of screen resolution. You change your monitor's display resolution in the Displays System Preferences pane. First, click the Display tab and then click the Scaled button, which makes a list of resolutions appear, as shown in Figure 27-1. Select the resolution you want to try from the list below the Scaled button.

Display tab

Scaled button

Available resolutions

Macs with Non-Retina Displays **Macs with Retina Displays**

FIGURE 27-1:
Lower resolutions
make things
larger onscreen.

You see many more items on the screen at native resolution, but you can make everything bigger by switching to lower resolutions.

Here's the deal on display resolution: The first number is the number of pixels (color dots) that run horizontally, and the second number is the number of lines running vertically. It used to be that fewer pixels refreshed faster. But with LCD and LED (flat-panel) monitors and notebooks, this usually isn't true — or if it *is* true, it's almost unnoticeable. Furthermore, because you can see more onscreen at higher resolutions, a higher resolution reduces the amount of scrolling that you have to do and lets you have more open windows on the screen. Finally, the highest resolution is almost always the native resolution of that display, which means it will usually look the sharpest. So you could just as easily say that higher resolutions can speed up your Mac experience as well.

On the other hand, if you can't discern icons in toolbars and other program components, using a lower resolution may actually enhance your work speed.

REMEMBER

Choose a resolution based on what looks best and works best for you. If things on the screen are too big or too small at your current resolution, try a higher or lower resolution until you find one that feels "just right."

And, if you have a Retina display, try all available resolutions to see which you prefer. The highest resolution on a Retina display will make everything on the screen appear very, very small, which may or may not be desirable.

Finally, check out the Accessibility System Preferences pane's Zoom tab, where you can enable keyboard shortcuts to zoom in and out instantly, and Hover Text, a highly configurable mode that enlarges only what's under your pointer.

Purchase a Faster Mac

Apple keeps putting out faster and faster Macs at lower and lower prices, and all current Macs now ship with at least 8GB of RAM. Although 4GB may be enough RAM to run Big Sur, if you like to keep more than one or two apps running all the time, it's not enough to run it at its best.

Check out the latest iMacs and Mac minis — they're excellent values. Or if you crave portability, MacBook Air, and MacBook Pro models are rocking good computers and have never been less expensive. You might even consider a used Mac that's faster than yours. eBay (www.ebay.com) has hundreds of used Macs up for auction at any given time. Shopping on eBay might just get you a better Mac at an outstanding price. Or try Craigslist (www.craigslist.org) if you prefer to see and touch the Mac before you commit.

Another excellent option is to visit the Apple website's refurbished and clearance section. You can frequently save hundreds of dollars by purchasing a slightly used Mac that has been refurbished to factory specifications by Apple. Another advantage to Apple refurbs is that they come with an Apple warranty. If you're on a tight budget, definitely check it out (http://store.apple.com/us/browse/home/specialdeals).

TIP

I always buy refurbished products when I can. In fact, it's been over a decade since I bought any (major) Apple product for list price when a refurbished one was available for less. And I always buy as much RAM and the fastest processor I can afford because I think both help to extend the lifespan of the Mac.

Add RAM

You get a lot of bang for your buck when you upgrade your Mac's RAM. Get an additional 4GB, 8GB, or even 16GB; you can never have too much. Your Mac will run better with at least 8GB of RAM, which will cost you less than $100 in most cases and can be installed by anyone. Yes, anyone — the instructions are right there in your User Guide booklet, or you can find them at the Apple Technical Support pages (www.apple.com/support; search for *RAM upgrade* and your Mac model).

Unless, that is, you own one of the many late-model Macs that aren't user-upgradeable. These models are exceedingly difficult to open, and Apple frowns upon users opening some models these days. Plus, some Macs have RAM soldered to the motherboard and can't be upgraded at all. If your Mac is upgradeable and you're uncomfortable with upgrading RAM yourself, opt for the services of an authorized, certified Mac cracker-opener.

TIP

The bottom line is that it's best to order your Mac with as much RAM as you can afford in the first place. It will cost you a little more up front, but it's worth it.

Add a Second Display

For almost as long as I've been using a Mac, I've used one with two displays. Almost all Macs today support a second monitor, and many support a third and fourth monitor. In my opinion, screen real estate is among the biggest productivity enhancers you can add — right up there with typing faster.

Screen real estate is the holy grail when working in multi-windowed or multi-paletted apps such as Photoshop, Final Cut Pro, and Logic Pro X. Two monitors are also great when you're working with two or more programs at the same time. With sufficient screen real estate, you can arrange all the windows and palettes for all programs in the way that's most expedient to the way you work.

You don't need an expensive 4K or 5K monitor. For a couple of hundred bucks, you can find a second display that will double your screen real estate. Or, if you have an iPad of recent vintage, read the next section.

Finally, in the words of my esteemed tech editor Ryan, "Why stop at two?" Because many Macs support three or more displays, all you need are the proper cables and available ports.

Use Your iPad as a Second Display

Catalina introduced a new feature known as Sidecar, which allows you to use a late-model iPad as a second screen for your late-model Mac.

The official list of supported hardware was unavailable at press time but should be available by the time you read this at https://support.apple.com (search for *Sidecar*). Or, just connect your iPad to your Mac with the USB cable and then open System Preferences. If you see an icon named Sidecar, your gear is new enough; if you don't, it's not.

If you have an iPad handy, give it a try; if your Mac and iPad are up to the task, enable the Show Sidebar check box. If applicable, enable the Show TouchBar and Enable Double Tap on Apple Pencil check boxes as well. Then use the Displays System Preferences pane to arrange the iPad's position relative to your other screen (or screens) — and you're done.

Hope you enjoy all that extra screen real estate as much as I do!

Here's a bonus tip: Some apps (Logic Pro X and MIMO Live come to mind) offer remote control apps so you can control them with your iPad (or iPhone)!

Upgrade to a Solid-State Drive (SSD)

The latest and greatest storage device to appear is the solid-state drive (SSD). It uses flash memory in place of a mechanical hard drive's spinning platters, which means, among other things, that it has no moving parts. Another benefit is that an SSD performs most operations at up to twice the speed of mechanical drives.

The bad news is that an SSD is more expensive — three or more times the price per gigabyte — of a mechanical hard drive or a hybrid drive with the same capacity.

That said, most users report that it's the best money they ever spent on an upgrade. I put the biggest one I could afford (1TB) in my MacBook Pro and I'll never go back to booting from a hard disk.

My MacBook Air's internal SSD died halfway through writing *macOS Catalina For Dummies*. Because that's the Mac I use for screenshots, I needed the fastest and easiest fix, so I bought a 500GB external USB 3 SSD (a Samsung T5) on sale at Fry's Electronics for $90.

I replaced an SSD with another SSD, but for those of you still booting from a hard disk, for under $100 you can speed up your Mac in a major way.

Honestly, folks, if you're only going to do one thing to make your old Mac faster, this is what you should do: Replace your hard drive with an SSD. If your Mac's SSD can't be upgraded, consider an external SSD as your boot disk (which is still what I use with my MacBook Air).

After switching to an SSD startup drive — internal or external — your old Mac will feel almost new again.

Get More Storage

Your Mac will run slower and slower as its startup disk gets fuller and fuller. If you can't afford to replace your startup disk with a bigger SSD or purchase a bigger external SSD to use as a boot disk, another option is to get a big external hard disk (much less expensive per megabyte than an SSD) and move some of your data off your startup disk and onto the external disk.

You can connect external hard disks (or SSDs) via USB 3 or Thunderbolt (or FireWire on older Macs). All three can be used to connect devices that require high-speed communication with your Mac — hard drives, SSDs, CD/DVD burners, scanners, camcorders, and such. Thunderbolt is today's speed champ, but FireWire is often the fastest bus that an older Mac will support natively.

TECHNICAL STUFF

The most recent Mac models that had FireWire used the type called FireWire 800, which has a different type of connector than does FireWire 400, which was available on older Macs. If you get a device that has only FireWire 400, and your Mac has only FireWire 800 (or vice versa), everything will work as long as you get a FireWire 400–to–FireWire 800 adapter cable, available at the Apple Store and many other places.

Thunderbolt, which is available on Mac models introduced since 2012, is the fastest bus around by far. That said, there are still relatively few Thunderbolt peripherals at this writing. Furthermore, the Thunderbolt devices that are out there are somewhat more expensive than their USB 3 counterparts. Although Thunderbolt shows tons of promise, at present, Thunderbolt hard drives are significantly more expensive than either FireWire or USB 3 drives.

And just to confuse things, all Macs since 2014 use USB 3 (Universal Serial Bus 3), which is many times faster than the previous generations of USB (and FireWire).

TIP

If you're buying an external USB drive, get one with USB 3. It shouldn't be much more expensive than a USB 2 drive and will be much faster. If your Mac has USB 3 ports, you'll be unhappy with USB 2 speeds.

Even if your Mac *doesn't* have USB 3 ports, you should get a USB 3 drive. It'll run at the same speed as a USB 2 drive on your current Mac — and will run a lot faster on your new Mac when you upgrade.

If you're not sure what generation of USB your Mac has, choose ➪ About This Mac, click the System Report button to launch the System Information application, and then click USB in the hardware list on the left.

The good news is that whatever connection you choose for your new disk — USB 2, USB 3, Thunderbolt, FireWire 400 or 800 — you can usually just plug it in and start using it. Unless the disk is preformatted for a PC and requires reformatting, there's nothing more you have to do!

Speaking of which, don't buy an external drive that's advertised as "for the Mac" or "formatted for the Mac." You can often save $20 or more by purchasing the generic (read: Windows) version of the disk and reformatting it as HFS+ or APFS with Disk Utility (see Chapter 25).

WARNING

Almost every Mac sold today has at least one USB-C port, which is a kind of hybrid USB/Thunderbolt port that doesn't appear on Macs prior to 2018.

To make things even more confusing, the same USB-C port also supports Thunderbolt 3 (the latest and greatest connection technology for storage and other devices requiring fast transfer speeds) and recharging.

Because the port is incompatible with every other type of USB cable ever made, you'll probably need a USB-C adapter (or USB-C hub or dock) to connect your USB devices to your new computer's USB-C/Thunderbolt port.

Whew. Now that you know all you need to know about your new external disk, the last step is to move some data from your startup disk to the new external disk. So copy the files or folders (your large files and folders are likely contained in your Pictures, Music, and Documents folders) to the new external disk; confirm that the files have been copied properly; make sure you have a backup, just in case; and then delete the files from your startup disk.

Subscribe to My Free Newsletter

Around once a month, I send out a short newsletter to my Working Smarter Insiders email list. In it, I offer hints, tips, techniques, humor, and advice on using your Mac better, faster, and more elegantly. Becoming an insider is free; you can join here: www.workingsmarterformacusers.com/join.

I guarantee you're gonna like it, but if for some reason you don't, you can unsubscribe (which is also free).

Chapter **28**

Ten Great Websites for Mac Freaks

A s much as I would like to believe that this book tells you everything you need to know about using your Mac, I know better. There's much more to discover about using your Mac, and new tools and products come out every day.

The best way to gather more information than you could ever possibly soak up about all things Mac is to hop onto the web. There you can find news, *freeware* and *shareware* (try-before-you-buy software) to download, troubleshooting sites, tons of news and information about your new favorite OS, and lots of places to shop.

The sites in this chapter are the best, most chock-full-o'-stuff places on the web for Mac users. By the time you finish checking out these websites, you'll know so much about your Mac and Big Sur that you'll feel like your brain is in danger of exploding. On the other hand, you might just feel a whole lot smarter. Happy surfing!

The Mac Observer

www.macobserver.com

The Mac Observer gives you Apple news, views, reviews, and much more.

Disclosure: I write a weekly column called "Dr. Mac's Rants & Raves" for The Mac Observer. But I loved The Mac Observer long before I begged for a job there. TMO (as we insiders refer to it) is known for insightful opinion pieces in addition to Apple news and product reviews. In my humble opinion, the quality and depth of the writing by the TMO staff is superior to almost any other site covering the Apple beat.

Macworld

www.macworld.com

Although the print publication and exposition became extinct years ago, the Macworld site still describes itself as: "Your best source for all things Apple." And it's still true, more or less. Macworld is perhaps the best and most comprehensive source of product information for Apple products. It's especially strong for reviews of Mac, iPhone, and iPad products. For example, when you want to know which inkjet printer or digital camera is the best in its price class, Macworld can almost certainly offer guidance, feature comparison charts, and real-world test results. And you won't merely find product information here — you'll find it accompanied by expert opinions and professional editing and fact checking.

Put another way, I trust the writers and editors at Macworld more than I trust the writers and editors of many other websites. Any other sites, that is, except the others in this chapter.

TidBITS

http://tidbits.com

TidBITS is an online newsletter and website with the motto: "Thoughtful, detailed coverage of everything Apple for 30 years." With some of the richest and most insightful writing on the web, TidBITS is another must-read for me. I always look forward to reading the latest issue (which comes out every Monday) as well as articles posted regularly throughout the week.

Disclosure: I have known the proprietors of TidBITS, Adam and Tonya Engst, since the 1980s and consider them friends. That said, they've prospered and grown for nearly 25 years because Adam, Tonya, and the contributors to TidBITS are as passionate about sharing information about Apple products and services today as they were in 1990.

I recommend subscribing to the email newsletter so that you get a new issue every Monday, like I do. But even if you don't choose to subscribe, you should check out the site; TidBITS is one of my all-time faves.

iMore

http://www.imore.com

If you live the Apple lifestyle, iMore is your go-to website. With in-depth articles on all Apple products and operating systems, and tons of tips, hints, and tutorials as well, it's one of the sites I try to visit daily.

AppleWorld.Today

www.appleworld.today

For the latest in Mac news, updated every single day, check out AppleWorld.Today, which arose from the ashes of The Unofficial Apple Weblog (TUAW) after its untimely demise. With a small staff of Apple newshounds, this site keeps you on the bleeding edge of Mac news — including software updates, virus alerts, and Apple happenings. It also offers extensive and unbiased reviews of many products soon after their release.

The Wirecutter

https://thewirecutter.com

When I want to see what others consider the best peripherals, tech tools, and toys, I visit The Wirecutter. Now a *New York Times* company, Wirecutter has the resources to objectively evaluate many products and declare one of them "the best."

I take the reviews with a grain of salt, and typically look at the Electronics and Office sections. I've also used it to research purchases as diverse as sunscreen, an insulated water bottle, and Bluetooth headsets.

I love this site and try to visit it at least once a week, regardless of whether there's anything I need. (I know — I should get a life.)

Apple Support

www.apple.com/support

Do you have a technical question about any version of Mac OS or any Apple product — including Big Sur? March your question right over to the Apple Support page, where you can find searchable archives of tech notes, software update information, and documentation. The Support pages are especially useful if you need info about your old Mac; Apple archives all its info here. Choose among a preset list of topics or products, and type a keyword to research. You're rewarded with a list of helpful documents. Clicking any one of these entries (they're all links) takes you right to the info you seek. The site even has tools that can help narrow your search.

The site also offers a section with user discussions of Apple-related topics. Although not officially sanctioned or monitored by Apple, it's often the best place to gain insights, especially on slightly esoteric or obscure issues not covered in other sections of the site.

Other World Computing

www.macsales.com

Other World Computing is the go-to place for Mac peripherals and upgrades, and my first stop when I need RAM, hard drives, SSDs, optical drives, video cards, processor upgrades, cables, discs, docks, or anything else you can think of. If it enhances your Mac, Other World Computing probably has it at a reasonable price.

And, if it's memory or internal storage, you'll usually get a comprehensive illustrated installation manual and (often) an installation video as well.

Because of its inexpensive and reliable delivery and a solid guarantee on every item it sells, you can't go wrong doing business with OWC.

I buy at least half my storage devices and other peripherals and almost all RAM from OWC, and I trust them to know Apple stuff a lot more than I trust BestBuy or Fry's.

dealmac/dealnews

www.dealnews.com/mac

Although now part of the larger dealnews site, dealmac is still a great place to find deals on software, hardware, training, and more.

Shopping for Mac stuff? Go to dealmac first to discover sale prices, rebates, and other bargain opportunities on upgrades, software, peripherals, and more.

"How to go broke saving money," this site boasts, and if you're a bargain hunter, it's not far from the truth. If you love a bargain, look here first.

Working Smarter for Mac Users

www.workingsmarterformacusers.com

I'm going to end this book with a bit of shameless self-promotion. Now that you know a bit more about Big Sur, I'd like to offer you an opportunity to become more productive using your Mac.

I'm obsessed with productivity and maintain a website and email list called *Working Smarter for Mac Users*. My mission is to help Mac users learn to do more work in less time so they have more time for things they love.

Sign up for my Insiders email list today and you'll receive tips, hints, techniques, tutorials, videos, and more every so often (but not more than once or twice a month, tops).

Did I mention that it's free?

Bottom line: If you want to take your Mac skills to the next level and become a raging thunder lizard of productivity, join my free Insiders email list today at www.workingsmarterformacusers.com/join. You have nothing to lose and much to gain; I hope you'll check it out.

This concludes our regularly scheduled programming. Thank you for your support.

Bob
"Dr. Mac"

Bob "Dr. Mac" LeVitus

Fall 2020

Index

C

Calculator app, 439–440
Calendar app, 204–209
  calendars
    adding, 205
    creating, 205
    deleting, 206
    merging, 206
    naming, 206
    publishing to iCloud, 206
  color-coding entries, 206
  Contacts app and, 208
  defined, 47, 204
  denying other apps access to, 436
  events
    creating, 207, 288
    editing, 207
    inviting others to, 208–209
    Quick Events, 207–208
    responding to invitations, 208–209
  Mail app and, 288
  navigating forward/backward, 204
  removing alerts, 209
  setting alerts, 209
  syncing across devices, 209
  views, 204–205
Camera app. See also images
  creating signatures, 103
  scanning, 399–402
Carbon Copy Cloner, 458
CDs and DVDs
  adding songs to Music app from CDs, 341–342
  burning Music app playlists to CDs, 348
  data CDs and DVDs, 348
  icon for, 67
  MP3 CDs, 348
  using for backups, 426–428
Character Viewer, 123–124, 127
check boxes
  defined, 33
  tri-state, 33
Chrome web browser, 260
Clipboard, 175–180
  copying items via, 176–177
  defined, 175

Edit menu items, 176–177
  pasting from, 179
  revealing, 175–177
  saving screenshots to, 107
  third-party enhancers, 176
  Universal Clipboard, 179–180
clock, displaying on screen saver, 118
Cohen, Dennis R., 350
Column view, 76–78
  displaying, 76
  preview column, 78
  resizing columns, 77
Command (Apple) key, 44
command line, 450–451
communication. See FaceTime app; Mail app;
    Messages app
compressing files/folders, 171
Computer folder, accessing, 137
Contacts app, 273–280
  adding contacts, 274–275, 288
  adding images to contacts, 301
  Calendar app and, 208, 274
  defined, 47, 273
  denying other apps access to, 436
  editing contacts, 275
  FaceTime app and, 271, 273
  groups, 276–277
    adding contacts to, 277
    creating, 276–277
    deleting, 279
    purpose of, 276
  importing contacts, 276
  Mail app and, 285–288
  mapping address of contacts, 233–234
  Maps app and, 233–234
  merging locally-stored contacts with those in
    iCloud, 280
  sharing contacts, 274
  smart groups, 277–279
    creating, 278
    deleting, 279
    purpose of, 277–278
  syncing contacts across devices, 279–280
containers, 71
contextual (shortcut) menus, 18, 39–40
Continuity Camera feature, 399–402

I

S

About the Author

Bob LeVitus, often referred to as "Dr. Mac," has written or co-written more than 90 popular computer books, with millions of copies sold worldwide. In addition to co-authoring fourteen editions of *iPhone For Dummies,* he has written versions of *OS X For Dummies* and *macOS For Dummies* covering every cat- and California locale–named operating system Apple has released since System 7 (all for John Wiley & Sons, Inc., of course).

Bob has penned the popular Dr. Mac column for the *Houston Chronicle* since 1996 and the Dr. Mac's Rants & Raves column for *The Mac Observer* for almost as long. He has also written thousands of articles, reviews, and columns for dozens of newspapers and magazines over his 30+ year career.

Bob is known for his Apple expertise, trademark humorous style, and ability to translate techie jargon into usable and fun advice for regular folks. He has presented more than 100 workshops at Macworld Expos in the United States and abroad, given Macworld Expo keynote addresses in three countries, and offered his own Macintosh training seminars in many U.S. cities. (He also won the Macworld Expo MacJeopardy World Championship three times in a row before retiring.)

From 1986 to 1989 Bob served as editor-in-chief of the first desktop-published Mac magazine, *The MACazine.* From 1989 to 1997, he was a contributing editor and columnist for *MacUser* magazine, writing the Help Folder, Beating the System, Personal Best, and Game Room columns at various times.

Bob's latest venture is *Working Smarter for Mac Users,* a website, blog, e-book, online training, and consultancy aimed at helping Mac users become more productive. He'd love for you to check it out at www.workingsmarterformacusers.com.

Prior to giving his life over to computers, Bob worked in advertising at Kresser/Craig/D.I.K., a Los Angeles advertising agency and marketing consultancy, and its subsidiary, L & J Research. He holds a B.S. in marketing from California State University.

Dedication

For the ninety-first time (I counted), this book is dedicated to the only woman I'll ever love — my wife and best friend Lisa, who taught me everything I know about pretty much everything I know that's not technology.

You are still the best!

And, again for the umpteenth time, this book is dedicated to my kids (now adults) Allison and Jacob, who love their Apple gadgets almost as much as I love them (my kids, of course, not my devices).

Author's Acknowledgments

A tip of the hat to super-agent, Carole "Swifty" Jelen, who has represented me for nearly 30 years. She's still the world's greatest literary agent in my humble opinion, and why she's the only agent I've ever had.

Special thanks to everyone at Apple who helped me turn this book around in record time — I couldn't have done it without you. And super, extra-special super-duper thanks to Keri Walker — after almost 30 years working with her she's still the nicest, classiest, and hippest PR person I've ever worked with.

Big-time thanks to the gang at Wiley: Steve "Is It Done Yet" Hayes; my absolutely superb editor, Susan Pink; my terrific tech editor, Ryan Williams, and everyone else at Wiley who put their heart and soul into getting this book to you.

Thanks also to my family and friends for putting up with my cranky demeanor during my all-too-lengthy hibernation sessions during this book's gestation.

Super-special thanks to Interstellar BBQ, Hops & Grain's *The One They Call Zoe* Ale, Black's Barbecue, Torchy's Tacos, and Saccone's Pizza for sustenance.

And last (but certainly not least), thanks to you, gentle reader, for buying my book.

Publisher's Acknowledgments

Executive Editor: Steve Hayes

Project Editor: Susan Pink

Copy Editor: Susan Pink

Technical Editor: Ryan Williams

Sr. Editorial Assistant: Cherie Case

Proofreader: Debbye Butler

Production Editor: Tamilmani Varadharaj

Cover Image: © Chris Axe/Getty Images

Take dummies with you everywhere you go!

Whether you are excited about e-books, want more from the web, must have your mobile apps, or are swept up in social media, dummies makes everything easier.

Find us online!

Leverage the power

Dummies is the global leader in the reference category and one of the most trusted and highly regarded brands in the world. No longer just focused on books, customers now have access to the dummies content they need in the format they want. Together we'll craft a solution that engages your customers, stands out from the competition, and helps you meet your goals.

Advertising & Sponsorships

Connect with an engaged audience on a powerful multimedia site, and position your message alongside expert how-to content. Dummies.com is a one-stop shop for free, online information and know-how curated by a team of experts.

- Targeted ads
- Video
- Email Marketing
- Microsites
- Sweepstakes sponsorship

20 MILLION PAGE VIEWS EVERY SINGLE MONTH

15 MILLION UNIQUE VISITORS PER MONTH

43% OF ALL VISITORS ACCESS THE SITE VIA THEIR MOBILE DEVICES

700,000 NEWSLETTER SUBSCRIPTIONS TO THE INBOXES OF *300,000* UNIQUE INDIVIDUALS EVERY WEEK

# of dummies

Custom Publishing

Reach a global audience in any language by creating a solution that will differentiate you from competitors, amplify your message, and encourage customers to make a buying decision.

- Apps
- Books
- eBooks
- Video
- Audio
- Webinars

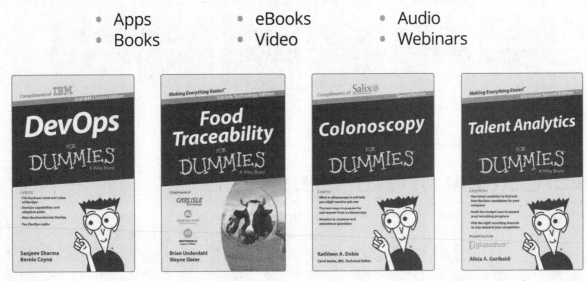

Brand Licensing & Content

Leverage the strength of the world's most popular reference brand to reach new audiences and channels of distribution.

For more information, visit dummies.com/biz

dummies®
A Wiley Brand

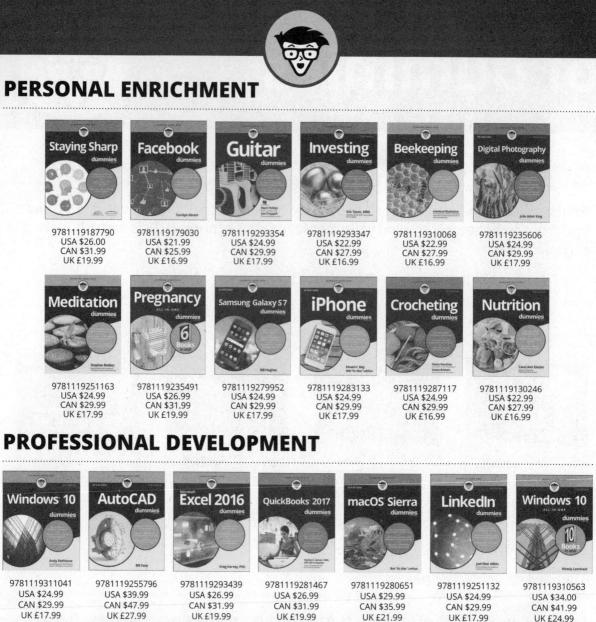

PERSONAL ENRICHMENT

Staying Sharp
9781119187790
USA $26.00
CAN $31.99
UK £19.99

Facebook
9781119179030
USA $21.99
CAN $25.99
UK £16.99

Guitar
9781119293354
USA $24.99
CAN $29.99
UK £17.99

Investing
9781119293347
USA $22.99
CAN $27.99
UK £16.99

Beekeeping
9781119310068
USA $22.99
CAN $27.99
UK £16.99

Digital Photography
9781119235606
USA $24.99
CAN $29.99
UK £17.99

Meditation
9781119251163
USA $24.99
CAN $29.99
UK £17.99

Pregnancy
9781119235491
USA $26.99
CAN $31.99
UK £19.99

Samsung Galaxy S7
9781119279952
USA $24.99
CAN $29.99
UK £17.99

iPhone
9781119283133
USA $24.99
CAN $29.99
UK £17.99

Crocheting
9781119287117
USA $24.99
CAN $29.99
UK £16.99

Nutrition
9781119130246
USA $22.99
CAN $27.99
UK £16.99

PROFESSIONAL DEVELOPMENT

Windows 10
9781119311041
USA $24.99
CAN $29.99
UK £17.99

AutoCAD
9781119255796
USA $39.99
CAN $47.99
UK £27.99

Excel 2016
9781119293439
USA $26.99
CAN $31.99
UK £19.99

QuickBooks 2017
9781119281467
USA $26.99
CAN $31.99
UK £19.99

macOS Sierra
9781119280651
USA $29.99
CAN $35.99
UK £21.99

LinkedIn
9781119251132
USA $24.99
CAN $29.99
UK £17.99

Windows 10 All-in-One
9781119310563
USA $34.00
CAN $41.99
UK £24.99

SharePoint 2016
9781119181705
USA $29.99
CAN $35.99
UK £21.99

Fundamental Analysis
9781119263593
USA $26.99
CAN $31.99
UK £19.99

Networking
9781119257769
USA $29.99
CAN $35.99
UK £21.99

Office 2016
9781119293477
USA $26.99
CAN $31.99
UK £19.99

Office 365
9781119265313
USA $24.99
CAN $29.99
UK £17.99

Salesforce.com
9781119239314
USA $29.99
CAN $35.99
UK £21.99

Coding
9781119293323
USA $29.99
CAN $35.99
UK £21.99

dummies.com

dummies®
A Wiley Brand